HISTORY OF THE BANK OF ENGLAND

HISTORY OF THE BANK OF ENGLAND

By

A. ANDREADES

TRANSLATED BY

CHRISTABEL MEREDITH

WITH A PREFACE

BY

H. S. FOXWELL, M.A., F.B.A.

TWO VOLUMES IN ONE

1640-1903

GYAN

Published by

Gyan Publishing House
5, Ansari Road
Daryaganj, New Delhi-110002
Phone: 011-47034999, 9811692060
E-mail: books@gyanbooks.com

Distribution Network
gyanbooks.com
India, USA, Canada, UK, Australia, France

ISBN : 978-81-212-9820-9 (PB)
First Published, 1909

2nd Impression 2023

Printed at: Gyan Press, Delhi.

HISTORY OF THE BANK OF ENGLAND
Author: A. ANDREADES

HISTORY OF THE BANK OF ENGLAND

By A. ANDREADES,

Professor of Political Science in the University of Athens

TRANSLATED BY

CHRISTABEL MEREDITH,

WITH A PREFACE

BY

H. S. FOXWELL, M.A., F.B.A.,

Fellow of St. John's College, Cambridge; Professor of Political Economy in the University of London.

TWO VOLUMES IN ONE.

1640—1903.

1909.

AUTHOR'S PREFACE.

THE Author of this book gladly welcomes the appearance of an English translation of so satisfactory a character. At the same time it may be well to remind the English reader that this is a history of an English institution written by a foreigner and intended for the use of foreigners. Difficulties must arise in any attempt to judge the institutions of other countries and to form an opinion with regard to advisable reforms. The task is especially hard in the case of a country like England, where more attention is paid to facts than to theories. Hence with respect to various questions, especially some arising towards the end of the work, when I have been unable to support my own views by the opinions of an English authority, I have chosen rather to confine myself to a statement of the facts than to set forth theories which might be disproved by subsequent events.

Moreover, in writing for French readers, I have described various matters and in particular historical events, the discussion of which may perhaps be superfluous for English readers. I must then ask the latter to remember that the political and economic history of Great Britain is less well known to continental readers than to themselves.

I am conscious of many other short-comings in this book, which is a product of youth; were it not for the pressure of University duties and other work I should have completed and revised it. In its present form it is the result of the conscientious study of several years; and as such I hope it will obtain the indulgence of my new readers.

It only remains for me to express my thanks to Mrs. H. O. Meredith, who has spared no pains in the work of translation, and to Professor Foxwell, whose instructive preface is sufficient in itself to give the book a special value.

A. ANDRÉADÈS,
Professor at the University of Athens.

PREFACE.

ENGLISHMEN may be pardoned if they regard the Bank of England as the greatest financial institution in the world. It is far inferior, no doubt, to many Continental banks, in the extent of its metallic reserves and of its note circulation; and there are even other English banks which hold a larger amount of private deposits. It can hardly be considered so essentially a *national* bank as the Banks of France and Germany, each of which does a larger business in the provinces than in the capital: it is not so democratic in the range of its operations as the Banque de France, perhaps not so directly associated with general enterprise as the Reichsbank. No existing bank can boast a history at the same time so long, so continuous and so distinguished; nor has any played so large and so worthy a part, not merely in the fortunes of a great nation, but also in the general financial activities of the world.

The history of this famous Bank, here presented in an English version by Mrs. Meredith, must be held to be in many respects a *tour de force*. It was written by a Greek, in French: and notwithstanding the double difficulty with which the author had to contend in describing an institution, so characteristically English, in a language not his own, it is the most comprehensive and most readable account of the Bank yet published. Dr. Andréadès, indeed, following Mr. Stephens, goes so far as to say that nothing deserving to be called a history of the Bank had previously been written, though the attempt had more than once been made. If this be so, the fact is sufficiently remarkable, and suggests reflections, some not too pleasant, to those who are concerned for the credit of English Economics. In what sense must we accept the statement ?

We must certainly agree, with M. Lyon-Caen, that no complete history of the Bank existed before the appearance of this book. Many valuable contributions to such a history had been published from time to time ; but all of them left something to be desired. Some were fragmentary, some were hardly scientific ; in the best of them history is often only incidental to the author's main purpose ; nearly all, a characteristically English fault, were unsystematic ; none of them covered the whole period, even approximately. We had no complete, formal and scientific account, such as would compare for instance with Alphonse Courtois' history of the Banque de France.

Let us glance at some of the more important existing works. The account given by Macleod, in his *Theory and Practice of Banking,* may be said to have held the field before the appearance of Dr. Andréadès' history. It is in many respects very good within its limits ; the present writer, like the late Henry Sidgwick, found it more suggestive and instructive than any other. But the historical work was merely incidental with Macleod, not his principal aim ; as may be gathered from the fact that the word 'history' does not even occur on the title of his book ; and his vigorous sketch deals with banking rather than with the Bank : a distinction, I will admit, which counts for less in earlier times than it would to-day.

Tooke and Newmarch (the former especially) have also contributed invaluable material in their well-known *History of Prices*, notably for the period of the Napoleonic war, but in hardly less degree for the whole period 1793-1857 covered by them. But Tooke's work might be regarded as a documented argument rather than a reasoned history: an objection which would apply to Macleod as well, though perhaps not quite to the same degree. The object of both writers was rather to establish a controversial thesis than to give a scientific explanation of the course of events. None the less, each work contains abundant and trustworthy historical material: the unconcealed bias of the writers does not seem to have interfered with their accurate record of the facts. Avowed bias, indeed, rarely misleads; what is really dangerous is the pretence of impartiality. Tooke, perhaps, sometimes puts upon the facts a construction they cannot fairly bear; on the other hand, he is most careful to give references, the lack of which is a principal defect in Macleod. It is certain that everyone who essays to deal with the history of English banking must be deeply indebted to both these writers.

There are some excellent authorities, too, upon the earlier years of the history of the Bank. First among them in merit, though not in time, I would mention Thorold Rogers, whose *First Nine Years of the Bank of England* has always seemed to me the most brilliant of his many contributions to economic history. It is, of course, only a fragment; but it is a model for the economic historian. Among others who have thrown light on the earlier history must also be mentioned Mr. Hilton Price, Mr. Maberly Phillips, and the late Mr. J. B. Martin whose numerous works and papers are full of valuable information as to early banking history, banking practice, and banking documents. Many others might be named, did space permit, who have made similar valuable studies of local banking, and individual banks. What seems to be an admirable sketch, covering a longer period in a more connected way, must be noted here; I mean Mr. W. R. Bisschop's *De Opkomst der Londensche Geldmarkt: 1640-1826:* S'Gravenhage, 1896. Unfortunately many of us are debarred by linguistic limitations from profiting as we otherwise might from the acute and critical exposition of this scholarly writer.

Returning to the larger works, Lawson's *History of Banking* is another book of considerable merit. It wants system, but has a great deal of interesting information about the early history of banking, is throughout well-informed on points of banking practice, and deserves special mention for the frequent references to the relations between the Bank and the Government, on which little has been written in English, though Dr. Philippovich, in his *Die Bank von England im Dienste der Finanzverwaltung des Staates*, has treated it exhaustively over the whole period up to 1884. Lawson's book too has an Appendix full of interesting matter, including a reprint of the Charter and By-Laws of the Bank. It has been objected to Lawson, and it is still more true of the better-known *History of the Bank of England* by Francis, that his history is too anecdotal and popular in form. Neither writer, however, appealed to an academic audience, nor would have found one at that time if he had. It may at any rate be said of both works that they contain matter of value, the result of pretty wide reading. Gilbart again is a writer of whom we must speak with respect. His contributions to the history of banking range wide over both time and place. He has written of banking not merely in the United Kingdom, but in America as well; and has not confined his studies to the period he knew best, the first half of the 19th century. No one could accuse him of being unduly readable; his writing is always methodical and often didactic to the verge of pomposity. As might be expected from the founder and manager of the first great London Joint Stock Bank, his works are full of details of administration, of which modern students may be a little impatient; but they are solid, well furnished with statistics, and of real value to the historian. They are not however so directly concerned with the Bank of England as with Joint Stock Banking. Passing over slighter sketches and papers, of which there are very many, as well as books like those of Maclaren, really a history of opinions, and of Doubleday, a notable criticism of the funding system, we come in conclusion to a writer of foremost importance, happily still active, Mr. Inglis Palgrave. He is our main source of information for the history of English banking in the last half-century. His mastery of English banking statistics is unrivalled; he has given us, partly in published works, partly in the *Bankers' Magazine* and elsewhere, a long series of studies of the discount rate and the changes in English banking structure and banking methods; and in his last work, *Bank Rate and the Money Market*, we have a collection of comparative statistics from 1844 to 1900 which seems to exhaust the available material on the subject.

If, then, we have no adequate history of the Bank, it is evident that very important contributions to such a history exist. Moreover, as Dr. Andréadès truly says, the records they contain are full of incident and attraction, almost of romance. Why have we had to wait so long for a worthy formal and fairly complete handling of such an interesting and fundamental chapter in our economic history? Dr. Andréadès makes a modest reference to the difficulty and magnitude of the task; but he does not seem convinced that this is quite an adequate explanation. Probably various reasons will occur to the reader. I will venture to suggest two considerations which may have given pause to others, as they certainly did to myself; and I write as one who for more than a quarter of a century has felt that special fascination in banking history to which our author refers.

The first is the remarkable absence of official records in connection with the Bank, especially for the first century of its activity. It has often been observed that the English are peculiarly fortunate in this matter of records; a result partly of their habits of publicity, and of the representative character of their political life. Speaking of our legal records, Maitland says they form "a series which for continuity and catholicity, minute detail and authoritative value has—I believe that we may safely say it—no equal, no rival, in the world." This is equally true in the case of many of our economic and political institutions. The Bank of England stands out as a striking exception to the rule. It never seems to have published any reports, or even to have preserved its own minutes and accounts. We have mainly to rely for any official knowledge of its operations on the occasional returns extracted by Parliamentary Committees, and on the weekly returns under the Act of 1844, which competent judges have declared to be the most valuable result secured by that Act. But the Committees throw no light on the period before the French war; and the returns under the Act of 1844 are very inadequate. Neither source gives the mass of valuable information contained in the Annual Reports of the Banks of France and Germany, and indeed of most of the foreign banks. Hence there are many questions of Bank policy which can only be studied upon such basis as is afforded by hearsay, and the articles or occasional utterances of individuals.

This absence of official records greatly increases the labour involved in writing a history of the Bank, and makes the result of it, after all is done, less complete and authentic than could be wished. But we should probably have had our history, authentic or not, if this had been all that stood in the way. It was not the absence of official records that left so many other chapters of English economic history to be first dealt with by foreigners. The main cause is to be found in the anti-historical bias of the dominant school of English official economists, most of them avowed disciples of that most unhistorical writer, David Ricardo. Their *doctrinaire* habits of thought, and their belief that they were in possession of a set of "principles" of universal application, led them to frown on historical research as at best mere waste of time. No physician, worthy of the name, will prescribe without some knowledge, direct or inferred, of the history of the case under treatment. To the typical English economist, however, who claimed that his "laws" were, would or should be (he was not *quite* clear about the tense) of world-wide pertinence, historical differences had no interest, and he relegated history to the antiquary. This, as we now see, is really the attitude of the quack. What is curious is, that in England, and to some extent in France also, the quack methods received the sanction of the professed practitioner, and it was left to the layman to follow the sounder practice. Hence for the half-century and more during which this "orthodox" school has been supreme, such economic history as was written in England was written outside academic circles, or at least by men whose work was under the ban of the dominant school. I well remember how completely this school ostracised Macleod. His admirable historical work, to which so many writers are indebted, was appreciated in every country but his own. Here, because of certain eccentricities in his theoretical position, his whole works were proscribed. Richard Jones in earlier days met a similar fate, though Whewell preserved him from entire neglect; and Cliffe Leslie in later times did not fare much better. There are many living economists who are not likely to forget the discouragement they suffered by this official blight on historical studies.

Fortunately this has all passed away, never, we may confidently assert, to return; passed away so completely that the younger men perhaps hardly realise how much it crippled and narrowed the work of the generation before them. Thanks mainly to the example of leaders like Archdeacon Cunningham and Professor Ashley, and later to the encouragement given to realistic studies at the London School of Economics, we now have a public which welcomes the results of historical research, and there is a large and growing number of scholars actively engaged upon it. The worst reproach on English economic achievement is now in a fair way to be removed.

With these attempts to explain what I cannot pretend to excuse, let me leave the question of our English shortcomings in this matter, and turn to the more agreeable work of considering the brilliant essay in which Dr. Andréadès has gone so far to supply what we lacked.

No two persons, reviewing so large a mass of situations and incidents, would be likely to agree in every estimate of evidence, or in all their judgments upon the actors in the drama. If I may venture to express an opinion, I should say that Dr. Andréadès seems, on the whole, to have shown a singularly sure instinct in his appreciations. There are of course a few points of fact, and some minor contentions, which might deserve examination, if this were the proper place for it; but in general, and notably on many much disputed issues, his conclusions seem to me, at any rate, to be sound and scholarly. Where I should differ most, is in regard to the period covered by the French war, and more particularly as to the conduct of the Bank during the Restriction.

This period is classical in the history of banking, and has attracted the attention of every writer on the subject. Never was the fate of England and her Empire more intimately bound up with the fortunes of her national credit; and there is no chapter in the long story of the Bank of England in regard to which her conduct has been so severely censured. On both grounds it must always be of special interest to an historian of our National Bank; and we might expect that the traditional verdicts would receive a very careful and critical scrutiny at his hands. It is just here that our author, who is not afraid to make excursions into party politics, and to shower censures on Pitt which will not commend themselves to everyone, seems to become less venturesome in dealing with the banking history, and follows too faithfully, as some may think, the generally accepted views. It may be worth while, then, to state briefly some considerations which he has perhaps under-rated.

Too much can easily be made of the iniquity of the Restriction itself, especially as a ground for reflections on the Bank. The difficulties of the Bank throughout were mainly due to its strong patriotism and loyalty to the Government. Even the Government, in the persistent demands upon the Bank which made the Restriction necessary, was only following the well-established policy of the time. In the eighteenth century nations exploited their banks in the same ruthless, impenitent way as they exploited their colonies and their trade. The contemporary *Caisse d'Escompte* in France, otherwise a very promising and well-managed institution, was completely wrecked by the insatiable demands of the State: and in later years the *Banque de France* was more than once brought by the same policy to a temporary suspension of payments. Nor is it so certain, quite apart from 18th century notions, that we could even now get through a first-rate war without an inconvertible currency. Gilbart, giving evidence before the Committee on Banks of Issue in 1841, says very frankly and emphatically that in the event of another war such as the war with France, "I would, immediately on the commencement of the war, issue an order in Council for the Bank to stop payment." He says he formed the opinion that the suspension of cash payments in 1797 "was not a matter of choice, but of necessity—it has since been confirmed by the writings of McCulloch." Quite recently again, at the discussion of Sir Robert Giffen's important paper at the Royal United Service Institution in March, 1908, several speakers expressed their conviction that a suspension of payments would be inevitable on the outbreak of a first-rate war; and Sir Felix Schuster said that we should certainly prohibit the shipment of gold to the enemy, which would involve a partial suspension. To find precedents for such a policy we need not go back to 1797. We have an excellent example to hand in the case of France in 1870. Suspension, then, must be considered as a still possible expedient, rather than as the scandal of a less enlightened age.

It is admitted by the severest critics of the Bank that there is no substantial ground for complaint as to its conduct during the Restriction until 1808-9. There does not seem indeed to have been any real depreciation of its paper until that date. The price of £4 per ounce which figures monotonously for the years 1803-9, was really an arbitrary price, fixed by the Bank itself as one at which it would purchase foreign gold.* The Bank, in fact, was adopting at its own expense the policy so common on the Continent to-day of strengthening the reserve by buying gold at a premium. No doubt it is less easy to defend the action of the Bank just after 1808. It might have done more than it actually did to check the speculative movement at that time. But events in South America were opening up splendid opportunities, which the English did well to seize, even at some risks. We must consider too, how limited were the means of control then at the disposition of the Bank. Regula-

*Cf. the Resolution of the Committee of Treasury, 28 Mar. 1804, in Appendix to Report of 1819.

tion by the rate of discount, the method now approved, was quite out of the question. The Usury law prevented a higher rate than 5%, and the Bank had long made 5% its minimum. It had to work therefore with a fixed rate of discount. Its policy in regard to the granting of accommodation seems very cautious, even in comparison with modern practice. Tooke tells us (I., p. 159) "The rule by which the Bank directors professed to be, and were in the main guided," was "the demand for discount of good mercantile bills, not exceeding 61 days date, at the rate of 5% per annum"; and he adds that this rule "did, with the necessary policy of Government in periodically reducing the floating debt within certain limits by funding, operate as a principle of limitation upon the total issues of the Bank." If the Bank wished to contract its circulation, what courses were open to it? To refuse accommodation altogether is always held to be dangerous. To make personal preferences is invidious, especially for a National Bank. It is just possible the Bank might have resorted to the expedient used in 1795-6, I mean the granting of *pro rata* discounts; but even so, it must have put severe pressure on the market, and risked the creation of panic. Further, its power over the market was seriously diminished by the rapid growth and reckless advances of the country banks. It was to these banks, and not to the Bank of England, that most of the troubles of the Restriction were due. The Bank was practically responsible for the solvency of this crowd of small, ill-managed institutions, but dared not call them to account, on peril of provoking a general collapse of credit. Thus the country banks over-traded without check, and on a moderate estimate had afloat a circulation of £30,000,000, a figure never touched by the circulation of the Bank itself.

Still there were those who held that, cost what it might, the Bank could and should have brought its paper and the exchanges to par. Tooke seems on the whole to have been of this opinion; but he clearly perceives and fairly states the extreme danger of such a course. After noting the difficulties imposed by the Usury law, he says, "Under these circumstances, and at such a time of unprecedented political difficulties, I am perfectly convinced that if the attempt alluded to had been made, there would have been a moment of total stoppage of business, something very like a general suspension of all payments except for retail purposes, and of all business excepting retail trade" (IV., p. 118). The alternative open to the Bank is admirably stated by him in another passage (I., p. 164), too long to quote here. The Bank had to choose between "violent changes in the state of the money market" and "extraordinary fluctuations in the exchanges." If the issues had been rigorously contracted so as to keep the exchanges at par, the most disastrous pressure would have been caused in the money market. In this earlier passage Tooke seems to think a financial crisis the lesser evil of the two. But there is much to be said for the opposite view.

We should remember that it was a main point with Napoleon to wreck our national credit. He regarded the remarkable credit development in England as a prime source of its military power, so long as it could be maintained; but he was equally satisfied that the development had proceeded to a dangerous extent, and that it would be quite possible to bring about its collapse.* To that object he directed many of his measures. He permitted the free import of corn to England, in the hope that it would cause a drain of gold. The Berlin and Milan decrees not only aimed at injuring our trade, but at destroying the basis of our credit, by causing drains of bullion; and they

*This has been clearly shown by Miss Cunningham, in an interesting paper, shortly to appear, upon *Napoleon's Attack on British Credit*, which I have had the advantage of reading in MS.

undoubtedly helped to bring about the high premium on exchange in 1810. If the Bank, in the attempt to correct this premium, had caused an internal stringency, and thereby provoked a general crisis, it would have exactly realised Napoleon's aims. Our credit, then (as now), was our strongest resource in war; then (as now), it was a vulnerable point, and its destruction was the first and main objective of the enemy.

Considerations of this kind, no doubt, rather than abstract arguments, led Parliament and the Bank in 1811 to reject the main recommendation of the Bullion Committee. For my part, I believe they were right; and that if at a time of such unprecedented disturbance to trade, the Bank had followed the counsels of the *doctrinaires*, the whole system of war finance would have collapsed. But the rejection of the Report, together with the passing of Lord Stanhope's Act in the same year, which put a check on the not too patriotic Lord King, and saved us from the danger of "two prices," enabled the Bank to pull through. As it was, and without the forced contraction of issues which resumption must have caused, prices fell, according to Jevons' investigations, from 164 in 1810 to 117 in 1819, or nearly 29 per cent. in nine years. It may be doubted whether, at such a critical time, the country could have supported a more rapid fall.

The situation, one would think, was so difficult and uncertain, that even if Parliament and the Bank had made an error of judgment, the error might have been pardoned, or at least gently handled; all the more too, inasmuch as many weighty authorities, merchants, bankers, and writers, inclined against the recommendation of the Committee. But the Bank had a consistent and uncompromising enemy in Ricardo. He came to the front in the currency controversies, and was soon to be the acknowledged head of the "new school" of economists; and his hostility is reflected in the unconsidered severity of traditional censure. Ricardo's animus was unconcealed; its origin I do not know, and it would be unprofitable to speculate upon it. In a letter to Malthus in 1815, he writes, "I always enjoy an attack upon the Bank, and if I had sufficient courage, I would be a party to it." He seems to have found his courage later. In 1822 he denounced the Bank in Parliament as "a company of merchants who . . . did not acknowledge the true principles of the currency, and who, in fact, in his opinion, did not know anything about it." It was precisely because they were a company of merchants that they saved the trade of the country from the crude prescription of the *doctrinaires*. However it is only fair to Ricardo to note that though he never tired of abusing the Bank, he was far from entirely approving the Report of 1810, which he is so often assumed to have inspired. For in a letter to that able writer Wheatley, dated 18th September, 1821, we find him writing "You rather misconceive my opinions on this question. I never should advise a government to restore a currency which was depreciated 30 per cent. to par . . . It was without any legislation that the currency from 1813 to 1819 became . . . within 5 per cent. of the value of gold,—it was in this state of things, and not with a currency depreciated 30 per cent., that I advised a recurrence to the old standard." The policy he here disclaims was precisely the policy recommended by the Bullion Committee. It is perhaps doubtful whether Ricardo's view was so qualified in 1810-11; and we may well be thankful that men of more cautious temper were at the helm then. Huskisson, who knew both the times and the man exceptionally well, pronounced a judgment on Ricardo in 1826 which we may extend to the whole party of the *doctrinaires*. "I believe," he said, "that if that gentleman, ingenious as he was, had been the sole director of the Bank of England, the country would before this have seen the stoppage of that establishment." (Speeches, II. p. 462).

Other critics have taken a kinder view of the action of the Bank. Baring in 1819, and Adam Smith fifty years before, both agree, that, as Smith puts it, the duty of the Bank to the public "may sometimes have obliged it, without any fault of its directors, to overstock the circulation with paper money." There was no severer critic of the Restriction finance than Doubleday, the opponent of funding in all its forms. But Doubleday, far from thinking that the Bank should have acted on the recommendation of the Bullion Committee, says that it "seemed to smack of a degree of fatuity that looked like political insanity" (p. 184). Senior, too, even when criticising the Bank for the extension of its issues, concludes with words of praise. "Such conduct," he says, "injurious as it was, is a model of sobriety and moderation when compared with that of any other individual or community invested with similar powers": and again, "The Bank directors exercised their power with extraordinary moderation." And Fullarton, in 1844, speaks of "the deep debt which the nation owes the Bank for its services throughout that long and trying crisis" (p. 68), and adds, "I believe they cannot be too highly appreciated; and I believe, further, that the same services could not have been so beneficially performed by any mere Bank of the State, or by any body whatever less intimately bound up in all its interests and relations with the commercial affairs and prosperity of the country."

This impression certainly grows upon me, the more I read the history of the period. I doubt whether the crowd of critics who have repeated Ricardo's censures of the Bank have sufficiently distinguished between the speculative views and the practical measures of the Directors. I think it will appear, the more the circumstances are examined, that their actual policy during the Restriction was generally guided by a sound instinct. It would be impossible to defend some of their arguments; but they were not there to argue. As so often happens with men of affairs, their policy was much better than the reasons they gave for it. The fact remains that where there was about an even chance of failure, the Bank succeeded: we may well be grateful to it for steering the country safely through the most critical period in the whole history of its banking and credit system. No doubt the Bank had the defects of its qualities; it may have laid rather too much stress upon the urgency of accommodating the trade and commerce of the country: but if so, its vices leaned to virtue's side. Its principal difficulties were due to its unwavering loyalty to the State; and to its endeavour, so far as lay in its power, to avert undue pressure on the commercial community. These are the ends for which a National Bank exists.

If we are to criticise the Bank, its conduct seems more open to objection in the twenty years *after* than in the twenty years *before* the Resumption of Cash Payments. As our author's account clearly shows, its management of the crises of 1825-6, and 1837-9 was far from prudent; and this after full allowance is made for the difficulties caused by the Usury Law and the conversion of the debt in the first period. One cannot help feeling too that much grave currency trouble might have been spared to our own times if the Bank had given a more favourable consideration to the currency proposals of Alexander Baring and Ricardo. But here again the Directors might plead that they were hardly free agents; the political situation was dominated by Cobbett, whose hostility to these schemes is well-known. For the worst blemish on the long and honourable record of the Bank we must go back to earlier times, to that fevered year 1720. It was the wild competition of the Bank with the South Sea Company which, more than anything else, as was ably argued by a contemporary writer, was the prime cause of the speculative mania of that year. The Bank was never nearer ruin than at that time, and only escaped, as Dr. Andréadès neatly puts it, by the rejection of its own proposals. His caustic judgment upon this episode seems fully warranted.

Dr. Andréadès apologizes for not having discussed more exhaustively the question of liberty of note issue, and the particular system of issue imposed by the Act of 1844, another legacy of the *doctrinaires*. English readers will hardly complain of this: the Act has been discussed *ad nauseam*. The vital question for us to-day is not so much liberty of issue, as the discovery of some means of regaining the elasticity of issue of which the Act of 1844 deprived us. The whole question of note issue, in so far as it is separable from the question of reserve, is of much less importance for England than for most other countries.

But there are some omissions in this history which strike one. It is hardly as strong as might be wished on the documentary and statistical side. One would have welcomed an Appendix containing some fundamental statistics: for instance, statistics of Capital, Dividends, Reserves, Discount Rates, and Note Circulation. A history of the Charter renewals would have been convenient: the original Charter and By-laws, the monopoly and other important Acts, and certain Orders and other documents might well have been printed. These are the things most useful, and generally most inaccessible, both to the student and the man of affairs. Again, some account of the various forms of Notes, Cheques, Bills, Tokens, etc., issued or handled by the Bank, such as might have been gathered from the writings of Maberley Phillips, Hilton Price, Bisschop and Philippovich, would certainly have been instructive. It may be said generally that the development of English banking is very closely connected with the currency development, and neither can be thoroughly understood without some reference to the other. Some of the incidents connected with the Recoinages of 1696 and 1774 have left their mark not only on the currency history of the world, but upon its banking history also, and certainly on the history of the Bank of England. It would be difficult, for instance, to exaggerate the importance of the rejection, in deference to Locke's plausible platitudes, of the very well considered Report of the Parliamentary Committee of 1695. Much the same may be said in regard to outside systems of banking. The development of banking in Scotland and Ireland is intimately connected at many epochs with the history of the Bank. More information also might have been given as to the relation of the Bank to various groups of other English banks. The growth of the country banks and the extent to which they were able to force the hand of the central institution, might have formed a special study, which would have thrown much light on the period 1793—1844. Another might have been devoted to the Bank's relations with the group of City bankers, and with the Clearing. More detail might been given, too, in regard to Joplin's movement, the relaxation of the Bank monopolies, the growth of the great Joint Stock Banks, and the effects produced by these changes upon the position of the Bank, and its control over the money market.

After all is said, however, the fact remains that we have in this work of Dr. Andréadès the best general survey of the subject which exists. It is the only one that covers the whole period of the Bank's history, and takes note of all the most important passages in it. Its author shows a remarkable familiarity with English methods and habits of thought, and his criticism is usually most just and temperate, and full of suggestion and stimulus. The earlier part of the history has never before been thrown into a form so convenient for English students; and they will find in the later part some new matter of interest, especially the sketch of the relations between the Bank and the Treasury, and a Memorandum by Sir Robert Peel which has not appeared in any previous work on the subject. The whole treatment is always alert and animated, the topics are vividly presented and well arranged, and above all, the book is eminently readable and attractive.

These merits seem to have been generally recognized. Dr. Andréadès' history has been everywhere well received, and by none more cordially, I think, than by those who best appreciate the great difficulty of the task. As I have ventured to touch on one or two matters in regard to which our points of view are not exactly the same, it is all the more pleasant to me to be able to congratulate the author upon his remarkable success, and upon the recognition it has received, not only in other countries, but in his own, where he now holds an important Chair in the University of Athens.

The work of the translator also calls for grateful recognition. The lucidity and vivacity of the original have been admirably preserved in Mrs. Meredith's effective and idiomatic version. While the translation is accurate, and keeps closely to the text, it has the unusual merit that it bears no trace, except perhaps in its clearness and point, of the original language from which it has been rendered. Perhaps it should be mentioned here that the translator did not attempt a general revision of the work, or the completion of the Bibliography; though many obvious slips and mis-spellings, and occasional inaccuracies of quotation and fact have been carefully corrected by reference to the original authorities.

It only remains to note that the appearance of the book is most timely. The question of the constitution and policy of National Banks is in some respects the supreme economic question of the day. The financier is in the ascendant; his is the dominating influence on modern economic activities. We are living in an age when financial fortunes and financial operations are upon a scale never dreamt of before; and when price manipulations and gold movements are constantly causing wreckage and dislocation of industry in greater or less degree. If disturbing forces of this magnitude are to be kept within due control, it can only be by institutions wielding national resources, and under the direction of men representing general public interests—men in touch with the national commercial and industrial conditions, and with the general aims of the State.

National Banks, then, are more necessary than they ever were; though their rôle has changed. If we look at their early history, either here or abroad, we shall find that the main object of the State in establishing relations with a Bank was to become its immediate beneficiary: indeed by the loans it exacted it very frequently crippled the Bank for its proper function of controlling the monetary position and securing due accommodation to industry and commerce. In modern times the public or national character of a Bank is mainly important in so far as it may be a guarantee that the Bank will safeguard public interests: that is to say, will realise that its chief duty is to the business world rather than to its shareholders, and its chief purpose to maintain financial security and stability rather than to make profit. It is from this point of view that National Banks will now be judged, and that we interest ourselves in their history. So regarded, the world's great National Banks have no cause to be ashamed of their record, the Bank of England least of all.

Cambridge, Xmas, 1908. H. S. FOXWELL.

CONTENTS.

VOLUME I. 1640—1819.

PART I.

PART II.

FOUNDATION OF THE BANK OF ENGLAND.

CHAPTER I.

CHAPTER II.

PATERSON'S LIFE AND WORK. FOUNDATION OF THE BANK OF ENGLAND.

CHAPTER III.

ORGANISATION OF THE NEW BANK.

CHAPTER VII.

PART III.

THE BANK OF ENGLAND UNDER THE HANOVERIAN DYNASTY UP TO THE TIME OF THE FRENCH REVOLUTION.

CHAPTER I.

CHAPTER II.

CHAPTER III.

PART IV.

THE BANK DURING THE REVOLUTIONARY AND NAPOLEONIC WARS

CHAPTER I.

CHAPTER II.

CHAPTER III.

CHAPTER IV.

CHAPTER V.

Part III.

PEEL'S ACT IN TIMES OF CRISIS.

CHAPTER I.

CHAPTER II.

PART IV.

GENERAL CONSIDERATION OF PEEL'S ACT—PRESENT POSITION OF THE QUESTION—SCHEMES FOR REFORM.

CHAPTER I.

CHAPTER II.

APPENDIX.

VOLUME I. 1640—1819.

HISTORY OF THE BANK OF ENGLAND.

INTRODUCTION.

Importance and Difficulties of the Subject. Reasons why no History of the Bank of England has ever been written. Examination of Sources: (*a*) Narrative sources and general works on Banking, (*b*) Official publications, (*c*) Pamphlets and tracts. Observations in reply to two criticisms likely to be made of the present work.

THE Bank of England is the oldest of the European national banks.[1] Established in 1694, it has seen the great banks which preceded it disappear one by one and has witnessed the collapse of many later foundations. At the present day it still remains the most famous, and from many points of view, the most original bank in the world.

A very slight study of English history shows the importance of this great institution to the Government and to the English nation. The loans made by the Bank to William III. and Queen Anne enabled England to regain that position among European nations which she had to all appearances hopelessly lost. The English Government sought help from the Bank on the eve of all the eighteenth

[1] The term national bank seems well-suited to those great establishments for the supply of credit facilities, such as the Banks of France, Spain, and Germany, which are, in fact, national institutions, performing, as they do, important services for the Government and for the public, and possessing more or less exclusive privileges of issue. The expression "national" bank also enables us to distinguish these institutions from genuine State banks.

century wars, and on the day of reckoning which followed the insanities of the Land Bank and of the South Sea Bubble.[1] Finally, not only the establishment of public credit by the formation of the permanent debt, but the organisation of the floating debt, and even the conversion of the national debt, are in the main the work of the Bank. Such services as these have not been forgotten by the English Government. The London commercial world, which was until 1694 a prey to usurers and without even a safe place of deposit for its money, has shown its gratitude to the Old Lady of Threadneedle Street[2] by the eagerness with which it has defended her in all times of danger.

Much has changed since these far-distant days. The machinery of credit has extended, and big loans have become customary. Now, when a Government wishes to borrow it makes direct appeal to the public, and individuals are familiar with more than one important bank which will discount their bills, or keep their deposits in complete security. But even to-day the importance of the Bank to the Government and to the public is hardly less striking than it was formerly. The Bank of England is, in fact, both the banker of the Treasury and the guardian of the gold reserve upon which the whole fabric of British commercial credit rests; it is this combination which makes it at once so powerful and so unique.

Certain questions naturally arise in respect to such a long-established and remarkable institution: Why, and in what manner was it founded? What position has it held during its long existence? What changes has it undergone? How has it acquired its present form? What, in short, has been its history? And this history proves to be so varied, so exciting, so full of life and instruction that the temptation to relate it is irresistible, even though the result be indifferently good or even very imperfect. This being so, it will be asked why the history of the Bank of England has never been written?

[1] See below pages 103 and 128.

[2] A nickname given to the Bank on account of its site.

Is it, as Mr. Stephens[1] thinks, on account of the great difficulty of such a task? Or is it that the practical conclusions which may be deduced will in all probability be disproportionate to the labour expended? It is perhaps somewhat late to suggest an answer to this question. It is besides, only fair to remark that although the Bank's history has never been written, it has at any rate been attempted more than once.

The first work of the kind was written in 1797, and is called *The History of the Bank of England, from the Establishment of that Institution to the present day*. The book consists of 110 small pages, and fulfils sufficiently well its author's intention, which was to give some account of the Bank, together with a concise history of the crises through which it had passed. The pamphlet is obviously inspired by the events of 1797, with which it is chiefly concerned; it is followed by a copy of the charter and of the principal regulations of the Bank.

The next account which I have been able to discover is an anonymous[2] pamphlet containing 62 pages, and called *The Life and Adventures of the Old Lady of Threadneedle Street, containing an account of her numerous intrigues*

[1] See *A Contribution to the Bibliography of the Bank of England.* The history of the Bank "from the scientific standpoint . . . has yet to be written." "Possibly," the author continues (p. ix., preface), "if anyone endowed with the necessary qualifications for writing a full and exact history of the Bank of England, the literary skill to deal with the vast mass of material, and the historical imagination to give it form and consistency, has ever contemplated the task, he may have been deterred by its magnitude, by the reflection that it must embrace a great deal of the commercial and most of the financial history of the country during more than two centuries. For the literature on the subject is enormous, and as the information it contains has never been collected and exhibited in a systematic form, it is the more necessary that record of it should be preserved."

Most likely if I had carefully estimated the difficulty of the task before me four years ago, I should not have entered upon it—unprovided as I am with any of the qualifications demanded by Mr. Stephens, and writing about a country and in a language which, alien to one another, are alike foreign to me. The charm of difficulty, or rather the natural presumption of youth, induced me to persevere. But this presumption, great though it may be, has not blinded me to the weaknesses and omissions in this attempt. I have, therefore, called Mr. Stephens to witness to the difficulties inherent in the subject, out of no feeling of pride at success, but in the hope that the kindly reader will allow me the excuse of extenuating circumstances.

[2] The author of it is probably W. Reid.

with various eminent statesmen of the past and present times. This purports to be an autobiography, but apart from its curious form the contents are wretchedly poor. The author, who is an ardent supporter of the Bank, thinks himself witty when he calls Louis XIV. Louis the Gascon,[1] or describes the Bank as being received by William III. in his palace at Kensington. When he refers to the newly opened branches, he compares the Bank to Sarah giving birth to a child in her old age, and he is guilty of a thousand other like absurdities. The book is one of the coarsest and dullest I have ever met with. It was published in 1832.

In 1848 Francis' *History of the Bank of England* appeared. Mr. Stephens[2] has accurately summed up its good qualities and its defects by describing it as "popular." It is certainly not a scientific work, and the writer lived at a time when those who wrote for the mass of the public were too much influenced by the author of the *Trois Mousquetaires*. Mr. Francis has, however, the credit of being a pioneer in a difficult task. His position at the Bank enabled him to give various interesting details, and I must confess to having read his book carefully and with advantage.

The one really scientific work which has been published on the history of the Bank of England unfortunately deals with but a very small portion of that history. I refer to *The First Nine Years of the Bank of England*,[3] by Thorold Rogers. It is no small praise to say that this book is a worthy companion to the same author's great work, *A History of Agriculture and Prices*. It is a matter for some regret that in this book, which was written but shortly before his death, Mr. Rogers has not dealt with the period leading up to the Act of 1694, and that he begins with the actual creation of the Bank of England. This, as he explains in the preface, is due to the fact that the work was taken up accidentally. During researches connected with his *History of Agriculture and Prices*, he came across

[1] pp. 6 and 13.
[2] Loc. cit.
[3] Oxford, 1887, 8vo.

a weekly register of the prices of Bank stock from August 17th, 1694, to September 17th, 1703; this register was found in a statistical paper published by a City apothecary called Houghton. In addition to some short articles on passing events, the paper contained a list of the prices of corn and other commodities on the markets of different English towns, as well as a great variety of notices and advertisements. Mr. Rogers applied to the Bank for an explanation of some obscure points, and found to his surprise that they possessed no record of the prices of the shares before 1705. He consequently determined to publish this register with comments; this was the origin of the book in question, and explains why it is limited to the brief period of nine years. If it was true, as Mr. Rogers[1] alleges, that the political and financial history of the Bank of England had never been written, he might congratulate himself that the gap was filled up to 1703, the last date referred to in his work.

These are, to the best of my knowledge, the only works especially devoted to the subject.

It is a curious fact that for a complete history of the Bank of England we must look, not to a book primarily concerned with the Bank itself, but to one dealing with banking in general, that is, to Macleod's treatise on the *Theory and Practice of Banking*.[2] In this book the Scotch economist gives the most complete existing account of the subject, especially with regard to the question of currency. Moreover, he supplies excellent analyses of the reports of Locke, Lowndes and Newton on the coinage question, and of the Bullion Report and the debates relating to it. Unfortunately, Mr. Macleod wrote history less with the object of discovering the truth than to supply proof of certain theories for which he was responsible, and of which he was for that very reason uncritical. This does not destroy the value of his work, but makes some caution necessary on the part of the reader.

Another general treatise deserving careful attention is

[1] Preface, p. 15.
[2] 2 Vols. 1855, 5th Edition, 1892-93.

Lawson's *History of Banking*.[1] This book appears superficial in form, but a more detailed study will show that, notwithstanding his stories of eccentric wills and celebrated frauds, of Quakers and adventurers, the author possesses a thorough knowledge of business and of the art of discussing a problem. Lawson is I believe the only English author who refers in his account of the Bank of England, to the close relations between this institution and the Treasury.[2] There are also interesting historical chapters in Gilbart's[3] and Mr. Collins'[4] books on Banking, but there is no reference to the history of the Bank in the best known of the general works, Bagehot's *Lombard Street*.

In addition to the histories mentioned above, and among what may be called narrative sources,[5] there are a large number of official publications devoted to the Bank of England, such as exist for all other English institutions, and which have greatly facilitated our study. These publications form a very complete series from the early nineteenth century, dating from the appearance in 1810 of the Bullion Report and the account of the preceding Inquiry. Since 1810 there have been numerous Committees and Reports on Banking. They have followed almost all the great crises which have shaken public credit to its foundations at intervals during the nineteenth century.[6] These reports are so valuable that the Bank of France has thought it worth while to have them translated.[7]

The Parliamentary debates[8] are no less important than the official publications. Some of the debates on banking in the

[1] London, 1850.
[2] On this point see the Appendix to Vol. II. of the present work.
[3] *History, Principles and Practice of Banking*. The last edition of this work was published in 1907.
[4] *The History, Law and Practice of Banking* (1882).
[5] Among these may be included *La Banque d'Angleterre et les Banques d'Ecosse* by Wolowski. This is a collection of studies, some of which are historical.
[6] The correspondence exchanged from time to time between the Chancellor of the Exchequer and the Governor of the Bank of England has also been published.
[7] *Extraites des Enquêtes anglaises sur la question des banques*. Edited by MM. Coullet and Juglar. 8 vols., 1865.
[8] *Parliamentary Debates from 1803 to the present time*. Edited by Hansard.

English Parliament are unrivalled in their completeness. Among these may be instanced the debates on the Bullion Report, on the resumption of cash payments (1819), on the crisis of 1826, on the Act of 1844, on the crises of 1847 and 1857; in the course of these discussions, orators like Thornton, Canning, Lord King, Ricardo, Peel, and Gladstone, delivered some of their finest speeches, and the problems raised were examined from an historical as well as from a theoretical and a practical point of view.

Before 1803 the Parliamentary debates were only published in a fragmentary manner. The summaries in Cobbett's[1] *Parliamentary History* cannot however be neglected; without them it would be impossible to study the South Sea crisis, or even the Act of Restriction.

Another source of quite a different character, but affording valuable information, is the innumerable mass of pamphlets, inspired in the first instance by the idea of a national bank, and later by the Bank of England itself. These publications began to appear about 1660.[2] Since then they have never entirely ceased, and have always been especially plentiful at times of crisis, when every quack has a sovereign remedy for the evils from which the country is suffering.

The study of these pamphlets is particularly indispensable for the period from the middle of the seventeenth to the beginning of the nineteenth century. During this long interval owing to the lack of newspapers and of economic treatises, scientific activity of every kind made itself known by means of pamphlets. Indeed, the economists of the period wrote in this form, in which appeared the studies of Petty, Child, and Locke, as well as those of Paterson, Godfrey, Chamberlain and everyone else who discussed banking questions, from Cradocke to Sir Francis Baring.[3]

After the beginning of the nineteenth century it becomes

[1] *Parliamentary History of England from 1066 to 1803.* Edited by Cobbett. 36 volumes.

[2] There were some even before this date.

[3] Many of the pamphlets devoted to the Bank of England are absurd or childish from an economic point of view, but none the less they have a vivid historical interest. They are often written in dialogue form.

an impossible and also a less useful task to look through all the pamphlets relating to the Bank. Impossible because of the excessive number of these productions, less useful because more complete works[1] are now obtainable in addition to these publications. Nevertheless, this form of expression is so firmly established among English customs that neither newspapers nor books have ousted pamphlets and tracts. The reform controversy due to the financial crisis of 1890 was carried on almost entirely in pamphlets.

This account of authorities would be incomplete without a further reference to Stephens' work, *A Contribution to the Bibliography of the Bank of England.*[2] This is, as stated in the title, merely a contribution to the bibliography, not a complete list of books. The author has indeed omitted several interesting works, but he has at any rate taken the trouble to read those mentioned, and often to give in addition a short and able analysis of them. Mr. Stephens has increased the value of his work by adding to the bibliography a chronological list of works on the English national debt, and biographical notices of the founders of the Bank of England.

Before concluding this introduction, I should like to reply in anticipation to two criticisms which will probably be made with regard to this book, viz.:

(*a*) That too much space has been devoted to general history; that while claiming to write a history of the Bank, something like a history of England itself has been attempted.

(*b*) That the dispute as to the respective merits of free issues and regulated issues has been treated rather negligently and with a certain lack of interest.

The first criticism is perhaps justified as far as certain minor questions are concerned,[3] but on the whole we believe it to be undeserved. The history of a national bank must be

[1] Among these may be included Lord Overstone's studies, which have been collected into a volume.

[2] London, 1897.

[3] Our excuse for this is the hope that the reader may be as much interested to hear about these questions as the author has been to write about them.

regarded as part of the general history of the country, and besides this, the creation of the Bank of England was so closely connected with political events, and was, indeed, so direct a result of some of these events that it cannot be described without taking them into account. Moreover, the Bank of England was distinguished at the outset from other Continental banks[1] by certain characteristic features introduced into banking operations by the goldsmiths; hence the importance of studying the business methods of these goldsmiths and their causes, which causes however, are purely historical. And further, the Bank when established did not remain in its original position but secured further privileges, and the explanation of this must be sought in political causes.

The Bank of England was thus created for political reasons. It was preceded by the goldsmiths and their banking methods, which again were due to political events and had received from them their peculiar form; it has been supported and attacked for political purposes. How then is it possible to avoid treating of general history in writing the special history of the Bank? In particular, no understanding of the position and transactions of the Bank during the first thirty years of its existence can be obtained without a knowledge of the events which preceded and accompanied its creation, and of the quarrels and prejudices, the Jacobite opposition, the political corruption, the hatred of the landed gentry for the commercial world, in the midst of which England was then struggling.

When once this period was passed frequent references to general history became less necessary and we have avoided making them. The Seven Years' War, the American Revolution, the Crimean War, have been barely mentioned. But on the other hand, we have had to emphasise the economic revolution which transformed England from an agricultural into a commercial and industrial country, and also the wars with the French Republic and with Napoleon. At this point, indeed, general history becomes once again

[1] See below, p. 80, etc.

closely connected with that of the Bank. Victimised by William Pitt's imprudence the Bank had to suspend cash payments in 1797, and was unable to resume them until four years after Waterloo. The transformation of England into an industrial country, on the other hand, not only enabled Great Britain to resist Napoleon, but also produced an upheaval of the system of credit which had hitherto existed, and thus led to crises which brought the Bank of England to the verge of destruction.

But the necessity for purely historical discussion has proved a fruitful source of difficulty. In the first place, it has not been easy to decide which historical events must be included and which might be neglected. When this was settled fresh difficulties arose with regard to the satisfactory combination of this historical information with economic discussions; in some cases it has seemed better to treat the history separately, and this has led to an apparent lack of unity in the book.

As regards the second probable criticism, that of neglecting in our discussion of the Act of 1844 the important controversy concerning freedom *versus* regulation of issues, we must acknowledge that we have here deliberately incurred the risk of blame. We judged that a discussion of this question would over-burden without compensating advantage,[1] a book already long enough. If however we had to give an opinion on this unsolved problem, this opinion while favouring in theory the idea of a certain limitation of issues, would resemble the definition once given by Émile Augier in an unspoken answer to a speech of M. Émile Olivier. There is a legend, says the dramatist,[2] that a Minerva was discovered fragment by fragment in

[1] Without compensating advantage because it would be hard to say anything new. This question, like many others of which people are beginning to weary, was formerly very fashionable, especially in France. Reviews, newspapers and economic societies gave it no peace, and the English crisis of 1866 aroused a famous controversy at the expense of the doctrine of liberty between Wolowski and Michael Chevalier. (The whole of this discussion together with the articles and letters of the two economists, will be found in Wolowski's *La Banque d'Angleterre*).

[2] Émile Augier, *Œuvres diverses*, p. 289.

successive excavations over a considerable extent of country. Each of the fortunate discoverers caused the portion he had found to be completed by a local sculptor, so that there were ten indifferent statues, each containing part of the masterpiece which was thus condemned to perpetual dismemberment.

Is not the history of truth somewhat of this nature?

The case in question may be an instance. Both systems have their advantages and their disadvantages. Regulation of issues may accentuate some crises by preventing the Bank from giving effective help to trade and industry. Free issues may bring about other crises by encouraging the Bank in an ill-judged excess. No doubt bank directors who are working under the latter principle may and ought to be guided by the course of the exchange and the prices of the precious metals. But experience shows that this precaution has not been always observed. On the other hand the case of the Bank of France may be noted; this institution, enjoying what is practically complete freedom of issue, has secured all the advantages of the system without falling into the excesses to which it might have led.

We may in fact conclude that the uses made of the system for regulating issues is of more importance than the actual system adopted. In this as in other cases it may be said that it is a bad workman who finds fault with his tools. Hence we have attached less importance to the theoretical value of Robert Peel's Act than to its practical working.

PART I.

ORIGIN AND DEVELOPMENT OF BANKING IN ENGLAND.

Political situation in England about 1640. Financial difficulties of Charles I. Seizure of Bullion deposited by the merchants in the Tower. Serious results of this proceeding. It encourages the development of banking, but delays the establishment of a National Bank.

Position and transactions of the Goldsmiths. Reasons for their success and their unpopularity.

Extension of English Trade. Projects for a National Bank. Pamphlets by Gerbier and Lamb. The return of the Jews, its influence upon banking.

The Bankers and the Government of Charles II. The King's Foreign Policy. Dutch War. First Run on the Banks. Financial Relations between Charles II. and Louis XIV. Second Dutch War. Suspension of Exchequer payments. Results and criticism of this Policy.

"BANKING, in the modern sense of the word, had no existence in England before the year 1640," writes Macleod.[1] This state of things might have gone on for a long time, for the merchants had acquired the habit of depositing their bullion and coin at the Tower, and there was therefore the less need felt for mere banks of deposit. But an incident, the precursor of the approaching internal struggles, hastened the appearance of bankers and of banking.

To explain this incident more clearly, the political situation must be briefly recalled. Charles I., who was then King of England, had ascended the throne not only believing in the political theories of his father, but firmly determined to put them into practice. To enforce these ideas, which were based on the theory of divine right and hence of absolute monarchy, a standing army was essential. And for the maintenance of this army money was required. The King

[1] Macleod, op. cit. (3rd ed.), Vol. I., p. 364.

was resolved to have this money, the Commons were resolved not to vote it. Things were at a deadlock as Charles was not long in realising. After dissolving two Parliaments and calling a third, he determined to dismiss this also and to summon no more. Thanks to the remarkable talents of Wentworth, better known by his title of Strafford, England was able to live for eleven years under a system of absolute monarchy. The great question throughout these eleven years was how to get money. The solution of the problem was not easy. As Dr. Cunningham points out,[1] Charles was more seriously in need than his father, and his requirements demanded both skill and invention. During the early years of his reign, although the Commons kept a tight hold on the purse-strings and only granted concessions in the form of tenths and fifteenths, a method of taxation which disappeared after this period, yet they did at any rate vote him numerous subsidies according to the custom which had originated under the Tudors. This source of revenue naturally declined under the absolute monarchy. But the expenses so far from decreasing proportionately, were increased by the necessity of keeping up the army which was urgently needed to strengthen the system of absolute monarchy so painfully built up.

It was thus important to invent a speedy remedy. One of the various methods of obtaining money was to grant monopolies under the pretence of developing the national industry, on which monopolies taxes were levied to compensate the Crown for the decrease in Customs duties.[2] But the device which was the most successful and which had the most disastrous consequences, was the illegal levying of a tax intended for use in emergencies, which is known in the history of English taxation as *Ship Money.*

This tax was levied as follows: the English maritime counties were bound, in case of a naval war, to provide a certain number of ships for the defence of the coasts.

[1] *The Growth of English Industry and Commerce* (Modern Times), p. 217.

[2] This was done in particular in the case of salt.

Money payments had sometimes been substituted for these ships. The Lord-Keeper Finch was of the opinion that this tax might be levied in time of peace, and a decree was accordingly issued under the pretext that pirates were capturing English ships in the Channel, and that it was necessary to provide for "the defence of the kingdom," and "the safeguard of the sea." This tax brought in £100,000 in the first year. Made covetous by this, the Government raised £200,000 by the tax in the following year, extending it to all towns, indiscriminately, whether maritime or not.[2] In this way a tax which ought only to have existed in emergencies, and then to have fallen upon a limited number of citizens, was levied in ordinary times, and throughout the whole kingdom.

This was too much, the two-fold illegality caused the failure of the plan; a vigorous protest was made. John Hampden, whose name afterwards became famous, took it upon himself to dispute the legality of the tax. He was condemned by the Court of the Exchequer, though by a very small majority. This decision only increased the general irritation, for everyone could see, as Strafford did, that if taxes intended for the fleet might legally be levied without authority, there was no reason why it should not be equally legal to collect in a similar manner taxes intended for the army.

This was the moment chosen by Charles to involve himself in fresh difficulties by provoking a religious crisis in Scotland. This affair, the details of which we need not discuss,[3] ended in civil war, and the maintenance of an army very soon exhausted the ill-supplied coffers of the royal exchequer.[4] The Scotch army had no such anxieties, for it was supported by subsidies from the national government,

[1] For the assessment of this tax, see Davenant, *Ways and Means of Supplying the War. Works*, Vol. I., p. 37.

[2] Dowell, *History of Taxation in England*, Vol. I., pp. 234, 263.

[3] For the Scotch crisis, see Clarendon, *History of the Rebellion and Civil Wars in England*, Book II., Vol. I., pp. 137-218, in Macray's edition in 6 volumes; and John Hill Burton, *History of Scotland*, Vol. VI., Chaps. 68-72

[4] It cost £300,000.

and above all, by the confiscations of its opponents' property. Charles had no resources of this kind; he had still to rely upon ingenious devices. He was delighted to find an excuse for summoning Parliament in an intercepted letter which contained, as he alleged, the proofs of an understanding between the King of France and the Scotch.[1] The said letter had actually been written. And in this conduct the King's enemies had only followed the traditional policy of Scotland, which was to apply to France for help in case of any quarrel with England.[2] Charles reckoned on the indignation aroused by this letter to produce a docile and generous Parliament.

Parliament met in the early spring of 1640. The new assembly according to the testimony of a famous author, was more moderate and showed more respect for the rights of the Crown than any of its predecessors since the death of Elizabeth. But apparently it failed to satisfy the King who hastily dissolved it after a session lasting three months without giving it time to pass a single Act.

The need for money continued to be no less urgent. Taxation was inadequate to supply means to maintain an army and to repel an impending invasion and a loan was suggested. To raise this the Government applied to the King of Spain, the Pope, and the City of London. The King of Spain refused the request for £400,000. The Pope was not prepared to give effective assistance unless Charles would become a Catholic. The City, being definitely opposed to the King, was determined to do nothing to help him.[3]

The King was more successful in dealing with individuals. Certain persons in official positions agreed to make him loans, which in all amounted to £60,000; the

[1] This letter, which was addressed, but not despatched, to the King of France by the Scotch, is given in Mazure, *Histoire de la Révolution d'Angleterre*, Vol. II., p. 405.

[2] The converse was equally true. See a reference to an old proverb in Shakespeare's *King Henry V.*, Act I., sc. 2:

"If that you will France win,
Then with Scotland first begin."

[3] When Parliament was summoned, the city did however grant a small loan, though it was only paid by instalments.

Catholics and the administration of the Crown lands advanced large sums. But amounts which were large for individuals were nothing to a government in extremities. The relief was thus of but short duration, and new expedients for raising money had to be devised.[1]

The first one suggested was not exactly new, it had formerly been a usual practice, and consisted merely in the debasement of the coinage. The proposal was to coin £300,000 of shillings, each containing three pennyworth of silver, with the motto, *Exsurgat Deus, dissipentur inimici.*[2]

This proposal caused great indignation. According to Macleod it was most warmly opposed by Sir Thomas Rowe in "a noble argument, which might have been studied with advantage two centuries later."[3] But in spite of this noble protest, the Mint was ordered to coin the new money, and the Attorney-General drew up a proclamation announcing the intention. The King although he had declared that the debasement was inevitable, now sent Cottington and Vane to the City to promise that if the merchants would grant the loan of £200,000 which had been demanded so long before there should be no more talk of debasing the coinage. The Common Council at a specially summoned meeting, replied that it had no power to dispose of the citizens' money. Renewed orders were sent to the Mint. When this was known general prices rose 10 per cent., and Charles gave way, having, as Mr. Gardiner[4] points out, drawn upon himself all the unpopularity of the measure, without gaining any of the immediate advantages which might have accompanied it.

His resources exhausted, and apprehensive of complete ruin, the King seized £130,000 in bullion which had been

[1] See Gardiner, *History of England,* Vol. IX., p. 169.

[2] These new shillings were reserved for civilians, the soldiers according to Strafford's advice, were always to be paid in good money.

[3] Macleod (p. 366) probably refers to a remarkable speech by Sir Thomas Rowe (*A speech touching the alteration of Coin*), published in 1641. This speech is often confused with one made by Sir Robert Cotton before the Privy Council in 1626, and published in 1651 in *Cottoni Posthuma.*

[4] Vol. IX., p. 174.

deposited in the Tower by the city merchants. This bullion had come from Spain, and was to have been despatched to Dunkirk, then a Spanish port.

The horror of the merchants may easily be imagined. This seizure—apart from the immediate loss—meant the ruin of the bullion trade which then flourished in London. They met at once and drew up a vigorous protest which they sent to Strafford. He answered that the step had only been taken in consequence of their refusal to lend money to the King. At length, after a whole day spent in argument, Charles agreed to give back the money he had seized, in return for a loan of £40,000, the Customs receipts being the security for the payment of interest and capital.

Before pronouncing judgment on the King's strange proceedings, his position must be remembered. It has been well summarised thus: "The enemy were proud and insolent, the army corrupt and disheartened, the country mutinous and inclined to the rebels, and the court . . . were all three."[1] The actions of the King could only be explained by the situation in which he found himself. Like a drowning man clutching at straws Charles committed folly after folly, each one more fruitless than the last. This interpretation of his behaviour is confirmed by the fact that in the case of the seizure of the bullion, as in the earlier scheme to debase the coinage, Charles dared not carry out his plans, and dishonour was all that he obtained. The seizure was nevertheless an exceptionally serious matter. and had not even the excuse of a precedent. As Francis remarks:[2] "If the short-sighted policy of the earlier kings of England had extorted money from the Jew and the Lombard, at least they borrowed from their English subjects; it remained for the polished Charles to sully his fair fame by robbing them." It is only fair, however, to remark that as regards "subjects," the "polished Charles," as Mr. Francis calls him in his figurative language, had none that were less faithful or less devoted than these very

[1] Macleod, p. 365.
[2] *Op. cit.*, p. 21.

city merchants who, reasonably enough, received him badly, refused to lend him money, showed no eagerness to pay taxes,[1] and in the approaching struggle were to be the strongest supporters of his enemies.

It would however be beside the point to discuss the policy of the seizure. The matter only concerns us through its consequences in which respect it is of supreme interest. It had two results which are in appearance contradictory:

(1) It led to the rise of banking.

(2) It delayed the foundation of a national bank.

We will begin by a few remarks on the second point, to save returning to it later on. This seizure so affected the country that it was long before the people could consider the possibility of an official bank, on account of the difficulty of protecting the precious metals in it from the depredations of royalty. The behaviour of Charles II. did not tend to allay these fears.

More needs to be said about the first result, the rise of banking. In this respect the King's action had such important consequences that we have not scrupled to study the question from the beginning, *ab ovo*. This explains indeed the starting point of the present work, a starting point which might otherwise seem to have but a slender connection with the subject.

We pass then to the history of the development of banking.

Rise and Development of Banking.

After such an experience the merchants could no longer think of entrusting their money to the Tower. They were reduced to keeping it themselves under the charge of their own clerks and employees. But the Civil War broke out, a warlike spirit seized upon everyone, and amongst others

[1] This, at least, was what the King alleged, when he summoned the Lord Mayor and the Sheriffs for their neglect to pay the taxes of "Coat and conduct."—See Gardiner, *loc. cit.*

upon the cashiers, who went off to join one or other of the opposed armies, taking their masters' money with them. It was a run of ill-luck, especially as even the more peaceful clerks were not more scrupulous, and secretly lent out to the goldsmiths at the rate of 4d. a day the sums entrusted to them. The goldsmiths inspired universal confidence. And consequently it soon occurred to the merchants that since their cashiers had treated them no better than their king, it would be both safer and more profitable to deposit their money directly with these goldsmiths. The country gentlemen very soon followed the example of the merchants, and, seeing their homes exposed to all the dangers of civil war, were only too glad to entrust their rents to the goldsmiths even without receiving interest. Thus rapidly and with but little trouble the goldsmiths found themselves in possession of considerable sums. A new field of business opened to them, and they anticipated the functions of a modern bank.

POSITION AND TRANSACTIONS OF THE GOLDSMITHS.[1]

The business carried on by the goldsmiths was varied in character, but all of it was exceedingly profitable, if not scrupulously honest.

(*a*)—In the first place along with their former trade as goldsmiths which many of them did not at once abandon,[2] they adopted very readily, thanks to their knowledge of coins, the extremely lucrative business of exchange.[3] Charles I. who let slip no opportunity of making money, had indeed

[1] See on this point a most valuable though very short pamphlet (it contains only 8 pages): *The Mystery of the New-Fashioned Goldsmiths or Bankers discovered* (1676). This booklet, which is adverse to the Goldsmiths, gives a very interesting account of their transactions.

See also Macpherson, *Annals of Commerce*, Vol. II., p. 427, etc., and various other works which we shall mention in the course of this study.

[2] Maitland states that even in his time many important bankers kept a goldsmith's shop in combination with their bank. Maitland's *History of London* was published in 1739.

[3] Copernicus in his *Traité de la monnaie*, maintains that the state of the coinage which was deplorable in his time, served only to bring profit to the goldsmiths. See Deschamps, *Cours de doctrines économiques*, 1897-98.

debarred them from this occupation by declaring it to be a Crown monopoly, and reviving the office of royal exchanger.[1] But this office disappeared with the King, and during the revolution the goldsmiths resumed the business of exchange, which was the more profitable since the coins struck in these disturbed times were very unequal in weight. They sometimes varied by as much as 3d. an ounce and many of them were heavier than the foreign coins of equivalent values. The goldsmiths did what is always done under such conditions; they put aside all the good coins, with a view to exportation. When it is remembered that Parliament about this time ordered the coinage of half-crowns to the value of seven millions, it will easily be seen what profits were to be gained from this business alone. Nor was this the only advantage which the goldsmiths derived from their knowledge of precious metals; they were expressly accused on all sides of debasing the coinage. It seems likely that these accusations were not without truth. One of the founders of the Bank of England remarks:[2] "If the bulk of the money of the nation which has been lodged with the goldsmiths had been deposited in the Bank four or five years past, it had prevented its being so scandalously clipped, which one day or the other must cost the nation one and a half millions or two millions to repair it." And the founders of the Bank of England were not unsupported in their accusations. One of their opponents says:[3] "As for the goldsmiths, no one expects any reformation from them, or that anything will make them honest but a catchpole."

[1] This office was a very ancient one. Its holder had to buy bullion with gold, to exchange coins of one metal for those of another, and also to exchange foreign and English coins. The arrangement appears to have hindered trade, and hence Henry VIII. abolished the office in 1539, on the advice of Sir Thomas Gresham. Charles I. revived it in 1627, on the pretence of preventing the shameful debasement of the coinage, and conferred it upon the Earl of Holland for 21 years.—(Ruding, *op. cit.*, pp. 383-385).

[2] Godfrey, *A short account of the Bank of England.*

[3] *Remarks on the proceedings of the Commissioners for putting into execution an Act passed last session for Establishing a Land Bank.* 1696, pp. 44, 45.

But whatever were the profits made by the goldsmiths out of their transactions as exchangers, they carried on another business which brought in yet larger gains, and through which they introduced banking into England.

(*b*)—We have seen how, thanks to the uncertainties of war and the dishonesty of some of the cashiers, a considerable capital had been collected in the hands of the goldsmiths. This capital, which they received at a very low rate, or even for nothing, they used for the discount of bills and for loans at high rates. The profitable nature of these transactions induced the goldsmiths to encourage the deposit of spare money with them by offering good interest and by allowing the depositors to withdraw their money without notice. This policy succeeded beyond all expectations, and in the course of a few years the citizens had generally adopted the habit of depositing their savings with the goldsmiths.[1]

Receipts were given for these deposits, which, under the title of goldsmiths' notes, soon circulated better than the actual coins whose scarcity they often supplied. Nor was this usage a temporary one, for even in 1696, during the crisis due to the restoration of the coinage,[2] Davenant[3] tells us that in the absence of coins, "All great dealings were transacted by tallies, bank bills, and goldsmiths' notes."

Goldsmiths notes must thus be regarded as the earliest form of bank-notes issued in England.

It is not surprising, in view of these profitable transactions, that the goldsmiths grew rich with prodigious speed. Five or six of them, Clarendon remarks, gained

[1] Sir Dudley North, on his return to London in 1680, after several years' absence, was surprised to find everyone depositing their money with the goldsmiths. He could not reconcile himself to such new customs, more especially as on the one occasion when he had the misfortune to entrust £50 to a banker, he chanced to select a bankrupt. See the life of Dudley North, by his brother Roger, in *The Lives of the Norths* (ed. by A. Jessop, 1890), Vol. II., p. 174.

[2] See below, Part II., Chap. V.

[3] *Discourses on the public revenues and Trade of England*, Vol. II., p. 161.

such a reputation on the London market[1] that people would have trusted them with all the money in the kingdom. "*And they then first came to be called Bankers.*"[2]

This immense prosperity naturally aroused some envy. And the conduct of the new bankers furnished excuse for numerous attacks. They were not only accused of debasing the coinage,[3] but also of a succession of other misdeeds, and this especially after they began to lend money to the Government. These accusations are expressed in the *Mystery of the new-fashioned Goldsmiths*, and, indeed, in most of the other economic pamphlets of the period.

In the first place, it was alleged that they lent money at exorbitant rates, and that they asked 33 per cent. or even more, whilst the legal rate was 6 per cent.[4] Complaint was made also of the inadequate security which they offered to depositors. According to Godfrey, two or three millions[5]

[1] The celebrated Sir Francis Child was the greatest of these goldsmiths. Mr. Collins supplies some details about the early London bankers in a chapter of some interest, the only one in his *History and Practice of Banking* which can be so described (Chap. IV., pp. 39-59. *The Early London Bankers*). Amongst other things he gives a list of people who had deposits with Sir Francis Child. We find among the number Cromwell, Nell Gwyne, Churchill (afterwards Duke of Marlborough), William III., and so on (see pp. 49 and 50). The firm still exists. Mr. Collins has indeed obtained most of his information from a study by one of its members, Mr. F. G. Hilton Price, who supplies interesting details about his own and other firms of goldsmiths. See *A Handbook of London Bankers, with some account of their predecessors, the early Goldsmiths*.

Some amusing anecdotes will also be found in an article by Disraeli, *Usurers of the Seventeenth Century* (see Curiosities of Literature, pp. 228-233). The stories are well told, and without pretence to scientific knowledge, like all the numerous and varied studies which the volume contains.

More detailed information about the goldsmiths and their London establishments are given in a book by one of their descendants, Mr. J. Biddulph Martin, *The Grasshopper in Lombard Street*. The grasshopper was the sign of a banking house in Lombard Street (now No. 68). It also formed part of Sir Thomas Gresham's coat-of-arms.

Finally, for the sake of completeness, we will mention a short pamphlet by Mr. A. F. Baker, *Banks and Banking*, which gives a brief summary of the history of the principal London banks.

[2] Compare Macleod, *op. cit.*, p. 367.

[3] See above, p. 22.

[4] *Bank of Credit: or the usefulness and security of the Bank of Credit examined in a dialogue between a country gentleman and a London merchant*, p. 18. An analysis of this pamphlet is given below (p. 50, *et seq.*).

[5] It is not clear whether Godfrey includes in this sum the money belonging to the goldsmiths which was seized by Charles II.

had been lost through the bankruptcies of goldsmiths and the disappearance of their clerks. Finally, the goldsmiths paid more attention to their profits than to the safety of their investments, and made loans to persons of no commercial solidity. This accusation at any rate is made by Dr. Lewis. Speaking of the Bank of Venice, he remarks:[1] "It had its first rise from the dishonesty of the Bankers. The Bankers at Venice did just as our Bankers have done here, they got mens' money into their hands at interest, and used it (as was necessary) to their best advantage, that they might make a better profit of their money than the interest they paied, they lent it out to insolvent persons, or laid out in desperate cases, as our Bankers did." This behaviour obliged the Venetian Government to interfere in the matter.

These accusations apparently contained elements of truth,[2] and all this serves to explain why, although the goldsmiths introduced banking into England, they did not succeed in adequately fulfilling the functions of a genuine bank and had later on to give place to the Bank of England; this institution supported as it was by the State, was able to avoid the mistakes of its predecessors.

We have now described the introduction of banking into England; it remains to observe its development under the successive governments of Cromwell and of Charles II. This development was favoured by a number of economic and political events which we shall proceed to describe, and the importance of the goldsmiths was increased by the fact that they began to make loans to the Government.

We shall study in succession the period of the Republic and that of the Restoration, but in order to give more unity

[1] *A Large Model of a Bank* (1678), p. 40. The author of the pamphlet about banking called *England's Glory*, which was published in 1694, and is often quoted, borrowed largely from Lewis.

[2] The goldsmiths published an answer to these attacks, under the curious title of *Is not the hand of Joab in all this? or, An Enquiry into the grounds of a late pamphlet, entitled, "The Mystery of the new-fashioned Goldsmiths."* This second pamphlet contains 17 pages. Unfortunately, it is not nearly so good as the first. There is nothing of interest in it. The author denies the accusations brought against the goldsmiths, and in particular (p. 4), 1, their crimes; 2, their insecurity.

to the account and to avoid repetition, we shall defer the question of State loans until we come to the reign of Charles II. Moreover, it was only in this reign that such loans became frequent.

SECTION I.

Banks Under the Republic and the Protectorate.

The condition of English trade and commerce improved greatly under the Republic and under the quasi-monarchical rule of the Protector. This was due in the first place to the natural progress of civilisation, but in the second place and more especially, to the restoration of order at home and to a varying but successful foreign policy, to the Navigation Act and the wars which attacked the Dutch monopoly of the carrying trade, and finally, to the liberal policy which opened England's gates to a race pre-eminently commercial, which had been ignominiously despoiled and ultimately banished several centuries earlier.

This commercial prosperity naturally favoured the development of banking, and in 1651 we may note the appearance of the first work which recommended the establishment of a bank. It was called *Some considerations of the two grand staple commodities of England,*[1] and is only nine pages long. It is written by Sir Balthazar Gerbier, the author of several economic tracts. The two staple commodities are fish and cloth;[2] the trade in these is in the hands of the Dutch, the problem is how to attract it to England. The question of the fishing trade is

[1] The complete title is: *Some considerations of the two grand staple commodities of England, and on certain establishments wherein the Public good is very much concerned. Humbly presented to the Parliament by Sir Balthazar Gerbier, Kt.* London, printed by I. Mab and A. Coles, 1651. This pamphlet has sometimes been referred to, but has not hitherto been honoured by an analysis, though it has at least the merit of novelty in default of other good qualities.

[2] p. 3.

foreign to our subject.[1] With respect to the trade in and manufacture of cloth, Gerbier cites the example of France, which established this industry at Sedan, and was afterwards able to supply half Europe. Moreover in order to furnish credit facilities to English business, a "bank of payment" ought to be set up in London. Gerbier points out the advantages other countries had gained from such institutions, and in particular he believes, for he is frankly mercantilist, that the capital of various foreign traders might be attracted in this way, and that a great benefit would result therefrom to the State.[2]

Some years later (in 1658), another still more characteristic proposal was published by Samuel Lamb, entitled, *Seasonable observations humbly offered to his highness the Lord Protector.* In this case the author's principal object is to advocate the establishment of a bank. He enumerates the advantages derived by the Dutch from theirs. Of these eight are important, and he considers that similar benefits, the chief being the increase of national capital and the reduction of the rate of interest, will be felt in England as soon as the bank is founded. Shortly afterwards Lamb issued a proposal in the form of a petition to Parliament.

[1] For the question of the fishing trade and the importance then attached to it, not only from a commercial standpoint but also as regards the maintenance of a fleet, see, among modern authors, Cunningham, *The Growth of English Industry and Commerce* (*Early and Middle Ages*, p. 443); Motley, *Dutch Republic* (Vol. I., p. 43); and among contemporary writers, H. Robinson, *England's Safety in Trade Increased* (1641), p. 16; John Smith, *England's Improvement Revived* (1673), p. 262.

There was a series of laws, dating from Henry VIII.'s time, to protect the fisheries, and especially the herring fisheries. The introduction of bounties was also advocated. See C. Reynal, *The true English Interest* (1674), p. 28. It is difficult to realise the importance attached to this trade. Dr. Cunningham remarks that it was believed to be the basis of Dutch prosperity. It is with regret that we limit our discussion to this note. We may add however, that the Navigation Act was evidently directed against the naval supremacy of Holland. (The Act was passed in 1651.) And similarly, the war of 1652 was due rather to commercial rivalry than to the relationship between the Stuarts and the Prince of Orange. See Morley, *Cromwell*, p. 336, and Seeley, *The Growth of British Policy* (Vol. II., Chap. I.). The latter work is full of original opinions and of interesting, though rather confused, detail.

[2] p. 9. Compare the Bank of Lyons.

A committee was appointed to consider it, but there is no record of the result.

It is unnecessary to contrast the two pamphlets and to estimate the superiority of the second. There had been an interval of seven years between the two publications, and during this time an event had occurred which, to judge by other countries, must have exercised considerable influence on the development of banks in England. I refer to the return of the Jews.

The return of the Jews to England. Its influence on banking.—The effect of the influx of Spanish Jews on the development of Dutch commerce is well known. The influence of the Jews at Venice was no less marked.[1] It was two Jews who first (in 1400) obtained the authority of the Senate to found a bank in the strict sense of the word. Their success was so great that many Venetian nobles established rival institutions. Abuses followed which, combined with monetary difficulties, determined the Government to establish the Bank of Venice.[2]

The same influence must have made itself felt in England. But at what date? In other words, when and for what reason were the Jews authorised to return to England? We will proceed to consider this question; it is not altogether easy to answer it.[3]

It is certain that as soon as Charles I. was dead, the Jews attempted to return to England. Public opinion was not

[1] Macleod, *Dictionary of Political Economy*, p. 216, article *Bank of Venice*. This dictionary which if finished, might have been of inestimable value, stops at the letter C. It was published in 1863.

[2] See above, p. 25, and below, p. 75.

[3] Cromwell's best known historians say little on this point. Morley and Carlyle devote little more than a page to it, and confine themselves to an appreciation of the event. See *Oliver Cromwell*, pp. 433-434, and *Letters and Speeches*, p. 175, Vol. IV. Goodwin (*History of the Commonwealth*, Vol. IV., Chap. XVII.), who devotes a chapter to the subject, does not tell us much more. Interesting information will be found in Gardiner, *History of the Commonwealth and Protectorate*, Vol. II., p. 30; in Leti, *Storia et memorie sopra la Vita di Ol. Cromwell*, Vol. II.; and especially in a published lecture by Mr. Wolf, *Resettlement of the Jews in England*. Guizot may also be consulted with advantage, *Histoire de la République d'Angleterre*, Vol. II., pp. 154-157.

unfavourable to them, partly on account of the biblical spirit which then prevailed, and partly because of the services rendered by them in Holland, a country which the English of this period constantly set before them as a model. Thus Gardiner mentions[1] the publication of a pamphlet about this time, in which in order to prove the importance of Dunkirk, it is stated that the Jews were prepared to give £60,000 to £80,000 in return for the toleration of a synagogue there, and that such permission would attract all the Portuguese merchants from Amsterdam, from which a still greater benefit would result.[2] The Amsterdam merchants had not expected such demonstrations of sympathy. They took the initiative, and two of them presented a petition in 1649 to Fairfax and the Council, for the revocation of the banishment of the Jews.[3]

Another petition is referred to by some historians. Certain Jews had asked for the repeal of the laws passed against them, and on condition that the Bodleian Library was made over to them, together with permission to convert St. Paul's Cathedral into a synagogue, they undertook to pay "six millions of livres" according to some, £500,000 according to others. It is stated that negotiations were broken off because the parties could not agree as to the price, the English Government asking eight millions or £800,000. It is unfortunate as far as concerns the authenticity of this tale, that the references given by the historians[4] are inade-

[1] Gardiner, *loc. cit.*; see also *Historical Review*, July, 1896, p. 485.

[2] For a similar opinion, see a letter from Major Whalley to Thurloë. *Thurloë's Papers*, Vol. IV., p. 308.

[3] See *Clarke Papers*, Vol. II., p. 172, note *a*. This petition is given at the end of Wolf's *Resettlement*.

[4] The historians in question are Francis and Goodwin. Francis (p. 24) refers to Thurloë. According to his habit he mentions neither volume nor page, in which indeed he is wise, for whenever he departs from this custom his references are false. Goodwin (Vol IV. p. 246, note), who does not himself believe the petition to be authentic, refers to Salmonet's *Histoire des Troubles de la Grande Bretagne* (p. 309). But Mentet de Salmonet on p. 309 is speaking of the year 1642 and the King's stay at York. Besides, this work which was published in 1649, deals with nothing later than 1646. Guizot and other historians make no reference to the affair. Neither have I found anything in Thurloë, a book researches in which are greatly facilitated by the excellent index.

quate or erroneous, hence we only refer to it as a curiosity.

These negotiations came to nothing. Mr. Wolf proves however, that notwithstanding this rebuff a number of Jews established themselves secretly in London in the time of the Commonwealth.[1]

The situation improved still more during the Protectorate. Cromwell's ideas were in advance of his times, and as Mr. F. Harrison remarks,[2] "Noble were the efforts of the Protector to impress his own spirit of toleration on the intolerance of his age; . . . He effectively protected the Quakers; he admitted the Jews, after an expulsion of three centuries; and he satisfied Mazarin that he had given to Catholics all the protection that he dared." Cromwell was particularly well-disposed towards the Jews, with whom he had, according to M. Guizot,[3] fairly frequent dealings. They seem to have done him numerous services. The Jews for their part were not unaware of the Protector's feeling towards them, and did their best to profit by it.

Rabbi Manasseh Ben Israel took the initiative in the matter. This Rabbi was a remarkable character. He was born in Portugal about 1604, but while still a child he emigrated with his family to Holland. There he became a brilliant student, wrote books, and even established the first Jewish printing press at Amsterdam. But his chief efforts were devoted to improving the lot of his co-religionists, and to securing their admission into the different European countries. In particular he tried by various means, such as petitions to the Protector, and even the dedication of his book, *Spes Israelis,* to the British Parliament,[4] to obtain permission for the Jews to return to England.

[1] See *The Crypto-Jews under the Commonwealth.* A lecture re-published from *The Jewish Chronicle,* and from the first pages of the "*Resettlement*" by the same author.

[2] Frederick Harrison, *Oliver Cromwell,* p. 216. See also Glasson, *Hist. du droit et des Institutions d'Angleterre,* Vol. V., pp. 194-195.

[3] *Op. cit.* p. 154. See also pp. 154-155 for the cause of these dealings. "Probably the Jews had more than once been useful to him, either as spies or in connection with his need for money."

[4] The English translation of this work was published in 1650.

A commission, presided over by Cromwell, was appointed to consider the question. It was composed of lawyers, priests and merchants.[1] The debates were long-winded and threatened to be interminable. Cromwell consequently dissolved the assembly, remarking that the matter, complicated enough to start with, now appeared more intricate than ever, and that, "although he wished no more reasoning, he yet begged an interest in their prayers."[2]

The conference was thus without result and Manasseh's hopes were apparently vain. As a matter of fact however, the Jews were tacitly allowed to live in England. Manasseh received a pension of £100 to console him for his disappointment. And three years later, on February 15th 1658, at a reception at Whitehall, Cromwell seems to have given an assurance of his protection to Carvajal and his co-religionists.[3]

Whatever may be the truth about this latter point, it is probable that Cromwell took no legislative action with regard to the Jews, but it is certain that he tolerated their return, and that at the end of the Protectorate a number of them were living in England. They must have taken an active part in trade, for shortly afterwards a petition was signed

[1] Collier, *Ecclesiastical History*, Vol. VIII., p. 380-382. Readers must not be surprised to find that this celebrated discussion is credited to the reign of Charles II. Collier was an uncompromising royalist, who never recognised the Revolution, and refused to take the oath to William III.

[2] Francis, p. 26.

[3] Perhaps Cromwell would have done more if it had not been for Manasseh's behaviour, which Mr. Wolf considers to have been most extravagant. According to the statement of Sagredo, the Venetian ambassador, he seems actually to have adored Cromwell, asking him if he were not a superhuman being. Moreover one or more of his companions, having obtained leave to visit Cambridge, went to Huntingdon, Cromwell's birthplace. The rumour spread that they had gone there to study the Protector's ancestry, to discover a Jewish origin for him, and to prove that he was the Messiah. (For this journey to Huntingdon, which has been disputed, see Leti, *op. cit.*, Vol. II., p. 443.) These rumours were made use of by Cromwell's enemies, and he, anxious to avoid ridicule and sarcasm, ordered the Rabbi's companions to return to London.

by numerous merchants complaining that the Jews were not subject to the alien law, and that in consequence the Treasury suffered a yearly loss of £10,000.[1]

SECTION II.

BANKING AFTER THE RESTORATION.

THE distinctive feature of this period is the transactions of the bankers with the Government, transactions which took the form of loans and advances in anticipation of the supplies. Loans of this sort had already been made under the Protectorate. Cromwell had to maintain a large army to carry on continual wars, one of which, that with Spain, was very unpopular, and he dared not ask Parliament to vote new taxes, owing to his somewhat strained relations with that assembly, which was jealous of his power, hence he was hard pressed for money,[2] and was often forced to rely on the help of the goldsmiths.

Charles II., when he returned to the throne of his fathers, was forced to have recourse to his predecessor's expedients, in this respect at least, with still greater frequency. It is true that he had not such a large army as the Protector's to keep up; indeed, he had no regular standing army, strictly speaking.[3] Neither had he a specially warlike disposition, since he entered upon only two European wars during the

[1] Stowe, *A Survey of the cities of London and Westminster*, Vol. II., p. 243. Others demanded that strict regulations should be made for the Jews, see T. Violet, *Petition against the Jews* (1661), and *England's Wants* (1667), p. 40. These unfavourable feelings lasted for a long time; the question of the naturalisation of the Jews gave rise to long Parliamentary debates. In 1753 naturalisation was conceded, and then, in the face of popular opposition, withdrawn. See Josiah Tucker, *A letter to a friend concerning Naturalisation* (1753). Even in this century Macaulay had to write an essay protesting against the civil disabilities of the Jews.

It is interesting to note that as soon as the Jews were placed on an equal footing with other citizens these feelings began rapidly to disappear. At the present day I have found no trace of anti-semitism in England.

[2] Goodwin, Vol. IV., p. 552.

[3] Charles' standing army was for a long time limited to his personal guards. This army was increased later on, but even at the end of his reign, after the evacuation of Tangier, the dowry of his wife, Catherine of Braganza, the King had no more than 7,000 foot and 1,700 horse and dragoons at his disposal.

twenty-four years of his reign, wars which indeed brought neither honour nor profit to England. The Parliaments, too, were liberal enough, and voted subsidies with unusual zeal, especially during the years immediately following the Restoration. Charles' vices and courtiers were however quite able to swallow up more money in one year than all Cromwell's armies and wars had cost in ten. And his urgent desires could ill adapt themselves to tardiness and delays, two qualities which usually accompany the collection of taxes. He wanted money and that at once, and the goldsmiths undertook to supply him.

It is however only fair to acknowledge that Charles was obliged to apply to the goldsmiths at the very outset of his reign. Cromwell's army had then to be disbanded, since it was at once an object of hatred to the people, a danger to the Crown and a heavy burden to the Treasury. But considerable sums were owing to the troops. Between two and three hundred thousand pounds had to be found in a few days. The House of Commons had readily voted this sum, but it could not be raised all at once by taxation. To put off the disbanding of the troops would have increased the nation's obligation each month in incredible proportions. "None could supply those occasions," writes Clarendon,[1] "but the bankers, which brought the King's ministers first acquainted with them; and they were so well satisfied with their proceedings that they did always declare 'that they were so necessary to the King's affairs that they knew not how to have conducted them without that assistance.'"

This satisfaction was indeed so great that soon the Crown could not do without the bankers, and entered into the closest relations with them.

According to Clarendon's[2] account, these transactions were managed as follows: As soon as the subsidies were voted, after discussion with his ministers as to the sums

[1] Clarendon, *Life*, Vol. II., p. 218.

[2] All that follows is taken from the *Life*, we have merely condensed the original to some extent. No one could have a better knowledge than the author, who was then Lord Chancellor, of the financial practices devised by himself.

needed at once, the King summoned the bankers to his presence, for no contract was arranged without him. Each banker was asked how much he could advance, and what security he would require. Each answered according to his own resources, for there was no combination between them. The bankers asked 8 per cent. for their money, which was not unreasonable, and the King was ready to pay it; but after mature consideration they decided to leave the rate of interest to be determined by the King's bounty, at the same time remarking that they were themselves paying 6 per cent. to their own creditors, which was, in fact, known to be true.[1]

They then received a transfer of the credits for the payment of the first taxes voted by Parliament, and tallies on those parts of the budget which were the least heavily burdened. But even this was not sufficient security, for the King and the Minister of Finance might devote the sums thus collected to other objects. Hence they had really no other security than their firm belief in the justice of the King and in the honour and integrity of his Treasurer; this was the real basis of the credit which supplied the needs of the Crown. The King, too, always treated them graciously as his very good servants, and the Ministers regarded them as very worthy people.

In this way for many years, even up to the unfortunate outbreak of the Dutch war, the public finances were, Clarendon states, managed with little difficulty, though perhaps at some slight additional cost, and no one said a word against the bankers, whose credit and reputation increased daily, and who had everyone's money at their disposal.

Probably at the time of which Clarendon speaks, that is before 1665, the goldsmiths did not ask more than 8 per cent., but this could not long continue, and their demands increased proportionately with the needs of the King, all the more since they were advancing money on more and more distant revenues, and had already anticipated all the payments to the Crown which would fall due in the near future.

[1] p. 219.

Soon, according to contemporary evidence,[1] they were asking 20 and 30 per cent. Pepys[2] tells us that as early as 1663 the Treasury was paying 15 and sometimes 20 per cent., which is, he says, "a most horrid shame," and ought not to be allowed, nor, he adds, should the goldsmith Maynell be suffered to make an income of £10,000 a year in this way.

Possibly the contemporary writers exaggerated a little, but there is no doubt that the goldsmiths got 12 per cent. from the King for their money.[3] And when it is remembered that they were paying barely half this interest to their depositors, the indignation of the public may be understood, an indignation which was further increased by the shame of seeing the King in the hands of usurers,[4] and by the harshness, common to all farmers of taxes, with which the goldsmiths collected those taxes which were made over to them. But even if the farmers derived as much profit from the King's vices as their enemies alleged, they were shortly to pay cruelly for their gains, thanks to this same royal immorality.

At this point the history of banking becomes once more closely connected with the general history of England. We must now consider in turn Charles' two European wars.

(a)—*The War with Holland. The Dutch fleet enters the Thames. First "run" on the banks.* Charles had entered upon a war with Holland. After several vicissitudes, and at the very moment when people were expecting the con-

[1] "Charles being in want of money, the bankers took 10 per cent. of him barefacedly, and by private contracts on many bills, orders, tallies, and debts of that King, they got 20, sometimes 30 per cent., to the great dishonour of Government. This great gain induced the goldsmiths to become more and more lenders to the King, to anticipate all the revenues, to take every grant of Parliament into pawn as soon as it was given; also to outvie each other in buying and taking to pawn bills, orders, and tallies, so that, in effect, all the revenue passed through their hands." See *The new-fashioned Goldsmiths, cf.* Macpherson, p. 428.

[2] Pepys' *Diary,* Vol. II., p. 97. This diary and that of Evelyn, are most valuable for any study of the history and customs of the period. Pepys was Secretary to the Admiralty during the reigns of the two Stuarts.

[3] W. D. Christie, *Life of Shaftesbury,* Vol. II., p. 57.

[4] "Sir John Hebden, the Russian Resident, cries out against the King's dealing so much with goldsmiths and suffering himself to have his kingdom kept and commanded by them."—Pepys, Vol. II., p. 170.

clusion of peace, De Ruyter sailed up the Thames, took Sheerness, burnt such ships as were at Chatham and seemed actually to threaten London. A description of this event will be found in Clarendon.[1] Consternation spread through London, the inhabitants of which thought themselves on the verge of destruction. Parliament, which had voted[2] large sums for the fleet and for the fortifications of the river, was terrified beyond description[3] at hearing the enemies' guns for the first time. It was believed that the Dutch had taken Greenwich, and had it not been for the presence of mind of the King and the Duke of York, the Tower would have been abandoned.

Everyone who had any money had deposited it with the goldsmiths. This money was known to have been lent to a Government which at the moment seemed to offer no security; each man then hastened to his banker in the hopes of being in time to save some remnants of his fortune, and London witnessed for the first time a phenomenon, with which, alas! it was destined to become familiar—a "run" on the banks.[4]

These fears were calmed by a royal proclamation[5] declaring that payments from the Exchequer would be made as usual, "And that we will not upon any occasion whatsoever permit or suffer any alteration, anticipation, or interruption to be made to our said subjects."

It will now be seen how Charles kept his promise, and what he called "our royal word and declaration."

(*b*)—*Second War with Holland. Treaty of Dover. Suspension of Exchequer payments.* A treaty of peace followed De Ruyter's expedition. During the years succeeding this treaty Charles seemed determined to enter upon friendly relations with the Low Countries. Through the good offices

[1] pp. 414-419.

[2] See contra, *Life of King James II.*, Vol. I., p. 425.

[3] For an account of this panic and its accompanying incidents, see Evelyn, *Diary*, Vol. II., pp. 24-25.

[4] The same phenomenon occurred in Amsterdam five years later.

[5] This is published at the end of a very interesting pamphlet by Th. Turnor: *The Case of the Bankers and their creditors, more fully stated and examined* (1675).

of Sir William Temple,[1] the ambassador to Holland, a Protestant Triple Alliance was made between the States General, England, and Sweden. Charles hoped by this to give temporary satisfaction to English public opinion, and, above all, to make a definite breach between Holland and Louis XIV. who had hitherto been allies, at any rate in name. Shortly after he made with Louis XIV. a second treaty, known to history as the Treaty of Dover,[2] at which town the King had personally carried on the negotiations. This treaty, in which Madame took such an important share, Charles was careful not to publish, not even communicating it to all his ministers. He bound himself to join Louis XIV. in a war against Holland, to be converted to Catholicism and to several other undertakings. In return he was to have two million francs in two instalments, and three millions a year during the war.

Charles II.'s principal object in signing the Treaty of Dover was neither foreign policy nor the conversion of the English to Catholicism, but to obtain power to satisfy the caprices of himself and his companions; in other words, to get money.

He was undoubtedly attracted by Catholicism, the faith in which he died, and his conversion to which seemed very rapid.[3] Doubtless, too, all his sympathies were for France, brought up as he had been by a French mother, and subject to the French influence of his sister and of his

[1] For this treaty, see Macaulay's essay, "Sir William Temple," pp. 418-468, in the one-volume edition, and, of course, Mignet's *Histoire des Négociations relatives à la succession d'Espagne*, Vol. II., p. 549, etc. An account of the varying feelings with which this treaty was regarded by the King of France will be found in the *Œuvres de Louis XIV.*, Vol. III., pp. 83-85.

[2] For the Treaty of Dover, see Mignet, Vol. III., and the text itself in the same volume, p. 187. For contemporary English writers, see *An account of the private league* in *State Tracts* (1705), 37-44; and also the *Secret History of Whitehall*, Letter xix. This last work, which was published in 1697, is evidently directed against France. It possesses some interest as an historical curiosity.

[3] Of this conversion, which must have taken place even before the Treaty of Dover, an account full of romantic and curious details, which seem however to be authentic, is given by an Italian Jesuit: *Storia della Conversione alla Chiesa Cattolica de Carlo II., re d'Inghilterra, Cavata de Scritture authentiche ed originali per Guiseppe Boere D.C.D.G. Estratto della Civilta Cattolica.* Rome, 1863.

cousin, Louis XIV., then at the height of his magnificence, and later of the Duchess of Portsmouth. But the subtle, intelligent and sceptical Charles II. was not the sort of man to risk his crown for the Pope and the King of France. He knew well how to exploit the fears with which Louis XIV. inspired Parliament, and the anxieties which Parliament aroused in Louis XIV., with the sole object of securing a few subsidies.

We shall shortly be able to watch him at his work. The Treaty of Dover was no sooner signed than the Lord-Keeper Bridgeman[1] urged Parliament to vote fresh supplies in order that the English navy might equal the constantly increasing navies of France and Holland. Parliament voted £1,300,000 to pay off debts and £800,000 to equip the fleet, adding a long report in which it prayed the King to take measures against the dangers of Popery. Charles promised all they asked, issued a religious proclamation of the character desired, prorogued Parliament, spent the £800,000 on anything but the equipment of the fleet, and at the end of the year signed a new treaty with Louis XIV. in which he secured even better conditions than those of six months earlier.[2]

Charles persisted in a policy which he had found so successful.[3]

After a temporary delay[4] however Louis XIV. deter-

[1] This minister, who acted as spokesman of the Government on the occasion, was not aware of the Treaty of Dover.

[2] Madame had died in the interval, but this had not caused that loosening of the relations between the two Kings on which some people had counted.

[3] "And so, in return for the prorogation of Parliament for fifteen months, which took place in November, 1675, Louis pays £100,000. Again, in 1677, when Parliament presents an address 'representing the danger from French aggression and imploring the King to strengthen himself by such alliances as may secure Flanders and quiet the fears of the English people,' Parliament is prorogued again, but this time Louis has to pay £180,000. On the other hand, at the beginning of 1678, when Charles demands £600,000 from Louis for a similar service and meets with a refusal, Charles begins to decide upon war, and obtains a grant of £600,000 from Parliament 'for enabling his Majesty to enter into actual war against the French King.'"—Seeley, *op. cit.*, Vol. II., p. 214.

[4] This delay was due to the fact that although Louvois had completed his reform of the army, the new army had not yet been tested. See Camille Rousset, *Histoire de Louvois*, Vol. I., p. 294. The affairs of Lorraine gave an admirable opportunity for a trial of the new system.

mined to begin the war with Holland. The Cabal[1] Ministry was in power. Charles was as usual without money, he dared not summon Parliament, and the French King's subsidies were no longer adequate. He determined on an action at once arbitrary, unjust and foolish, which was inspired by Clifford, though it has often been attributed to Shaftesbury, who in fact, according to his biographer, Mr. Christie, both condemned and opposed it.[2]

Clifford's remedy was as follows: An order was issued on January 2nd, 1672, just two months before the commencement of the war, suspending all payments out of the Exchequer on whatever warrant, order or security, for a period of twelve months.

When this order was issued the Government owed £1,300,000 to the goldsmiths, of which £416,724 belonged

[1] "Cabal," from the initials of the names of Charles' five ministers—Clifford, Arlington, Buckingham, Ashley, and Lauderdale.

[2] Lord Ashley, afterwards the Earl of Shaftesbury, even sent a written protest to the King against the suspension of payments from the Exchequer. See also a letter from him to Locke, and the corroborating evidence of Sir W. Temple in Christie, Vol. II., pp. 58-70. This account is supported by Evelyn, Vol. II., p. 70. Burnet, however (*History of his own time,* Vol. I., pp. 532-533), formally accuses Shaftesbury of instigating the King: "Shaftesbury was the chief man in this advice." He alleges that he had this from Shaftesbury himself, who had moreover withdrawn his money from the bankers before the seizure. J. Lingard (*History of England,* Vol. IX., p. 202, note *b*) is inclined to agree with Burnet. I do not believe that Burnet was right. But nevertheless I feel some doubt as to Christie's assertions, because, to say nothing of the morality of Shaftesbury—he would have served for a model for Otway's Senator in *Venetia Preserved*—his biography, published with the consent and assistance of his family,—the 7th Earl of Shaftesbury, to whom the book is dedicated, having supplied numerous documents,—his biography, I say, has somewhat the tone of an apology. Mr. Christie's work has however nothing in common with those biographies of which Macaulay speaks as the result of an agreement by which the family provides the documents and the historian the flattery. On the contrary the book is one of the best there is on the reign of Charles II. In this connection it is regrettable to have to state that we possess no good history of Charles II.'s reign, and worse still, that the gap is not unique. There are hardly more than two periods of modern history about which scientific works exist, that dealt with by Gardiner, and the fifteen years (1685-1700) to which Macaulay's *History of England* is devoted. It is true that pictures of Charles II.'s reign are to be found both in Macaulay's work and in Fox's *James II.,* but however good these may be, they remain little more than pictures, serving as an introduction to more serious studies.

to Sir Robert Vyner.[1] This proceeding, which was nothing less than a declaration of national bankruptcy, was accomplished so suddenly, and was so entirely unexpected by the public, that indescribable confusion at once spread through the town and caused a number of financial disasters. This confusion can be easily explained, since, although the number of bankers directly injured was comparatively small, yet, as everyone who had any money had habitually entrusted it to these bankers, the total number of people brought to ruin was not less than ten thousand.

The bankers indeed stopped their payments immediately, and those merchants who had deposited capital with the goldsmiths declared themselves bankrupt.[2] Colbert who, in the interests of the war, approved of the measure, refers to the great opposition it aroused, and remarks that bills of exchange to the value of £30,000 had to be sent back to Italy dishonoured.[3]

Four days later (on January 6th), an explanatory announcement was made, promising the bankers 6 per cent. interest and declaring that the suspension of payments should not last more than six months. The next day the King summoned the goldsmiths to the Treasury. He pacified them and persuaded them to repay the money deposited with them by the merchants. This was done, and the evil was so far diminished, but the bankers were no nearer payment. The King probably had some idea that Parliament would provide the means of repaying them when the twelve months were over. But nothing of the sort happened, the House of Commons rejected the repeated demands made on it to adopt such a course. All that was

[1] Collins, *op. cit.*, pp. 43-44, gives a list of bankers and of the sums of which they were respectively defrauded :—

Sir Robert Vyner ...	£416,724.	J. Snow	£59,780.
E. Blackwell	£295,994.	J. Colville	£85,832.
G. Whitehall	£248,866.	Thomas Rowe	£17,615.
J. Horneby	£22,548.	T. Portman	£76,760.
G. Snell	£10,894.	Divers	£93,505.

[2] Vivid details of this crisis will be found in Turnor's pamphlet referred to above.

[3] See Christie, *loc. cit.*, Letters of January 4th and 8th (1672) in the Archives of the Ministry of Foreign Affairs. Colbert too estimated the number of those affected at ten thousand.

done was to pay the 6 per cent. interest, and in 1677 the King granted a yearly rent on his hereditary excise for this purpose. All payment of interest ceased, however, in 1683, and was not resumed after the Revolution, in spite of a lawsuit of a unique character which was carried on by the goldsmiths.[1] At length (in 1701) an Act was passed charging the hereditary excise with a yearly interest of 3 per cent., payable from 1705, not on the actual amount of the debt, but on the original capital. Moreover, these 3 per cent. annuities were counted as redemption, and were to cease when half the original capital, that is, £664,263, had been repaid. The Act of 1701 was simply a fraud, for six times this amount was owing to the bankers. It was calculated that they had lost three millions in the affair, without counting their legal expenses. But what was most remarkable was that this debt, known as the "Bankers' Debt," was never paid, and still forms part of the English national debt, having been consolidated with the South Sea annuity.

[1] Substantially the same accounts are given of this lawsuit by Macleod, 3rd Edition, Vol. I., pp. 373-375, and Broom, *Constitutional Laws* (*The Bankers' Case*), pp. 228-234. The latter discusses the duties of a sovereign to his subjects: combined with the right to personal liberty, there exists the right to private property. It is in connection with the latter that Broom gives a very detailed account of the whole dispute.

The ground for quibbling was that the letters patent, in which Charles had recognised his debt to each of the goldsmiths and to their heirs, had been ratified by the House of Lords, but had never been presented to the House of Commons, and had not passed into law.

Thus, when the goldsmiths brought an action before the Court of the Exchequer in 1689, and finally won their case after a delay of two years, the Government raised two questions, viz.:—

1.—Whether the letters patent were good and valid to bind the Crown.

2.—Whether the Court of Exchequer was competent to decide the case, or whether the petitioners ought not to have applied directly to the King.

The discussion turned chiefly on the second point, since the first was not seriously disputed. Somers, the Lord Chancellor, in spite of the opinion of the majority of the judges, declared that the Court of Exchequer was not competent in the case.

The question whether Lord Somers could give a decision contrary to the opinion of the majority of the judges gave rise to an appeal to the House of Lords, the Supreme Court, which, on January 23rd, 1701, reversed Lord Somers' judgment. But—and this is the most surprising part of this remarkable suit—as Macleod aptly points out, although this Court recognised the indisputable rights of the petitioners, it made no attempt to redress their grievances. And this was the conclusion of a lawsuit of twelve years' duration.

This melancholy history brings us to the conclusion of our first part.

It is not possible to treat Charles II. as we treated his father in a similar case, *i.e.*, to find excuses for him. On the other hand, it is evident how well this suspension of Exchequer payments accorded with the general character and with the political ideas of this prince, a charming person, but born with tastes in excess of his resources, and with no idea of sacrificing these tastes to the interests of his country. An economist of well-deserved reputation, M. Wilfredo Pareto,[1] has however defended him as follows: "Charles has been much blamed for a deed which differs but slightly from the actions which have been done and continue to be done by governments who appropriate the treasures of banks." It might equally well be said that William III.'s Government treated the defrauded bankers very little better than Charles' had done. But these after all, are meagre excuses.

[1] *Cours d'Économie Politique, professé à la Faculté de Lausanne* (Vol. I., p. 363).

PART II.

FOUNDATION OF THE BANK OF ENGLAND.

CHAPTER I.

NECESSITY FOR A NATIONAL BANK.

Sketch of the commercial requirements. The rate of interest. Importance attached to a low rate. Theories of Sir J. Child. The paper currency. In what way this could be made less variable than a metallic currency. Account of the proposed schemes. The *Bank of Credit.* Failure of the schemes. Reasons for this failure.

Bad state of the public finances. Heavy expense of the War against Louis XIV. Inadequate returns from taxation. Montague's financial expedients. The Tontine and the Lottery Loan. Montague and Paterson's scheme.

In spite of defeats abroad and disorder at home, industry and commerce prospered under the Restoration Government. The comparative peace enjoyed by England and the wars into which Louis XIV.'s insatiable ambition plunged the rest of Europe, largely contributed towards this commercial expansion. The natural progress of civilisation also counted for something, and vigorous legislation for a great deal. Numerous protectionist measures were in fact passed by Parliament.[1] Some of these laws, such as the extension and improvement of the Navigation Act, were of great service to the country. Others were marked by the absurdity to which extreme protection often leads: for instance, the law quoted by M. Glasson, which ordered that corpses should be buried in flannel shrouds so as to encourage the growing woollen industry.

This commercial prosperity required to be supplemented by the foundation of a bank, an institution which would strengthen England's position in a remarkable degree by regulating and securing the paper currency, by reducing

[1] Glasson, *op. cit.*, Vol. V., pp. 201-202.

the rate of interest and by looking after a thousand other secondary interests. The goldsmiths had perhaps delayed the creation of such an institution, but had not succeeded in making it superfluous. Even before they had been despoiled by the King, their greed had made them hopelessly unpopular.[1]

Throughout Charles II.'s reign there was accordingly a spontaneous outburst of pamphlets advocating the establishment of every variety of bank, whose proposals were very favourably received by the public. The promoters also could readily point to the services done by the banks to Venice and to Genoa, and, above all, to Amsterdam; and this latter case had no small weight in a country and at a time when the imitation of the Dutch and their institutions was exalted into a regular system.[2]

These projects came to nothing for accidental reasons which we shall notice presently, but from this time onwards the commercial world actively desired the creation of an institution of which it felt in serious need. Very soon it was not alone in this wish.

The Revolution of 1688 had occurred, involving a war with France. William III.'s Government having engaged in an expensive and, for a long time, an unsuccessful struggle, and unable to count on a satisfactory payment of the taxes, and having tried all kinds of financial expedients, at length realised that the creation of a bank would be of immense service to them, for nothing but a national bank could raise an important loan and subsequently maintain the King's financial position.

Henceforth the interests of the Government were in accordance with those of the country. A suitable proposal, easily carried out, was brought forward by Paterson. *The Bank was founded.*

Our first chapter, dealing with the causes which led to this foundation, thus falls naturally into two divisions:

[1] See above, pp. 25 and 35.

[2] For the general effects of this imitation on English industry and commerce, see Cunningham, *op. cit.*, (Modern Times), p. 101.

1. The commercial necessity for the foundation of a bank.
2. The political necessity.

The first part, besides describing the requirements of commerce, will deal with the various systems proposed for satisfying them; that is, the different projects suggested for banks and the reasons for their non-success.

The second part will deal with the financial and political reasons which induced the Government to found a bank, and these reasons will explain the opposition with which the institution met from the beginning.

SECTION I.

THE COMMERCIAL NECESSITY FOR THE FOUNDATION OF A BANK.

A.—*Account of the requirements of commerce.* We have already pointed out the chief reasons which influenced the commercial world in favour of the establishment of a bank; they correspond to the three main classes of business which a bank undertakes: the receiving of deposits, the lending of money, and, in the case in point, the issue of bank-notes. The deposits made with the goldsmiths have been discussed, and it has been shown that the system did not always offer desirable guarantees of security. The chief remaining services which the public expected from a bank were:—(1) that it would reduce the rate of interest; (2) that it would guarantee a paper currency.

(1).—*The rate of interest.* Interest was first forbidden in England by two synods in 787. But the codification of the canon law was only begun in England in Henry III.'s reign, under the influence of researches into the law which were initiated by Theobald, bishop of Canterbury. Even at this period, however, we find documents against usury and bishop's edicts against it, but no royal edict.[1] It was not until 1364 that Edward III. empowered the city of London to issue an *Ordinatio contra Usurarios.* An Act

[1] *Dictionary of Political Economy, English Early Economic History,* Vol. I., p. 721.

having the same object was passed in 1390. The usurers evaded these laws by numberless devices and consequently a very stringent Act was passed in 1487. But this proved equally vain and was repealed by a law passed in 1495, which, while condemning usury, allowed the "*poena conventionalis, or usura punitoria.*" This in fact sanctioned the very practice it pretended to forbid. At length an Act of Henry VIII. (1545) legalised the demand for interest and fixed the rate at 10 per cent. In 1552 there was a fresh prohibition, which again failed, and the legality of interest was recognised anew by Elizabeth,[1] with the former limit of 10 per cent. The limit was reduced to 8 per cent. in 1624.

This reduction[2] was followed by a second in 1651, which made the limit 6 per cent. And Sir Josiah Child,[3] believing that the low rate of interest had largely contributed to the prosperity of Holland,[4] and considering the 6 per cent. limit too high, proposed an additional reduction to 4 per cent., which he calculated would double the national wealth in twenty years.[5]

Very soon the controversy as to the legality of interest changed into one as to the legal rate. William Petty, in his

[1] It has been alleged that this was due to Protestant influence; and a letter from Calvin to Oekolampadius on the Aristotelian theories is quoted in support of this. Besides this, it is pointed out that Holland, where interest was early permitted, was a Protestant country, whilst about the same time Dumoulin's *Tractatus contractarum et usurarium* was censured in France. I believe, however, that it is difficult to form a definite opinion on this matter; the canonists were less severe than people try to make out, and objected chiefly to loans to consumers.

[2] The reduction of 1624, like that of 1652, was chiefly due to Sir Thomas Culpepper, who thus helped to put into practice the theories which he had set forth as early as 1621 in his *Tract against the high rate of usury.* His son also wrote various works on the same subject.

[3] See the first edition of *A New Discourse of Trade,* published in 1668 under the title: *Some brief Observations concerning trade and interest of money,* pp. 7-16.

[4] The legal reduction of the rate of interest was, as Professor Edgworth justly remarks, Child's panacea, his *unum magnum.* Child alleged for instance, that the sole reason why Holland was able to capture English trade in spite of the Navigation Act, was that the rate of interest was 3 per cent. lower there than in England. John Law of Lauriston shared Child's views on this matter. See *Premier Mémoire sur les Banques,* in Guillaumin's edition, *Économistes et financiers du xviiie. siècle,* p. 550.

[5] p. 10. Child declared that a high rate of interest encouraged luxury and hindered the development of commerce.

Quantulumcunque,[1] condemns all laws regulating interest. Locke's arguments, as expressed in his *Considerations on the Lowering of Interest and Raising the Value of Money,* tend to the same conclusions.

As regards the period in question, it appears that the merchants had little ground for complaint, since the legal rate was no higher than 6 per cent. which was in no way immoderate considering the financial condition of the country.[2] Unfortunately this limit was theoretical and nothing but theoretical. The goldsmiths were not the kind of people to be satisfied with so little.[3] We have seen the interest which they asked from the King; and they were even more exacting in dealing with ordinary merchants, especially with the poor ones, from whom they demanded exorbitant rates.[4] Hence there was urgent need to remedy a situation which was most irksome to the commercial world, and a national bank was the only institution which would be sufficiently influential to improve matters, and to secure for trade that credit which is "one of the essential conditions of its expansion."[5] Such a bank would also do good service in another matter, that of the paper currency.

(2).—*The paper currency.* The future bank must also issue notes. Contemporary thinkers had clearly analysed the advantages which might follow from the use of the metallic coin thus made available. Sir William Petty, for instance, in his pamphlet, *Quantulumcunque,*[6] to which we

[1] Question 23. For Petty's theories on interest see a recent work by M. Maurice Pasquier, *Sir William Petty,* pp. 186-192.

[2] This is pointed out by the author of the pamphlet, *The Interest of Money mistaken,* who attempts to refute Child, and remarks very justly that the latter throughout his argument is mistaking cause for effect.

[3] This was, besides, the rate which they themselves were paying to their own depositors, see above, p. 34.

[4] This is an undoubted fact, and is proved by a number of authorities to whom reference has already been made. The author of *Bank of Credit,* p. 18, states that although the rate of interest had been reduced to 6 per cent., private enquiry showed that poor men could not obtain loans for less than 33 per cent., and were lucky not to be asked 60, 70, or even 80 per cent., as had been known to happen. (See also above, pp. 25 and 35).

[5] Lyon-Caen and Renault, *Manuel de Droit Commercial,* p. 510. We imagine that the loans were not to take the form of discounts, but were to be advanced on the security of goods held in deposit.

[6] Question 26, p. 165 of McCulloch's reprint in *Select Tracts on Money.*

have already referred, answers the question: "If there is any way to know how much money is sufficient for any nation," by saying, "I think it may be pretty well guessed at." A nation, like "a particular merchant, may have too much money, I mean coined money." If there is too little money, the best remedy is the erection of a bank "which well computed doth almost double the effect of our coined money."[1] Again, if there is too much coin, "we may . . . turn it into . . . vessels or utensils of gold and silver, or send it out as a commodity where the same is wanting or desired, or let it out at interest, where interest is high."

These opinions had been originally stated by Francis Cradocke,[2] a merchant who in 1660 wrote to Charles II. concerning the advantages which would follow from the establishment of a bank. He believed that the profits would be so great that it would be possible to abolish all taxation, and hence he called his pamphlet: "An expedient for taking away all impositions, and for raising a revenue without taxes by creating banks for the encouragement of trade." This pamphlet is seven pages long, but the theories in it are not demonstrated scientifically, and the author exaggerates the effects of his device.

Petty's pamphlet dates from 1682. Hence it is a mistake to credit Adam Smith with having discovered how the issue of paper money might increase the riches of a given country. In this case as elsewhere, the father of political economy discovered nothing, he merely worked out the idea, and above all, was able to render it tangible by a most happy simile, that of the "waggon-way through the air."

The second advantage which the public hoped to gain from paper money is more unexpected. Whenever a comparison has been made between a paper currency and a metallic coinage, economists have always been careful to note among the drawbacks of the former that it is much

[1] See Question 26. He remarks also that a country is not always "the Poorer for having less Money." "For, as the most thriving Men keep little or no Money by them, but turn and wind it into various commodities, to their great Profit, so may the whole Nation."

[2] For Fr. Cradocke, see the *Quarterly Journal of Economics*, published at Boston by Harvard University, Vol. II., p. 485.

more variable in value than the latter. But at the time of which we write the metallic currency was in such confusion and the English coins were so debased, clipped and falsified, that people could not recognise them, and they preferred to take a bank-note which they might reasonably hope to pass the next day at the same price as that for which it had been received.

In addition to these two principal advantages the public anticipated certain secondary benefits from the bank, on which it is superfluous to dwell, but which helped in the production of a number of projects on the subject. This brings us to our second point, the description of these suggested projects.

B.—*Description of the projects suggested.* This description seems to us necessary. It is true that none of the projects in question was fully carried out, but they prepared public opinion, which was thus ripe to receive Paterson's scheme. On this account alone, apart from the interest possessed by some of them for their own sake, they deserve not to be neglected.

For reasons already stated, the schemes proposed were exceedingly numerous. Their publication was encouraged by the policy of the city of London. This city had had for a long time the charge of children of deceased freemen. The property of these children was administered by the Court of Orphans. In this way a large sum of money had been accumulated which was known as the Orphans' Fund, and this, being rashly lent to the King, had been much diminished. The corporation tried to fulfil their obligations by means of the profits which might result from the creation of a bank, and the Lord Mayor appointed a committee to examine "all such propositions as should be made by any persons for the improvement of the Chamber of London." Amongst the suggestions made was one which the committee accepted, and which it only remained to carry out. To assist in this was the object of a very compact little work called *Corporation Credit or a Bank of Credit made current by common consent in London more useful and safe than Money.* This pamphlet, which appeared in 1682, was four pages long (numbered six), and concluded with an appeal to would-be supporters of the scheme to sign their names as such in various specified taverns. This appeal was apparently unheard.[1]

Apart from these municipal schemes there was the project for a land bank, which was put forward by Dr. Chamberlain, a project which nearly ruined the Bank of England, and of which we shall have to speak more at length.[2] The propositions contained in a pamphlet by M. Lewis, *Proposals for a large model of a Bank*, published in 1678, must also be referred to, and we may then pause to consider a bank of credit which was actually established and carried on business for a certain time.

The functions and the utility of this bank of credit are stated in the form of a dialogue between a country gentleman and a London merchant in a lucid and most amusing pamphlet called, *Bank of Credit, or the usefulness and security of the Bank of Credit examined in a dialogue between a Country Gentleman and a London Merchant*. The scheme however referred only to a bank of credit, there was no question of a deposit bank.

The somewhat curious reason for this omission is given in the merchant's answer to the country gentleman, who was inclined to think highly of the advantages of such a combination.[3] The directors, he says, "are unwilling to meddle with Money, . . . because . . . the scarcity thereof (on any occasion) would perhaps, by ignorant or malicious men, be

[1] A more complete account of this scheme will be found in *England's Interest, or the great benefit to the trade by the Banks and offices of credit in London, as it hath been considered and agreed upon by a Committee of Aldermen and Commons appointed by the Right Honourable the Lord Mayor* (1682). This pamphlet contains 8 pages.

[2] See below, p. 103. Before proposing a land bank, Dr. Chamberlain had apparently had a share in Mr. Murray's scheme to establish shops where merchants could deposit goods which they did not immediately require, and receive in return loans to enable them to carry on their business successfully. See Murray, *Proposals for advancement of Trade* (1676)—4 pages.

[3] The gentleman had said (p. 16): "Let me ask you for what reason the Bank will not meddle with money; for in my opinion, considering the great security and safety of their constitution, they might very well, and without any damage to themselves, have secured the running cash of the Nobility, Gentry, Merchants and Traders of this City and Kingdom from all hazard of loss. That would have been a great ease and benefit to all concerned, who know not now where to deposit their cash securely; especially if running cash should prove, as some imagine, to be within the state of bankrupt."

imputed to them; and as that can never be their Crime, they would also avoid the Imputation."[1]

What then was the business which the directors proposed to undertake?

Their first object[2] was thus described: "that Tradesmen, when they have a considerable quantity of goods or wares made, . . . they know not what to do therewith . . . whereas by the help of this Bank they may deposit their Goods, and by raising a credit on their own dead stock imploy their Servants, and increase their Trades, untill they get a good Market, without spending their time . . . to look out Chapmen, who usually take advantage of such men's necessities . . . they being many times forced to sell their Goods and Wares to loss."

Traders might offer as security not only merchandise but any other kind of unproductive goods, such as silks, ribbons, jewellery, toys, linen,[3] which they could thus make use of in case of emergency. The bank also made loans on real property and even on long leases, "without hazard or trouble of their Friends."

The interest on the loans was 6 per cent.

Should the goods deposited be lost, the bank forfeited the sums advanced on them. These sums might not exceed two-thirds or three-thirds of their value. But as regards the surplus value, the risk might be avoided by insurance through a monthly payment of two shillings per £100.[4]

The directors also intended to encourage any "ingenious invention tending to the Increase of and Promoting of any Linnen, Woolen, Silk, Lace, Paper, Salt; or any other useful Manufacture. . . ."[5]

Notes were to be issued: but the merchant was quite undisturbed by the dangers of forgery.[6] "I am well as-

[1] p. 17. The directors' fears were not ill-founded, for this very accusation was afterwards brought against the Bank of England.

[2] See pp. 5, 6, 7. In short, this bank was to be especially useful in cases of over-production, but it was dangerous on that very account, for by temporarily saving the merchants from the dangers of a glut, it would encourage them to speculate by excessive production or by ill-judged purchases.

[3] The Bank of Hamburg, established in 1619 on the model of the Bank of Amsterdam, made advances on jewellery as readily as on bullion.

[4] p. 15. [5] p 16.

[6] The promoters of the bank of credit were moreover not alone in their belief that the solution of this problem was a simple matter. In *England's Glory*, a work published in 1694, the author remarks incidentally that the notes will be printed on special paper so as to prevent imitations. The odd

sured," he asserts, "that the bills are so contrived that it is morally impossible that they should be counterfeited." He enumerates the precautions[1] taken, and the list is so long that his questioner remarks, "I cannot but admire and applaud the care and caution of the bank in this particular."

The London merchant was no more disturbed by the dangers which might arise from the note issue. The bearers would he considered, have sufficient guarantee in the honour of the directors, who would besides be liable up to the full value of their property.[2] This satisfied the country gentleman, who—like a wise man—was content with very little.

The arguments used by the London merchant were not stated here for the first time.[3] They might have been read seventeen years earlier in a pamphlet called: *A description of the office of credit.*[4] The first part of this, consisting of 11 pages, is devoted to an explanation of the working of the system, and the second, consisting of 15 pages, answers the objections which may be raised. The pamphlet, *Several objections sometimes made against the office of credit fully answered,*[5] is merely a later, slightly revised edition of this second part. Finally, *An account of the constitution and security of the general Bank of Credit*[6] contains nothing which has not already been noticed.[7]

thing is that these optimistic views were actually justified by facts for a long time. The first conviction for counterfeiting was not until 1758, sixty-four years after the foundation of the Bank of England. The guilty person was a Stratford draper called Richard Vaughan.

[1] pp. 12-13.

[2] It must be remembered that, owing to the narrow limits of the commercial world at that time, the personality of the directors would play a much more important part than at present, and that the Bank of England itself offered little more security to the bearers of its notes.

[3] See Murray's pamphlet referred to above, p. 50.

[4] The full title is: *A description of the office of credit by the use of which none can possibly sustain loss, but every man may certainly receive great gain and wealth.—Printed by the order of the Society,* 1665.

[5] Undated, Mr. Stephens in his *Contribution to the Bibliography of the Bank of England,* refers it to the year 1682. Two circulars announcing the establishment of the *Bank of Credit for the City of London* will be found in the British Museum bound up with the pamphlet in question.

[6] 1683, 14 pages.

[7] The same may be said of the arguments in *England's Interest.* See above, p. 50.

This bank of credit was at length established after numerous vicissitudes; its offices were in Devonshire House, Bishopsgate Street. Its transactions suggest those of some of the Italian *Monti*. Advances were made of three-quarters of the value of the goods deposited and notes for this sum were given to the depositor. To ensure the circulation of these notes a company had been formed of persons engaged in various branches of commerce, who undertook to accept the notes in payment. Anyone possessing notes might purchase goods from this company as easily as if he offered coin. The bank does not seem to have been a success. Its organisation was too complicated and the risk of depreciation in the value of the goods was too great.

Failure of the projects.—Reasons for this failure. To be brief, none of these schemes, to which must be added a project for mortgage on land, the Land Bank, could be realised successfully.

The cause of these failures must be sought not only in the intrinsic weakness of the schemes, in the very genuine dread of royal confiscation,[1] and in the distaste felt by some nations for novelty, but above all in a speculative mania which had suddenly spread and was diverting public attention from serious schemes which would take time to mature, to the advantage of charlatans who offered rapid profits to be made in lotteries, by the exploitation of unknown mines and pearl fisheries, or from treasures hidden at the bottom of the sea.

Anderson draws a vivid picture of what was truly a raging fever, which we shall find reappearing in England with the South Sea scheme, and in France with the *Compagnie des Indes*. The promoters of these enterprises made much stir in the town, says Anderson, in order to induce the public to support them, and employed a variety of devices and stratagems. They stated that a vein of gold, silver or

[1] See in Pepys' *Diary* (Aug. 17th, 1666) a discussion which took place during an excursion which Pepys made with several friends. The fear of confiscation was not peculiar to England. Compare Law's remarks on this point, *op. cit.*, p. 574.

bronze, had been found in a piece of land which they knew, that they had made a contract with the owner of this land, and that he, in return for a small life- annuity or for a share in the profits, had leased the mine to them for 21 years, it remaining for them to exploit it and to extract its wealth. Then they formed a company, generally with 400 shares, and declared their intenton of dividing the resulting profits between all the shareholders. The shares were at first sold at very little, perhaps for ten or twenty shillings. Then, suddenly, the price was raised to £3, £5, £10, and even £15. At this stage the promoters hastily sold out and the company shortly collapsed.[1]

Under these circumstances it is not surprising that a serious scheme for a bank should come to nothing. The speculators who were in the majority in these days, did not care to invest capital in lengthy undertakings which could not yield more than from 10 to 15 per cent., when they might triple their fortune from one day to another. Prudent people for their part, only noticed the failures, which were of daily occurrence,[2] and to be on the safe side, refused to involve themselves in any project whatever.

It must not be concluded from this however that the fundamental reasons for creating a bank no longer existed.

On the contrary the economic necessities which have been described were now strengthened by political necessities which we must next consider.

SECTION II.

The Political Necessity for a Bank.

We have attempted to describe in a few words the embarrassment of the Government; it was excessive. William when he came to the English throne, found that

[1] For a similar account see De Foe, *Essay on Projects*, pp. 11-13 (1697), published in 1698; one of the very numerous economic writings by the author of *Robinson Crusoe*.

[2] An echo of the failures due in these days to speculation will be found in the anxieties of the country gentleman so often quoted. *Bank of Credit*, p. 20.

the financial situation was as follows:—The total revenue of the Kingdom, after he had abolished the hearth tax[1] in the hope of gaining popularity, was between £1,600,000 and £1,700,000, of which £1,101,839 had to be devoted to the needs of an insignificant army and a fleet in very bad condition.

These supplies were small enough in time of peace; in time of war they were absurdly inadequate. But William was soon successful in his policy of joining England to the European coalition. And a civil war in Ireland and Scotland was shortly added to the war with France.

Attempts were made to supply these needs by a series of taxes.[2] The poll-tax, both burdensome and unpopular, was introduced from Holland. From thence also came the stamp tax;[3] the customs and excise were considerably increased; even hearth-money was revived in the form of a window tax,[4] and a large number of direct taxes were levied.[5]

The administration was however so corrupt that the revenue did not increase in proportion to the taxes voted.[6]

[1] The tax known as hearth-money or chimney-money was imposed in 1662 on all dwellings excepting cottages. The tax was 2s. on every hearth or stove in every dwelling-house. It was extremely unpopular on account of its inquisitional character, and was at first collected with much difficulty (Davenant, Vol. I., p. 208). This tax was profitable, being farmed at £170,000. It was abolished by an Act of William and Mary (1 and 2, c. 10) when it was yielding £200,000 (see Sir Robert Howard's report, *Commons' Journals*, Vol. II.).

It is interesting to note that a similar tax, the Kapnikon, existed at Byzantium, and was also abolished for political reasons by the Emperor Theophilus.

[2] For these taxes see the section in Dowell's *Taxation and Taxes in England* referring to William III.'s reign, Vol. II., pp. 37-63.

[3] In 1694.

[4] In 1696.

[5] There were besides the land tax and the window tax, taxes on pedlars (1697), on hackney coaches (1694), on births, marriages, and burials (1695), and finally on bachelors (1695). Recent proposals have invested the latter tax with some importance: it was not a succession tax, but really a direct tax, each paying according to his rank. Dukes paid £12 11s. a year, persons at the other extremity of the social ladder 1s. only; gentlemen paid 6s., esquires and Doctors of Divinity, Law, or Physic £1 6s. See the list in Dowell, Vol. II., p. 544. This tax was abolished in 1706.

Another suggestion which Macaulay qualifies as confiscation, was to impose a tax of £100,000 on the Jews. The Jews, however, prevented this imposition by threatening to leave England if it was voted Macaulay, *History of England,* Chap. xv., p. 125 of the popular edition in two volumes.

[6] The returns were sometimes even less than those in 1688.

The poll tax only produced half of what it ought to have done and the other taxes succeeded little better.

Even had the finances been honestly administered the revenue would not have covered the war expenses, not only because these were enormous, but because the army commissariat and the army contractors were such that the taxes collected never reached their destination. The King was left without his carriage, and the soldiers went shoeless.[1]

The administrative machinery, both civil and military, was rotten throughout. When not in use and looked at from a distance it might perhaps still have imposed on the ignorant.[2] But when after the fall of the Stuarts, people wished to set it going, the structure crumbled to dust. William did much to improve matters, but his throne was insecure and he recognised his unpopularity, and hence dared not introduce changes except with the utmost caution.

His ministers too could not resort to the plan so much used by their predecessors of mortgaging the taxes voted by Parliament, for the policy had been adopted of granting subsidies for short periods only, and soon Parliament voted taxes only for the service of the current year. This limitation was due to want of confidence in William III., and was regarded as the best guarantee that the nation could have that Parliament would be summoned regularly.

Taxation then was insufficient to meet the expenses of the war. Nowadays this is the usual state of things, and we find Governments raising a loan on the outbreak of war. Then matters were different, the public were unaccustomed

[1] Macaulay, Chap. xiv., Vol. II., p. 89 of the edition referred to above. He says with regard to the Irish campaign, and more especially with regard to the Commissioner General, Henry Shales: "The beef and brandy which he furnished were so bad that the soldiers turned from them with loathing: the tents were rotten: the clothing was scanty: the muskets broke in the handling: great numbers of shoes were set down to the account of the Government, but two months after the Treasury had paid the bill the shoes had not arrived in Ireland. . . . An ample number of horses had been purchased . . . But Shales had let them out for harvest work to the farmers of Cheshire, had pocketed the hire, and had left the troops in Ulster to get on as they best might."

The fleet fared little better, see Macaulay, Chap. xv., Vol. II., p. 127.

[2] I say "the ignorant," for men like Bonrepaux, who had been sent by Louis XIV. in 1686 to investigate the state of the English navy, were not deceived as to the real condition of things.

to State loans. It may have been that William could not readily have procured money, for he had no credit; not to mention the bankers' recollections of Charles II.,[1] the public had no confidence in the stability of this Government, the Jacobites were numerous, and Louis XIV. continued to be victorious.[2] William was forced to beg a loan of £100,000 from the city of London. Paterson[3] says that to get the money the ministers and aldermen had to go from shop to shop and from office to office. In the end they could only raise the whole amount by allowing commissions and giving premiums, which reduced the total by nearly 30 per cent.

The war expenses had however to be met, and Montague took upon himself to attract the public by ingenious devices.[4]

The first of these devices, which strict-minded people might be inclined to call shifty, was a loan raised in 1692 in the form of a tontine.[5] "The subscribers were to receive 10 per cent. until 1700, and after that £7,000 per annum was to be divided among the survivors till their number was reduced to seven, when, on the death of each, his annuity was to lapse to the Crown." The ingenuity of the scheme was greater than the credit of the Government and only

[1] The lawsuit of the goldsmiths was then in full swing. It was suggested that they should be offered 6 per cent. for their money on condition that they would advance, at the same rate, a sum equal to the debt, which was estimated at £1,340,000. But these proposals met with little success.

[2] At the time of which I write Ireland was not yet completely re-conquered and rebellion was raging in Scotland. Tourville had control of the Channel, and Luxembourg was fighting William in Flanders. And this, apart from the personal exploits of Louis, the capture of Mons, and the taking of Namur, which last event inspired such terror in Europe and such bad verses in France.

[3] See *Wednesday Club in Friday Street.*

[4] One of these had important results, though in itself a small matter. A tax was put on the shares of the East India and of the Hudson's Bay Companies. "This tax," says Mr. Dowell (p. 51), "had the effect of a caution to the public creditor. No one is more easily alarmed than the man about to lend his money." Even after the repeal of the tax "it was found expedient, if not necessary, to introduce into the Loan Acts a proviso that Government annuities should be clear of all taxes and duties whatsoever."

As regards the loan demanded from the City, the Council refused to help the King except on receipt of a commission. See on this point *Remarks on the proceedings of the Commissioners for putting into execution the Act passed last session for establishing a Land Bank* (1696).

[5] Macleod, *op. cit.* (3rd Edition), p. 376. The interest on the loan was to be met by a new tax on beer.

£108,000 was collected. Better results were obtained after the addition of a clause by which subscribers could get 14 per cent. during the life of any person they liked to indicate.[1]

This loan, which in the end brought in £881,493, and the money from the land tax,[2] which was raised in 1692 to 4s. in the £ and produced £1,922,000,[3] joined to a relative improvement in the political situation, enabled things to go on until 1694. But at this date political affairs were as bad as they had been two years earlier. The estimates for the year were enormous, over five millions; more than half this was needed for the army alone.[4] In order to meet them all possible taxes were imposed and a lottery loan was agreed to; the latter was a new invention of the indefatigable Montague.

This lottery had nothing in common with modern lotteries except the name. The sum to be raised was divided into 10,000 £10 shares. The yearly interest payable on each of these shares was 20s., that is, 10 per cent. for 16 years. But as this was not enough to attract the public, prizes were added. £40,000 was to be divided each year among the fortunate winners.[5] This sum, and also the 10 per cent. interest, was to be raised by means of a new tax on salt.

A million was secured by this means, and another was needed to make up the required sum of £5,030,000; there was only one way of obtaining it, which was to adopt

[1] Many people received incomes throughout the 18th century in return for a few pounds lent to William III. in their youth. For instance, £100 was entered in the name of Charles Duncombe, then three years old, who afterwards translated Horace. This author received 77 annual payments under the Act of 1692.—Macaulay, Chap. xix., Vol. II., p. 398.

[2] A tax imposed on the rental value of land.

[3] In 1693 the land tax did not, as Macaulay (Chap. xix.) states, bring in two millions, but £100,000 less than the year before. The total rent was stated this year by the taxpayer on oath. Davenant (*Essay upon Ways and Means, Works,* Vol. I., p. 33) attributes the decrease to this method of assessment.

[4] The King wished to increase the army to 94,000 men; he was in the end allowed 83,000. Things had advanced a long way since Charles' 8,700 men, and since his budgets of £1,500,000.

[5] The largest prize, a £100 annuity, was won by four Huguenots who had given up their country to keep their religion. The English public thought that the hand of God was recognisable in this result.

Paterson's plan.[1] Montague, who had known of this scheme for several years, now turned his attention to it, and the Bank of England was founded.

It is now time to learn something of Paterson and his scheme. We shall first give a biographical sketch of this remarkable man and then proceed to examine his scheme, or rather schemes, and point out their main features.

[1] See the reports of F. Bonnet to Frederick III., Elector of Brandenburg, which were found among the Secret Archives at Berlin by Leopold Van Ranke, and were published by him at the end of his *History of England principally in the Seventeenth Century*, Vol. II., pp. 144-278. These letters are of great interest, the writer describes vividly the financial difficulties in which William III.'s Government were continually involved. See especially the letter of January 12-22, in which the future Bank is discussed, and pp. 238, 239, 240.

The letter of April 20-30, 1694, (p. 246), is the most interesting of all. Bonnet explains the organisation of the Bank and the reasons for its foundation. He concludes by stating that the paper tax has been passed and that possibly a tax on hackney coaches will be passed; but, he adds, "this last contribution is regarded as an extra one, because the House has only agreed to raise a sum of £5,030,000 this year, which is to be produced as follows":—

Land Tax,	estimated at	£1,500,000
Poll Tax,	,,	£0,700,000
Paper Tax,	,,	£0,330,000
Lottery,	,,	£1,000,000
The Bank,	,,	£1,200,000
Annuities,	,,	£0,300,000
		£5,030,000

CHAPTER II.

PATERSON, HIS LIFE AND WORK.—THE FOUNDATION OF THE BANK OF ENGLAND.

Birth and youthful adventures. Return to England after 1688. Active share in public affairs. Explanation of his leaving the Bank of England shortly after he had founded it. The Darien Expedition. Last years of his life. His claims on public gratitude.

Paterson's first scheme, 1691. His Pamphlet in 1694, "*A Brief Account of the Intended Bank of England.*" Principles on which the new Bank should be based.

Political opponents; Jacobites and Tories; Commercial rivals; the Goldsmiths. Hostility of the landed gentry; its causes. The dissentient Whigs. Arguments used by the Bank's opponents. Opposition in Parliament. Bill only passed because the Government wanted money and could not obtain it otherwise.

SECTION I.

THE LIFE OF WILLIAM PATERSON.

WILLIAM PATERSON was born at Trailflat,[1] in the county of Dumfries, probably in 1658.[2] He came to England when very young and afterwards spent a long time in travelling, as is shown by one of his letters to George I.[3] In particular he visited the West Indies, and was able to point out the importance which would be acquired by a colony on the isthmus of Panama, or of Darien, as it was then called. But the tale[4] according to which he joined some American buccaneers, after having started from England as a missionary, while it is possible, yet rests on no sufficient foundation.

[1] See Pagan, *The Birthplace and Parentage of W. Paterson.*

[2] This date may be deduced from his will, made in July, 1718, in which he says that he is 60 years old. The farm where he was born was only pulled down in 1864.

[3] Paterson, *Memorial to George I.* (March 8th, 1714).

[4] Francis, pp. 45-46. The profession of buccaneer was not then accounted dishonourable and it was alleged that Blackburn, Archbishop of York from 1724-1743, had followed it in his youth. See Thorold Rogers, *The Industrial and Commercial History of England*, p. 12.

About 1685 Paterson went to Amsterdam—then the head-quarters of the English Whigs; he apparently took part in the revolutionary movement of 1688, and must have been deeply involved in the Liberal agitation which preceded the campaign in England. At any rate like many politicians, he diligently frequented the coffee-houses.

After the revolution he settled in London where he became rich and influential. In 1691 he, in association with Michael Godfrey and other London merchants, proposed the foundation of the Bank of England, at the same time pointing out the need for a restoration of the coinage. Paterson was the chief promoter of this scheme, but in spite of his repeated efforts, nothing came of it for three years. During this time Paterson, who was by no means the mere adventurer people have tried to make out, took part in various important undertakings, helped to supply North London with drinking water, and in 1692 was the chief witness before the Parliamentary Committee appointed to receive proposals for raising supplies.

It was during these negotiations that he had the good fortune to become acquainted with Montague, then one of the Commissioners of the Treasury, who recognised the advantages to the State which might follow the realisation of Paterson's scheme, and whose influence proved invaluable two years later, when the proposal came to be voted upon.

When the Bank was founded Paterson became a director, with a salary of £2,000, but the Bank did not completely fulfil his expectations, and a year later he resigned, after a disagreement with his colleagues.

As a matter of fact the exact cause of Paterson's retirement is not known. In his *Enquiry*[2] he expresses himself purposely in vague terms. Sir W. Scott and Chambers both incline to the belief that his colleagues having made use of his experience, wished now to make use of his post. Mr. Stephens[3] considers this view quite mistaken; he believes it to be impossible that a body of people having such

[1] *An Enquiry by the Wednesday's Club in Friday Street* (1717), p. 68.
[2] See *Enquiry, loc. cit.*
[3] See the notice of Paterson by Mr. Stephens at the end of his *Contribution to the Bibliography of the Bank of England*, p. 160.

high reputations should act so meanly and should be blind enough to get rid of so experienced a colleague.

The explanation of these disagreements seems to me easy enough to find when we remember the differences of character and financial training which distinguished Paterson from his colleagues.[1] Paterson was a genius, bold even to rashness, quick to undertake difficult enterprises and to accept the risks of untried experiments, experiments which, as we shall see, were not always successful. His colleagues were of quite a different type; they were merchants, the heads of important firms, not having like him made a rapid fortune, but on the contrary, having amassed their wealth by prolonged effort, and on this very account not caring to risk in a day what had cost them so much labour to acquire. The long practice which they had had in business inclined them to excessive prudence. Paterson in spite of his many good qualities, had the adventurer's temperament, which must have frightened not a little the good citizens who were his colleagues. As long as Godfrey lived he was able to keep the peace between these two inharmonious factors. After his death the differences of opinion came to the surface, and Paterson realised that there was nothing for it but to retire, which he did in a perfectly dignified manner.[2] However he was soon to be involved in fresh adventures. He took up once more a scheme with which he had previously dallied, and to promote which he had applied to the Elector of Brandenburg, and had even gone to Prussia, but without success. I refer to the famous project of the Darien or Panama expedition.

This is not the place to give an account of this disastrous

[1] See also the pamphlet: *Observations upon the Constitution of the Company of the Bank of England, with a narrative of their late proceedings.* The author complains amongst other things of a director, who expected an "unreasonable reward," and was inclined to express his opinions on the matter in the coffee-houses. It is possible that Paterson is the person referred to, and this would give a new explanation of his resignation.

[2] Apparently however he continued to feel a certain resentment at the incident, for some years afterwards, in a petition to Godolphin, the Lord Treasurer, dated the 4th of April, 1709, he refers to the services he rendered and states that he received no reward for his efforts and for the expense to which he was put.

adventure,[1] into which the whole Scotch nation threw itself blindly and with unexpected fervour. The result was deplorable, but Paterson's share in the matter was absolutely honourable.[2] Indeed on his return to London[3] he was most graciously received by William III., who accorded him numerous interviews and requested him to formulate his schemes in writing. These schemes related to various financial questions and occasionally to political matters: such as the real union between England and Scotland.[4] Many of these proposals subsequently formed the basis of important financial reforms, such as Walpole's Sinking Fund, and the consolidation of the national debt in 1717.[5]

William Paterson died in London in 1719. According to some writers he passed the concluding years of his life in want.[6] He certainly lost £10,000 in the Darien expedition, and he complained of poverty unceasingly until the end of his life.[7] It seems however, that in 1715 he was recompensed for his losses in the Scotch expedition, for not only did Parliament, at the request of the King, vote him a sum of £18,241 at this time, but it is probable that he actually received the money since in his will he left considerable bequests to different people.[8]

[1] Details as to the Darien Expedition will be found in Macaulay, Chap. xxiv., and in John Hill Burton, *History of Scotland,* Vol. VIII., chap. lxxxiv. The Scotch numbered 1,200 and the expedition went in five large ships.

[2] Paterson nearly lost his life in this expedition, during the whole of which he displayed great courage and energy. His fellow-countrymen never blamed him for their common failure, disastrous though it was for Scotland. Dumfries elected him a Member of the first United Parliament. The last Scotch Parliament had already recommended him to Queen Anne on account of his good services.—De Foe, *History of the Union,* p. 525.

[3] April, 1701.

[4] *Enquiry,* p. 84.

[5] I have omitted to say that Paterson, who certainly took a part in everything, was concerned in the question of the Orphans' Fund. There is in the British Museum a pamphlet called: *Some account of the Transactions of Mr. W. Paterson in relation to the Orphans' Fund* (1695). The catalogue states however that this document is "wanting all but title page," and it adds for our more definite information, and out of respect to the memory of M. de la Palice, that the work is *incomplete.*

[6] Dalrymple, *Memoirs on Great Britain and Ireland,* Vol. II., Part III., pp. 89-123.

[7] The last petition which he made to the Government is in a letter sent a month before his death, in December, 1718, to Lord Stanhope.

[8] He left £6,000 to different relatives, £1,000 to Paul Daranda, his legal executor, etc. The will was made in 1718.

Such was in outline the life of the founder of the Bank of England.[1] There have been none more eventful and, it must be acknowledged, none more fruitful or more honourable. On all the occasions when he was the promoter of an enterprise, Paterson showed much talent and energy, and whatever mistakes he may have made, he never spared either himself or his fortune. His courage and the nobility of his character were proved during the Panama expedition, an undertaking which was happy in its conception and which deserved to succeed. He gave evidence of diplomatic skill in the negotiations with Scotland with which the Queen entrusted him about 1706, and of statesmanship in the various measures which he brought forward between 1701 and his death, and which others had the honour of carrying out. In addition he not only possessed great facility, which was a sufficiently common gift at that time,[2] but also exceptional gifts as a political writer.[3] Nevertheless, his name will be chiefly remembered in history on account of his share in founding the Bank of England.

He had the honour of proposing the first really workable and matured scheme; and possessed talent and perseverance to carry it out in the face of innumerable obstacles, as much political as financial. He was it is true but ill-rewarded for his labours. He never held any of the official posts to which he might have aspired; and though I do not think it accurate to say that he died in poverty, he at any rate passed

[1] Those who are interested to learn more details of Paterson's remarkable life may consult in addition to the works already mentioned, a biographical notice at the beginning of S. Bannister's edition of his works; Laing's *History of Scotland,* Vol. V., p. 299; Chambers' *Domestic Annals of Scotland,* Vol. III., pp. 121, 124, 131; and, finally, a French work by Paul Coq on the *Monnaie de Banque,* dedicated to Paterson, and preceded by an essay on the ingenious Scot. Paterson was also the hero of an historical novel published in 1852, *Darien,* by Eliot Worburton, which had its day of celebrity.

[2] Daniel De Foe's work is the most famous instance of the prolific and diverse character of the writings of the authors of the period. M. Taine says of him: "He wrote in verse, in prose, on every subject, political and religious, ephemeral and fundamental, satires and romances, travels and pamphlets, business treatises and statistical studies, in all 210 works."—*Histoire de la Littérature anglaise,* Bk. III., Chap. vi., p. 264.

[3] Bannister's edition, *The Writings of William Paterson, with a biographical notice,* is not complete. A full list of Paterson's works will be found at the end of Stephens' notice of him.

a large portion of his concluding years in this condition. Posterity will do him more justice than his contemporaries, and his name will always be connected with the famous institution which owes its origin to him.

SECTION II.

William Paterson and the Bank of England.

The scheme which was accepted by Montague and was destined to be realised in the form of the Bank of England was not Paterson's only project; there were two others.

As early as 1691, he proposed, in company with various city notables, to lend a million to the Government, in return for a yearly payment of £65,000, of which £5,000 were for the expenses of management, on condition that the notes of the bank to be founded should be legal tender. The committee to whom these proposals were submitted refused to make the notes legal tender, but were ready to authorize their issue. Paterson was willing to accept this, but his colleagues would not support him.[1]

The second scheme, which offered to provide two millions for the Government, also came to nothing. And it was to compensate for this failure that Montague devised the lottery loan; but as we have seen, the sums yielded by this were inadequate, and application was made to Paterson, who in the interval, had drawn up his final scheme.

The plan now was to raise £1,200,000 to be lent to the Government in return for a yearly interest of £100,000. The subscribers to the loan were to form a corporation with the right to issue notes up to the value of its total capital. The corporation was to be called, "The Governor and Company of the Bank of England."[2]

Paterson wrote a pamphlet demonstrating the economic principles on which the future Bank of England was to rest.

[1] See Macleod, 5th edition, Vol. I., p. 47. Bannister, *Paterson's Works*, Vol. I., pp. xxviii., xxix. (2nd edition).

[2] See Bonnet, letter referred to above, p. 246. "The high profit of 8 per cent. paid to those who lend the sum of £1,200,000, only affects a small number of persons and the majority of the Lower House, who are in a position to advance ten, twenty, or thirty thousand pounds. For the whole

He notes the old mistake "that the stamp or denomination gives or adds to the value of money." The fallacy contained in this was pointed out by those who had suggested the foundation of the Bank some years earlier. Its promoters had seen that the institution ought to be based on the following principles :[2]

"1. That all money or credit not having an intrinsic value, to answer the contents or denomination thereof, is false and counterfeit, and the loss must fall one where or other.

"2. That the species of gold and silver being accepted, and chosen by the commercial world for the standard, or measure, of other effects, everything else is only accounted valuable as compared with these.

"3. Wherefore all credit not founded on the universal species of gold and silver is impracticable, and can never subsist neither safely nor long, *at least till some other species of credit be found out and chosen by the trading part of mankind over and above or in lieu thereof.*"

After describing the strong position of the Bank and its prospects of success, and stating that no dividend would be paid without several months' notice, in order to give the shareholders the choice of selling or retaining their shares, Paterson remarks that "The politicians . . . distinguish between the interest of *land and trade*, as they have lately done between that of a king and his people,"[3] but "if the proprietors of the Bank can circulate their own *fundation* of twelve hundred thousand pounds without having more than two or three hundred thousand pounds lying dead at one time with another, this Bank will be in effect as nine hundred

amount is divided into shares of £10,000 each, of which not less than one nor more than three may be taken. . . . The subscribers are to form a company, here called a corporation, . . . which will pay them at the rate of 4½ per cent., and from which they can withdraw their money at any time and in any quantity that they wish, hence the proprietors will make 8 per cent. on the money they have lent, and 3½ per cent. on what is lent to them. . . . But Parliament makes the corporation responsible for all the sums which it receives above £1,200,000, and makes the proprietors jointly and severally liable."

[1] *A brief account of the intended Bank of England* (1694), p. 3. Bannister, *op. cit.*, Vol. III., p. 80.

[2] pp. 9, 10. Bannister, pp. 83 and 84.

[3] p. 12, an allusion to the Land Bank. Bannister, p. 85.

thousand pounds or a million of fresh money brought into the nation." The Bank, far from being a source of danger to borrowers, traders or landowners,[1] will benefit them by reducing the rate of interest, as has been done by the Banks in Amsterdam and Genoa.

Paterson concludes that the enemies of the Bank are only "Jacobites who apprehend it may contribute to lessen their monarch of France, with some few usurers and brokers of money; and the third sort are commonly such as have not wherewith to trade, unless it be like Haman of old, for whole nations or peoples at once."[2]

This conclusion leads us to refer to the objections which greeted the announcement that the Government[3] had accepted Paterson's scheme, and the inclusion of the plan of the new Bank in the Tonnage Bill. These objections came from all sides, and though the Bank opponents may if necessary, be classified in Paterson's three categories, such a division requires to be explained and defined. This will be the aim of the third part of our second chapter. We shall also explain why their opposition was ineffectual.

SECTION III.

The Opponents of the Bank.

These opponents were both political and commercial.

In the first place, the Tory party and the Jacobites were afraid that the Government would be strengthened by a

[1] Paterson is trying to pacify the merchants and above all the landed proprietors, who had been led to believe that the bank would absorb all the money in the country, and would only make loans at abnormal rates. Godfrey, the second founder of the Bank, also did what he could to dispel such fears. He writes (p. 7 of the pamphlet already referred to, Francis, *op. cit.*, Vol. II., p. 247): "The Bank will reduce the interest of money in England to 3 per cent. per annum in a few years, without any law to enforce it, in like manner as it is in all other countries where banks are establisht, . . . the lessening the interest of money will infallibly raise the value of land . . . for the falling the interest of money . . . will unavoidably advance the price of land to above thirty years' purchase, which will raise the value of the lands of England at least 100 millions, and thereby abundantly reimburse the nation all the charges of the war." Godfrey does not however say on what ground he promises this remarkable rise, and appears mainly concerned to disarm the opposition of the landed proprietors.

[2] Bannister, p. 87.

[3] The statute establishing the Bank had received the royal assent on April the 25th.

successful bank, while if the scheme failed it would be powerless from lack of funds.

Then there were all the country gentry, whose opposition was due not only to their political opinions, but also to the horror which merchants and financiers, such as were the promoters of the Bank, have always inspired in small landowners, condemned to lead a miserable existence on their estates. Moreover, these landowners had been induced to believe that the Bank would attract all the money in the country and that borrowing would no longer be possible except at exorbitant rates.[1]

The new Bank had also to meet the opposition of the goldsmiths and money-lenders who were deprived of their most obvious profits by the new undertaking; and of the promoters of rival schemes, chiefly that of Chamberlain and the other supporters of the Land Bank.

Finally, these various opponents were joined by a few dissentient Whigs, whose opposition was not altogether without effect.

This union between all the enemies of the Government served to rouse its partisans.[2]

But nevertheless the arguments of the opponents did not appear valueless to contemporaries. The principal ones were as follows:[3]

(1) It was alleged that the Bank, which was nicknamed the Tonnage Bank, would absorb all the money in the kingdom and would subject commerce to usurious exactions. A remarkable objection this to come from the goldsmiths, who had never enjoyed the reputation of lending their money for nothing; none the less they talked of the risk of honest merchants "if they got into the clutches of this harpy of Grocers' Hall."[4]

(2) It was alleged that the Bank would attract to itself all the money in the country by its high rate of interest, and

[1] We have seen that Paterson and Godfrey tried to allay these forebodings. The latter even went to the length of making rash promises. See above, p. 67 note.

[2] Burnet, *op. cit.*, Vol. IV., p. 246.

[3] Thorold Rogers, pp. 9, 10.

[4] From the name of the headquarters of the company.

that no capital would be available for trade and industry. This is the objection made by Davenant,[1] who writes: "The funds . . . are so inviting and of such infinite profit that few now are willing to let out their money to traders at 6 per cent. as formerly; so that all merchants who subsist by credit, must in time give over."

(3) It was alleged that the Bank would grow too powerful, and would become the keystone of the commercial world, and that if it failed, it would drag down with it the whole of English trade.

(4) It was alleged that the Bank could only favour a limited number of merchants, and that these, thanks to a very low rate of discount and to facilities of all kinds, would soon be able to ruin their competitors.[2]

(5) From a political point of view the Tories declared that a State Bank would be one step towards a republic, because such institutions are not compatible with a monarchy.[3] Indeed the facts seemed to give some plausibility to this theory, since the three great banks then existing were established in three republics.

(6) Starting from a similar standpoint but arriving at totally different conclusions, the dissentient Whigs feared lest the foundation of a bank should lead to absolute monarchy, since the King would be supplied with means of procuring money through this institution and might thus escape the financial control of Parliament.

To meet this criticism, a clause was introduced into the law prohibiting the Bank from lending money to the Government without the express authority of Parliament. The full wisdom of this prohibition was not realised until it

[1] *Essay upon Ways and Means* (2nd edition, 1695, p. 44). [*Works*, Whitworth's Edition, 1771, Vol. I., p. 24.]

[2] This objection was not, to be strictly accurate, brought forward until 1707. It is the only original objection contained in a work opposing the renewal of the Bank's charter: *Reasons offered against the continuation of the Bank. In a letter to a Member of Parliament.* Perhaps it is partly due to considerations of this kind that the Bank of France is obliged by its charter to allow the same rate of discount to everyone alike.

[3] Paterson, *Intended Bank*, p. 8. "Another tells us that in all his peregrinations he never met banks but only in Republics. And if we let them get footing in England, we shall certainly be in danger of a commonwealth." See also pp. 7 and 9.

was disregarded by William Pitt, from which neglect a crisis resulted whose description will occupy the whole of the IVth Part of this volume.

All these criticisms, contradictory though they appear, greatly excited public opinion, and aroused many fears among the landed proprietors who formed the House of Lords. The project was only passed because the Government needed money and could not obtain it otherwise.

Bonnet[1] thus describes the debate in the House of Commons: "People think that this institution has its good and its bad points, but had it not been that time pressed, they do not believe that it would have been passed by the Lower House, for there was strong opposition at the last moment, one of the chief objections being that this will be a Bank in the State without being under the control of the Government." The Bill however passed without a division. "No question," writes our author, "has been more vigorously debated in this Parliament than that of the establishment of a Bank in the hands of a corporation. It came before the Upper House yesterday, and the assistance of all the Lords of the Court party was needed to get it through. The Marquess of Halifax, and the Earls of Rochester, Nottingham and Monmouth, spoke several times against this institution, and brought forward a number of arguments to show that it would be injurious to the King, since it was not to his interest that the management of such large funds should be in other hands than those of the Government. That it would be still more injurious to the public, since instead of money being invested in trade, it would be deposited in this bank; and that it would be no less injurious to individuals, since it was obvious that they would no longer be able to sell or to mortgage lands without great loss. The Marquess of Caermarthen and the Earl of Mulgrave were the chief among those who maintained that the Bill must be passed without alteration; not because the arguments against the Bank were not good ones, but

[1] *Op. cit.*, pp. 246, 247.

because the difficulties which would follow from a refusal, and the departure of the King, which would at least be delayed ten or twelve days by a consent, seemed more real than those with which they were threatened. But the number of votes, not the number of arguments, carried the day, for in the division which they were forced to take there was a majority of twelve in favour of passing the Bill unaltered, and it has been read to-day for the last time."[1]

[1] Letter of April 24th to May 4th, p. 248.

CHAPTER III.

ORGANISATION OF THE NEW BANK.

The Tonnage Act. The Bank Supported by Government and by the commercial world. Enthusiastic subscription for its stock. The Bank Charter.

The Bank of Venice. Primitive Venetian Banks; their transactions resembled those of modern Banks. Reasons for the establishment of a single Bank by the Senate. The Banco della Piazza del Rialto (1584) and the Banco del Giro (1619). Amalgamation of these two establishments. Their transactions. The Bank of Genoa. Origin and original character of the Bank of Saint George. The biglietti di cartulari di San-Giorgio. The Bank of Amsterdam. Its importance. Its exceptional position up to the end of the eighteenth century. Distinctions between the Bank of England and the three continental Banks. Bank money and the English bank notes. Resemblance in this respect between the Banks of England and Sweden. The use of the continental bank notes forced, and the English ones not even legal tender. No monopoly enjoyed by the Bank of England when first founded. Gradual disappearance of these distinctions. Close resemblance between the Bank of England in the present day and the primitive Banks of Italy and Holland.

Character of the new notes. Not guaranteed by any metallic reserve. The discounts and deposits.

THUS notwithstanding the violent opposition, the project was finally passed, and the Tonnage Bill became the Tonnage Act. We shall proceed to study its provisions. Then we shall compare the Bank of England with the principal Continental banks of the period, and shall point out the original character of the new institution, and in what way it marked a definite advance. This comparison will lead us to examine the business which the youthful bank proposed to transact.

SECTION I.

CHIEF PROVISIONS OF THE "TONNAGE ACT."[1]

The Act of Parliament by which the Bank was established is called "An Act for granting to their Majesties several Rates and Duties upon Tunnages of Ships and Vessels, and

[1] Gilbart, *History, Principles and Practice of Banking*, Vol. I., p. 31 (edition of 1907), gives a good analysis of this Act. It is almost the only thing in which this book has proved of service.

upon Beer, Ale, and other Liquors; for securing certain Recompenses and Advantages, in the said Act mentioned, to Such persons as shall voluntarily advance the Sum of Fifteen hundred thousand Pounds towards carrying on the war against *France*."

After various articles referring to the imposition of taxes, the Act authorised the raising of £1,200,000 by subscription, the subscribers forming a corporation to be called, "The Governor and Company of the Bank of England."[1] No person might subscribe more than £10,000 before the 1st of July following, and even after this date no individual subscription might exceed £20,000. The corporation was to lend the whole of its capital to the Government, and in return it was to be paid interest at the rate of 8 per cent., and £4,000 for expenses of management, in all £100,000 per annum. The corporation was to have the privileges of a bank for twelve years, then the Government reserved the right of annulling the charter after giving one year's notice to the company. The corporation were not authorised to borrow or owe more than their capital; if they did so, the members became personally liable in proportion to the amount of their stock. The corporation were forbidden to trade in any merchandise whatever, but "they were allowed to deal in bills of exchange, gold or silver bullion, and to sell any wares or merchandise upon which they had advanced money, and which had not been redeemed within three months after the time agreed upon."[2]

The subscription list was opened at the Mercers' Chapel,[3] then the headquarters of the corporation, on Thursday, June 21, 1694. According to Luttrell, £300,000 was subscribed on the opening day alone, the Queen having contributed £10,000. "To encourage capitalists, £2 10s. per cent. rebate on the amount subscribed was allowed on the first three days, and £2 on the subscriptions of Monday,

[1] This is the official title still in use. The word "company" is even preserved in the Italian form then fashionable; the Bank notes are issued in the name of the Governor and *Compania* of the Bank of England.

[2] Gilbart, Vol. I., p. 32.

[3] The Bank continued at the Mercers' Chapel until September 28, when it moved to Grocers' Hall, which had been taken for 11 years, and where it remained for 40.

June 25; after which the advantage was reduced by five shillings per cent.[1] for each of the successive days."[2] This reduction was justified, since £900,000 had already been subscribed, and the £600,000 which came in during the first three days sufficed to make the subscribers into a corporation.

After this great success the Charter of Incorporation was granted on July 27, 1694. Its main provisions were as follows:[3]

"That the management and government of the corporation be committed to the governor, deputy-governor, and twenty-four directors, who shall be elected between the 25th day of March and the 25th day of April each year, from among the members of the company duly qualified.

"That no dividend shall at any time be made by the said governor and company save only out of the interest, profit or produce arising out of the said capital stock or fund.

"They must be natural born subjects of England, or naturalised subjects; they shall have in their own name and for their own use, severally, viz., the governor at least £4,000, the deputy-governor £3,000, and each director £2,000 of the capital stock of the said corporation.

"That thirteen or more of the said governors or directors (of which the governor or deputy-governor shall be always one) shall constitute a court of directors for the management of the affairs of the company."

It may be noted also that according to the terms of the Charter, each director must have at least £500 capital stock; "four general courts" must be held in each year, conditions are specified under which additional meetings may be summoned, and finally, the general courts are to issue "by-laws and ordinances for the government of the corporation."[4]

[1] "These premiums were defrayed from the civil list,"—Postlethwayt, *History of the English Revenue*, p. 10.

This fact, joined to that of the Queen's subscription, shows the intense interest which the Orangist party had in the success of the Bank.

[2] Thorold Rogers, *First Nine Years of the Bank of England*, p. 2.

[3] See Gilbart, Vol. I., pp. 32, 33.

[4] The laws and ordinances of the Bank, "not repugnant to the laws of the Kingdom," were drafted according to the advice of Sergeant Levinz, a celebrated barrister of the period.

The new institution was started on a sufficiently modest scale. "The secretaries and clerks altogether numbered but fifty-four, while their united salaries did not exceed £4,350."[1] Business was carried on in a single room with primitive simplicity. Even sixteen years later Addison[2] writes: "I looked into the great hall where the Bank is kept, and was not a little pleased to see the directors, secretaries and clerks . . . ranged in their several stations according to the parts they hold in that just and regular economy."

SECTION II.

COMPARISON BETWEEN THE BANK OF ENGLAND AND THE BANKS OF VENICE, GENOA, AMSTERDAM, AND SWEDEN.

At the time of the foundation of the Bank of England, at least three important banks existed in Europe, those of Venice, Genoa, and Amsterdam. An examination of the constitution of these banks, and a comparison between them and the Bank of England, will prove both interesting and important.[3]

A.—*The Banks of Venice, Genoa, and Amsterdam.*

1.—*The Bank of Venice.* A persistent error dates the Bank of Venice from the 12th century, from 1156 or 1171.

[1] Francis, p. 65.

[2] *Spectator* No. 3 (March, 3, 1701). This essay will be found in Chalmers' collection, *The British Essayists, with prefaces historical and biographical*, Vol. VI., p. 13. I was surprised not to find it in the edition of Addison's *Essays* brought out by Sir John Lubbock in 1894. See *Sir John Lubbock's hundred Books*. The essay in question contains an allegory illustrating the close union between the Bank and the Whig party; we shall refer to it again below, see p. 119.

[3] For this two-fold purpose the following works may be consulted: Law, *Mémoires sur les Banques;* Guillaumin's edition, *Économistes et Financiers du XVIIIe siècle;* and Rota (P.), *Storia delle Banche*. For the Bank of Venice in particular: Lattes *La Liberta delle Banche a Venezia dal Secolo XIII. al XVII;* and C. F. Dunbar, *The Bank of Venice* (*Quarterly Journal of Economics*, April, 1892). For the Bank of Genoa: Carlo Cuneo, *Memorie sopra l'antico debito publico mutui, compere, e banche di San Giorgio in Genova;* and Adam Wiszniewski, *La Méthode Historique appliquée à la réforme des banques; Histoire de la Banque Saint-Georges de la République de Gênes.* Finally, for the Bank of Amsterdam: Mr. Pierson, *Principles of Economics*, English translation, p. 488, mentions a Dutch work by Dr. W. C. Mees, *Proeveener geschiedenis van het Bankwezen in Nederland.* The various books to which we refer in the text may also be read with advantage.

As a matter of fact, this Bank was not created until four centuries later. Probably however, private banks existed in Venice from an early date, doubtless as a supplement to the business of the exchangers. These exchangers, the *campsores,*[1] soon began to accept deposits, and in a law of September 24th, 1318, some security was given to the depositors. But it should be noted that an earlier law, passed in 1270, which regulates the transactions of the *campsores,* makes no mention of deposits. From this it seems likely that this new business developed between 1270 and 1318. At all events, the laws following that of 1318 frequently use the terms *bancherius* and *bancus.*

The new banks grew and multiplied. *Their business was very similar to that of modern banks.* They were banks of deposit and of discount. Moreover payments by means of transfers on the banker's book existed from the early 15th century. These transfers were simplified by the issue of certificates of deposit, the *contadi di Banco,* to which reference is made as early as 1421, and which were used, according to Rota,[2] like coin; in this way these primitive Venetian banks resembled our *banks of issue.*

Some of these private banks became very powerful, but many of them ultimately failed. Thomas Contarini, in a speech that well repays reading,[3] states that out of 103 banks which had been established only 9 had succeeded.[4]

The series of failures in 1489[5] and 1523, and in 1504 the failure of the Pisani and the Tiepolo, with liabilities of

[1] For the *campsores* see Rota, pp. 35 and 36.

[2] p. 104.

[3] Contarini's speech in favour of the establishment of a public bank, and that of a senator opposing this policy, both delivered during the great debate of 1584, were published by Lattes in 1869 at the end of his book.

[4] One of the causes of the failure of the private banks was the perpetual loans made to the Government—loans which were indeed enforced by law, for it was decreed that the banks might not employ in trade more than one and a half times the amount of the money lent to the Government. Another cause of these failures may have been the greed of the bankers, who, tempted by high interest, lent money to persons of no commercial solidity.

[5] The failures were in some cases due to "runs." A description of the most important of these, which occurred in 1489, is given by Malpiero in the *Archivio Storico,* Series I., Vol. VII., p. 715.

500,000 ducats, apparently convinced the Venetian Senate that the system of private banks must be abandoned,[1] and a fresh one introduced, for it did not even occur to them that banks might be dispensed with altogether; without a bank, Contarini remarked, Venice could not exist.

After some remarkable debates, it was decided to establish a public bank, and the *Banco della Piazza del Rialto* was founded by the laws passed in 1584 and 1587. Another law in 1593 decreed that all bills of exchange should be paid only through bank transfers.[2]

Unlike the private banks which it replaced, the Bank of Rialto was not a bank in the modern sense of the term. The new bank had not been created for any fiscal purpose but solely to ensure security in trade. Hence the republic very wisely refused to undertake the investment of the funds entrusted to it, and did not attempt to make any profit out of the credit of the bank. In theory at any rate, it restricted itself to keeping the depositors' money in security, and to paying it out or transferring it according to the wish of its owners.[3]

The private banks had been suppressed in 1587, but the need for a second bank soon made itself felt, and in 1619 the famous *Banco del Giro* was founded, which is often made to date from the 12th century.[4]

Hardly was this bank established than it made a temporary loan to the republic of 500,000 ducats;[5] this incident accounts for the tradition according to which the Bank of Venice owed its origin to a national debt. In other respects the *Banco del Giro* transacted business in exactly the same way as the *Banco della Piazza del Rialto,* which it ultimately (in 1637) absorbed.

The republic was not, however, able to pay its debt to the

[1] Lewis, *op. cit.*, p. 40; compare above, p. 25.

[2] See Lattes, pp. 170-171, for the reason of this.

[3] Dunbar, p. 321. See also below, p. 81, for some remarks on the transactions of Continental banks in general.

[4] Dunbar gives numerous instances of this mistake, he noted it in most of the Dictionaries of Political Economy, and even in the *Dictionnaire des Finances,* Vol. I., p. 291.

[5] Rezasco's *Dizionario di Linguaggio Italiano Storico e Amministrativo,* p. 85.

Banco del Giro, and after many struggles, the latter was obliged to suspend cash payments from 1717 to 1739.[1] This suspension had the effect of reducing almost to nothing the premium on bank money, which had sometimes amounted to 20 per cent., and had existed throughout the 17th and 18th centuries.[2]

In 1739 the Bank of Venice resumed cash payments, and continued them until the French occupation of Venice. At this time, that is in 1797, the Bank had a reserve of 522,000 ducats against liabilities of 1,500,000 ducats. The *Banco del Giro* nevertheless survived the French occupation, and was not suppressed until 1806, after the peace of Presbourg.

2.—*The Bank of Genoa.* Perhaps the Middle Ages produced no institution more unique than the *Compania* or *Casa di San Giorgio* of Genoa; an association of State creditors who managed the revenues of the republic, owned colonies and possessions, maintained armies and fleets, made war and concluded treaties, and combined with all these various functions the duties of a bank of deposit.

This institution was founded under the following circumstances:

In 1148, the republic, which had previously had no public debt, was obliged to raise a loan, and its creditors were formed into a company to which was entrusted the administration of certain taxes, whose returns were to be devoted to paying the interest and capital of the loan. This system was extended, and gradually there came to be as many distinct companies as there had been loans. These companies were called *compere,* and this organisation of *compere* recalls that of the *monti* of Venice, Florence, and Sienna. Complications resulted from the increasing number of *compere,* and they were united about 1250 into one institution called the *Compera del Capitolo.*[3]

In 1407, Jean le Maingre, marshal of France, changed

[1] Apparently there had been previous suspensions between 1631 and 1669 during the war in Crete. Compare what Savary writes in 1679 in *Le Parfait Négociant,* Part II., p. 128.

[2] Dunbar, p. 330.

[3] Rota, p. 185.

this *compera* into the *Ufficio di San Giorgio,* a company intended to advance to the Government the money needed for the conversion of the numerous existing debts. In this respect the *Ufficio* never changed its character, and from 1441 to 1736 it supplied the Government with frequent loans.[1]

Soon the *Ufficio di San Giorgio* became a State within a State, and much surpassed in importance the most powerful of chartered companies. The East India Company never held in England a position one-quarter so great as that which the *Ufficio* occupied at Genoa.

The republic began by ceding to it in 1453 Péra and its Black Sea colonies. In the same year Corsica, in which the republic, torn by internal discussions, could not maintain its authority, was made over to it. Many other such concessions were made. "The citizens," says Machiavelli,[2] "preferred the authority of the company to that of the State, on account of the tyranny of the latter and the excellent administration of the former."

It has often been stated that the Bank of Genoa did not begin to carry on banking business until 1675. This view, as has now been proved, is a mistake.[3] The error can be explained as due to a confusion. It was, in fact, at this date that it was decreed that bills of exchange should be paid in *biglietti di cartulari di San Giorgio.*[4] Amongst the instruments of credit of these early banks the cartulary notes of St. George are those which most resemble bank-notes. They were certificates of deposits, deposits which the Bank of Saint George used in whatever way it considered expedient.

The crisis of 1797 ruined the Bank of Saint George, and between 1799 and 1804 the Ligurian Senate tried vainly to restore it. In 1816 Genoa was annexed to Sardinia and the debt of the Bank of Saint George was consolidated with the Sardinian national debt.

[1] For the amounts and dates of these loans see Wiszniewski, p. 106, *et seq.*

[2] *Le Istorie Fiorentine,* Bk. V., III. Giraudet's French Translation, Vol. IV., p. 389, *et seq.*

[3] Rota, p. 141. The name Bank of Saint George was in use before 1675.

[4] Compare the laws at Venice and Amsterdam.

3.—*The Bank of Amsterdam*. This bank was at the height of its glory when the Bank of England was founded. Established at the time when the Netherlands were about to conclude their first truce with Spain, the Bank of Amsterdam was continuously prosperous. In 1608 and 1609 a monopoly was granted to it by the decrees which abolished the offices of the exchangers, and a subsequent law still further increased its power by enforcing the use of its receipts for all payments exceeding a certain amount, an arrangement which obliged every merchant of importance to have a deposit account at the Bank. And its credit became boundless after Louis XIV.'s invasion of Holland and the consequent run on the Bank resulted in proving that its treasure was absolutely intact.[1]

The prosperity of the Bank of Amsterdam was so continuous and it was so generally looked upon as a model bank, even in the time of Steuart and of Adam Smith, that these economists felt it necessary to study the organisation of the Bank of the Netherlands in preference to that of the Bank of their own country.[2]

Unfortunately, at the time of the invasion of the revolutionary armies it was discovered that all the Bank's treasure had been lent to the East India Company. This was the end of the Bank of Amsterdam.

B.—*Contrast between the Bank of England and the three Continental Banks.*

Without pausing over certain points of resemblance to the Bank of Genoa, such as a similar origin (both banks came into existence through the organisation of a loan, and found their privileges increasing in return for successive advances made to the State),[3] and without pausing either to

[1] The marks on those coins which had been injured in the fire at the Stadthauss could be easily seen.

[2] *An Enquiry into the Principles of Political Economy*, Chap. 36-39, and *Wealth of Nations*, Vol. IV., Chap. iii. Adam Smith was helped in his study by his friend Hope.

[3] Other banks owed their existence to a loan, *e.g.*, those established at Florence in 1336 and 1357, at Chieri (Piedmont), in 1415, at Barcelona in 1349. (See W. Pareto, p. 356). In modern times the National Bank of Austria was founded in 1817 in order to withdraw from circulation the paper

notice that the Bank of England never possessed the political powers of the Italian Bank, we must bring out at once the ways in which the Bank of England was original and differed essentially from its Continental rivals.

(*a*) The chief distinction was that the Continental banks were merely banks of deposit while the Bank of England was something more and something better.

We must explain. The Continental banks, with the exception indeed of the Bank of St. George, accepted from merchants coins of all countries of repute and held them "as the equivalents of the bills issued against them. In theory the notes of these earlier banks were of the nature of dock warrants, entitling the holder to claim not only the sum which they expressed, but, theoretically at least, the very coins which were deposited against them."[1]

The Bank of Amsterdam guaranteed that its depositors should always receive the same weight of money, that is a value equal to what they had deposited. Accounts were kept in terms of an ideal money, bank money.[2] In this way the paper issued by the banks was much superior to metallic money which was liable to all kinds of depreciation. Hence it was at a premium.[3]

The Bank of England from the outset adopted a different

money issued by the Government. The Banks of Genoa and Turin also lent 20 millions to the Piedmontese Government, which authorised their amalgamation into a single bank; this bank continued to make loans to the Government and became the national bank of Sardinia and then the Bank of Italy. The Bank of Spain was founded in 1874 to raise a loan of 125 millions of pesetas for the State. Since then its advances have continued under various forms.

As examples of a different origin the Bank of Amsterdam may be noticed and more recently the Scotch banks. The Banks of France and Belgium were created by private enterprise but they received a more or less direct assistance from the Government.

For further details on the above points see du Hays du Gassart, *Des prêts consentis aux États par les Banques de Circulation*, Chap. I.

[1] Thorold Rogers, p. 8.

[2] Gide, p. 336. The incident of 1672 showed that the obligation of keeping the deposits was not at first an illusory guarantee. According to Davenant, the Bank of Amsterdam held regularly £36,000,000.

For a long time the public believed that this policy was always followed, but Law (*Mémoire sur les Banques*, edition already quoted, p. 553), and Galliani (*Della Moneta*, Vol. II., p. 212, edition of the *Economisti classici Italiani*), were sceptical, and future events showed that they were justified.

[3] Pierson, p. 489. The same thing happened at Venice. See above, p. 78, and Savary, *loc. cit.*

policy, that already followed by the goldsmiths and by the Bank of Sweden.[1] "It purported to give in its bills the equivalent of what it had received, but it never pretended to take the deposit for any other purpose than that of trading with it. It never professed to make its issues square exactly with its coin and bullion, though, of course, it made its liabilities square with its assets, plus the capital of its shareholders, and in time, plus its rest or reserve also, *i.e.*, its accumulated and undivided profits. At first, these profits were derived from the dividends it received from Government, and from the gains it made out of the notes which it put into circulation in exchange for, or in addition to, the cash which it took. It coined, in short, its own credit into paper money."[2]

(*b*) Another important distinction between the Bank of England and the other Continental banks consisted in the fact that its notes were not legal tender, whereas in the case of the three banks described above, debtors were obliged to offer and creditors to receive the paper money issued by the banks.[3] The Republic of Venice, for instance, forbade the use of metallic money for sums exceeding 300 ducats, and ordered such payments to be made by bank transfers. At Amsterdam payments of sums exceeding, at first 600 and later 300 ducats, had to be made in bank receipts. Finally, at Genoa, an ordinance of 1675 ordered all payments, however small, of bills of exchange or other remittances, to be made through the Bank of St. George.

There was nothing of this sort in the case of the Bank of England. The English Government did not make the Bank's notes legal tender, and moreover the Bank had no

[1] The Bank of Stockholm, established in 1656, had already issued banknotes (Law, *op. cit.*, p. 556). Voltaire writes that the Bank of Sweden, which is the oldest bank in Europe, had to be created because the currency was copper and iron, the transport of which was too difficult (*Histoire de Charles XII.*, Bk. I., p. 1). On this point see also Palgrave, *Notes on Banking in Great Britain, Sweden, and Hamburg*, p. 87.

On the Bank of Palmstruch an American work: *History of Banking in all Nations*, Vol. IV., pp. 393-395, and the *Economiste Français* for Feb. 2nd, 1901, may be consulted.

[2] Thorold Rogers, *op. cit.*, p. 9.

[3] On this point see Wilfredo Pareto, *op. cit.*, Vol. I., p. 360, *et seq.*

thought of asking that they should do so, for the directors were not in favour of such a measure. One of them remarked,[1] "It's nothing makes bank bills currant, but only because that all those who desire it, can go when they will, and fetch their money for them."

(*c*) A third important distinction is that the Continental banks enjoyed a monopoly while the Bank of England was granted no such privilege at the time of its foundation. The Government even threatened it with a formidable rival by the creation of the Land Bank. It was only after the collapse of this institution, which nearly ruined the Bank of England, that the Government (in 1697) conceded to the latter a partial monopoly; twelve years later a genuine one was granted.

The distinction between the Bank of England and the Banks of the late Renaissance will be better understood if we study the business which the new English bank undertook from the outset of its career. But before doing this, we must point out that the important differences which we have tried to describe exist no longer.

At the present time the Bank of England enjoys a monopoly, which, originally limited to London, has been extended throughout the country; its notes are legal tender, and have been so since 1833; and in addition to this, it has shown for some time a tendency to return to the position of the primitive banks, whose chief function was to manage the exchanges, to supply good money, and to take charge of the capital of individuals.[2]

The Act of 1844 obliges the Bank to buy all the gold offered to it at a fixed price. And besides it can be shown that for some time—more than ten years—the value of the Bank of England notes in circulation has always been less than that of its metallic reserve. The character of the bank-notes has thus completely changed; like the old certificates of deposit, they are to-day approximately warrants. In fact the Bank of England to-day is less a credit institution than a

[1] Godfrey, *op. cit.*, pp. 7-8. [Francis, *op. cit.*, Vol. II., p. 248.]

[2] Leroy-Beaulieu, *Traité théorique et pratique d'Économie politique*, Vol. III., p. 604.

repository of cash. It is the guardian of the cash reserves for the whole of English commerce, *i.e.*, almost for the world's commerce.[1]

SECTION III.

THE TRANSACTIONS OF THE BANK.[2]

These transactions were various, but they were not undertaken according to the principles which seem to regulate the business of modern banks.

In the first place all the capital up to the last shilling had been lent to the Government. The only security the shareholders had was the good faith of the debtor. But only two years had passed since the system of a national debt had been first introduced by the Government through the annuities. The lottery loan of a million was undertaken at the same time as the foundation of the bank. It was speedily successful, but this debt also was temporary, and was to be liquidated in sixteen years. Thus the loan from the Bank was the first permanent loan, if not in theory, since the Government reserved the right to pay it off in 1705, at any rate in fact, since everyone foresaw that the Government would never want to destroy an institution so useful to itself and to the public.

The capital of the Bank was thus in the hands of the Government.

In what way, then, could it make any profit?

1st.—Besides the income of £100,000 paid to it yearly by the Government, the Bank had the power to issue notes.

It issued these to an amount equal to the sum advanced to the Government. These notes, as we have seen, were

[1] We shall see at the end of the present work (Vol. II., appendix) that the English Government has avoided the inconvenience of keeping the public money by entrusting this to the Bank. It is interesting to note that as early as the eighteenth century the Republic of Venice proposed to hand over the duties of the Treasury to the *Banco del Giro*—see Besta, *Lezioni sulla Contabilita di Stato*, Bk. VII., Chap. iii.

[2] For an account of these transactions see Godfrey, *A short account of the Bank of England* (1695). This pamphlet also describes the immediate results of the Bank's foundation. It is most useful and we have already referred to it. All references are to the reprint which Francis gives at the end of his own book.

not legal tender; an interest of 2d. a day was allowed on them, which cost the Bank £36,000 a year, but attracted to it the patronage of the goldsmiths. This policy made people use these notes less often in making payments; but it also deprived them of that fixity of value which is one of the main characteristics of a well-managed currency.

It seems incredible that the Bank took no precaution to ensure the convertibility of its notes, and during the restoration of the coinage it was reduced to the most desperate expedients to maintain its credit. It would not have succeeded in doing so had it not been for the sacrifices made by its directors and shareholders.

2nd.—Nominally the Bank discounted at 4½ per cent. in the case of foreign bills of exchange, and at 6 per cent. in the case of English bills and notes for debts. But considerable reductions were made to such of its customers as kept their money deposited with it.

3rd.—This was not the only favour shown to depositors. In order to increase the profits which could be made on deposits the Bank endeavoured to attract them by paying 4 per cent. interest to depositors.[1] This practice aroused great indignation among the Bank's opponents who declared that it would cause the withdrawal of capital from commerce and industry.[2]

4th.—Its first charter authorised the Bank to lend money on pawned articles. According to Godfrey it lent money on "pawns of commodities" and "real securities" at 5 per cent. per annum. If the titles to land had been more certain, advances would have been made on mortgages at 4 per cent., and in time of peace, at 3 per cent. The Bank does not seem to have made much use of its power to lend on pawned goods, and it never bore any resemblance to a pawn-dealer.

[1] Another feature distinguishing it from the primitive banks, whose depositors, so far from making any profit on their deposits, were obliged to pay for them.

[2] Davenant, *Discourses on the Public Revenues and Trade of England* (1698), Part I., p. 205.

CHAPTER IV.

RESULTS OF THE FOUNDATION OF THE BANK.

Political and economic condition of England at the time of its foundation. Success of the Bank. Causes of this success. Michael Godfrey, his salutary influence on the commercial world, his pamphlet, "*A Short Account of the Bank of England.*" Services of the Bank to the Government and the public.

THE Bank was created under gloomy auspices. The political outlook was bad,[1] the March equinoxes had been extremely severe[2] and the financial situation was deplorable; not only was the market constantly upset by the gambling fever,[3]

[1] Marlborough had disclosed to James II. the plan for an assault on Brest, and had thus converted into a disaster an attack which it had been believed must ruin the French navy. (This letter from Marlborough is published among the *Stuart Papers*. See also Henri Martin, Vol. XIV., pp. 196-197).

At home the Government was not strengthened, an attack on the coasts of Britain was feared, and it was rumoured that the Pope was going to advance considerable sums to James II. to support this expedition.

[2] One of these alone seems to have done damage to the amount of £400,000, a considerable sum when the English navy according to Rogers' estimate, hardly exceeded 200,000 tons burden. In 1702 the total tonnage according to Macpherson, did not exceed 212,222 tons. At present it is 9,164,342, as compared with 1,639,552 for Germany, and 957,756 for France (these figures are taken from very detailed statistics published in the *Times* for February 5, 1901). In 1898, 761 merchant vessels were constructed in England whose total tonnage amounted to 1,367,250 tons, without counting 33 warships of a total tonnage of 120,560 (see Victor Bérard, *L'Angleterre et l'Impérialisme contemporain*). In other words, the annual construction is now seven times the total tonnage of the English merchant navy two centuries ago.

[3] We have already referred to this (p. 53), and to the companies formed, often entirely without foundation, and whose shares fluctuated incessantly. These fluctuations were the more numerous owing to the ease with which a panic regarding the shares of such-and-such a company could be spread or an artificial rise in the shares of others produced. The public was unaccustomed to manipulations of this kind and was easily deceived. The speculators used to meet at the coffee-houses, especially at Garraway's and Jonathan's, which in London history are the equivalents of the Rue Quincampoix; they had no qualms about producing fluctuations to an extent of which a few figures will give an idea. The stock of the Hudson's Bay Company fell from £250 to £80 in three years. That of the East India Company, which had stood at £146 at the beginning of 1693, fell to £37 in May, 1697, to rise again to £142 by the beginning of 1700. The stock of the English East India Company, the young rival of the former, with which it ultimately combined, suffered a like fate; from £46 in March,

but the lack of sound metallic coinage[1] on which to base the credit currency might at any moment have forced the Bank to the verge of ruin. However, in spite of all, the Bank prospered at the outset.[2] This was due to the prudence and ability of its directors and shareholders. Michael Godfrey, who had done for the Bank in all that related to the City what Montague had done for it in matters concerning the Government, not only gave it the support of his personal influence, which was great, but also took pains to surround it with wealthy financiers of high reputation. There was Sir John Houblon,[3] the first governor, afterwards Lord Mayor of London, Gilbert Heathcote, and several other merchants of excellent commercial standing. The personality of the directors had more influence then than to-day and that of Godfrey's colleagues was such that even his death,[4] followed by Paterson's resignation, did not appreciably diminish the credit of the new establishment.[5]

The success of the Bank had also a political side and political causes. Its promoters were all active Whigs, and although this exposed it to attacks as we know, it also ensured to it the support of the Government and the sympathy of the commercial world, who rallied round the new institution when they saw it attacked.

Whatever the exact causes, the success was brilliant.

1699, it rose to £219 in March, 1703. And these were well-established companies of good repute. I have chosen them on that very account. The enormous fluctuations in the stock of other companies now long forgotten may easily be imagined.

[1] The condition of the coinage will form the subject of the next chapter.

[2] On all these points see Thorold Rogers' excellent work: *The First Nine Years of the Bank of England.*

[3] These Houblons, for Sir John had four brothers, were of Flemish origin. Their father had taken refuge in England on account of religious persecutions. He made a good deal of money in London, but always continued a member of the French colony, of which he was for a long time the president.

[4] Godfrey was killed at the siege of Namur on July 15, 1695. He had come to bring subsidies to William, who was besieging the town, and like a good courtier accompanied his sovereign into the trenches, where he was shot. His enemies alleged that he ventured into such an exposed position only out of excess of prudence, believing that the one place of safety was with the King.

[5] This death only caused a fall of 2 per cent. on the stock.

Godfrey lived long enough to witness it and some little time before his death he published his famous pamphlet, in which he expressed his delight with some complaisancy.

The primary advantage which followed from the establishment of the Bank was, according to him,[1] that a loan was granted to the Government at an exceptional rate. This is quite true and it was this that enabled William to take the offensive in Flanders and to secure his first successes. Moreover, the Bank helped the Government by making the voting of taxes more effective, as well as by actual loans. It accepted the tallies at par so that they soon rose to a premium, whereas until 1694, even the most secure of these tallies which had but a short time to run, such as those on the land tax, had been at a discount of from 1½ to 2 per cent., while tallies which offered less security were discounted at a loss of 15 to 30 per cent. over and above the interest.[2]

The advantages which the Bank afforded to the public were no less great. The citizens now had a place where their deposits would be in security,[3] and would bear interest although the money could be withdrawn at will.

The Bank also had a beneficial influence on the rate of discount. Godfrey remarks as a thing both surprising and unexampled that after six years of war and after an expenditure of thirty millions,[4] there had been a great fall in the rate of interest instead of the rise usual in such cases. The author prophesied that in a few years, thanks to the Bank, the rate of interest would be reduced permanently to 3 per cent., and the value of the lands of England increased by nearly 100 millions.[5]

The Bank was undoubtedly an immense benefit to both Government and public; Godfrey's statements are confirmed on all sides. And what is more, the benefit was mutual, since the Bank lost nothing.

[1] p. 3

[2] p. 3.

[3] Godfrey takes the opportunity of making various accusations against the goldsmiths. See above, pp. 22 and 25.

[4] p. 6.

[5] p. 7, and see above, p. 67 for reference to the result thus anticipated.

This is evident from the price of its stock, which soon rose to par and on October 25th, 1694, was at 105. After some fluctuations, of which Rogers gives a most detailed account,[1] it rose again to 99 on March 25th of the following year, fell slightly, then rose once more, so that in January, 1696, it reached the unprecedented height of 108.[2] All seemed to be going well when two dangers made their appearance, which proved to be among the most serious of those with which the new institution was threatened: these dangers were the reform, now become unavoidable, of the coinage and the project for the Land Bank. They will form the subjects of the two next chapters.

[1] See his Table I., giving the "Weekly Prices of Bank Stock."

[2] These fluctuations were due either to the political events, favourable and otherwise, which occurred during these years, such as the taking of Namur, the death of the Queen, etc., or to events particularly affecting the Bank, such as Godfrey's death, or the announcement of a dividend, or, finally, to the scandals and political intrigues which marked the period. Macaulay (Chap. xxi.) describes the scandals connected with the East India Company and with the City of London Orphans' Fund. On this occasion the Speaker was accused of corruption, and had himself to put the question to the House over which he was presiding. The vote was against him, and he was expelled from the House. Seymour and Leeds were also implicated, and their accusers were no better than they.

These scandals threw discredit upon the stock of all the great financial companies, and that of the Bank was further affected by the manipulations of Lord Godolphin and Charles Duncombe, who sold all their stock in order to produce a fictitious fall. The effects of this sudden and combined sale may be imagined when it is remembered that Duncombe alone had £80,000 of stock. This same Duncombe, a man of the worst character, who had been convicted of forgery but released in default of a legal penalty for his crime, ended by becoming Lord Mayor of London by means of unrestrained corruption. He had made his fortune in all ways imaginable. The account of his life would form a curious chapter in the history of the social behaviour, and in particular, of the electioneering habits of his time. Bribery in every form ran rife at elections without concealment or needless beating about the bush. It is one of the things not least to the credit of modern England that she has freed herself from these scandalous methods, which, with the connivance of the Hanoverian monarchy, persisted down to the end of the eighteenth century.

CHAPTER V.

THE RESTORATION OF THE COINAGE.

Scandalous condition of the English coinage. Laws powerless to prevent clipping. The *Re-Coinage Act* of 1696. Examination of this Law. Montague's difficulties, (*a*) Great expense involved in the successful completion of the operation, (*b*) The standard of the new coins. Controversy between Lowndes and Locke. Decision of the House of Commons.

In William III.'s time the coins were struck at the Tower by a mill worked by horses. But until the introduction of a machine for stamping the coins, this had been done by a hammer; the metal was first cut into pieces and then stamped. These two sorts of coins circulated together, in theory at least, in actual fact the bad money soon drove out the good. Folkes,[1] indeed, states that during the re-coinage in 1696 the coins brought to the Mint had all been struck between the 6th year of Edward VI.'s reign and 1662, the year in which milling had been introduced.

At the time of which we write at all events, the state of the currency had become scandalous; coins dating from the Plantagenets were still in circulation, as well as debased coins of Henry VIII. and Edward VI., which had escaped the re-coinage[2] in Elizabeth's reign and which were valued accurately by the dealers in money, for coins were found offered for sale and valued as half alloy. "The English Mint levied on the bullion coined a pretty heavy seignorage to cover charges,[3] for the coin had to carry, not only the fourteen pence per pound charged for manufacture, but the cost of melting and refining. Now such a seignorage

[1] Martin Folkes, *A Table of Silver Coins*, p. 42.

[2] Some details as to this re-coinage will be found in our fourth part, chap. vi., in connection with Robert Peel's speech. It was this re-coinage which gave Gresham the opportunity of stating the law called by his name.

[3] At the present day all the expenses of minting are met by the taxes, and the English sovereign is the only coin which really possesses its face value.

charge must have led to a considerable importation of foreign coin, which in the exchanges was estimated at its bullion, as opposed to its Mint value."[1] The disadvantages of such a situation were continually making themselves felt, and had been the subject of petitions to the House of Commons and of various Bills. But in 1694 the matter became insupportable. The silver currency was depreciating daily, and at the end of the year, the guineas which were nominally equivalent to 20 shillings, rose gradually to 30 shillings. The exchange on Holland fell 25 per cent. although the balance of trade was favourable to England.

This state of things could not fail to attract the attention of Parliament.[2] The difficulties were so great that trade was at a standstill and the taxes were no longer collected. The silver money had been getting clipped for a long time and the damage was done so secretly and was so well concealed by all who were interested in dealing in the currency, that all the coins had greatly decreased in value, five pounds in cash being hardly worth forty shillings. There were also in circulation a quantity of coins of iron or copper silvered over.[3]

The committee requested that the money should be re-coined and calculated that this would cost a million. It also recommended that the new money should be of the same weight and fineness as the old; that the crown should be valued at 5s. 6d.; and that numerous penalties should be imposed on those who debased the coins.

An Act was passed in 1695,[4] the preamble of which states that it was notorious that the currency had been greatly debased by various devices, that many false coins had been clipped to make them like the good ones, and that these

[1] Thorold Rogers, *op. cit.*, p. 31.

[2] A committee was appointed as early as 1689, but it presented no report. References to the monetary crisis are found in many of the literary writings of the period, in Dryden's correspondence, for example; in Blackmore's *Satyr against Wit,* and even in Cibber's comedy, *The Fool of Fashion,* the hero of which, in language reflecting the licence which then prevailed in the English drama, declares that "Virtue is as much debased as our money, and faith, Dei gratia, is as hard to be found in a girl of sixteen as round the brim of an old shilling."

[3] *Parliamentary History,* Vol. V., p. 955.

[4] 6 and 7 W. and M., c. 17.

practices had been carried on by persons who made a trade of exchanging good money for bad, or other like devices. The law therefore forbade anyone to exchange, lend, sell buy, or receive any coins, clipped or unclipped, of gold or silver, for more than their nominal value, under a penalty of 10s. for every 20s. so traded in. The law added (art. 4) that anyone who bought, sold or knowingly possessed, any of the clippings of the coins, should forfeit them, and should be liable to a fine of £500 and to be branded on the right cheek with a capital R. Moreover everyone, except those who were goldsmiths by profession, was forbidden, under penalty of imprisonment, to buy or sell bullion, and various penalties were imposed on those who exported coin.[1] In addition, this law, which Rogers describes as "a striking illustration of that unwisdom and ignorance of monetary laws which pervaded the legislature," contains two even more characteristic sections.

Section 8 allowed the Warden, with two assistants of the Goldsmiths' Company, or two justices of the peace, to enter any house suspected of containing bullion, and if any was found, it rested with the owner of the house to prove that it was not the product of melted coin or of clippings. The law went even further in ordering the sheriffs of counties, on and after May 1st, 1695, to pay £40 to anyone who procures the conviction of a clipper; and the informant may sue the sheriff if the latter neglects to pay him his reward.

This was sufficient to put a premium on denunciation. But the law went still further in this direction. Any clipper who could prove the guilt of two others was pardoned and an apprentice who informed successfully against his master was at once made a freeman of the City. His denunciation served him instead of a "masterpiece."

We have thought it necessary to dwell upon these pro-

[1] See sections 5, 6, and 7. The provisions are as follows:—Section 5 disables every person from exporting bullion unless it be stamped at Goldsmiths' Hall and oath be made that it is not the produce of English coin. Bullion thus "sworn off" was worth about 1½d. an ounce more than other bullion. As Mr. Rogers witily remarks, "this meant that three halfpence an ounce in gold was the price of perjury."

Section 6 permits unstamped bullion to be seized and confiscated by the Customs' House. Section 7 authorises goldsmiths alone to deal in bullion.

visions, because they are not peculiar to the law of 1695. They recur in all similar legislative attempts, and it is not too much to say that the prohibition of keeping money coined or in bullion, and the encouragement of informing, are the necessary outcome of measures by which statesmen have hoped to restrain the free action of monetary laws. To refer only to France, we find similar provisions under the Regency, when sons denounced their fathers, and in the laws of the revolutionists with regard to assignats. The French laws only served to bring trouble and disorder and fulfilled none of the hopes with which they were passed. The effects of the English laws may be deduced from the facts which follow.

During the months of May, June, and July, 1695, 572 bags of silver coin, of £100 each, were brought into the exchequer. They should have weighed 18,451-lbs.; they did, in fact, weigh 9,480-lbs., that is, there was a difference of nearly 50 per cent.

A contemporary writer[1] says: "Upon trial I have found that 5s. of milled money weighed 8s. of the present current money, and 3s. of the 8s. was not clipped, only worn. Again, I have found 10s. in milled money to weigh 21s. of the clipped money. Again, 20s. of milled money to weigh 43s. of our now current money."

The officers of the Exchequer, according to Lowndes,[2] weighed £57,200 of hammered money. Its weight ought to have exceeded 221,418 ounces, it was actually 113,771 ounces. The weight per bag was as follows:

1st bag,	correct weight	15,483	ounces	-	actual weight	8,095
2nd ,,	,,	28,645	,,	-	,,	14,375
3rd ,,	,,	51,483	,,	-	,,	27,318
4th ,,	,,	46,451	,,	-	,,	23,469
5th ,,	,,	40,645	,,	-	,,	20,899
6th ,,	,,	38,709	,,	-	,,	19,588
		221,418				113,771

[1] *An Essay for the Regulation of the Coin*, By A. V. (Sept. 2nd, 1695).

[2] *Some Remarks on a Report containing an Essay for the Amendment of the Silver Coins* (1695), p. 159 of the original edition, and p. 253 of MacCulloch's reprint in *A Collection of scarce Tracts on Money.*

See also Martin Folkes, *op. cit.*, p. 117, note. L'Hermitage also says (Dec. 9th, 1695) that three well-known London goldsmiths were asked to supply £100 of current silver coin; the £300 ought to have weighed 1,200 ounces, they actually weighed only 624.

The anonymous author quoted above gives a similar calculation.[1] He went to several London goldsmiths and asked them to take out of their strong-boxes a bag of £100; he found that these bags weighed as follows:

1st bag	- - -	230 ounces[2]
2nd ,,	- - -	222 ,,
3rd ,,	- - -	198 ,,
4th ,,	- - -	190 ,,
5th ,,	- - -	182 ,,
6th ,,	- - -	174 ,,

The whole £600 weighed 17,198 ounces, which would have been the weight of £310 of milled money. The author adds that he is informed that the money paid into the Exchequer weighs from 13 to 20-lbs. per £100 sterling and that it is worth less than two-thirds of its nominal value. "But,[3] since it was thought that the money in the country is generally not one-half as bad as it is in and near London," he obtained an account from various cities as follows:

At Bristol -	1st bag	of £100	weighed	240	ounces
	2nd	,,	,,	,,	227	,,
At Cambridge -	1st	,,	,,	,,	203	,,
	2nd	,,	,,	,,	211	,,
At Exeter - -	1st	,,	,,	,,	180	,,
	2nd	,,	,,	,,	192	,,
At Oxford -	1st	,,	,,	,,	216	,,
	2nd	,,	,,	,,	198	,,
					1,668	ounces

The £800 weighed no more than £431 15s. of milled money, so that the difference from the London figures was very small.

Our author exaggerates slightly, for some parts of the North escaped the infection. Macaulay relates with his usual wit, the tale of the Lancashire Quaker, who during a

[1] *Essay for Regulation*, p. 8, Chap. iv.

[2] I omit fractions, so that the totals given are slightly higher than those of the figures actually quoted. The same remark applies to the preceding table.

[3] p. 9.

journey to London, found to his amazement that the value of his money changed and increased as he drew nearer to the Capital. When he got there his wealth was half as great again as when he started.[1]

What was the reason for this incessant clipping of the coin? It could not be explained by the negligence of the law. The laws were only too severe, and were actually enforced: instances of condemnation to death followed by execution occur by dozens.[2] Godfrey accuses the goldsmiths. Rogers considers that the crime was fashionable, and that the morals of the Court after the Restoration afforded a bad example to the public.

It is certain, at any rate, that these practices were extraordinarily profitable;[3] the bullion had become so much dearer than the coined money that people were irresistibly tempted to clip the coins,[4] more especially since the connivance of the boatmen on the south coast made the exportation of bullion extremely easy.

Another equally certain fact is that people were so tolerant of these crimes that the clergy thought it incumbent upon

[1] Chap. xxi., p. 544, Vol. II., in the two-volume edition. Vol. IV., p. 627 in the first edition.

[2] Seven men were hanged and a woman burnt in a single morning for a crime of this kind.—Macaulay, p. 543, Vol. II., or p. 625, Vol. IV.

[3] Luttrell says that many people made fortunes in this way, and instances Moor of Westminster, who, when his crime was discovered, offered a considerable sum in order to save his life. See Thorold Rogers, *op. cit.*, p. 32.

[4] The trade of clipping coin, says L'Hermitage (Oct. 1st), was so profitable and seemed so easy that, no matter what was done to suppress the clippers, others were always ready to take their places. The author of the *Essay for regulation of the coin* (p. 3) in his second chapter, headed, *Setting forth what is become of the great quantities of money coined in the reign of King Charles II. and the preceding Reigns,* points out that 4d., 6d., or even 12d. may be gained by melting an unclipped 5s. piece. He adds, "And 20 per cent. advantage is a good allay for any scruple of conscience that may have those that practice it, and those that receive and pay one thousand pounds a day, and meet with but one hundred pounds amongst it of unclipped Silver may in a year (accounting but three hundred days) get six hundred sterling."

Another reason given by the same writer (p. 4) for the disappearance of the coin was the fashion for gold and silver plate, and for chains, buttons, and buckles of the precious metals, a fashion which must have caused the melting of more than 7 million sterling, involving an annual loss of interest of £420,000. The author suggests that the use of such plate should be forbidden or that it should be licensed and a tax of 5 per cent. imposed. Such complaints of the inconveniences of fashion recall those made by Bodin in his answer to the paradox of M. de Malestroit.

them to protest and to recall the faithful to a truer view of the matter.[1]

The Re-coinage Act of January 21, 1696.[2] Meanwhile, the sermons did little to alter the situation, which grew worse daily, and the price of gold and the foreign exchanges[3] were continually disturbed by it.

During 1694 the price of gold varied from 80s. to 81s. 6d. That of guineas from 21s. 10d. to 22s. 6d., and that of the ounce of silver from 5s. 2d. to 5s. 5d. In 1695 the prices of the precious metals began to rise.[4] On January 11th, the price of an ounce of gold was 80s. 6d., and that of guineas 22s. 9d. These prices rose steadily, and on June 14th, were

1 Two sermons on this subject are particularly remarkable. The first and most striking was preached by Fleetwood, afterwards Bishop of Ely, then chaplain to the King, before the Lord Mayor and Aldermen, and was printed by order of the court (Ruding, p. 36, note 2). Fleetwood was one of the most interesting characters amongst the English clergy, he was an ardent Whig and continually introduced politics into his sermons. (We have of his a *Chronicon Pretiosum, or an account of English gold and silver Money,* published anonymously in 1707, and various sermons on passive obedience and in opposition to the peace of Utrecht). In this case he showed considerable knowledge of economic questions. He took for his text Genesis xxiii., 16, and in reference to the grave of Sarah found opportunity (p. 19) to point out the evils of debasing the coinage, especially in regard to payments to foreigners which could not be made in clipped money. "For it is not Cæsar's face and titles, but weight and goodness that procure credit." "Now," he concludes, "if the exportation of our weighty money be a mischief to the nation, we see it is occasioned chiefly by the clipping."

The other sermon was preached by G. Halley at York Castle, before some "clippers" who were to be hanged the next day.

2 For this Act, its causes, and some interesting details, see Shaw, *The History of the Currency*, pp. 222-227.

3 Rogers gives five tables which are of great value for the study of this question. I.—The Weekly Prices of Bank Stock from Aug. 17, 1694, to Sept. 17, 1703. II.—The Rates of Exchange on Amsterdam. III.—The Discount or premium on bills of exchange, London and Amsterdam. IV.—Discount of Bank Bills. V.—Changes in the value of gold, silver, and guineas. Rogers made considerable use of a book by Alexander Justice, *General Treatise on Moneys and Exchanges* (1707). I have not been able to consult this work, for the only copy is in the Oxford Library. The Director of the British Museum, to whom I applied, promised to procure the book if possible, but apparently the attempt has not hitherto been successful. [There is now a copy in the Goldsmiths' Library.]

4 The price of silver fluctuated less, because silver was in fact the standard coin of the country, and during this crisis the Government, so far as a Government can exercise influence in such a matter, was able to control partially the price of this metal through the quantity of coin issued. Gold did not become the English standard until 1816, and the single standard was adopted less for theoretical reasons than on grounds of economy. Silver was then at a premium. For the present monetary system in England see Cauwès' *Cours d'Économie Politique,* Vol. II., p. 542.

109s. and 30s. respectively, which were the maximum prices for the year.[1]

The rate of exchange fell in a corresponding manner. In June, 1695, the exchange on Amsterdam, which is important both on account of the prominent position held by this town and also because the sums necessary to support the English troops in Flanders were sent through it, was at 22.2 per cent. below par, and in August English bills of exchange on Amsterdam were at a discount of 30 per cent.

This latter fact hastened the decision arrived at by Montague and Somers that the currency must be reformed at all costs and that this could only be done on condition that the debts to individual creditors and to the public remained unaltered in value.

It was, in fact, out of all the numerous results of the deplorable state of the currency, its effect upon the rate of exchange which most disturbed England at that moment. Whatever might be the state of home trade, the sufferings of those who were dependent on their salaries, the disturbance produced in credit, the immense profits of the goldsmiths and exchangers, all these evils seemed small compared with the fact that the subsidies voted for a war upon whose result, as was commonly thought, the very existence of England depended, were always reduced by 20 or 30 per cent. owing to the expenses incurred in conveying the sums voted to their destination.

The new Parliament met in November, 1695, and the reform of the currency was its first subject of discussion. The law which decreed the reform of the currency was 7 William III., c.i.[2] The remedy came almost too late, for the distress continued to be extreme during the first year after its application. The currency reform under William III., like that under Elizabeth, was an undertaking of fundamental importance and extreme delicacy, and it was unlike

[1] In April, 1696, after the new coins had been issued, guineas fell again to 22s., and the price of gold, on July 10, to 82s.; silver at the same date was 5s. 2d.—See Rogers, p. 36.

[2] *The Statutes at Large*, Vol. IX., pp. 380-386.

Elizabeth's re-coinage in that so far from yielding a profit it was a great expense.[1]

The re-coinage Ruding[2] states, was not completed until 1699, having occupied the greater part of this and the three preceding years. According to the reports of the directors of the Mint, the new currency amounted to £6,882,908, of which £5,091,121 were struck at the Tower, and £1,791,787 at various mills established in the provinces.[3] The expenses were met by a tax on houses and windows, and amounted in all to £2,702,164, which was far in excess of the original estimates.[4]

Criticisms of the Act of 1696.—Difficulties which Montague had to encounter.[5] It is well known that the Act of 1696 was due to Montague and a difficult enough task he had had.

Montague received much help from his colleague Somers, and above all, from two men of genius for whom political economy had not been a primary object of study—I refer to Newton and Locke. The latter was not content merely to advise, he also wrote a masterly pamphlet, of which we shall presently give an analysis. These four men, each so distinguished in his own province, had many difficulties to solve, of which the two chief were—(1) the question of the expense which must necessarily be incurred by the re-coinage, (2) the question whether, when the re-coinage was accomplished, the coins should keep their old standard or be issued at a lower one.

First difficulty. The £2,703,164 required for the undertaking had to be covered; a considerable sum at any time, and for that period enormous. Most likely if this expense

[1] Elizabeth's re-coinage left a net profit of £14,079 13s. 9d. See below, p. 240.

[2] Vol. II., p. 57.

[3] These mills for minting were at Bristol, Exeter, Chester, Norwich, and York.

[4] On this point see Lord Liverpool, draft of an intended report on the state of coinage. Mr. Leake (*An Historical Account of English Money*, p. 369) points out that all the expenses might have been avoided if the matter had been taken up in time. Some details interesting from a technical point of view, on this reform and on the statutes relating to it, will be found in a work by Edward Hawkins, curator of the antiquities at the British Museum, *The silver Coins of England*, pp. 391-392.

[5] See Thorold Rogers, p. 44 *et seq.*

had been clearly instead of vaguely foreseen, Montague would have argued in vain. Possibly too, if the Bank had realised the difficulties it would have to face—the depreciation of its stock and notes, the suspension of payments and of dividends—its directors, in spite of their courage and intelligence, would have refused to enter upon such a formidable adventure, more especially since they were already threatened by the Land Bank. Godfrey estimated the cost of the re-coinage at from one to two millions. To spend three million pounds, a sum equal to more than a year's revenue in time of peace, was as serious a matter at the end of the 17th century as the loss of a hundred million pounds to-day.

Second difficulty. The second difficulty encountered by Montague was a more delicate matter. The harvest had been bad, prices had risen, and the distress was great. "Would it not be better to keep the same names for the crown, the half-crown, the shilling, and the sixpence, but to coin an ounce of silver into seven shillings instead of five? There are people who even now believe that the Government can give an intrinsic value to a coin which it does not possess in bullion.[1] But many more people believed in this theory in 1695."[2] Parliament had fixed and was to go on fixing for some time the prices of crowns and guineas, of beef and salt, of labour and of money (by deciding the rate of interest); why might it not evade the expense of the re-

[1] At all events this opinion had not entirely disappeared some years ago. In England, in 1819, when cash payments were to be resumed after a suspension lasting 22 years, Lord Lauderdale proposed that the standard should be lowered, and maintained that gold ought to be valued at £4 1s. an ounce. It was also suggested that it should be valued at £4 10s. or at £5, since these prices, reckoned in Bank notes, had prevailed some time before the resumption of cash payments. People also said that as a great part of the national debt had been incurred during a period of forced currency, it was fair to pay the interest on it in depreciated coin. But wisdom prevailed and the old standard of the coins was re-established. This was not accomplished without opposition, and Robert Peel who advocated the policy, was treated as a lunatic by his own father, the statesman who had taken such a large share in drawing up the first labour laws. Montague's example must have been in the minds of those who were managing the business of resumption.

[2] Thorold Rogers, *op. cit.*, pp. 45-46.

coinage by lowering the standard of fineness of the coins and continuing to call the coins by their former names?[1]

These opinions were developed in a report by William Lowndes, the Secretary of the Treasury, published under the title: *A Report containing an essay for the amendment of the silver coins* (London, 1695). This work which contains much interesting historical information, called forth a reply from Locke.[2] The latter took Lowndes' arguments in turn, and after stating them very impartially, proceeded to refute them or rather to crush them to powder, in a masterly manner.[3] Locke's opinions had been stated before, but never with so much authority and skill.[4] That celebrated philosopher had written the pamphlet in question for the private use of Somers. Somers was delighted with it, and ordered it to be printed. The little treatise concludes as follows:

"The increase of denomination does or can do nothing

[1] The King, and afterwards Somers, proposed that the money should be weighed and not counted, but these suggestions were negatived by the council.

[2] *Further considerations concerning raising the value of money.* This pamphlet and two other economic essays by Locke, *Some considerations on the lowering of interest and raising the value of money,* and *On the Coining of Silver Money,* have been reprinted at the end of McCulloch's *Principles of Political Economy.* See Macleod, 5th edition, Vol. I., p. 468.

[3] See note, pp. 322-349 of McCulloch's reprint.

[4] We may mention among works whose authors agree with Lowndes: *A Discourse of Coin and of Coinage,* by Rice Vaughan, a book in which the author in spite of his talent, has been unable to escape the idea that the stamp affects the real value of the coin. The book, which is worth reading, was printed in 1675, but must have been written some time earlier, at any rate before 1643, when Louis XIII. died, for (p. 29) reference is made to an edict of the present King of France, in 1614. In connection with Locke's work, I cannot resist giving some extracts from *Quantulumcunque* which refer to the question. William Petty seems to me to be far in advance of the ordinary thought of his time on all the points with which he deals, both in the boldness and in the decision of his answers, and his short pamphlet—it is only ten pages long—deserves to be remembered. See Question 8 (p. 65, *Select Tracts*)—"If the new shilling were but three-quarters of the weight as formerly . . . the Merchant would export them, just as before, only he will give but three-quarters so much Pepper or other Indian Goods for the new retrenched shilling as he did for the old. . . . And consequently there would be no difference, but among a few such Fools as take money by its name and not by its weight and fineness."

Question 9.—"If a shilling was by new Coinage reduced to three-quarters of its present weight, should we not thereby have one-third more money than we now have, and consequently be so much the richer? Answer—You would indeed have one-third part more of the new christened shillings, but not an

in the case, for it is silver by its quantity and not denomination that is the price of things and the measure of commerce; and it is the weight of silver in it, and not the name of the pieces, that men estimate commodities by and exchange them for.

"If this be not so, when the necessity of our affairs abroad, or ill-husbandry at home, has carried away half our treasure, . . . it is but to issue a proclamation that a penny shall go for two pence, sixpence for a shilling, half a crown for a crown, etc., and immediately, without any more ado, we are as rich as before. And, when half the remainder is gone, it is but doing the same thing again, and raising the denomination anew. And so on, and if the denomination were raised 15 or 16 times, everyone would find his wealth in silver turned into gold.

"If this be not so, I desire anyone to show me why the same way of raising the denomination, which can raise the value of money in respect to other commodities one-fifth, cannot, when you please, raise it another fifth, and so on." The name, Locke goes on, is an arbitrary matter; the shilling might be called a penny, and *vice versa;* similarly, the existing proportion between the two coins might be changed.

"But this, however ordered, alters not one jot the value of the ounce of silver, in respect of other things, any more than it does its weight, this raising being but giving of names at pleasure to aliquot parts of any piece." No human power can "raise the value of our money their double in respect of other commodities, and make that same piece or quantity of silver, under a double denomination, purchase double the quantity of pepper, wine, or lead, an instant after such proclamation, to what it would do an instant before."

Ounce more of Silver . . . of Foreign Commodities . . . Nor even of any Domestic Commodities. . . . Suppose you buy a Silver Vessel from a Goldsmith weighing 20 ounces at 6s. per ounce, making 6 pounds or 24 ounces of Coined Silver; now suppose that the said 6 pounds were reduced from weighing 24 ounces to weigh but 18 ounces upon the new Coinage, but be still called 6 pounds even by the King's Proclamation. Can it be imagined that the Goldsmith will give his Vessel weighing 20 ounces of wrought for 18 ounces of unwrought Silver? . . . Now this Absurdity is the same in all other commodities."

Locke's conclusions seem unanswerable,[1] and nowadays no one would seriously deny that Lowndes' suggestion would have given a severe blow to the credit of the Government, and would have involved the spoliation of creditors for the benefit of debtors. Many interests were opposed to an alteration of the standard. Creditors would have lost a part of their incomes, landlords a part of their rents, and everyone who had a contract not yet fulfilled would have suffered in like manner. But the notion that the name of shilling carried the thing with it was powerful and Lowndes' reasoning answered well to the prevailing frame of mind. The resolution to preserve the old standard of the coins, vigorously supported by Montague, was, however, passed by a majority of 111.[2]

[1] His premises were no less important. He began by stating as a principle that there is only one difference between the Government which debases the coins and the criminal who clips them, viz., that the Government can oblige people to accept the debased coin. He then points out that such conduct will cost the State dear. The debasement of the coin in fact "will defraud the King, the Church, and the universities and hospitals, and of so much of their settled revenue as the money is raised. . . It will weaken, if not totally destroy the public faith, when all that have trusted the public and assisted our present necessities upon Acts of Parliament, in the million lottery, Bank Act, and other loans, should be deprived of twenty per cent." Later on, p. 338, Locke adds that it is alleged that the lowering of the standard will enable more debts to be paid, which shows evidently that there is a fraud involved which it would be impossible to sanction.

[2] Macaulay, Vol. II., p. 552.

CHAPTER VI.

THE LAND BANK.—RENEWAL OF THE BANK CHARTER.

(*a*) Dr. Chamberlain. His economic theories and scheme for a Land Bank. Bill for the Land Bank passed by the House of Commons. Collapse of the Land Bank. (*b*) Position of the Bank of England after the re-coinage and the foundation of the Land Bank. Partial suspension of the Bank's payments. First Exchequer Bills issued. (*c*) Grievances and demands of the Bank of England. Renewal and extension of the Charter. Chief provisions of the Act of February 3, 1697. Question of a monopoly.

THE price of Bank stock, which on February 1st, 1696, stood at £107, had fallen to £83 on the 14th of the same month. It was at this time that the House of Commons sanctioned the scheme for a Land Bank, best known by the name of its promoter Dr. Chamberlain.

Chamberlain was an accoucheur who had written two or three medical books, and who had for some time been endeavouring to found a Land Bank, or indeed, a bank of any kind.[1] Four years after the failure of his scheme in England he made another attempt at Edinburgh, but with no better success than on the former occasion.[2]

[1] As early as 1693 Chamberlain had submitted his scheme for a Land Bank to the House of Commons, who considered it and pronounced it to be useful and practicable. Before this a formal allusion to Dr. Chamberlain's schemes occurs in the pamphlet so often referred to, *Bank of Credit*. The City merchant remarks that Mr. Murray and the Doctor have drawn up a very ingenious scheme for a bank of credit, but since they have received no encouragement from the City, they have made a proposal for a bank of a more general character, including not only London and its suburbs, but the whole kingdom. This pamphlet is dated 1683. Possibly this opposition explains Chamberlain's hatred of the City commercial men.

[2] Rogers is uncertain whether Hugh Chamberlain, the author of the *Manuale Medicum*, is to be identified with the promoter of these schemes. If he is, the latter was physician in ordinary to Charles II. and a member of the Royal Society. It is certain that Hugh Chamberlain of the Land Bank was summoned to attend the confinement of Queen Mary of Modena in 1688, but was at Gravesend and arrived too late. He wrote a *Narrative of the Birth of the Prince of Wales*.

John Briscoe was another promoter of the new scheme.[1] He was supported by Harley, afterwards Lord Oxford, and by Foley, the Speaker of the House of Commons. Both were political opponents of the Bank of England and very jealous of Montague.

Chamberlain maintained that he could raise a public loan double of that subscribed by the Bank, upon the security of landed property, could make the loan the guarantee for the interest which would be paid on the notes issued, and lend the capital directly to the Government, and subsequently to landowners on mortgage security at 3½ per cent.

The projectors regarded it as axiomatic that everyone who owned real property ought to have in addition paper money equivalent in value to that property. For instance the owner of an estate worth £2,000 ought also to have £2,000 in paper money. Briscoe and Chamberlain alleged that over-issue was impossible so long as corresponding to every £10 note there was a piece of land in the country of equivalent value. No one, they said, will accuse a goldsmith of over-issue so long as there are guineas and crowns in his vaults equal in value to the notes in circulation which bear his signature. Why should not an acre of fertile land have the same virtue as a bag of gold or silver? The promoters did not deny that the public preferred the precious metals, and that in consequence if the Land Bank were forced to pay in gold, it would soon have to suspend its payments. But they proposed to overcome this difficulty by making the notes inconvertible and legal tender.

"The speculations of Chamberlain on the subject of the currency," writes Macaulay,[2] "may possibly find admirers even in our own time. But to his other errors he added an

[1] See two pamphlets by the two promoters. 1.—*A proposal by Dr. Hugh Chamberlayne, in Essex Street, for a Bank of Secure Current Crédit, to be founded upon Land, in order to the general Good of Landed men, to the increase of the value of Land, and the no less benefit of trade and commerce* (1695).

2.—*Proposals for the supplying their Majesties with money on easy terms, exempting the Nobility, Gentry, etc., from taxes, enlarging their yearly estates and enriching all the subjects of the Kingdom by a National Land Bank.* By John Briscoe. With the motto: *O fortunatos nimium bona si sua norint Anglicanos.* 3rd edition, 1696.

[2] *Op. cit.*, p. 481, Vol. II., of edition in two volumes.

error which began and ended with him. He was fool enough to take it for granted, in all his reasonings, that the value of an estate varied directly as the duration. He maintained that, if the annual income derived from a manor were a thousand pounds, a grant of that manor for twenty years must be worth twenty thousand pounds, and a grant for a hundred years worth a hundred thousand pounds. If, therefore, the lord of such a manor would pledge it for a hundred years to the Land Bank, the Land Bank might on that security instantly issue notes for a hundred thousand pounds."

On this point Chamberlain was proof against ridicule, arguments and even arithmetical demonstration. "He was reminded that the fee simple of land would not sell for more than twenty years' purchase. To say, therefore, that a term of a hundred years was worth five times as much as a term of twenty years, was to say that a term of a hundred years was worth five times the fee simple; in other words, that a hundred was five times infinity. Those who reasoned thus were refuted by being told that they were usurers; and it should seem that a large number of country gentlemen thought the refutation complete."[1]

On Monday, February 10th, the Commons met in Committee to find a means of procuring two millions. It was decided that this sum should not be raised by the Bank of England. Mr. Neale then proposed to "raise it upon the Exchequer" (*i.e.*, by Exchequer bills), but, this being also rejected, it was ultimately agreed that a Land Bank should be founded and should provide the capital required by subscription. Moreover anyone concerned in the Bank of England was forbidden to take a part in the management of the new institution.

This law received the royal assent on the 27th of April.

How the King and his Dutch advisers, who were the leaders of financial science in Europe, could have risked the campaign of 1696 on such a scheme, is inexplicable. As to the success of the enterprise in Parliament, this

[1] For a reply to these doctrines see *A Bank Dialogue between Dr. H. C. and a Country Gentleman.*

must be put down to the hatred felt by the landowners for the financiers and the commercial world. This hatred was so keen that they were ready to believe anything that appealed to their passions, and no scheme could have done this better than Dr. Chamberlain's, promising them, as it did, loans at an unhoped-for rate, and the ruin of the Puritan usurers of Grocers' Hall.[1]

As in the case of the Bank itself the measure relating to the Land Bank was included in what is known in England as a *Ways and Means Bill.* The object of the law was to raise a loan of £2,564,000 over and above the ordinary revenue. Harley, Foley and Chamberlain undertook this task. The interest on this loan, *i.e.*, £179,480,[2] was to be secured by a salt tax imposed for the purpose.

Most of the other provisions are also copied from the Tonnage Act.

The King was to appoint a certain number of commissioners to receive subscriptions before August 1st, 1696. It was intended to issue letters-patent recognising the company under the title of the Governor and Company of the National Land Bank, on condition however, that half the loan were subscribed before August 1st, and the remainder by the New Year. In order to avoid speculation, each subscriber, as in the case of the Bank of England, must pay a quarter of his subscription at once.

The bank might not negotiate bills of exchange or issue notes in excess of the sum paid to the Exchequer. It must lend at least £500,000 on land securities at an interest not exceeding 3½ or 4 per cent., according to whether the interest was paid quarterly or half-yearly. The company was authorised to sell lands on which it had received no interest for two years.

These are the chief provisions of this famous scheme, which was not however destined to come into force. Its collapse was absolute.

[1] Evidence of this two-fold appeal will be found in the Doctor's pamphlets and in his three successive advertisements. Analogous reasons had influenced the Commons to declare three years earlier that Chamberlain's project was useful and practicable.

[2] The rate was 7 per cent.

The subscription list was to be opened at Mercers' Hall before May 25th. The preceding weeks were not passed in silence by Dr. Chamberlain. But his advertisements had so little effect that on June 11th the promoters were reduced to expedients, and announced that they were ready to accept "old clipped money that cannot be passed away without loss." On August 1st the Land Bank, in accordance with the Act constituting it, ceased to exist. The total subscription amounted to £2,100, to which must be added £5,000 contributed by the King.

This collapse put the Government into a very awkward position and the landed interest was disappointed in its dearest hopes, but the country was saved from bankruptcy, the real victim of Dr. Chamberlain's scheme being the Bank of England, which was threatened in the first instance by the project itself, and was subsequently obliged to grapple with a most perilous situation.[1]

Position of the Bank of England after the creation of the "Land Bank" and the reform of the currency.—Partial suspension of payments. The Bank suffered, in the first instance, from the project itself, and its stock fell from £107 to £83.[2]

Besides this, the currency reform went on too slowly. The old coins ceased to be current on May 4, but there were no new ones to take their place. Hence on May 6, when the goldsmiths organised a run on the Bank of England, the

[1] A clever defence of the Land Bank was set forth some time after the failure of the company in a little work already mentioned: *Remarks on the proceedings of the commissioners for putting in execution an Act passed last session for establishing a Land Bank* (1696). This posthumous pamphlet was not the last appearance of the Land Bank. Pamphlets commending Dr. Chamberlain's system continued to appear from time to time. The two last were published after the South Sea disaster; they are called, *Proposals for restoring credit, for making the Bank of England more useful and profitable, and for relieving the sufferers of the South Sea Company* (1721).—*An honest scheme for improving the trade and credit of the nation* (1727).

[2] The creation of a rival establishment even to-day causes some disturbance in the prices of the stock of the original institution; in these days these disturbances were much more violent, for the public instantly became alarmed without troubling to consider whether both institutions could not exist side by side without serious mutual damage. Thus, when Montague raised up a political and economic rival to the old East India Company by creating the English East India Company, the stock of the old Tory company fell from £158 to £33. Five years later the shares of the old company stood at £134 and those of the new at £219.

latter had not enough coin to meet the suddenly increased demand. Sir John Houblon, who was at once Lord Mayor, Governor of the Bank, and one of the Lords of the Admiralty, endeavoured to reassure the claimants by offering to pay a tenth of their demands in cash, and by promising on behalf of the Bank, to pay the remainder as soon as the Mint could supply the coins.

"On Wednesday, May 13, the directors held a general court of the proprietors, who agreed to put off their dividend and to offer to such persons as distrusted the notes of the Bank the tallies which they themselves held of the Government as security for their loans. Meanwhile the Lords of the Treasury pledged themselves to pay £60,000 a week in the new money into the Bank till their whole stock was re-coined."[1]

By about June 11 the failure of Chamberlain's scheme had become evident to all, and the Treasury had to apply to the very institution which the Land Bank had expected to ruin. The Bank of England did not open a subscription, it borrowed 20 per cent. of their capital from its subscribers for six months at 6 per cent. only, and paid this into the Treasury, while it applied to the Bank of Amsterdam for an additional sum of £100,000. The total amount advanced to the Government was £340,000.

The issue of the new coins was meanwhile going on fairly rapidly but the Treasury continually put off paying the sums promised to the Bank. The Bank was obliged to limit its cash payments to 3 per cent. of the amounts payable. It was at this point that the Lords of the Treasury at length determined to come to the rescue of public credit by issuing an order on July 13th "that no public notary should enter a protest upon any bill of the Bank of England for fourteen days."[2] This was not without effect, for three days later the discount on bank bills fell from 16 to 8 per cent.[3]

[1] Thorold Rogers, *op. cit.*, p. 63.

[2] Rogers, p. 66. "In those days the protesting of a commercial bill could only be effective when drawn up by one of these functionaries."

[3] Rogers, *loc. cit.* The notes did not rise to par until September 17, 1697, when a dividend was declared to the shareholders, who had received none for two years.

Issue of the first Exchequer Bills.[1] At this same time the Government opened an office at the Exchequer for the issue of Exchequer bills to supply the want of currency. This was done at Montague's desire and as a result of a clause inserted into the Ways and Means Act of the last session. Meanwhile, nearly a million of the new money had been coined.[2] The new Exchequer bills, for £10 each, bearing interest at the rate of 3d. a day and payable on demand, were issued on July 23rd.

The Bank bills were at a discount of 10 per cent. on July 28th, and the King secured the promise of a loan of £500,000 from the Dutch Government, on condition that security was provided. Several persons of high standing in the City, almost all of them Tories, undertook to guarantee the money. On August 15th, the Bank made a further advance to the King of £200,000 at the urgent request of Portland, one of its principal shareholders.

The Bank's grievances and demands.—The second Bank Act.—Renewal and extension of the Charter of the Bank of England. The situation forced upon the Bank of England in 1696 was scandalous. The Government had borrowed its last shilling, had forced it to incur liabilities in Holland, to forgo its dividends, and even, by not keeping its own promises with regard to the delivery of the new coins, to suspend its payments. To crown all it had supported the Land Bank, and then as soon as this absurd scheme had collapsed, it had had recourse once more to the assistance of the Bank. Finally, it wanted to oblige the Bank to increase its capital and to accept depreciated tallies in payment of the new subscription; this proceeding, by largely diminishing the number of tallies, would have helped to raise their value and so to restore the credit of the paper currency which was then in confusion, but, of course, always at the Bank's expense.[3]

[1] Hamilton, *Inquiry Concerning the National Debt,* p. 122.

[2] Altogether £2,975,550 of gold money and £7,014,047 of silver were coined. The amounts coined since Elizabeth's re-coinage had been £14,669,949 in gold and £20,355,651 in silver.

[3] See *The arguments and reasons for and against engrafting upon the Bank of England with Tallies, as they have been debated at a late general*

Under these circumstances the directors, urged by the shareholders, thought it their duty to demand guarantees which would enable them to carry on their business successfully and to strengthen their position. This position had not improved since the collapse of the Land Bank. In 1697 the price of stock was even lower than in the midst of the crisis. The Bank notes too, had met with dangerous rivals in the new Exchequer bills, which were easily negotiated, and were less liable to depreciation than the old tallies, hence the notes did not rise to par until after the announcement of the peace of Ryswick and of a heavy dividend. The grievances and demands of the Bank are set forth in the two pamphlets to which we have just referred in the note. The three principal demands are as follows:

I.—*The concession of a monopoly.* This had become essential for the following reason. The notes, according to the author of *A letter to a friend,* will only circulate if the funds on which they are issued are safe, secured and sufficient. No compulsory expedient can supply the place of public confidence. Hence the Bank must be the only institution of its kind, for competition causes distrust and contracts credit instead of enlarging it. The Bank, to be useful to the State, must be the general repository of cash for all the inhabitants of London. This is the policy which

court of the said Bank. Not dated, but no doubt written at the beginning of 1697. The chief argument brought forward against the proceeding is that it would cause such an increase of capital that the corresponding interest would be out of proportion to the profits. The author, nevertheless, thinks that the scheme would be practicable if additional privileges were conceded to the Bank, amongst others that of a monopoly. These privileges might be granted in return for the great services rendered to commerce by the Bank, in particular the reduction of the rate of discount, which was now 3 per cent. instead of 12 per cent. as in the days of the goldsmiths.

The author of *A letter to a friend concerning the credit of the Nation, and with relation to the Bank of England, Written by a Member of the said Corporation for the public good of the Kingdom* (1697), gives similar arguments against the proceeding, which he considers both unjust and stupid. Stupid because the credit of the Government depends on the good faith with which it carries out its promises; unjust because the shareholders of the Bank have a right to the profits due to their foresight and their efforts, not to mention the reward due to them for all the sacrifices, including even that of their dividends, made to help the Government in its times of difficulty. In addition to all these good reasons, the anonymous author suggests another which must in his opinion have seemed excellent, viz., that he had invested a large part of his fortune in the Bank, and had already suffered considerable loss. This explains the eloquence of his remarks about justice.

has caused the strength and utility of the Banks of Venice, Amsterdam and Hamburg.

II.—*The payment through the Bank of sums due to the Government.* This would be a great advantage to the Bank and would inconvenience no one.

III.—*A certain number of secondary reforms.* Amongst others, a renewal of the Bank's privileges and a more efficient protection against the possible counterfeiting of notes.

Parliament and the Bank were agreed upon the two main points, viz.: 1st—That the privileges of the Bank should be renewed and extended. 2nd—That in return the Bank should make a loan to the Government. It remained to determine the amount of this loan. The House of Commons asked for 2½ millions, guaranteed by a tax on salt.[1] On January 5th the Bank declared that, having regard to the scarcity of coin, it could not agree to such a large loan,[2] but that it was ready to increase its capital under certain conditions which were ultimately accepted by the Commons, and which were sanctioned by the Act of 1697.

Chief provisions of the Act of February 3rd (8 and 9 William III. c. 20).—*The monopoly and its results.*

(1) The Bank was to add £1,001,171 to its original capital.

(2) Anyone might subscribe, and the subscriptions might be paid four-fifths in Exchequer tallies and one-fifth in Bank notes.

(3) All the subscribers were to be incorporated in the company.

In return for these sacrifices, the Act conferred on the Bank a number of privileges with which we are already familiar through the claims made in the two pamphlets referred to.

(1) The time when the Crown might put an end to the corporation by repaying the sums owing to it was pro-

[1] The tax in question was that voted on account of the Land Bank.

[2] The directors must have made this decision in order to please the shareholders, who objected strongly to the policy of making loans to the Government. See *A second part of a Discourse concerning Banks* (undated, but almost certainly 1697).

longed, and was fixed at twelve months after the 1st of August, 1710.

(2) During this period a genuine monopoly was granted to the Bank of England, since no other corporation of the nature of a bank was to be established by Act of Parliament.

(3) An interest of 8 per cent., guaranteed by a tax on salt, was allowed on the tallies accepted in payment by the Bank of England.

(4) Before opening the subscription the original capital was to be estimated and made up to 100 per cent. for each proprietor.

(5) The Bank was authorised to issue notes to the amount of its original capital of £1,200,000, and to the amount of the sums to be subscribed, on condition that they were payable on demand;[1] in case such payment was not made, these notes might be presented at the Exchequer, and would be payable out of the funds constituting the annuity due to the Bank.

(6) All the property of the Bank was exempt from taxation.

(7) Finally it was made a felony, without benefit of clergy, to forge or tamper with Bank notes.

These privileges were important, and the consequences of the Act were no less so. Bank notes to the amount of £200,000 and tallies to the amount of £800,000 were drawn out of circulation, and hence the value of the remainder rose so that by the end of the year the notes were at par and the interest-bearing tallies at a premium.[2] Soon Godfrey's wish was realised, and bank-notes could circulate as nowadays we are accustomed to see them, *i.e.*, without bearing interest.

The Bank was the chief gainer by this Act. The benefits it secured were extensive. Macleod[3] thinks them excessive and attributes a large proportion of the subsequent crises to the monopoly granted to the Bank. There is no doubt that

[1] But the debts of the corporation might not exceed its capital, otherwise the shareholders became personally liable.

[2] From 50 per cent. below par they rose to 112.

[3] p. 479 (5th edition).

this monopoly had a very bad effect on the organisation of provincial credit,[1] but possibly most of the crises which we shall describe below might have been avoided if the advice of a contemporary author[2] had been followed, and the Bank of England had established branches in every commercial town in the kingdom.

Be this as it may, it must be acknowledged that the immediate effects of the Act were highly satisfactory. The Bank notes rose to par, the stock did the same, and a second dividend of 7 per cent. was paid on September 21st, 1698.[3]

At this time the Bank undertook a transaction of a more prolonged character which it was able to bring to a successful conclusion. This was the repayment of the new debt of £1,001,171 subscribed in January, 1697. The first instalment was paid on September 10, 1698, and for the next ten years the Bank paid both a dividend and a bonus. But although the debt was finally paid off in March, 1707, the Bank continued to reckon it as part of its capital.

A fortiori it seems probable that the Bank repaid to its shareholders the loans of £240,000 and £200,000 of June 11 and August 15, 1696, respectively. One writer[4] even alleges that the Bank offered to advance a million to the Government without interest for 21 years, on condition that its charter was prolonged for the same period. This statement may be correct, but it does not seem to be confirmed by other writers, and in any case, the transaction referred to was not carried out.

[1] See below, Part IV., Chap. i., pp. 170-173, dealing with the country banks.

[2] See *Some Thoughts in the Interest of England.*

[3] Later on the profits were greater, and it is said that Sir Gilbert Heathcote, one of the directors of the Bank, made more than £60,000 for himself alone. See Francis, p. 80.

[4] *A letter concerning the Bank and the Credit of the Nation.*

CHAPTER VII.

THE BANK OF ENGLAND AND THE WAR OF SUCCESSION.

(*a*) Economic condition of England in 1700. Problem of the Spanish Succession. Political position of William III. Unpopularity of a War with France. War declared. (*b*) Policy of the Bank during the War. Bank's close alliance with the Protestant Monarchy. Attacked by the enemies of the Government, but secures the continuation and extension of its Charter. Run of 1707. Act of 1709. Criticism of this Act: (1) Bank secures a genuine monopoly. Results of this, (2) Bank undertakes to circulate Exchequer Bills. Is authorised to double its Capital. The Sacheverell affair. Attack on the Bank.

THE year 1699 passed uneventfully. The situation continued to improve and the year 1700 opened under the most favourable auspices. The stock, which had been quoted at £117½ at the beginning of the previous year, rose towards the middle of March to the hitherto unheard-of price of £148. This happy state of things was not confined to the Bank. The prosperity was general; the harvest of 1699 had been very good and that of 1700 promised to be excellent; industry flourished and trade had expanded rapidly, having no longer anything to fear from the French privateers. Proof of this is to be found in the noticeable rise in the prices of the stock of the two East India Companies and in the Customs returns, of which the average for 1700-1701 exceeded that for the period 1700-1714,[1] although the duties were considerably increased during these later years.

The rate of interest too, had fallen enormously. The extent of this fall and the abundance of capital available may be estimated from a project which is attributed by Rogers[2] to the Bank's old enemy, Duncombe. This was nothing less than the formation of a company for the purpose of advancing four millions to the Government at 5 per

[1] The average for those fifteen years was £1,352,764.—Macpherson, Vol. III., p. 45.

[2] Rogers, p. 101, and Davenant, Vol. III., p. 320.

cent., with the ultimate object of paying off the Bank of England and the new East India Company, to which the Government had granted extensive privileges two years earlier in return for a loan at 7 per cent.

This scheme, which was never carried out, was published on October 5. Bank stock fell £12 at once. The fall may also be explained as due to another cause, *i.e.*, to the news of an event which attracted the attention of the whole civilised world, which everyone had long been expecting and fearing, and which when it took place, inevitably destroyed all the good results of the peace of Ryswick and involved Europe in a crisis which she will never forget: I refer to the death of Charles II., King of Spain.

The news of his death when first announced was false, but the actual event was not long delayed.

The King of Spain died on November 1, and shortly afterwards the Duke of Anjou was proclaimed his heir.

If William III. had had absolute power, the doubt whether it was not better to keep quiet and to acquiesce in the fact that the Spaniards had acknowledged the Duke of Anjou, would never even have been hinted at. William hated Louis XIV., and his great political ambition was always to humiliate France. He was naturally eager to join the European coalition. It was however difficult for him as a constitutional monarch to carry out his wishes and enter upon a war, which was likely to prove both long and costly, without the good wishes and the support of his people. But he had neither the one nor the other. The idea of a fresh war was as unpopular as he was himself. He was disliked as a foreigner, and for his cold manners, his accent, and his advisers, who were foreigners like himself. As he had himself foreseen, the great services which he had done for England were forgotten. His high intelligence, his military ability, and indeed all the other talents which made him, with the exception of Cromwell, the greatest man who has ever ruled England, were overlooked, and instead, his stern personality was contrasted with the charm and elegance of Charles II., and regrets were lavished on the peaceful and merry times of the Stuarts. Nine-tenths of the clergy and all the country squires were still Jacobites. Even those who would have been most vigorously opposed to the return of James II. and his family only looked upon William as the lesser of two evils, and so long as there was no immediate danger of a counter-revolution, were quite ready to oppose and thwart their sovereign. And although in case of need they were prepared to support him at the risk of their lives and fortunes, they continued meanwhile to be gloomy and dissatisfied. As Somers pointed out in a remarkable letter to the King: "There is a deadness and want of spirit in the nation universally."

This state of mind is easily explained. William's reign had been one long series of wars and commercial crises, which had so disturbed the country that even after three years of peace, it had not entirely recovered. It had been necessary to raise loans at high rates, and heavy taxes had to be levied to pay the interest on the borrowed money. Besides this, and what was more important, the executive power was extremely weak, notwithstanding William's genius and the high ability of the men whom he had placed in office. At that time the parliamentary customs which now prevail were not yet established in England. The Government did not require the support of a majority in Parliament; and indeed, during William's reign, it hardly ever had this. The Opposition could therefore reject without scruple the financial measures brought forward by the Government, since this rejection did not oblige them to assume the reins of government themselves and devise an alternative policy. Taine[1] most justly remarks in reference to an analogous situation: "Generally in a supreme assembly, when one party is in the ascendant and has a majority, it appoints the ministry, and this is enough to give it or to restore to it some glimmerings of good sense. Its leaders, having the control of the Government, feel themselves responsible for it, and are forced to take account of the effects of such laws as they may either propose or

[1] *Les Origines de la France contemporaine*, Vol. III., p. 205 (Vol. I. of *La Révolution*), Hachette's edition, 1899.

agree to accept. It is rare for a Minister of Finance to advise expenditure which his revenue will not cover, or a system of collection which will hinder the payment of taxes. But," continues the author,[1] "this source of instruction and good sense had been cut off from the outset. On November 6, 1789, influenced by principle and by the fear of corruption, the assembly had declared that none of its members might hold office as a minister. Henceforth it was deprived of all the lessons supplied by the direct management of affairs. Worse still, and what was another result of the same mistake, it was a victim to continual terrors. It had placed in lukewarm or suspected hands the powers it would not take upon itself, and hence it was perpetually uneasy, and all its decrees are not only marked by the voluntary ignorance in which it persisted, but by the exaggerated or illusory fears from which it suffered." Taine concludes:[2] "For want of having the control of the driving-wheel which would have enabled it to guide the engine, it was suspicious of all the machinery, both old and new."

Taine's words are as true of the English Parliament of our period as of the Constituent Assembly. The English Opposition, very suspicious of all new machinery, rejected without consideration all proposals for financial reform, and William's Government found itself without weapons in face of a corrupt Parliament. It is not surprising under the circumstances, that an unpopular king, who had no prerogative allowing him to dispense with his subjects' consent, could not undertake a war against which so many excellent arguments, both political and financial, were brought forward.

To take the financial point of view only: in the first place the expenses of the war would have to be met, and for this recourse must be had to a loan or to taxation, and in particular to taxation, a method of raising money for which the public always feels the strongest distaste; a distaste which was the more natural when we remember the irksome character of the taxes of that time, and that, thanks to the

[1] p. 207. [2] p 210.

corruption of the officials who collected them, only a small part of the money raised ever reached the Exchequer.[1]

The merchants for their part, feared that a new privateer war would ruin their trade, which was beginning to revive since the peace, and were particularly anxious about the trade with India, to which the new company had given a great stimulus, and which had already much difficulty in defending itself against piracy.

Public opinion, also (except in Kent), was opposed to the war, and the House of Lords, in its reply to a warlike King's speech, stated that its members were prepared to "support his Majesty and his Government, and take such effectual measures as may best conduce to the interest and safety of England, the preservation of the Protestant religion, and *the peace of Europe.*" The House of Commons, by its behaviour with regard to various matters, such as the impeachment of the four lords and the petition of Kent, showed an even greater dislike for the war and a very characteristic suspicion of the King.

England's neutrality thus seemed to be certain, when an act, either of thoughtless sentimentalism or of malicious provocation, changed the whole situation, strengthened William on his throne and caused the outbreak of one of the longest and most expensive of modern wars. James II. died at Saint-Germain on September 16, and Louis XIV., affected as some think by the dignity of his death and by the grief of the excited queen, or believing, as others allege, that William's throne was so unstable that this prince might be insulted with impunity, acknowledged James II.'s son as King of England.

The indignation of the English people at this news, the break in diplomatic relations with France, the dissolution of Parliament, the crushing defeat of the Tories in the elections which followed, the beginning of the War of Succession, the European coalition and the speedy abandonment of Louis XIV. by his last allies, belong to the province of

[1] In Scotland, especially, throughout almost the whole of the 18th century the cost of collecting the customs exceeded the amount collected.

[2] Feb. 15, 1701.

general history. We must content ourselves with examining the influence of this war on the Bank, the part played by this institution, and the way in which its fortunes became permanently bound up with those of England.

Policy of the Bank during the war.—Run of 1707.—The Bank's Charter renewed and extended.—The Sacheverell affair. The policy followed by the Bank at this period was marked by the same characteristics as its policy during the preceding war.

The Bank supported the quarrels of the Protestant dynasty, and it supplied the Government with the means of carrying on the war;[1] on this account it had to suffer from the calumnies and the attacks of the enemies of the Government; but, on the other hand, it secured the renewal and the extension of its privileges.

In substance the changes made were merely in name. William III. died at the beginning of the struggle, but his sister-in-law made no alteration in his policy, and even did more than he for the Bank since she avoided encouraging such rivals as the Land Bank. The Bank for its part, supported to the best of its ability the Protestant succession with which its own interests were henceforth bound up.[2] Addison has described the position excellently in an allegory in which he relates how: In Grocers' Hall he saw Public Credit "on a throne of gold. At the upper end of the hall was the Magna Charta. At the lower end of the hall was the Act of Settlement, which was placed full in the eye of the

[1] This war was very expensive. See the list given by Dowell (2nd edition, 1888, Vol. II., Appendices V. and VI.) of the cost of each of the wars carried on by England between 1688 and 1815, and the amount of the national debt which accrued in each case.

	Cost of each war.	*Debt accrued.*
1688-1697	£32,643,764	£14,522,925
1702-1713	£50,684,956	£21,483,098
1739-1748	£43,655,192	£29,173,771
1756-1763	£82,623,738	£59,633,000
1776-1785	£97,599,496	£117,285,000
1793-1815	£831,446,449	£504,889,452

[2] The importance of the Bank may be judged from the following fact reported by Burnet (Vol. VI., p. 8). Some years after the outbreak of hostilities, the Queen obliged Sunderland to resign and gave the seals to Lord Dartmouth. This caused alarm both at home and abroad which was only allayed when the Queen declared to some of her subjects, and notably to the "governors of the Bank of England," that she would make no other changes.

virgin that sat upon the throne. . . . The floor on her right hand, and on her left, was covered with vast sums of gold, that rose up in pyramids on either side of her. But this I did not so much wonder at when I heard . . . that she could convert whatever she pleased into that precious metal." All at once the door opened, and the Pretender hastened in, carrying in one hand a sponge and in the other a sword, which "he often brandished at the Act of Settlement." Credit, "the beautiful virgin, fainted and died away at the sight." The charm by which she changed all about her into gold was broken. The money bags burst like bladders pricked with a pin. "The great heaps of gold . . . now appeared to be only heaps of paper or little piles of notched sticks." This allegory is to be found in the third number of the *Spectator,* in the same essay in which Addison describes the simple way in which the work of the Bank was carried on.[1]

Crisis of 1707.—*Run on the Bank.* On several occasions, after the first outbreak of war the Bank found itself involved in difficulties, but it was not until 1707 that it ran any serious risk. At this date the agitation of the Jacobite party, stimulated by the announcement of a French invasion, spread panic through the country. The price of the public stocks fell 14 or 15 per cent.[2] The enemies of the reigning dynasty combined with those of the Bank to organise a run upon the latter.[3] The private bankers tried to ruin their great rival and Sir Francis Child refused to accept Bank notes; he explained afterwards that he was only applying the law of retaliation to the Bank.

This panic served to show that although the Bank had enemies, it had not lost its powerful and devoted friends.

[1] See above, p. 75.

[2] See a pamphlet entitled, *The anatomy of Exchange Alley.* Many details are here given about this affair and the part played by two leading goldsmiths —"Knights also and one of them Member of Parliament, too,"—Sir R. Hoare and Sir Francis Child.

[3] The Bank had already suffered from a run organised by Duncombe and some of his colleagues after the elections of January 23, 1701. On this point all the details that can be desired will be found in a pamphlet written directly afterwards, and which is well worth reading notwithstanding its eccentric title: *The villainy of Stock-jobbers detected and the causes of the late run upon the Bank of England discovered and considered.*

Help came from all sides. The Dukes of Marlborough, Newcastle and Somerset, as well as other nobles and a number of merchants, offered to advance considerable sums One individual, whose whole fortune amounted to £500, brought this sum to the Bank. The Queen, when she heard of this, sent him £100, with a bill on the Treasury for the repayment of the £500. The Lord Treasurer, Godolphin, who recognised that the credit of the country was bound up with that of the Bank, told the directors "that the Queen would allow, for six months, an interest of 6 per cent. on their sealed bills."[1] Finally, the Bank itself made a call of 20 per cent. on its shareholders, and the danger was overcome by the combination of all these efforts.

Act of 1709.—The Bank's Charter renewed and extended. In 1708 the Government was once more involved in financial difficulties. The receipts from the taxes hardly covered half the expenditure. In this dilemma the Ministry applied to the Bank of England for help, offering it in return a continuation of its privileges. This proposal roused violent opposition; the old enemies of the Bank were unconquered, and they proceeded to set forth their opinions in numerous pamphlets. The author of one of these[2] was not content to propose the abolition of the Bank, which he regarded as beyond all doubt a harmful institution, but, in addition, he suggested a remedy for the financial necessities of the moment. This remedy, cleverly set forth, was that adequate revenues should be collected by improving the Excise, and in particular by authorising the officials to taste the liquors and to tax them according to quality instead of quantity. But this writer and his companions could not

[1] Francis, Vol. I., p. 87. Such a thing has never happened again.

[2] *Arguments against prolonging the Bank, with proposals for advancing the Revenue of the excise and making more useful to the Nation than ever the Bank can be, without any danger to the Publick. In a letter to a Member of Parliament* (1708). For other protests against the continuance of the Bank see also, *Remarks on the Bank of England with regard more especially to our trade,* By a Merchant of London and a true lover of our Constitution. *A short view of the apparent dangers and mischief from the Bank of England. More particularly addressed to the Country Gentlemen. Reasons against the continuance of the Bank of England.* I give the titles of those pamphlets without an analysis, which would tell us nothing new, for they merely reproduce the arguments already brought forward against the Bank at the time of its foundation.

hinder the Government from making the following agreement with the Bank:

1.—It was agreed that the interest upon the original capital of £1,200,000 should be reduced from 8 to 6 per cent., with an allowance of £4,000 a year for expenses of management.

2.—It was also agreed that the Bank should advance a fresh loan of £400,000 at 6 per cent.

3.—Since the Government wished to circulate Exchequer bills on the security of the house duties, the Bank undertook to put them into circulation and to pay £1,775,027 for these at once. The Bank was to receive 6 per cent. of this sum, 3 per cent. as interest, and 3 per cent. as repayment of the capital.

In return for these concessions the Bank secured:

1.—The continuation of its privileges for 21 years from August 1, 1711.

2.—Permission to double its existing capital of £2,201,171, the new shares of £100 being issued at £115.

Anderson states[1] that in spite of these somewhat severe conditions, the subscription list, which was opened on February 22, 1709, was entirely filled between nine o'clock and mid-day: "Near one million more," he says, "would have been on the same day subscribed, had there been room for it, so great was the crowd of people coming with their money to the books." After these transactions the total capital of the Bank amounted to £6,577,370, viz.:

Capital of the Bank - - - - - -	£2,201,171 10s.
This Capital doubled - - - - - -	4,402,343
And increased by the £400,000 now advanced -	4,802,343
To which must be added for the Exchequer Bills	1,775,027
Total -	£6,577,370

Finally, and this was the most important of all, the Bank's monopoly was strengthened.

[1] Vol. III., p. 33.

The Act of 1697 had decreed that no other bank should be allowed by Act of Parliament; but it did not forbid the formation of other joint-stock companies, nor of any company which undertook banking business. One company, called the Company of Mine Adventurers of England, had constituted itself into a bank of issue and circulated notes, a power allowed it under the Act of 1697.[1] To put a stop to this it was now enacted: "That during the continuance of the said corporation of the Governor and Company of the Bank of England, it shall not be lawful for any body politic or corporate whatsoever, erected or to be erected, . . . or for any other persons whatsoever, united or to be united in covenants or partnerships, exceeding the number of six persons, in that part of Great Britain called England, to borrow, owe, or take up any sum or sums of money on their bills or notes payable at demand, or at any less time than six months from the borrowing thereof."

At this time the power to issue notes was looked upon as so essential a part of the business of banking that its prohibition was considered to prevent the formation of any bank whose shares were held by more than six persons, and thus to prevent any private company from exercising an influence dangerous to the Bank. This seemed so evident at the time that the clause did prevent the formation of any joint-stock bank. It was not until much later that it was realised that the consequences of the prohibition need not be nearly so stringent.[2]

The Bank's monopoly of issue was only limited by the formal order not to issue notes to an amount exceeding its capital.

These provisions with regard to note-issue have been

[1] Sir Humphrey Mackworth was at the head of this company, and he showed an ability worthy of a better cause. He deceived the shareholders for five years by the payment of fictitious dividends and other frauds; he bought the products of other mines, and caused them to be coined at the Mint as produced by the silver mines of the company, etc. But, in spite of all this, he could not succeed for long. Everything came out, and the Company of the Mine Adventurers was pronounced a bubble by the House of Commons, and Sir Humphrey Mackworth was declared guilty of scandalous frauds.

[2] See below, Part IV., Chap. i., p. 171.

severely criticised by Macleod.[1] In the opinion of this eminent economist, they amounted to this: that every loan made to the Government was attended by an equivalent increase in the paper currency. "Now, to a certain extent, this plan might be attended with no evil consequences, but it is perfectly clear that its *principle* is utterly vicious. There is nothing so wild or absurd in John Law's *Theory of Money* as this. His scheme of basing a paper currency upon land is sober sense compared to it. If for every debt the Governments incurs an equal amount of money is to be created, why, here we have the philosopher's stone at once. What is the long-sought Eldorado compared to this? Even there the gold required to be picked up and fashioned into coin. . . . But let us coolly consider the principle involved in this plan of issuing notes upon the security of the public debts. Stated in simple language, it is this: *That the way to* CREATE *money is for the Government to* BORROW *money.* That is to say, A lends B money on mortgage, and, *on the security of the mortgage, A is allowed to create an equal amount of money to what he has already lent!!* Granting that to a small extent this may be done without any practical mischief, yet, as a general principle, what can be more palpably absurd? The ravings of Chamberlain himself are not more wild."

In 1713, the last year of the war, the Bank made another loan to the Government, and secured the continuation of its charter until 1743.

In the following year Queen Anne died. The fear of civil war roused by the question of the succession caused some anxiety in the City, but all was soon as quiet as usual. The Hanoverian dynasty now established on the English throne, could hardly be ill-disposed towards the Bank, and in 1716 a new agreement was made with the Bank in respect to the Government debt. The Act of 1716 was passed in return for the redemption of the previous debts and for further advances at 5 per cent. This Act also exempted the Bank from the usury laws,[2] which were becoming a heavy burden on the commercial world.

[1] pp. 416 and 417 (5th edition, pp. 487, 488).

[2] Macleod, Vol. I., p. 488 (5th edition).

The Sacheverell Affair.[1] The history of this period would be incomplete without a reference to the dangers incurred by the Bank of England in 1709 owing to a sermon preached at St. Paul's by Dr. Sacheverell.

"A sermon at St. Paul's," says Mr. Morley,[2] "was like a modern demonstration in Hyde Park. . . . Dr. Price's discourse at the dissenting meeting-house in the Old Jewry on 4th November, 1789, laid the train for Burke's *Reflections on the French Revolution*. It was Dr. Sacheverell's sermon on November 5th, 1709, that provoked the most violent Tory explosion of the century."

This sermon was violent in tone and apparently directed against the dissenters; in particular, it declared the principle of passive obedience and non-resistance to Government, with allusions to the opposite views which had inspired the revolution of 1688. The Lord Mayor who was present and who was a Tory M.P., asked the preacher to dinner, thanked him for his sermon, urged him to publish it and allowed it to be dedicated to him.

This publication made a scandal. The sermon referred to the First Lord of the Treasury as Volpone. The author was arrested on account of the liberties he had taken with the Government. The populace supported his cause which was that of the Church of England, and the preacher was escorted to Westminster, where his trial was honoured by the presence of the Queen,[3] by a guard of butcher boys. The crowd pressed round the doctor, struggling to kiss his hand, and money was thrown to it by the gentry,

[1] References to this affair are numerous. The best authorities to consult are Morley, *Walpole*, pp. 13-17; Smollett, Vol. VIII., pp. 72-79; Stanhope, *History of Queen Anne's Reign*, Chap. xii., p. 4. See also as curiosities, White Kenett, *Wisdom of looking Backward with an account of Dr. Sacheverell's proceeding*, and the opinion of the famous Duchess of Marlborough in *Account of my Conduct*, p. 247.

[2] p. 14.

[3] People cried out as the Queen proceeded to Westminster—"God bless your Majesty and the Church, we hope your Majesty is for Dr. Sacheverell." —Morley, p. 16.

The English Church regarded the accused as a hero and a martyr, prayers were said in all the churches for his acquittal, his behaviour was praised in sermons and the royal chaplain himself expressed his admiration and apprqval.

who followed the procession in hackney coaches. The people could not rest contented with these peaceful demonstrations, they plundered the dissenting chapels and burnt the books and other spoils collected from them, in Lincoln's Inn Fields. They even pillaged accidentally one of the orthodox churches whose appearance was not sufficiently distinctive. The riot very soon acquired a purely political character and the Bank, always an object of attack, was warned that it was to be assaulted. The assembled directors appealed to the Secretary of State for a guard to defend their establishment. No troops were available, but the Queen sent her own foot and horse guards, preferring to be left unprotected rather than risk the capture of the Bank. "Am I to preach or fight?" Captain Horsey inquired, when he received the royal commands. There was no need to do either, the mere appearance of the troops sufficed to put the rioters to flight.

The Bank was thus saved from plunder by the Queen's devotion. As to the Sacheverell affair—it ended as follows: Sacheverell, notwithstanding the excellent defence which he read before the House of Lords and which was probably the work of Atterbury, was condemned by 69 votes to 52.[1] But the light penalty imposed[2] caused the sentence to be looked upon as a victory for him and his supporters. Shortly afterwards Godolphin resigned and the Tories were conspicuously victorious in the elections which followed.

To gain a better understanding of these continual riots and scandals and of the state of England during the period, the third chapter of Taine's *Histoire de la Littérature Anglaise,* Vol. III., should be read.

"There was nothing to be seen," writes the great critic, "but corruption in high places and brutality among the common people—a group of intriguers leading a populace of brutes. The human animal, drunk with political passions, expressed itself in cries and violence, and swaying to

[1] Out of the 13 bishops who voted, only 7 were against him.

[2] He was forbidden to preach for three years and his sermon was ordered to be burnt.

and fro under the hand of each party by turn, seemed ready to destroy society by its blind outbursts.

"Every political event was the signal for riot, for disorder, for blows and broken heads. When Dr. Sacheverell was tried, butcher boys, chimney sweeps, fruit sellers, prostitutes and the dregs of the population, believing the Church to be in danger, accompanied him with howls of rage and enthusiasm and in the evening devoted themselves to the burning and pillaging of dissenting chapels."

Taine goes on to describe the burning of Admiral Byng's effigy, the stoning of Lord Bute, Pitt's unpopular successor, who was obliged to surround his carriage with a guard of boxers, the judges not daring to condemn drunkards, the House of Commons afraid to pass Walpole's Excise Bill, and the Gordon Riots. He might easily have lengthened the list, for Royalty was no more respected than the Ministers, and the Duke of Bedford's house underwent actual sieges and assaults.

The gulf between this state of things and the England of the 19th century is immense. Indeed I know of nothing which is more to England's credit than the transformation this produced in less than a hundred years. It shows how much can be accomplished by the persevering work and devotion of all ranks of citizens for the public welfare. It shows also, what could be done by the active and intelligent interference of the middle classes, who, not submitting to be set on one side or submerged, were able to take the lead in public affairs and to revolutionise the country. They afford an excellent example of that patriotism which refuses to be put off with mere words. English history is accordingly a splendid study for nations which, like the English nation of the 17th and 18th centuries, are numerically small, unorganised, and the victims of demagogues. It proves that these evils are not such as need be suffered involuntarily, and offers encouragement, combined with a good example.

[1] Vol. III., p. 5, of the edition of 1863.

PART III.

THE BANK OF ENGLAND UNDER THE HANOVERIAN DYNASTY.

CHAPTER I.

THE BANK OF ENGLAND AND THE SOUTH SEA COMPANY.

The South Sea Company. Offers to take over all the Public Debts. Proposals of the Bank in this matter. Government accepts the proposals of the South Sea Company. Speculative mania. Multiplication of schemes of every kind. The South Sea Company's lawsuit against the new Companies. Results of this lawsuit; Ruin of the South Sea Company. Trial of the Company's Directors. End of the crisis. Part played and risks run by the Bank during the crisis.

WHILST France was in the throes of the financial crisis which marked the period of the Regency, England was passing through a similar crisis. Although she had not her man of genius like Law, she had her *Compagnie des Indes Occidentales* in the South Sea Company. The results of this crisis were less severe in England than in France, but the crisis itself was no less alarming. For more than a year the history of England is bound up with that of the South Sea Company.

The South Sea Company was formed in 1711 by Lord Oxford with the object of strengthening public credit which had been severely shaken by the fall of the Whigs. Like all such contemporary institutions it originated in a State loan. The company undertook to provide the money due to the army and navy, as well as for other parts of the unfunded debt. This was to be done in return for a 6 per cent. interest on the security of various duties and the monopoly of trading in the South Seas (*i.e.*, the Pacific Ocean), from which the company took its name.

It carried on its trading business quietly until 1720 at which date it won its melancholy notoriety.

The year 1720 was, according to Anderson,[1] "a year remarkable beyond any other which can be pitched upon by historians for extraordinary and romantic projects." The public rage for speculation approached insanity. But the rulers too were partly responsible for the misfortunes which followed. The crisis originated, if Smollett is to be believed, from the King's recommendation to the Commons to consider the "proper means for lessening the national debt."

The South Sea project was then brought forward by Sir John Blount, who had the coolness and audacity required for such an enterprise. He submitted his scheme to Aislabie, the Chancellor of the Exchequer, and to one of the Secretaries of State, both of whom were already prejudiced in its favour for self-interested reasons. Hence he was able to meet their objections without much difficulty.

The scheme was adopted by the Government; its primary object was to lighten the burden of the national debt by reducing all the public debts into one.

On January 22, 1720, the House of Commons met in committee to consider the project. The South Sea Company offered to take over all the debts of the State, which were estimated at £30,981,712, in return for an interest of 5 per cent. until 1727, and of 4 per cent. after that date. In exchange for this it was to pay 3½ millions. These proposals were brought forward unexpectedly by the Government, who hoped thus to secure a favourable vote. The House however received them somewhat coldly, and the friends of the Bank of England, by pointing out the great services rendered by this institution to the State, and the harm which the passing of this scheme would do to it, secured a delay of five days.[3]

The Bank took advantage of this interval, and before it

[1] *An Historical and Chronological Deduction of the Origin of Commerce*, Vol. III., p. 91. This work, dating from 113 years ago, gives most valuable information about the whole of this affair. See also Macpherson, *Annals of Commerce* (1805) Vol. III., p. 76. Up to 1764 this work is however merely a revised edition of Anderson's.

[2] *History of Scotland*, Vol. VIII., p. 238.

[3] Brodrick was the chief supporter of the Bank during a very stormy debate.

was over offered to undertake the same responsibilities as the South Sea Company and to pay five millions in return with less delay[1] than the rival company had required to raise the smaller amount tendered by it.

The proposals of the Bank were no sooner announced than the directors of the South Sea Company called a general meeting of their shareholders and received instructions to secure the preference at all costs. They accordingly offered to increase the sum granted to the Government from 3½ to 7½ millions. The Bank however threw all its strength into the desperate struggle, and began in its turn to make the most insane proposals. It offered to give £1,700 Bank stock for every annuity of £100 for 96 or 99 years. "Let any-one," writes Anderson, "consider how this was possible." Luckily for the Bank these proposals were rejected. At one time there was some idea of dividing the undertaking between the two establishments. But Sir John Blount is said to have refused to agree to this Solomon's proposal, exclaiming "No, sir! we will never divide the child."

The proposals of the South Sea Company were only accepted after prolonged and violent debates in Parliament. In the House of Commons, where, after a discussion lasting two days, the scheme was passed by 172 votes to 55, Robert Walpole was the principal speaker for the Opposition. In the House of Lords, where the debate was very short and where there was no division, the most notable speech was that of Lord North and Grey. Earl Cowper also spoke against the Bill, saying that, "like the Trojan horse, it was ushered in and received with great pomp and acclamations of joy; but was contrived for treachery and destruction."[2]

The royal assent was given on the 7th of April. On June 11th when he dissolved Parliament, the King con-

[1] These proposals are to be found in two or three contemporary pamphlets, such as *The schemes of the South Sea Company and the Bank of England as proposed in Parliament for the reducing of the National Debt;* and *A comparison between the proposals of the Bank and the S.S. Company. Wherein is shown that the proposals of the first are much more advantageous than that of the latter.*

[2] See *Parliamentary History,* Vol. VII., pp. 644-646, for the debates in the House of Commons, and pp. 646-648 for those in the House of Lords. The principal supporters of the scheme were Aislabie and Lord Sutherland.

gratulated the two Houses on having set the liquidation of the national debt on a firm basis without violation of the public faith.

The mere report that the South Sea Company intended to take over the consolidated debt made its shares rise in 1719 to £126. When the law was passed they were at £310. After the success of the first subscriptions, due to more or less correct rumours, the shares rose to £500,[1] then (June 2, 1720), to £890;[2] they did not even stop there for a wave of veritable madness had turned everyone's heads. At the end of June their price had reached £2,000.[3]

Recourse was had to devices and promises of all kinds in order to maintain this artificial level; promises were made of profits of 50 per cent., and of the acquisition of distant and invaluable markets; it was whispered that mines and hidden treasures had been discovered. All these devices had been employed before, and we have already had to describe them at sufficient length; but this was no reason why they should not be successfully used once again.

The great majority of the public was caught in the snare. The same thing happened in Change Alley in London as had happened in the Rue Quincampoix in Paris; nobles and citizens, merchants and country squires, judges and bishops, women belonging to all classes of society, [4]crowded

[1] May 23.

[2] One of the reports which contributed most to this rise was that a treaty of peace had just been signed between Spain and England, as a consequence of which Port Mahon and Gibraltar were to be exchanged for part of Peru. This exchange was exceedingly profitable to the company; it strengthened its position in the Pacific and secured to it the trade of a country of legendary wealth (Smollett, p. 244).

[3] In the interval the company had opened a third subscription list at £1,000 per share; four millions were subscribed. Some of the directors also were made baronets for their great services.

[4] See Pope's description in his *Epistle to Allen, Lord Bathurst.*

"At length corruption, like a general flood
Did deluge all, and avarice creeping on
Spread like a low-born mist and hid the sun.
Statesmen and patriots plied alike the stocks,
Peeress and butler shared alike the box,
And judges jobbed and bishops bit the town,
And mighty dukes packed cards for half-a-crown—
Britain was sunk in lucre's sordid charms."

See also Swift's poem: *The South Sea Project,* in *Complete Works* (edition 1824), Vol. XIV., pp. 146-155, and the satirical poem, *South Sea Ballad, or*

together there. The King himself did not escape the infection[1] and his mistress is accused of making considerable profits from the affair, which gains she hastened to send to Hanover.

Fashion even was affected. South Sea carriages, coats, and neckties made their appearance; the ladies wore no jewellery except that bearing this name, and there were South Sea servants.

The artificial rise in the shares produced an artificial increase of wealth, and an unprecedented luxury appeared in the country. Speculators and adventurers, says a contemporary author, drunk with their imaginary riches, bought the rarest food and the finest wines that could be imported; with neither taste nor judgment they purchased the most gorgeous furniture and carriages; they gave way freely to the most shameful excesses and their speech was characterised by pride, insolence and a ridiculous ostentation.[2]

The result of all this was an immense rise in general prices. If the level of prices reached in France was not attained and if no one gave £200 for a chicken,[3] this was only because the Bank was not involved in the South Sea Company, so that there were no over-issues; nevertheless the prices were such that people with moderate incomes were forced either to speculate or to live in poverty.

The clerks of the company were among the few people who made genuine profits. Since the passing of a single

Merry Remarks upon Exchange Alley Bubbles. We give these numerous literary references not to display a vain erudition, but because in actual fact it is from such sources as these that the best descriptions are obtained, in default of a history of the crisis. Finally, see Smollett, p. 244, and compare Thiers *Histoire de Law*, p. 93. The two crises are so much alike that a description of the one might easily be read as applying to the other.

[1] It is certain that the King vigorously supported the project, if he did not actually make money by it. The Duchess of Ormond wrote to Swift: "You remember, and so do I, when the South Sea was said to be my Lord Oxford's brat, and must be starved at nurse. Now the King has adopted it and calls it his beloved child: though perhaps you may say, if he loves it no better than his son, it may not be saying much; but he loves it as well as he does the Duchess of Kendal, and that is saying a good deal. I wish it may thrive, for some of my friends are deep in it; I wish you were so too."
This letter will be found in Swift's works, Vol. XVI., p. 335.

[2] Compare Thiers, *op. cit.*, p. 103.

[3] Thiers, p. 107.

day might mean a difference of £100, people often gave them a £20 note to hasten the transaction. The profits which they made in this way were so great that they used to wear clothes trimmed with lace, and replied to those who criticised them that "if they did not put gold upon their clothes, they would not make away with half their earnings."

It would have been fortunate if the evil had ended here. But the success of the South Sea Scheme gave rise to all kinds of other projects. Some of these were serious and deserved to succeed,[1] but the absurdity of the others was such that according to Francis, their popularity "stamped the minds of those who entertained them with what may be truly termed a commercial lunacy."[2] A few examples will illustrate this.[3] One project was for the "discovery of perpetual motion," another to found a company "for importing a number of large jack-asses from Spain," a third "for building of hospitals for bastard children," a fourth "for extracting silver from lead," and, finally, the most remarkable of all was a project to found a company "for carrying on an undertaking of great advantage, which shall in due time be revealed." Each subscriber was to deposit two guineas, in return for which he would subsequently receive a 100-guinea share, and would at the same time hear the nature of the scheme! It is difficult to believe that in five hours the ingenious promoter had collected 1,000 subscriptions, *i.e.*, £2,000, with which he decamped in the course of the evening.

Any subscription was accepted for projects of this kind, even a shilling for £5, *i.e.*, 1 per cent.[4] And since no one ever asked for the remainder of the subscription, the poor man with his few pence could build the same castles in the air as the rich man with his millions of pounds.

[1] Among the schemes which succeeded were the Royal Exchange and the London Assurance Company, which still exist.

[2] Francis, p. 127.

[3] Still more extravagant projects are given by Mahon, pp. 16 and 17, and by Anderson, p. 108.

[4] There were even some promoters who asked only a shilling for £100.

Another fraud of the period[1] was that of the "Globe permits," small squares of playing cards, on which were printed pictures of the Globe tavern with the words, "Sail cloth permits." These cards were merely permits to subscribe to a future Sail cloth company, and were sold currently for 60 guineas apiece. The crush and confusion were so great that the same shares were sometimes sold simultaneously for £10 more at one place in Change Alley than at another.[2]

The new companies enjoyed the patronage of the highest nobility. The Prince of Wales, afterwards George II., consented to be governor of the Welsh Copper Company. According to Lord Mahon,[3] the Speaker and Walpole tried in vain to dissuade him; it was not until the company was threatened with an action that His Royal Highness had the prudence to retire with a profit of £40,000.

The Duke of Bridgewater founded a company to build houses in London and Westminster and the Duke of Chandos was the head of the York Buildings Company. Practically all the other nobles followed these examples. The Dukes of Argyll and of Roxburgh and Lord Stanhope were apparently the only persons among the nobility and ministers who escaped the infection.

This state of things afforded excellent opportunities for satire. Announcement was made of a company for "making butter from beech-trees," and of various analogous projects. But the most brilliant satires and the most biting

[1] Mackay, *Popular Delusions*, p. 54. This work also contains an essay on Law, and one on the "Tulipomania" in Holland.

[2] The way in which business was carried on may be gathered from the account of a contemporary. The *London Journal* for June 11, says: "The hurry of our stock-jobbing bubblers has been so great this week, that it has exceeded all that was ever known. There has been nothing but running about from one coffee-house to another, and from one tavern to another, to subscribe without examining what the proposals were. The general cry has been, 'For G—'s sake let us but subscribe to something, we don't care what it is!' So that, in short, many have taken them at their words, and entered them adventurers in some of the grossest cheats and improbable undertakings that ever the world heard of; and yet by all these the projectors have got money, and have had their subscription full as soon as desired."

[3] See p. 15, and Morley, *Walpole*, p. 64.

epigrams are to be found in the contemporary verse.[1] "The print shops teemed with caricatures," says Mackay, "and the newspapers with epigrams and satires upon the prevalent folly. An ingenious card-maker published a pack of South Sea playing cards, . . . each card containing, besides the usual figures, . . . a caricature of a bubble company, with appropriate verses beneath. One of the most famous bubbles was 'Puckles' Machine Company' for discharging round and square cannon-balls and bullets, and making a total revolution in the art of war. Its pretensions to public favour were thus summed up in the eight of spades:

"A rare invention to destroy the crowd
Of fools at home, instead of fools abroad.
Fear not my friends, this terrible machine,
They're only wounded who have shares within."

Each company of the same kind was ridiculed in turn. Mackay[2] gives most of the verses, and a reproduction of the very curious cards.

Unfortunately, so long as the speculator was putting money into his pocket, he paid no heed to the satires, and laughed at those who ridiculed him. It was estimated that the total amount subscribed to the different projects exceeded £300,000,000,[3] and the price of their shares[4] rose continually. Things reached such a pitch that sensible men could no longer hide from themselves the dangers of the situation. Walpole, the Jeremiah of this period of insanity,[5] was continually prophesying the most terrible

[1] Amongst the best known the following may be quoted:—

"A wise man laughed to see an ass
Eat thistles and neglect good grass,
But had the sage beheld the folly
Of late transacted in Change Alley,
He might have seen worse asses there
Give solid gold for empty air."

[2] pp. 60-62.

[3] Tindal, *History of England from the Revolution to George II.*, Vol. VII., p. 357, and Smollett, p. 245. Anderson gives (pp. 104-107) the amounts actually subscribed for each project.

[4] For the prices of shares during this period see Anderson, pp. 103-104, Bank of England stock itself was quoted at £260.

[5] Walpole's gloomy prophecies did not prevent him, with characteristic elasticity of conscience, from making £40,000 by speculation in South Sea

misfortunes. The King, roused to anxiety, issued a proclamation on June 11, against "Such mischievous and dangerous undertakings, especially the presuming to act as a corporate body, or raising stocks or shares without legal authority." But this proclamation had no more effect than the satires and epigrams, and it remained for the South Sea Company itself, jealous of its rivals, to put an end to the folly and to bring about its own ruin.

Alarmed by the success of all these projects, the South Sea Company obtained a writ from the Lord Justices rejecting all petitions and dissolving all the bubble companies.[1] This writ, issued on July 12, was followed by a list of those companies which were considered to be of this kind. There were no fewer than 86 and this list is still amusing to read, both for the number and the absurdity of the inventions.[2]

The company was apparently triumphant but the bursting of the bubbles caused general uneasiness; everyone wished to realise his gains. People quickly found out the difference between the prices in Change Alley and the real value of the shares of the different companies, and the South Sea Company found itself involved in the ruin it had caused.

When the legal proceedings began the company's stock stood at £850. It kept up to £700 until September 2, but on the 13th it was only £400 and on the 29th, after a continuous fall, it was selling at £175. The anxious directors promised a dividend of 30 per cent., and guaranteed one of 50 per cent. for the following years, but their promises had no influence on the now incredulous public which was very soon in a state of absolute panic. Everything collapsed, thousands of families were reduced to beggary, many people were unable to survive the disaster and the fortunes

Stock; he managed to choose a good moment for selling out, see Coxe, *Memoirs*, Vol. I., p. 730. Mr. Morley remarks (p. 134), "His firm and wise conviction of the folly of the South Sea schemes did not prevent him from turning his wisdom to account by dealing in South Sea stock."

[1] These companies collapsed after June 20, 1720, in consequence of the Bubble Act.

[2] This list is given by Anderson, pp. 104-112. But the author only mentions 80 companies.

secured by a handful of individuals only served to aggravate the prevailing ruin.

The directors of the company vainly sought to delay the catastrophe by the help of credit. Several goldsmiths and private bankers who had advanced money on the shares were obliged to stop payment owing to the depreciation of these, and the Sword Blade Association which had been the company's chief cashiers, now shared its disgrace.

In vain they even applied to the Bank itself. Urged by Walpole the directors had indeed undertaken to circulate £3,500,000 of the company's bonds at £400, but this agreement, which was made on September 13, was no longer tenable, and the directors took advantage of the fact that the contract drawings had not been legally ratified, and refused to execute it.[1] Indeed, had they been forced to carry it out, they would only have shared the South Sea Company's ruin. The Bank had difficulty enough to maintain its own credit and it was only able to meet the run made upon it by devices which Macleod[2] thus describes: "It employed a number of clerks to tell out the money which was demanded, as well as what was brought in. Payments were made in light sixpences and shillings, and large sums were paid to particular friends, who went out with their bags of money at one door, to deliver them to people placed at another, who were let in to pay the same money to tellers, who took time to count it over. These persons were, of course, always served first. By this means time was gained, the friends of the Bank rallied round it, and made large subscriptions to support the company. The festival of Michaelmas, at which it was usual at that time to shut up the Bank, came, and, when it was opened again, the public alarm had passed off."

The directors of the South Sea Company thought at one time of taking legal measures to force the Bank to execute its contract, but they soon remembered that the lawsuit

[1] For the part played by Walpole on this occasion, see "*The case of the Bank Contract*," 1735, a reply to the attacks printed by Aislabie in the *Craftsman*.

[2] 3rd Edition, p. 428.

must throw light on their own proceedings and would do them more harm than good. Besides, they had triumphed so insolently in their days of prosperity, and had so oppressed well-meaning people by their ill-judged luxury, that they could not find a single supporter in the day of misfortune, and during the Parliamentary inquiry they suffered more on account of their gorgeous past than on account of their frauds.[1]

The crisis, however, continued, and George I., who according to habit, was never in England, had to leave Hanover and return to his new kingdom at the beginning of November. Several remedies were suggested. The most important of these was that nine millions of the capital should be made over to the Bank of England and an equal amount to the East India Company; this would leave twenty millions to the South Sea Company. This measure which was ably drafted by Walpole, was passed, in spite of the objections of the Bank and of the two other companies concerned; but the vote of the two Houses did not result in the execution of the arrangement, which was optional in character and remained a dead letter.

Meanwhile, the debates and the Parliamentary inquiry were revealing the most scandalous proceedings, and the tone of the discussion reflected the unmeasured wrath of the public against the company and its promoters.[2] No one seemed to realise that the nation had been as guilty as the company. The nation was composed of simple, hard-working, honest people, despoiled by a group of thieves who deserved to be cast out without mercy. This was the unanimous opinion in the country and Parliament was hardly more reasonable. The protest there was the more violent, since several members tried in this way to throw dust in the eyes of the public.

The King, in his speech at the opening of the session, hoped that it would be remembered that "all your prudence,

[1] Mackay, p. 69.

[2] For this celebrated affair see the whole session from December, 1720, to August, 1721, in *Parl. Hist.* (pp. 678-911).

your temper, and resolution, are necessary to find out and apply the proper remedies to our misfortunes."

These words were scarcely heard. The House of Lords was content to urge that the property of the criminals should be confiscated. But in the Commons, Lord Molesworth[1] demanded that extraordinary penalties should be inflicted on extraordinary crimes, and recalled the example of the ancient Romans, who, having no law against the unforeseen crime of parricide, yet made one as soon as it was committed, and threw the guilty wretch sewed up in a sack into the Tiber. He should, he added, be content to see these speculators, as the parricides of their country, treated in a like manner and thrown into the Thames. These views were shared by Parliament, and Walpole who was the only person who kept his head, had much difficulty in calming the audience; indeed, on the following day he could not do so, and penalties with retrospective force were passed against "the Infamous practice of Stock-Jobbing."

A committee of inquiry was appointed.[2] The governors, directors and officers of the company were summoned before the bar of the House of Commons, and since Knight, the treasurer, had thought it prudent to escape, a proclamation was issued, forbidding any of the accused to leave the kingdom.

General Ross,[3] with more vigour than elegance, described to the House how "The committee had discovered a train of the deepest villainy and fraud that had ever contrived to ruin a nation." Bribery had been used to pass the Act, all the directors who were members of the House were expelled and all the officers of the company who held Government posts were dismissed. The inquiry was hampered by obstacles of every kind: the company's cashier was in France and the most important of the books had been tampered with or entirely destroyed. It was discovered however, amongst other things that £574,500 of stock, said

[1] For Lord Molesworth's speech see *Parl. Hist.*, pp. 682-683.

[2] It included the chief opponents of the South Sea project, amongst others Molesworth, Jekyll and Brodrick; the latter was elected president of the committee.

[3] For this speech see *Parl. Hist.*, p. 711.

to have been sold, had been distributed among ministers, influential nobles and the King's favourites. The Earl of Sutherland had had £50,000; Mr. Secretary Craggs, £30,000; Mr. Charles Stanhope, one of the secretaries of the Treasury, £10,000; the Sword Blade Company, £50,000. The Duchess of Kendal having accepted £10,000, the other favourite, the Countess of Platen, received a like sum—an impartial treatment which Lord Mahon thinks worthy of praise—and her two nieces were not forgotten.

But the person most compromised by the inquiry was Aislabie, the Chancellor of the Exchequer.[1] He had advised the company to increase its second subscription by half a million, on no authority but his own, and had apparently been well paid for this permission; he had also received a large share of the stock which had been distributed in the manner just described. Speedy and well-deserved punishment fell upon him. He was expelled from the House with ignominy, sent to the Tower, and all his property was confiscated for the benefit of the victims.

This sentence was welcomed with extraordinary enthusiasm. London was illuminated, fireworks were let off and a huge crowd assembled on Tower Hill to witness his degradation. But the demonstration was caused less by pleasure at Aislabie's condemnation than by indignation at Stanhope's acquittal on the previous day.

Charles Stanhope had been the first to be sentenced,[2] and although his defence, skilful as it was, had convinced no one, he had been acquitted by a majority of three. The most powerful influence had been exerted to save him. Lord Stanhope, Lord Chesterfield's son, had approached the members of the House in turn and was able to induce a large number of them to vote for the acquittal, or at least, to abstain from voting. The verdict roused much discontent in the country and was the cause of numerous troubles in London. Similar dissatisfaction was caused by the acquittal of the Earl of Sutherland. It was stated that

[1] For his trial see *Parl. Hist.*, p. 748. The Secretary of State, Craggs, could not be tried since he had died in the interval.

[2] *Parl. Hist.*, pp. 746-747.

this acquittal was due to the necessity of staving off a political crisis and preventing the return of the Tories to power.[1]

The rest of the accused, the directors of the South Sea Company, many of whom had themselves been ruined by the business, were all condemned. More than two millions were confiscated; the fines were based more on the guilt of the speculators than on the extent of their property.[2]

These proceedings,—a justice indulgent to the great and harsh to the poor, to quote Figaro,—were rightly condemned by the great historian, Gibbon.[3] He complains that, "Instead of the calm solemnity of a judicial inquiry, the fortune and honour of thirty-three Englishmen were made the topics of hasty conversation." All the accused —not as individuals but in a body, absent or unheard, and often on paltry evidence—were condemned to arbitrary fines by a passionate and bitter assembly, some of whose members were glad to be able to satisfy their personal animosity by a secret vote.

The force of these criticisms, which Gibbon sets forth with a remarkable eloquence, is undeniable. But, nevertheless, before condemning the judges, it is well to imagine oneself living at that time and in the circumstances under which they were called upon to give judgment.

No doubt injustices were committed. The accused were not spared either insults or ridicule, and many Members

[1] Lord Mahon, pp. 31-32, is inclined to justify this acquittal; he bases his argument on the fact that there was no written evidence against Sutherland, and that the witnesses were not to be trusted. Sutherland was however forced by public opinion to resign his post of First Lord of the Treasury.

[2] The values of the estates and the amounts of the fines will be found in *Parl. Hist.*, Vol. VII., pp. 834-835. This list is given by Francis but according to his habit he does not mention the source of his information.

[3] *Memoirs of Life and Writing,* p. 12 of the 1st edition (1796); a large portion of this work is in French. In writing these fine pages Gibbon, if not avenging his own wrongs, was at any rate performing an *officium pietatis,* for his grandfather and namesake was one of the directors of the South Sea Company and lost a large part of his fortune through it; he was condemned to pay a fine of £10,000; his estates had been valued at £106,543. Gibbon, however, was not the man to yield to personal feeling, even in a chapter devoted to the origins of his family, and his evidence, which is supported by the facts, is worthy of attention.

seized their opportunity of revenging themselves for the vanity and insolence displayed by the directors of the company in their days of prosperity. Evidently, too, Parliament hardly attained the standard of a calm and impartial tribunal. It was excited by passions which were exciting the whole nation and by which any tribunal must have been affected. But it should be noticed in its favour that, although we may think the sentences severe, contemporaries looked upon them as mild and considered the gallows the only fate worthy of those whom they called the cannibals of Change Alley.[1] Similarly, the French nation showed but scant mercy to Law, who was yet a thoroughly honest man, and who, like some of the South Sea directors, had gone into the affair rich and emerged from it poor.[2]

The sentences having been passed, it remained to deal with yet more serious problems. It was easier to punish the guilty than to comfort their victims. Something was accomplished in this respect however, thanks to the ability of Walpole, who, when his first scheme failed, was ready to devise a second. The capital of the South Sea Company according to the estimate made at the end of 1720, was in round numbers £37,800,000, whilst the stock allotted to the various shareholders amounted only to £24,500,000; so that there remained £13,300,000 belonging to the company in its corporate capacity and representing the profit which it had made out of the national disaster. The State had a claim to £7,500,000 out of this sum, this being the payment promised when the company was founded. But to set a good example, the Government cancelled five millions of this debt; there was thus £8,900,000 to divide among the shareholders, *i.e.*, 33½ per cent. of their stock. Many of these shareholders were, however, so dissatisfied, and interrupted the meetings of Parliament[3] by such constant disturbances, that the Government ended by cancelling the

[1] For the feelings of the English public, see the letter of Britannicus in the *London Journal* of November 19, 1720.

[2] Levasseur, *Récherches historiques sur le système de Law*, p. 315 and Dubois, *Histoire des doctrines Economiques*, Vol. I., p. 326.

[3] These disturbances were so violent that it was necessary to read the Riot Act, to which the crowd retorted: "You pick our pockets and then imprison us for complaining."

rest of the company's debt to it, and the shareholders were paid a second dividend of 6¼ per cent.

In this way the credit of the South Sea Company's stock was maintained. The Bank which had hitherto been powerless, now took action in its turn, and purchased annuities to the value of £200,000, which the company had been authorised to sell.[1] To enable it to make this payment the Bank's capital was increased by £3,400,000 and now stood at £8,959,955. The stock was subscribed for at 118 per cent. so that the Bank made a profit of £610,169 by the operation.

The Government payed £632,698 for long and short annuities, and now had its annual revenue consolidated into a redeemable fund for which it had only to pay 4 per cent. after 1727. It thus secured a yearly advantage of £339,631. This was, according to Coxe,[2] the signal for a reduction of the rate of interest on several loans.

But all these must not lead us to infer that the South Sea crisis was beneficial to England. It had produced enormous agitation and an unjust redistribution of wealth and had very nearly ruined the Hanoverian monarchy.[3] Besides this the crisis had a deplorable influence on public morality. Queen Caroline compared the South Sea scheme to the Triple Alliance of 1735. Those who shared in it knew perfectly well that it was only a fraud, but hoped notwithstanding to make some profit out of it. Each reckoned that he would be the first to withdraw after making his own fortune, and each thought himself clever enough to leave his companions in the lurch. I believe no more accurate analysis of the speculators' state of mind has ever been given. These speculators—and this is one of the most painful features of the crisis—represented all classes of

[1] This profitable transaction was at first the cause of some anxiety; an expression of this will be found in a contemporary pamphlet: *A letter to the Governor of the Bank of England (Against the purchase of annuities from the South Sea Company)*, 1722, the year of the purchase.

[2] Coxe, *op.* and *loc. cit.* The French Government secured a similar advantage from the crisis of the *Compagnie des Indes.* The national debt remained the same, but the rate of interest was much reduced, and the Treasury had only to pay 37 millions instead of 80.

[3] For the hopes raised among the Jacobites by this crisis, see Mahon, Chap. xii.

society, and things were so arranged that the poorest man might ruin himself as easily as the millionaire. Hutcheson,[1] borrowing the language of the gambling-house, says: "The South Sea stock must be allowed the honour of being the gold-tables, the better sort of bubbles the silver-tables, and the lower forms of these are the farthing-tables for the footmen." The evil was thus as widespread as it was serious, and it was the less skilful rather than the more guilty of the gamblers who were ruined, so that the punishment was as objectionable as the offence.

The crisis of 1720 was especially serious in the effect it had on the Bank of England. It twice forced this institution to the verge of ruin.

In the first place it led the directors to make proposals of so absurd a kind that, had they been accepted, they would, as Aislabie[2] very plainly showed, have much intensified the crisis instead of staving it off. This was partly because the offers of the Bank were even less practicable than those of the South Sea Company,[3] partly because the Bank would inevitably have tried to keep up the credit of its new stock by that of its notes, would have made over-issues, and, in a futile endeavour to fulfil its rash promises, would have compromised an institution which had already done great services to England and was destined to do still greater ones. It was in this way that Law in trying to keep up the stock of the India Company, compromised and finally ruined the *Banque d'Escompte*, which had previously been both useful and prosperous.

[1] *A collection of calculations and remarks relating to the South Sea Scheme and Stock*, p. 87 (1720), Published at the end of *A collection of treatises relating to the National Debts and Funds*.

[2] See his speech in the House of Lords.

[3] The impossible nature of the South Sea Company's promises was clearly pointed out even in 1720 in a pamphlet by Hutcheson, *Some calculations relating to the proposals made by the South Sea Company and the Bank of England to the House of Commons*. The author shows that the South Sea Company's assumption of all the public debts, funded and unfunded, would raise its capital to £43,558,000. And he proceeds to ask how it can undertake a trade so extensive as to enable it to pay an interest exceeding the total revenue obtained from the Customs and Excise of the whole kingdom.

The Bank owed its escape from this first danger to its enemies, who secured the rejection of its proposals. It escaped the second and later danger which resulted from the failure of the South Sea Company[1] only by breaking its word, and it only withstood the run upon it by using methods unworthy of a great establishment.

[1] See above, p. 137.

CHAPTER II.

THE BANK OF ENGLAND IN THE REIGN OF GEORGE II.

Establishment of a Reserve Fund. Renewal of the Charter in 1742. Contemporary idea of the privilege of *Exclusive Banking*. Definition given by the Act of 1742. Importance of the Act. The Bank and the Jacobite rising of 1745. Black Friday. The Bank and the conversion of 1750. Relation between the Bank and the Treasury.

THE last years of George I.'s reign and the first years of his successor's were very peaceful. Walpole was the true ruler of England and, despicable as he was in many respects, he had at least the indisputable merit of securing tranquillity at home and preserving peace in Europe.[1] Commerce and industry flourished under his influence and the history of the Bank of England became uneventful. One important fact deserves notice, viz., the establishment of a reserve fund, and the renewal of the Charter in 1742 which confirmed and extended the Bank's privileges, must also be mentioned. The period of peace continued until 1745 when the great Jacobite rising endangered the Bank's existence once again.

We shall consider these three events in succession. Then we shall conclude the chapter by examining the relations between the Bank and the Treasury during this period.

[1] I attribute to Walpole's love of peace what otherwise appears to be the rather exaggerated admiration felt for him by Mr. Morley. *The English Historical Review* published in 1901 a series of remarkable articles by Mr. Basil Williams on *The Foreign Policy of England under Walpole*.

"The good effect of Walpole's financial management was proved by the high price that the funds had reached. A 3 per cent. loan issued in 1727 stood at *par* in 1736, and in the next year at 107. Under such conditions it is plain that the whole redeemable debt might have been reduced to 3 per cent. or even lower. Political expediency, which made it an object to favour the fundholders, who were strong supporters of the Hanoverian dynasty, prevented this useful measure" (Bastable, 2nd edition, pp. 631, 632). It will be remembered that the conversions made in France under the Restoration at first aroused much discontent.

SECTION I.

Establishment of a Reserve Fund.

Until 1722 the Bank divided all its profits amongst the shareholders, and provided no reserve fund. As a consequence, the dividends had been exceedingly variable, and had ranged from 18¼ per cent. in 1716 to 6 per cent. in 1722. The disadvantages of this state of things were keenly felt and also the dangers due to the absence of any reserve fund on which to rely in case of an emergency. Urgent needs had indeed been met hitherto by a call upon the shareholders, but this policy became increasingly inconvenient in practice as business developed and the personal connection between traders was proportionately loosened, so that in 1722 it was found necessary to establish a reserve fund, known in England as *The Rest.*

SECTION II.

Renewal of the Charter in 1742.

Each time that the question of renewing the Bank charter came to the front during this period there happened in England what still happens in many countries on like occasions. There were always some persons who opposed the renewal, and the Government took advantage of this opposition to secure conditions from the Bank that were more to the public interest, or sometimes merely more advantageous to itself. It was upon such conditions, and more particularly in return for a loan, that the Bank secured the renewal of its privileges in 1742, as well as in 1764 and 1782.

As the year 1742, the date of the expiration of the monopoly, drew near, the controversy was renewed even more fiercely than before and the Bank's privileges were even more seriously endangered. But when the fatal date arrived the Government was as usual involved in financial difficulties,[1] and the Bank agreed to lend it £1,600,000 with-

[1] The long peaceful interval ended in 1739. When peace was concluded in 1748 the total of the national debt had reached £78,000,000.

out interest.[1] In order to raise this sum the directors made as usual a call upon the shareholders, the response to which increased the capital to £9,800,000. In return the Bank's privileges were continued, and it was provided that they should not be cancelled without a preliminary twelve months' notice, which notice could not be given before 1764. The Bank thus obtained complete security for 22 years apart from the additional guarantee that the Government would have to pay off all the capital lent to it should the privileges be cancelled.

Moreover the monopoly introduced into the charter of 1709 was confirmed and defined. The new Act (statute 1742, c. 13, s. 5) conferred on the Bank the privilege of "exclusive banking." The clause in question explains the nature of this privilege: "It is the true intent and meaning of the Act that no other bank shall be erected, established or allowed by Parliament, and that it shall not be lawful for any body, politic or corporate, whatsoever, . . . united or to be united in covenants or partnerships, exceeding the number of six persons, in that part of Great Britain called England, *to borrow, owe, or take up any sum or sums of money, on their bills or notes payable at demand, or at any less time than six months from the borrowing thereof,* during the continuance of such said privileges of the said Governor and Company." As Macleod[2] remarks, this clause merits "the most earnest attention," firstly, "because it is the one which contains the sole monopoly of the Bank of England," and secondly, because "it is a penal clause, and therefore, of course, to be construed strictly."

"The sole monopoly granted to the Bank . . . is that, during the continuance of its charter, no partnerships exceeding six persons . . . should issue notes payable on demand, or at any less time than six months after issue."

Banks of any other kind and all other methods of carrying on the business of banking are left free and unaffected.

[1] This in fact reduced the interest paid hitherto on the original capital of £1,600,000 from 6 per cent. to 3 per cent. The amount lent was doubled without increasing the interest paid, which was equivalent to a reduction of 50 per cent. in the interest.

[2] 3rd Edition, p. 430.

And in fact there was nothing to prevent a foreign company from opening a London branch and carrying on all forms of banking, with the exception of the issue of notes payable in a less time than six months.

SECTION III.

The Bank of England and the Jacobite Rising of 1745.

This was not the first occasion on which the Bank had suffered from the Jacobites. In 1722, the Duke of Orleans had revealed to George I. the existence of a Jacobite conspiracy.[1] A proclamation by the Pretender was distributed, and the most absurd rumours were current. All was said to be in readiness, money collected, officers appointed, arms and ammunition stocked. One of the intended victims was the Bank of England which was destined to be pillaged. These rumours were believed. The Jacobite party was still powerful and the Regent could hardly be suspected of making such statements without foundation; hence the stock of the Bank fell, and, as usual, the public hurried to its doors. But vigorous measures were taken, the royal troops were at once assembled, and the Jacobite peril vanished into smoke.

The crisis could not be thus stifled when, in 1745, the Pretender landed in Scotland at the end of July, almost alone, without anyone's support, trusting to his lucky star and to the help of a few Highland chiefs.[2] The history of the rising is well known, for its romantic side has been frequently depicted on the stage and in novels, and the personality of Prince Charles has always had a strange fascination for historians.[3] Hence it would be superfluous

[1] Mahon, Chap. xii.

[2] The Highlanders formed hardly a twelfth part of the Scotch nation.

[3] See Chambers, *History of the Rebellion.* John Hill Burton, *History of Scotland,* Vol. VIII., pp. 431-505. Mahon, Vol. III., pp. 301-470. There is also an excellent summary in Lecky, *England in the Eighteenth Century,* Vol. I., pp. 421-423. See in addition Mr. Andrew Lang's recent book, *Prince Charles Edward,* a work containing much information. The author was allowed to consult the *Stuart Papers* at Windsor, and were it on this account alone his book would have the attraction of a novel treatment of a hackneyed subject.

to describe its extraordinary success at the outset: the defeat of Sir John Cope, and the triumphal entry into Edinburgh. In a few weeks the royal adventurer was master of Scotland, and on the 5th of November he invaded England.

Fortune seemed always in his favour; he took Carlisle on November 15th after a short resistance,[1] and marched as far as Derby without opposition.[2] The alarm caused in London by this news may well be imagined. The Pretender was only 127 miles away and what was worse, had numerous supporters in the City.[3] The Duke of Newcastle was uncertain what policy to adopt and debated whether he should not join the enemy. The fear of a French invasion added to the general terror. A panic resulted, the funds fell to 49,[4] all the shops were closed, and the 6th of December was known for a long time as Black Friday.[5]

Finally there came the inevitable accompaniment of all panics—a run on the Bank, for which the directors were not prepared. This run was instigated not only by political opponents, but also, it appears, by some of the Bank's rivals.[6] The Bank managed to resist it, thanks partly to

[1] This siege of Carlisle forms a somewhat amusing interlude. The town was defended by a Colonel Durand, and by a Mayor whose name suggested a Scotch origin, and who changed it in order to inspire greater confidence. See Walter Scott, *Tales of a Grandfather*, p. 419.

[2] According to a letter sent to the Duke of Cumberland from Manchester, this town "was taken by a sergeant, a drummer, and a girl," who entered it in view of thousands of spectators. See the whole of this exceedingly curious letter in Mahon, pp. 400-401.

[3] The chief of these was a City Alderman called Heathcote.

[4] The Pretender had tried to calm the fears of the public by declaring in the second article of his manifesto, that, although the national debt had been contracted under an illegal government and was a heavy burden on the nation, his father would consult Parliament before coming to any decision about it. But a mere declaration was not enough to satisfy the public creditors, who distrusted an unknown Parliament and had not forgotten what the promises of the Stuarts were worth.

[5] See note to a letter from Horace Walpole to Sir Horace Man in the collection of these letters, Vol. I., p. 409. See also Fielding, *The true Patriot*. Friday, May 11, 1866, received the same name. See below, Vol. II., p. 358.

[6] If it is true that the Bank's rivals took an active share in the run, they were only paying it back in its own coin. According to Francis (p. 164) the Bank had organised a run on the firm of Messrs. Child. Jealous of the reputation of this house, it had secretly collected the firm's

the device already described of paying in sixpences, but more especially—for this alone would have been insufficient—thanks to the support and loyalty of the London merchants who agreed to accept Bank notes in payment, and thus bore witness to the important position the Bank had attained in the commercial world.

A similar manifesto was issued with equally good results fifty-two years later. That of 1745 was as follows:

"We, the undersigned, merchants and others, being sensible how necessary the preservation of public credit is at this time, do hereby declare that we will not refuse to receive Bank notes in payment of any sum of money to be paid to us, and we will use our utmost endeavours to make our payments in the same manner."

This declaration was signed in the course of a single day by 1,140 merchants and fundholders.

The retreat from Derby, followed by the retirement from England, happened shortly afterwards, and improved the situation, relieving the Bank from all danger, though not from all anxiety, for in the following year the Government was obliged to apply again for its assistance on account of the difficulty of meeting the expenses of the expedition against the Pretender, and also those of the struggle intended to safeguard the integrity of Hanover. The directors were empowered to cancel £986,000 of Exchequer bills in return for an annuity of 4 per cent. and to issue new stock for the purpose. This transaction increased the paid-up capital to £10,780,000. This was the only increase in the Bank's capital until 1782.

receipts which circulated like cheques, intending to present them for payment at a time when there would be difficulty in meeting the demand. Mr. Child was only saved by the intervention of the Duchess of Marlborough, who sent him a cheque for £700,000 on the Bank. Thus armed Child awaited his rival's demands; as soon as they were presented he sent one of his partners with the Duchess' cheque to the Bank, and the whole value of the receipts, about £500,000 or £600,000 was paid in Bank notes. Francis says that he has taken this story from Ireland, but gives no reference, so that it has not been possible to verify the authenticity of the incident. Compare the run in 1707, above, pp. 120-121.

SECTION IV.

THE BANK OF ENGLAND AND THE CONVERSION OF 1750. —RELATIONS BETWEEN THE BANK AND THE TREASURY.

In the middle of the 18th century there occurred one of the most remarkable events in the financial history of England—the conversion of the rate of interest on the national debt to 3 per cent.[1] On this occasion the consolidated 3 per cent. stock was issued, which existed until the conversion of 1888.

The credit of this conversion rests with Pelham and Sir John Barnard. The operation was carried out gradually. The interest was at first reduced to 3½ per cent.; this rate was to be paid until 1757, when it was to fall automatically to 3 per cent. The conversion so successfully carried out by Mr. Goschen in 1888 resembled that of 1750 in this particular, for the rate of interest was at first reduced to 2¾ per cent., and then after a certain date, it fell automatically to 2½ per cent.[2]

The Government debt to the Bank at the time of the conversion was composed as follows:[3]

		Funded Debt.	*Capital.*	*Interest.*
1.	Original Capital - - -	£1,600,000		
	New Loan in 1742 - - -	1,600,000		
	(Interest already reduced to 3%)			
		£3,200,000	£3,200,000	£96,000
2.	For cancelling the remainder of the Exchequer Bills (1709) at 4% since 1727 - - -		500,000	20,000
3.	For purchasing the Stock of the South Sea Company at 4% -		4,000,000	160,000
4.	Annuity of 1728 at 4% - -		1,750,000	70,000
5.	Annuity of 1729[4] at 4% - -		1,250,000	50,000
6.	For cancelling Exchequer Bills (1748) at 4% - - -		986,800	39,472
	Total National Debt -		£11,868,000	£435,472

[1] For an account of the conversion of 1750, see Sir John Sinclair, *The History of the Public Revenue of the British Empire*, Part II., p. 86

[2] For the conversion of 1888, see Hamilton (E. W.), *An Account of the operations under the National Debt Conversion Act*, 1888, *and the National Debt Redemption Act*, 1889.

[3] Martinuzzi (Pietro), *La Banca d'Inghilterra nei riguardi del servizio del Tesoro*, p. 35.

[4] A loan made for the war with Spain.

Out of this annual payment of £435,472, £96,000 represented interest already reduced to 3 per cent. in 1742, which was not therefore affected. The rest of the annuity, £339,472, was reduced to £297,038 until December 25, 1757, and to £254,604 after that date.

We may also note before concluding this chapter, that from this time (1751) the Bank of England was entrusted with the administration of the permanent debt.[1]

[1] See the Appendix to Vol. II. In particular the section dealing with the Bank of England and the administration of the national debt. See also Lawson, *History of Banking*, p. 171.

CHAPTER III.

THE BANK FROM THE DEATH OF GEORGE II. TO THE FRENCH REVOLUTION.

Renewals of the Bank Charter (1764 and 1781). Commercial Crises of 1763, 1772, 1783. Re-coinage. Gordon Riots.

THE history of England during this first part of George III.'s reign includes the end of the Seven Years' War, the Rebellion and the recognition of the Independence of the American Colonies. It includes also an unprecedented commercial and industrial development with which we shall deal when we come to describe the economic condition of England at the time of the Revolution.

As regards the history of the Bank the period of twenty-five years covers two renewals of the charter (in 1764 and 1781), three economic crises, following somewhat closely on one another; another re-coinage, which need only be briefly touched upon, and an attack on the Bank during the disturbances known as the Gordon Riots. These various events, grouped according to their character rather than in chronological order, will supply material for four paragraphs.

SECTION I.

RENEWALS OF THE BANK CHARTER.

The first of these renewals was in 1764. The charter was continued until the repayment of the Government debt, and for this six months' notice was required, which notice could not be given before August 1st, 1786.

This was in fact a renewal, in the usual form for twenty-two years. As usual also this renewal was paid for by a financial sacrifice. The Bank gave £110,000 to the nation, and lent the Government a million on Exchequer bills for two years at 3 per cent. These advances were of great service to the country which was just concluding a glorious and profitable war, which had however been an immense expense.[1]

By this same Act, "it was made felony, without benefit of clergy, to forge powers of attorney, or other authorities, for receiving dividends, transfering or selling stock, or for personating the proprietors of any stock, for such purpose."[2]

Similarly by an Act of 1773, the forging of bank-notes was made punishable with death. This crime was a recent innovation. As we have noticed above the first instance of it did not occur until 1758. In order to prevent imitation of any kind, it was made illegal to manufacture any engraved bill or promissory bill bearing the words "Bank of England," or "Bank post bill," or even to state any sum in white letters on a black ground so as to resemble "Bank paper," under penalty of six months' imprisonment.

According to the law of 1764 the possibly fatal date when the charter might be cancelled was 1786. Five years before this limit was reached the second renewal of the Bank's privileges was granted, and in the usual formula these were continued until 1812 in return for a loan of two millions at 3 per cent. During the following year a call of 8 per cent. was made on the Bank's shareholders, which brought in £862,000 and increased the company's capital to £11, 642,400.

This renewal of the privileges five years before they expired roused animated discussions; but the Ministry paid a well-deserved tribute to the services rendered by the Bank and refused to make any modification in its charter. They were supported by a large majority and the new agreement was passed by 109 votes to 30. When it is remembered that the 3 per cent.'s stood then at 58, the Bank's offers must be considered very advantageous to the State, impoverished as

[1] The total cost of the Seven Years' War is estimated at £82,623,738. It added £59,633,000 to the national debt.

[2] Francis, *op. cit.*, p. 173.

it was by the American War which had cost no less than £97,599,496 and whose results had been very different from those of the Seven Years' War.

SECTION II.

COMMERCIAL CRISES OF 1763, 1772, 1783.

The year 1763 was noted for the number of serious bankruptcies on the Continent. The Seven Years' War seems to have given rise to much speculation. With the peace came the day of settlement bringing with it the collapse of many of the speculators, a collapse which ruined the merchants who had traded with them. The most important of these failures was undoubtedly that of Neufville Brothers at Amsterdam. This firm left liabilities of 330,000 guineas and not only ruined 18 important Dutch houses but also a large number of rich Hamburg merchants.[1] The shock was so great that for some time business was only transacted for cash. These disasters could not of course be confined to the two great commercial cities in question. There were numerous failures in Germany and the crisis spread to England, where according to Smith, the Bank advanced nearly a million to the merchants.

England was shortly to be the headquarters of a similar crisis, which, like that just described, was not confined to the country where it began.

The years 1770 and 1771 had been years of great commercial prosperity throughout Europe, but this was especially the case in England, whose export trade in particular expanded to an extent previously unknown and which was not again reached until 1787. Macpherson[2] remarks that a number of failures often follow after too great commercial prosperity, just as certain diseases in mankind are the result of an undue confidence in health.

[1] The Amsterdam merchants had been warned by their Hamburg colleagues that if they did not support Neufville Brothers the Hamburg merchants would suspend payment. Unfortunately, the warning came too late and the Hamburg firms had to carry out their threat.

[2] Vol. IV., p. 524.

This theory was fully borne out by the facts in the particular case before us. Speculative mania had broken out afresh, and a partner in the firm of Heale having disappeared with £300,000, this house failed on June 10th, 1772, dragging down several others with it. The Bank and certain merchants endeavoured to maintain credit and for several days were apparently successful; but at length they could do so no more and a general collapse followed. The number of failures reached the amazing figure of 525 whereas since 1728 there had never been as many as 300.[1] It was a return to the South Sea year, and this crisis is memorable as the first of those great modern panics which played so important a part in the history of the Bank. In the following year the evil spread to Holland, and it soon affected all Europe, thanks to the general mania for speculations, whether commercial or in the public funds. Macleod estimates the total losses at £10,000,000.[2]

The evil was cured in England by a series of vigorous measures. The Dutch merchants behaved with their customary good sense. The Bank of Stockholm lent its aid to all the firms of really good standing and the Empress of Russia, Francis[3] asserts, secured the English merchants at St. Petersburg from risk by giving them unlimited credit at her own bankers. Thanks to these combined efforts the crisis of 1772 was calmed and for eleven years the commercial world of Europe was at peace.

The crisis of 1783 like that of 1763, followed upon a treaty of peace. When the independence of the United States was acknowledged in 1782, international trade which had suffered greatly from the war, developed very rapidly. This increase of business and the opening up of new markets, led to extravagant transactions which were combined with a considerable over-issue of notes. An alarming drain of precious metals from the Bank produced a crisis which nearly ended in the suspension of cash payments.

[1] There had been 425 Bankruptcies in 1726, 446 in 1727, and 388 in 1728. Since then there had never been as many as 300 except in 1764, when there were 301. For the failures between 1700 and 1793 see Chalmers, *Estimate of the Strength of Great Britain* (1810), p. 36.

[2] 3rd Edition, p. 433. [3] p. 177.

Fortunately, the directors had noticed that if the issues could be restricted even for a short time, the coin, instead of being exported, flowed back even more quickly than it had been withdrawn; they had thus arrived at the following rule:[1] "That while a drain of specie is going on their issues should be contracted as much as possible, but that as soon as the tide had given signs of ceasing, and turning the other way, it was then safe to extend their issues freely." The Bank therefore determined not to apply to the Government, but merely to restrict its issues for a time until the exchanges were once more favourable. The anxiety was at its height in May, 1783. All further advances to the Government on the loan of that year were then refused, though they did not demand the repayment of the advances previously made which amounted to nine or ten millions. This policy was maintained until October when the withdrawal of precious metals finally ceased and a movement in the opposite direction began to show itself. As soon as these favourable signs were confirmed, the Bank made considerable advances to the Government upon the loan, although the coin then at its disposal was only £673,000, and was less than it had been at the time when the greatest alarm had been felt.

SECTION III.

Restoration of the Coinage.

The year 1774 brings us back to a subject with which we have previously dealt at length but which can now be much more briefly disposed of—the subject of the restoration of the coinage. During the 18th century the currency had increasingly deteriorated. In the report of a committee appointed by the House of Commons, it was estimated that there was a deficiency of gold in the coins of nearly 9 per cent. An ounce of gold which had been worth £3 18s. 6d. in 1730, was £3 18s. 10d. in 1761, and actually £4 1s. 0d. in 1772. Consequently, in 1774 the Government

[1] This rule is due to Bosanquet. See Macleod, 3rd Edition, p. 437.

ordered a re-coinage, which reduced the value of an ounce of gold to £3 17s. 6d. at which price it continued until September, 1797.

SECTION IV.

THE GORDON RIOTS.—THE BANK ATTACKED.

The anti-Catholic disturbances in 1780 involved the Bank in serious dangers. At first the excitement was confined to the neighbourhood of the Houses of Parliament where the rioters and their leader, Lord George Gordon, treated the members of the two Houses with deplorable violence, hoping to prevent the passing of a Bill favourable to the Catholics.[1]

But, as generally happens in disputes whose pretext is religion, the objectors soon became rioters, and the members of the Protestant Association,[2] as Gordon's supporters called themselves, began to plunder the chapels and houses of the Catholics, destroying the objects of veneration, and not forgetting to carry off the valuable pictures and the gold and silver plate. The police seemed powerless to prevent or suppress these proceedings, and the rioters, no doubt in a spirit of tolerance, ceased to be content with plundering the Catholics, but laid hands on the property of all who came in their way, without regard to sect or creed; they even went so far as to take Newgate Prison by assault and to set free their imprisoned comrades.[3] Emboldened by this success, the mob proceeded to the Bank of England. The Government which had been warned, sent some help, and fortunately this was supplemented by a band of Volunteers formed by the London citizens. The rioters were daunted by these measures: they only made a half-hearted attack where a more vigorous effort would probably have succeeded. This attempt is of historic interest. It was only

[1] The object of the Bill was to remove some of the disabilities under which Catholics suffered owing to a law of William III.

[2] The association had been in existence for two years, but had hitherto contented itself with peaceful agitation.

[3] An account of these riots will be found in all the histories of England. Dickens has given an especially vivid description in *Barnaby Rudge*, one of his best novels.

after it had been made that the bank was guarded day and night.

The next day an army of 20,000 men was assembled, and after a somewhat severe fight the rioters were defeated, 300 men being abandoned on the field of battle. Shortly afterwards, 192 of them were condemned, and 25 were executed.[1] As for their leader, Lord George Gordon, he was acquitted after a lengthy sojourn in the Tower. He died in 1793, after being condemned to five years' imprisonment for two libels against Marie Antoinette, and, a curious experience for a champion of Protestantism, after being in all probability converted to the Jewish faith. Most people thought him a little mad, but he had warm admirers, one of whom, Watson, has left us a history of his life.[2]

[1] *Notes and Queries. A medium of intercommunication for Literary Men, etc.* Second series, Vol. I., p. 518.

[2] Robert Watson, *Life of Lord George Gordon, with a philosophical review of his political conduct.* For an account of these trials see—(1) *Cobbett's State Trials*, xxi., pp. 485-687; and (2) *The whole Proceedings on the Trials of two Informations against Lord George Gordon*, 1787.

PART IV.

THE BANK OF ENGLAND DURING THE FRENCH REVOLUTION AND THE NAPOLEONIC WARS.

CHAPTER I.

ECONOMIC CONDITION OF ENGLAND AT THE TIME OF THE FRENCH REVOLUTION.

Sketch of the Industrial Revolution in England. The Cotton and other industries. The canals. The steam engine. Results of the transformation of England from an agricultural and commercial into a commercial and industrial Country. Its effects on the Revolutionary and Napoleonic Wars. Its effects on the Organisation of provincial credit. The Country Banks.

TWENTY years before the French Revolution, England was still an agricultural and commercial country. Agriculture employed the great majority of the population and was the chief source of the country's wealth.[1] Industry was indeed already flourishing in the 18th century, but, as M. Bry writes,[2] it showed no signs of concentration of capital or of masses of workpeople in large factories. Big fortunes at this time were still in the hands of the trading companies. The masters were artisans who often worked themselves with their wives and children, in the villages or in the country. The prevailing system was a combination of agriculture and industrial work.

[1] The population of England was estimated at 8,500,000, and the total annual income at £119,500,000. The agricultural population was 3,600,000, with an income of 66 millions, and the industrial population was 3,000,000, with an income of only 27 millions. (See the list of the different classes of inhabitants with the amount of their respective incomes, given by G. Bry, *Histoire Industrielle et Économique de l'Angleterre,* p. 453). The agricultural section was thus not only the most numerous but also the richest; and all the evidence goes to show that it was contented and prosperous. See especially Young's comparison between its condition and that of the French peasant, *Political Arithmetic,* pp. 133, 158, not to speak of the *Tour in France.* See also Sir J. Stewart, *Enquiry into the Principles of Political Economy* (1767), Bk. I., Chap. xviii, and Adam Smith, Bk. I., Chap. viii.

[2] *Op. cit.,* p. 447.

Twenty years after the Revolution, England was in miniature the England of to-day.

To give one instance only, that of the cotton industry. This industry was introduced into England at the beginning of the 18th century owing to the infatuation of the public for the calicoes and other materials imported from India, but its importance was still so small that even in 1750 the value of the cotton goods exported was only £45,000, while that of the woollens was two millions. In 1833 the woollen exports had increased to £6,539,731 and the cottons to £18,486,408.[1]

In the interval an industrial revolution had taken place.

When it is remembered that during the period we are considering, that is, from 1793 to 1815, England was engaged in a struggle which cost her more than 80 millions a year, and in all, more than 830 millions,[2] and that during this same period she witnessed the conquest of her allies, the frequent defeat of her own troops, the increase of her national debt from 247 to 861 million pounds and of her yearly burden of taxation to 70 millions; when it is also remembered that English industry and commerce was faced by extraordinary difficulties, by the Bank of England's suspension of cash payments, by the sudden closing of the markets of the Continent and of South America to English goods,[3] and by the Berlin decree, devised by Napoleon, which was a most formidable weapon against British trade, it is easy to infer that there must be a close connection between England's final triumph and her economic revolution.

Indeed England's policy during this period can hardly be explained and her financial history is incomprehensible if the economic transformation is neglected—a transformation which can only be compared to that which Europe

[1] The cotton export now exceeds 70 millions and the home consumption equals this in value, so that this industry supports a commerce of 140 millions. The export of woollens amounts to 24 millions.

[2] The exact cost of the war was £831,146,449.

[3] In addition to all this there was the difficulty of obtaining certain raw materials, such as Spanish wools, which were indispensable to English industry.

underwent after the discovery of the new world, and of which some brief account must be given.

Sketch of the Industrial Revolution in England.[1] We will begin with the cotton industry to which we have already referred, and in which the changes were most striking. Between 1697 and 1764[2] the importations of cotton increased from 1,976,359-lbs. to 3,870,392-lbs. Progress was small and the work was done by hand. In 1767 Hargreaves invented the spinning jenny, which by means of a wheel, enabled eight spindles to be worked at once, and afterwards a still greater number, so that one man could spin 100 threads of cotton at a time. Another important innovation was that of roller spinning, which was done at first by men and later by water power.[3] Arkwright perfected this machine and made it for the first time an important factor in the manufacture of cotton.[4]

These great inventions were followed by a series of others, such as Crompton's mule and Berthollet's use of chlorine for the bleaching of cotton cloth, and the process was so revolutionised that a single man could now work 2,200 spindles.

These important discoveries, which made England the leading industrial country in the world, were at first greeted with terror, for it seemed evident that to enable one man to do work which had hitherto employed 2,200 was to turn his 2,199 fellows into the streets.[5] But it soon appeared that these fears were ill-founded for whilst at the beginning of George III.'s reign the cotton industry only employed

[1] Amongst general works on this question the reader may consult: Cunningham, *op. cit.*, Bk. III., Part II.; H. Traill, *Social England,* Vol. V., Chaps. xviii. and xix.; Bry, *op. cit.*, Bk. V., Chaps. i. and ii.; Lecky, *op. cit.*, Vol. VI., Chap. xxiii.; McCulloch, *Account of the British Empire,* and *Essay on Manufactures* (in *Treatises of Economic Policy*); De B. Gibbins, *Industrial History of England.* [Also Paul Mantoux, *La Révolution Industrielle.*]

[2] For a complete list of the fluctuations during this period see Baines, *History of the Cotton Manufacture in Great Britain* (1835), p. 109.

[3] The first idea of this process is attributed sometimes to John Wyatt, sometimes to Lewis Paul. See for the first opinion Baines, and for the second French, *Life and Times of Crompton.*

[4] Arkwright took out his patent in 1769.

[5] Lecky (pp. 209-210) gives an account of the persecutions suffered by Kay, Hargreaves, Arkwright, and Peel, the grandfather of the Prime Minister.

40,000 men, in 1785 it employed 80,000, and in 1831, 833,000.[1] The population of Lancashire, the headquarters of the industry, was only 166,200 at the beginning of the 18th century; at the end of the century it was 672,000; now it is over four millions. The towns of Manchester and Liverpool have each more than half a million inhabitants.[2]

We have seen that between 1697 and 1764 the quantity of cotton imported hardly doubled, while the exportations increased in an even smaller proportion. During the last twenty years of the 18th century, the former multiplied seven-fold and the latter fifteen and a half-fold.[3]

The enormous growth of the cotton industry, though the most striking, is not the only sign of the progress which made the second part of the 18th century the most memorable period in the history of English industry. Something must be said too of the manufacture of pottery and china, which was introduced in the first instance, like so many

[1] McCulloch, *Account of the British Empire*, pp. 218, 219, 360. Wages, however, fell considerably between 1795 and 1815; Cunningham (p. 468) estimates that during this period they were only two-thirds of what they had been during the preceding decade. On three occasions, in 1795, 1800, and 1808, it was proposed to fix a minimum wage, but this idea was rejected as likely rather to increase the evil (on this point see the Report of the Committee of the House of Commons, *Reports*, Vol. II., p. 97). Things were in fact in the state of crisis distinctive of all periods of transition.

[2] According to the census of 1901 these two towns have populations of 543,969 and 686,332 respectively. See *Encyclopædia Brit.*, Supplement, Vol. XXX.

[3] I quote from Baines' yearly list for the period 1781-1832 some figures which will give a more exact idea of the increase in the cotton imports:—

Year.	*Cotton imported for spinning.*	*Year.*	*Wool imported.*
1781	5,198,778 lbs.	1771	1,829,000 lbs.
1784	11,482,083 ,,	1790	2,582,000 ,,
1789	32,576,023 ,,	1800	8,609,000 ,,
1792	34,907,497 ,,	1810	10,914,000 ,,

Decline for five years, followed by another increase in 1798.

Year.	*Cotton imported for spinning.*
1799	43,379,278 lbs.
1800	56,010,732 ,,
1802	60,345,600 ,,
1807	74,925,306 ,,
1810	132,488,935 ,, (maximum for the war period).
1813	50,966,000 ,,
1815	99,366,343 ,,
1831	280,080,000 ,,

other industries, by the Huguenots,[1] and of the iron industries.

The iron industries were old-established,[2] but never really expanded until after the inventions of Darby of Colebrook, and especially of Cort of Gosport, who in 1783 introduced the process of puddling and rolling iron. The industry did not attain its full development until the 19th century,[3] but even in the previous century it had made considerable progress.[4]

One of the reasons for the growth of the iron industry was that after the discovery of the Darbys, father and son,[5] coke could be used for smelting instead of the wood charcoal which had been employed before and which was very scarce. The demand for coke increased daily and stimulated the exploitation of coal mines,[6] which soon grew to an importance of which the list given below will give some idea.[7]

The Canals. All this industrial development would have been impossible if it had not coincided with increased facilities for attaining coal. Progress in manufactures pre-

[1] For this industry see Lecky, pp. 210-211, and Bry, p. 500. Its head-quarters are in Staffordshire, which stands fifth among English counties as regards population. These industries owe their development to Josiah Wedgwood, for whose life see Eliza Meteyard, *Life of Wedgwood.*

[2] McCulloch, *Essay on Manufactures,* p. 466 of *Treatises on Economical Policy.*

[3] For further details as to the iron industry, see Fairbairn, *Iron, its history, properties and manufacture.*

[4] In 1740 the total quantity of pig-iron manufactured in England and Wales was estimated at 17,000 tons. In 1796 it was 125,079, and in 1806, 258,206. It increased to 678,117 tons in 1830. Birmingham, Sheffield and a number of other towns owe their prosperity, it may be even said their very existence, to this industry.

[5] As early as 1621 Lord Dudley took out a patent for a similar invention. He started some works which came to an untimely end and then the matter was forgotten in the confusion of the Civil War. But Dud Dudley, the natural son of this Lord Dudley, published in 1665 an account of what had happened under the title of *Metallum Martis.* This pamphlet, which had become very rare, was reprinted fifty years ago.

[6] For the working of the mines and its difficulties see Traill, *Social England,* p. 314.

[7] Cunningham (p. 463) gives the following statistics of the output of coal at different dates :—

1660	2,148,000 tons.	1770	6,205,400 tons.
1700	2,612,000 „	1790	7,618,728 „
1750	4,773,828 „	1795	10,080,300 „

supposes and encourages improvement in the public roads; it also stimulates great undertakings such as those which entirely changed the methods of internal communication in England. I refer to the construction of canals.[1]

Canals had been used for a long time on the Continent.[2] England on the contrary, was very backward in this respect.[3] Consequently transport rates were very high. The carriage of a ton of goods between Manchester and Liverpool cost 40s. by land and 12s. by river. It was not until 1761 that it was determined to make a canal between Worsley and Manchester. This canal, the first made in England, was constructed by Brindley entirely at the expense of the Duke of Bridgewater. It halved the cost of coal in England and its extension supplied an easy and cheap means of communication between Liverpool and Manchester.[4]

After this canal Brindley made another 139 miles long, connecting the pottery centres.[5] He died in 1772 at the age of 56. For a long time his schemes had been rejected or laughed at, but he lived long enough to witness their success. Eighteen years after his death canals were constructed according to his plans to connect the four great ports of London, Bristol, Liverpool and Hull. In the same year a canal joining the Forth and Clyde, whose construction had

[1] H. D. Traill, *op. cit.*, pp. 322-326, and Phillips, *A general History of Inland Navigation.*

[2] Not to mention Italy and Spain, where canals had been constructed at a very early date, the undertakings of Charles XII. and of Peter the Great may be noticed, and in France the canal from the Seine to the Loire, begun under Henri IV., and the canal *du Midi*, finished under Louis XIV.

[3] As early as 1656, it is true, Francis Mathew suggested joining the Isis to the Avon by a canal, and various similar projects were brought forward, but nothing was done beyond the improvement of certain rivers.

[4] This first canal cost the Duke £220,000, but Brindley's pay formed but a small part of this sum, for he was only paid 2s. 6d., and afterwards 3s. 6d. a day. He was uneducated as well as inexpensive, his letters being full of uncouth spelling mistakes, but he was none the less a man of genius who made important changes in his country. (His biography will be found in Smiles, *Lives of the Engineers*).

[5] Canals are a means of transport peculiarly adapted for pottery since they offer little risk of breakage, hence they are still used for this industry. In Brindley's time there were additional considerations, the carriage of pottery cost nearly a shilling per mile per ton and the expense put a stop to all trade. After the construction of the canal the cost of transport from Etruria to Liverpool fell from 50s. to 13s. 4d. (Traill, p. 324).

taken twenty-two years, was completed. During the next four years Parliament passed no less than 81 Acts authorising the construction of navigable canals.[1]

Undertakings of this kind are still of much importance. Canals continue to be the best means of internal transport for heavy goods and for such as do not require rapid transit. Hence great nations still devote considerable sums to their extension and improvement. But whatever may be the actual importance of canals, it is as nothing compared with what it was a century ago, or to speak generally, before the invention of railways. In those days the method of transport they offered was the cheapest, the safest, the easiest and not the least rapid. In fact had it not been for them the greatest industrial discoveries would have had but limited results, and English industry and commerce owes an eternal debt of gratitude to Brindley.

It is estimated that before the introduction of railways no less than 2,600 miles of navigable canals had been constructed, without counting those in Ireland[2] and Scotland, which owned respectively 276 and 225 miles, and that 50 million pounds had been invested in these undertakings.

But if inventions may be judged by their consequences, the most important of all was James Watt's[3] improvement in the steam engine.

James Watt, who was born at Greenock in 1736, and details of whose life will be found in Lardner's works and in the biographies of Muirhead and Smiles, took out his first patent in 1769, but it was not until long afterwards that he succeeded in giving to the steam engine, which had hitherto moved only vertically, "a rotary motion and a parallel motion, and, by the regulating centrifugal force of the governor, in placing the machine in all its various com-

[1] Lecky, p. 214.

[2] With regard to Ireland see Newenham, *View of the circumstances of Ireland* (1809), especially p. 202.

[3] R. H. Thurston, *History of the Steam Engine*, gives an account of Denys Papin, the Marquis of Worcester, Savery, Newcomen and other forerunners of Watt. There are no doubt excellent works in French on the subject, but it has not been easy to find them, since the present book has been written entirely in England.

bined motions under the complete control of the mechanic."[1]
When once this result was secured the steam engine became a real influence in industry, and Watt may be said to have brought about an unprecedented revolution.

These were the chief among the inventions which transformed England from an essentially agricultural country into an essentially industrial country, and in the course of a few years produced those vast accumulations of wealth[2] and those great agglomerations of population which are now her predominant characteristics. There is nothing more striking from this point of view than the persistent growth in trade and population. The following figures are quoted from the statistics given by Cunningham.[3]

	Population.
1700	5,475,000
1760	6,736,000
1770	7,428,000
1780	7,953,000
1790	8,675,000
1801	8,892,536
1811	10,164,256
1821	12,000,236

	Year.	*Trade.* *Exports.*	*Imports.*
England.	1613	£2,487,435	£2,141,151
	1662	2,022,812	—
	1688	4,301,000	7,120,000
	1720	6,910,899	6,090,083
	1750	12,699,081	7,772,039
	1783	13,896,415	11,651,281
	1796	29,196,198	21,024,866
United Kingdom	1805	31,064,492	28,257,781
	1810	43,568,757	39,301,612
	1815	58,624,550	32,438,650
	1850	197,330,265	100,460,433

Volumes would not be long enough for a study of all the results of these changes from a political and from a social point of view. The emigration of workpeople to the manufacturing centres, the decline of agriculture, and even of the agricultural industries,[4] the labour laws,[5] the abolition of tariffs and the adoption of free trade principles, all follow directly from this revolution. These however were not the only consequences, and it is safe to affirm that the effects

[1] Lecky, *op. cit.*, Vol. VII., p. 279 (edition 1899).

[2] This accumulation was the more rapid owing to the immense profits made in the early years. Pitt, when he imposed the legacy duty, thought it absurd to consider the possibility of any inheritance exceeding a million. But things changed so rapidly that after a short time a year rarely passed without such a case occurring.—William Johnston, *England as it is*, Chap. xii.

[3] *Op. cit.*, p. 694-695.

[4] Especially when water-power was no longer the principal driving force in use.

[5] The first of these laws was passed in 1802 and was introduced by Sir Robert Peel, the father of the Prime Minister.—Jay, *Cours de Législation Industrielle*, 1897-1898.

can be traced throughout English social life and in all the characteristic marks of the English temperament.

During this period of thirty years, from 1789-1819, we must confine ourselves to our particular subject, and shall deal only with the effects of the change on the course of the French wars and on the development of provincial banking.

1.—*The Revolutionary and Napoleonic Wars.* It may be confidently asserted that had it not been for the industrial revolution, England, even with a commercial monopoly, would never have been able to muster the resources needed to resist the Republican army and to conquer Bonaparte. Attempts have been made in vain to explain this extraordinary vitality and energy by other causes. It has even been alleged that England could not have provided the capital expended during a struggle of a quarter of a century without the inconvertible currency, which enabled her to coin boundless wealth from every piece of money. It will not be difficult to show how far removed this opinion is from the truth, for the fact is, that England made no attempt during Pitt's lifetime to profit by the situation and to urge the Bank to excessive issues, and that later on, when this policy was adopted, the result was a cruel disillusionment. On the contrary, it is due to Arkwright, Watt, Brindley and their companions, that England was able to raise the capital for her immense loans, to impose taxes to pay the interest on them and to provide for the expenses of the war. This fact is eloquently stated by Mr. Lecky :[1]

"The first and most obvious fact is that the triumphant issue of the great French war was largely, if not mainly, due to the cotton mill and the steam engine. England might well place the statues of Watt and Arkwright by the side of those of Wellington and Nelson, for had it not been for the wealth which they created, she could never have supported an expenditure which, during the last ten years of the war, averaged more than 84 millions a year, and rose in 1814 to 106 millions, nor could she have endured without bankruptcy a national debt which had risen in 1816 to 885 millions."

[1] p. 218.

2.—*The Country Banks.* The second point which we have to consider is the effect of the industrial and commercial development in extending country banking. Necessarily this effect was immense, but for special reasons the extension was not of a very advantageous kind.

Bank of England notes did not circulate outside London and the Bank did not establish any branches in the provinces. At the same time the enormous increase in industrial undertakings demanded a greater extension of credit facilities and in particular, an increased supply of paper money; this need was supplied by the issues of country banks formed for this one object.

The Bank itself assisted in the formation of these banks in the following manner:

During the crisis of 1783 which we have described, the Bank succeeded in putting a stop to the drain on its reserve by an exceptional contraction of its issues. When the crisis was over there was a continuous stream of gold into its coffers, and the supply of currency was necessarily increased by the issue of notes in payment for the gold. Hence the issues which between 1783 and 1785 had not exceeded six millions, rose to £11,121,800 and the bullion increased to £8,645,865.[1] This increase in the coin and in the issues of the Bank occurring thus in time of peace, naturally caused a decline in the rate of interest, whilst the Bank did not reduce its rate of discount. This enabled the country banks to increase their issues in order to discount bills, some of which at any rate, would have been discounted at the Bank had the rate of interest been higher. The Bank's discounts were actually reduced from £4,973,926 in 1785, to £2,035,901 in 1789, and, taking into account the general increase in business, it may be concluded that the discounts of the country banks increased by more than the difference between these two amounts.

For all these reasons the development of the banks was very rapid, but owing to the deficient organisation of credit the extension was not, as we have said, very advantageous.

[1] Tooke, *History of Prices*, Vol. I., p. 194.

The situation was as follows. The Act of 1742 (c. 13, 5)[1] conferred on the Bank a monopoly of issue in "that part of Great Britain called England." The only banks not affected by the monopoly were those having less than six partners.[2] The Bank of England, playing in this matter the part of dog in the manger, not only did not found branches to issue notes, but was even unwilling to allow powerful and well-established companies to be formed for the purpose, although this might on occasions have helped to strengthen its own credit. Further, when the country notes were at a discount, it refused to supply issues which would have taken their place. The consequence was that wealthy and respectable companies were unable to issue notes, and that, since the country needed a circulating medium and could not get a good one, it was soon supplied with a bad one. A number of shopkeepers, chemists, tailors and bakers, taking advantage of the clause authorising banks formed by less than six persons, became bankers[3] and flooded the

[1] See above, p. 148. A criticism of the organisation of the country banks is given by W. Boyd, *Letter to the Honourable W. Pitt on the Influence of the stoppage of Issues in Specie at the Bank of England* (1801), p. 20 of the edition of 1811, revised by the author; and more particularly by H. Thornton; *An Enquiry into the Nature and Effects of the Paper Credit of Great Britain*, Chap. vii., entitled, *Of Country Banks; their advantages and disadvantages*, pp. 236-261 of McCulloch's reprint. For a special discussion of the relations between these banks and industry, see p. 245.

[2] The privileges conferred by this Act were limited in fact to borrowing or owing money on bills or notes payable on demand. The business of banking was at that time actually confined to this. Since the clause was strictly interpreted the device of using cheques, which was borrowed from Holland, was not forbidden by the law. Hence there was nothing to prevent companies from being formed and carrying on banking by this means. This did happen by degrees and without occasion arising for Parliamentary interference. The custom passed unnoticed until it was too widespread to be forbidden, and shortly afterwards Mr. Joplin pointed out that the foundation of deposit banks was absolutely legal (see *Supplementary Observations to the third edition of an Essay on Banking*, p. 84—1823). In 1833 some joint-stock companies were established in London and undertook banking business, but without issuing notes. The Bank of England tried vainly to have them condemned as illegal. At the present time there are numbers of these joint-stock banks in London, which enjoy an excellent reputation and well-deserved prosperity. For this whole subject see below, p. 258, *et seq.*

[3] In 1775 an attempt was made to remedy matters by an Act forbidding the issue of notes of lower value than 20s., and two years later the limit was increased to £5. See below, p. 253, Lord Liverpool's speech in February, 1826, describing the persons who took up the profession of banking, in connection with the crisis of 1825 and the part played by the country banks.

country with worthless paper. In 1750 there were not 12 banks outside London: in 1793 there were 400.

Some of these 400 banks were no doubt well-established, and of these a few still survive, but the remainder did not offer the same guarantee of solidity, and in their eagerness for profit, they made the mistake of keeping an inadequate reserve of coin to support their issues, so that they collapsed at the first unusual demand for cash.[1]

The two great crises of 1793 and 1797 were due to the defective organisation of the provincial credit system.

The Bank of England had not chosen to lend any substantial aid to the organisation of credit and it now suffered the punishment of its careless selfishness. The speedy collapse of the country banks left it to maintain credit unassisted. As we shall see, it accomplished the task in 1793, thanks to the active interference of the Government who issued five millions of Treasury bills. Four years later, however, it was thrown upon its own resources and gave way.

Nor did the evil cease with the year 1797; the same thing happened in 1810 and 1812. Macleod[2] informs us that during the three years 1814-1816, 92 commissions in bankruptcy were issued against country banks, and that during the 28 years, 1791-1818, there were no less than 273 commissions of this kind.

The Act of 1826 permitted the formation of joint-stock companies to carry on the business of banking and with power to issue notes, at a distance of not less than 65 miles from London. In 1844 however the law deprived both private banks (banks having less than six partners) and

[1] According to Sir Francis Baring, banks had been established throughout the country in the interval between the failure of the Ayr Bank in 1772, and 1793. This was an important change and as long as credit was well established it was a change beneficial to the country, in that it increased the currency. Unfortunately these banks were founded upon an insecure basis, and they were quite unable to withstand any sudden disturbance, for they allowed interest on all deposits and hence could not afford to keep even a small reserve of idle and unproductive capital (see *Observations on the Establishment of the Bank of England*, p. 15.)

[2] 3rd Edition, Vol. II., p. 380. The author goes on to remark that if we allow the usual proportion of three or four suspensions to one bankruptcy we may readily calculate that upwards of a thousand banks stopped payment during this period.

joint-stock banks of the right of issue. But those actually in existence, viz., 72 joint-stock banks and 207 private banks, retained their privilege of issuing notes though only up to a fixed limit.

The number of these banks with issue rights has greatly decreased and continues to decrease; in 1888 there were only 19 private banks and 44 joint-stock banks.[1] Whenever one of these banks disappears its right of issue passes over to the Bank of England. The note issue of private and joint-stock banks was limited in 1866 to £8,648,008;[2] it is now only £2,762,323.[3]

[1] M. Octave Noel, *Le Banques d'émission en Europe* (Vol. I., pp. 78, 82), gives a very complete list of the banks of issue then in existence and of the respective limits of their rights of issue.

[2] £5,153,000 for the private banks, and £3,495,000 for the joint-stock banks.

[3] The actual issues are much less. See below, p. 297, *The issue department*

CHAPTER II.

FINANCIAL POLICY OF WILLIAM PITT.[1]

Pitt's financial policy before 1789. Pitt and the Revolution. Connection between Pitt's financial policy and the suspension of cash payments. Sketch of this policy. Mr. Gladstone's speech. The subsidies paid to the Allies. The rate at which the loans were raised. Loans *versus* taxation. Criticism of Pitt's policy. The Sinking Fund. Conclusion.

WHEN the French Revolution broke out, Pitt had been in power since 1784; his general policy was peaceful and his financial policy especially fortunate.[2] He began to pay off the debt; a million a year was set aside for this object. This million was to be devoted to the purchasing of Government stock and was to be increased each year by the interest

[1] I have thought this chapter essential as an explanation of those which follow, but I have not written it without many hesitations and with considerable difficulty. It is very difficult to judge of a financial policy during such a remarkable period, and Pitt could not reasonably be expected to foresee all the events of which he was to be an eye witness. To this first difficulty is added a second, that of finding data for an opinion. The political struggles were exceptionally violent and they influence nearly all the books on the subject. Moreover, Mr. Lecky's work stops at 1793. There is no general history whatever for this period. Lord Stanhope's *Life of the Right Honourable W. Pitt* (4 volumes) is anything but a scientific work.

The following may be consulted for the subject matter of the chapter:—A masterly speech by Gladstone, delivered on May 8, 1854 (see *Parliamentary Debates*, third series, Vol. 132, columns 1472-79 devoted to this matter). McCulloch, *Collection of Tracts on the National Debt* (with a preface); *The History of the Bank of England* (1798), a work already mentioned, whose standpoint is essentially liberal. G. K. Rickards, *The Financial Policy of War*, an answer to Mr. Newmarch. Grellier, *Terms of all the public Loans, with an appendix by R. W. Wade* (1812); very important.

William Newmarch, in a valuable pamphlet which contains much documentary evidence, *On the Loans Raised by Mr. Pitt during the first French War*, has given a brilliant defence of Pitt's financial policy. More recently the question has been discussed very ably, but unfortunately too briefly, by Lord Rosebery, *Pitt*, pp. 148-156. The appendices A and B may also be read with advantage, since Lord Rosebery's figures are more accurate than those given by Newmarch.

Finally, the Parliamentary Debates may be consulted, especially, of course, the speeches of Pitt and Fox, but they cannot be read with too great caution. Amongst other speakers, William Smith and his report of February 9, 1796, deserves mention.

[2] Rosebery, *op. cit.*, Chaps. IV. and V.

on the stock already acquired. A special commission, independent of the House of Commons, was to carry out this plan and to administer the Sinking Fund. This system on which exaggerated hopes were based, continued to work throughout the wars of the Revolution. It reduced the national debt by £10,250,000 between 1786 and 1793.

At the first outbreak of the revolution Pitt apparently intended to continue the same policy. If he did not actually ignore the Revolution, as Lord Rosebery says,[1] at least he appeared to do so. There is ample evidence to show that he had no thought of interference, and he did all that he could to avoid the conflict.[2] Further than that he did not go.

After the 10th of August, the English Government recalled Lord Gower, the ambassador at Paris, and from this time onwards the hostility to France felt by the King and the English people continuously increased. Pitt tried to resist the current but the French victories in the Netherlands were calculated to weaken his resistance; the beheading of Louis XVI. dispelled his doubts. The English, who regard the execution of a king as their special monopoly, received the news of this unfortunate prince's death with extraordinary demonstrations. The theatres were closed, everyone put on mourning, pulpit and platform re-echoed with the murder committed in France, and the King's chariot was surrounded by a mob demanding "war with France!" "Since the massacre of St. Bartholomew," writes Lecky,[3] "no event in a foreign country had produced such a thrill of horror in England." Pitt, the author con-

[1] p. 96.

[2] In February, 1792, on introducing the budget, Pitt made a famous speech, one of those exceptional speeches which he revised with a view to publication. He proposed the removal of certain taxes, the increase of the sinking fund, the suppression of the subsidies paid to the Hessian mercenaries, and a reduction in the number of seamen from 18,000 to 16,000. Moreover he declared that: "Unquestionably there never was a time in the history of this country when from the situation of Europe we might more reasonably expect fifteen years of peace than at the present moment."

Lord Rosebery, pp. 118 to 123, gives numerous other proofs of Pitt's state of mind. This view is corroborated by Newmarch, p. 5, and Lecky, pp. 2-4. See also for Maret's mission to England and his interview with Pitt (Nov., 1792), Ernouf, *Maret, duc de Bassano*.

[3] p. 122.

tinues, at once seized the opportunity of breaking with France, and on January 24th, Grenville, the Foreign Secretary, ordered Chauvelin to leave the country within eight days. On February 1st the Convention made the only response possible, and declared war against both the King of England and the Stadholder of Holland.[1]

The war concerns us only in so far as it affected the Bank of England.

Between February 1st, 1793, and March 17th, 1801, the Government was obliged to increase the English national debt by £325,211,460.[2]

The Bank, on the other hand, had to suspend its cash payments in February, 1797.

Was there any connection between these two facts? Would a wiser administration of the public finance have avoided this disaster? This is the question into which we must now inquire.

Yearly loans had to be raised from the outbreak of the war until the peace of Amiens.

These loans, which were at first small, rapidly increased in amount, and after 1795 became excessive, but decreased slightly between 1798 and 1800. After this the upward movement began again, so that at the end of 1801, the total English funded debt had increased by £271,980,000 during the nine years of Pitt's administration, the average yearly increase being £30,000,000.

[1] Mr. Lecky, with his customary talent and learning, tried to justify the behaviour of England and to mark it off from that of the Continental monarchies. It would be out of place to discuss the question here, but if I had to express an opinion I should sum up the matter thus: that, while the behaviour of England in these wars against Louis XVI. and Napoleon was justifiable and did good service to Europe, her conduct during the whole period 1789-1793, now before us, was unjust, deceitful and full of hypocrisy. And yet I am not inspired by any excessive admiration for the Revolution, and willingly acknowledge that the Convention, by indulging in incongruous and unsuitable demonstrations, played into the hands of its enemies and supplied them with their strongest arguments.

[2] This sum did not indeed represent the whole debt, for besides their shares, the subscribers received a certain number of terminable annuities as part of their security. Those annuities, known as "Long Annuities," expired in 1860, and their value reckoned at 5 per cent. interest would be £9,323,976. But during this time the Sinking Fund continued in operation and £42,518,832 was redeemed through it, which sum must be subtracted from the total amount.—Rosebery, pp. 150-151.

And, since the shares in all these loans were issued considerably below par, the Government only actually received £202,375,000 out of the 271 millions[1] for which it was indebted.

For the same reason, the interest, nominally 3 per cent., was actually much higher.[2]

This increase was mainly due to the disinclination felt at the outset to impose fresh taxes. The taxes levied during the four years 1793-1797 amounted to £70,000,000, or £17,500,000 a year, whilst during the four years 1799-1802 the taxes amounted to £134,750,000, *i.e.*, there was an increase of 92½ per cent.[3]

And finally, a large part of the money raised by these loans was not used in the public service but was absorbed in subsidies paid to the allies. These were of two kinds: (1) direct subsidies, (2) Imperial loans, guaranteed by the English Government and raised in England. These loans ultimately became a charge on the English Treasury.

Pitt's financial policy has been severely attacked on all these accounts. We will proceed to examine these criticisms, and will begin with those of Mr. Gladstone, rendering honour where it is due. During the debate of

[1] Newmarch, p. 39, gives the annual amounts of the loans contracted and the sums actually raised as follows:—

	Loans contracted.		*Money actually raised.*	
1793	6.250	millions.	4.500	millions
1794	15.676	,,	12.907	,,
1795	55.537	,,	42.090	,,
1796	56.945	,,	42.755	,,
1797	28.275	,,	14,500	,,
1797	3.669	,, (Imperial loan)...	1.620	,,
1798	39.624	,,	20.000	,,
1799	27.125	,,	15.500	,,
1800	32.185	,,	20.500	,,
1801	49.209	,,	28.000	,,
	314.495	,,	202.372	,,

But out of the 314.495 millions contracted, 42.515 were cancelled by the Sinking Fund, so that the actual debt incurred by the State was 271.980 millions.

[2] Most of the loans, *i.e.*, 271.597 millions of the debt., were issued at 3 per cent. There were, however, 35.593 millions issued at 5 per cent. and 7.305 millions at 4 per cent. The average rate at which the loans were actually raised was £5 5s. 9d. per £100.

[3] Bastable, *Public Finance*, 2nd edition, pp. 589-591.

May 8, 1854, this great statesman, who was then Chancellor of the Exchequer, set himself the task of proving that all war expenses ought to be met by taxation,[1] an attempt which gave evidence of a rare degree of uprightness and political courage. After a statement of the economic and moral grounds for his opinion, Gladstone passed on to discuss the lessons of history, and criticised Pitt strongly for the policy he adopted at the beginning of the war.[2] He ridiculed the view which had gained for Pitt the title of "Heaven-born minister," though at the same time he acknowledged a profound respect for his memory, and pointed out how he recognised his mistakes, changed his policy and whole-heartedly sought the aid of taxation.[3]

The speaker in fact, entirely condemned the continued resort to loans.[4] Others[5] have criticised the rate at which the loans were issued, on the ground that, as only an inadequate interest of 3 per cent. was offered, much larger sums had to be borrowed than were actually received, and above all, the possibility of future conversions was cut off. Finally, Pitt has been almost unanimously blamed for the subsidies given to the allies.

Let us examine these various points.

[1] See the whole of this speech, *Parl. Debates*, Vol. 132 (March-May, 1854), pp. 1414 to 1479.

[2] p. 1472.

[3] p. 1474. This is indeed no accident in Pitt's career but an instance of one of his distinctive characteristics. It is surprising that this has not attracted more attention. Pitt made mistakes readily, but, the fault once committed, he as quickly realised it, and never persisted in it obstinately. Witness his behaviour in the war with France: he soon recognised that it had been a mistake to enter upon the struggle; and when the Directory gave him an excuse for changing his policy, he at once opened negotiations and did all he could to conclude an honourable peace. Witness his behaviour to the Bank: he exploited that institution so ruthlessly as to force it to suspend cash payments; but when the paper money was actually in use he took every precaution to avoid abusing this dangerous weapon. Other examples of the same kind could be given.

[4] Gladstone also condemned the Sinking Fund, but since everyone agrees with his condemnation, this matter can be deferred till later.

[5] See Bastable, *op.* and *loc. cit.*

SECTION I.

Subsidies Paid to the Allies.

These subsidies, as we have said, were managed in two ways. Either the money was paid over directly,[1] or security was given for the loans raised by the German Empire, security which, considering the state of the Imperial finances, was equivalent to a loan. The first of these loans was for £4,600,000,[2] the second, guaranteed in 1797, was only for £1,620,000.

Most English writers, not even excepting Newmarch,[3] condemn the payment of these subsidies.

It is true that some of the allies deserved the name of "treacherous" given them by Fox,[4] and that they employed the money for anything rather than the support of England in her struggle against revolutionary France. It was also true that even when the allies were honest, there was little or no agreement between them and the English troops, that the combination did more harm than good to both parties, and that ultimately England gained little advantage from the 15 millions and more which she spent between 1793 and 1801. But it cannot therefore be asserted as has too often been done in England, that Pitt's policy was nothing but a mistake and a delusion. In my opinion this is perhaps the very point where he is least to blame.

In fact, these payments only formed a small part of the war expenses, and it cannot be said either that they were wholly ineffectual, or that England was not justified in hoping for still better results. It is curious that these subsidies have been thought to play such an important part in

[1] The amount paid directly was £9,024,817. Details of the distribution will be found in Rosebery, *Appendix A*, and Newmarch, p. 51, *Appendix I.* We may again point out that the figures given by the former are more accurate than those of the latter.

[2] The first loan was guaranteed, at the request of the King, on February 5, 1795. The guarantee gave rise to lively debates. The opposition did not lack arguments which were, indeed, justified subsequently by facts, for after 1798 the loan became a charge on England. The grant was passed by 173 votes to 58.

[3] pp. 12-13, *contra* Rosebery.

[4] Speech on February 5. The whole speech, which is entirely devoted to this question, should be read.

the crisis from which England suffered after 1795. Macleod still holds this view. At the time they were believed to be the sole cause of the drain of bullion. The opposition repeated this persistently and the commercial world was convinced of its truth. People apparently attributed the exportation of precious metals entirely to the subsidies, forgetting the fleets and armies which England had to maintain abroad. Sir Francis Baring[1] pointed this out clearly enough: "It must be indifferent to the country, if bullion is exported, to what service it shall be applied; but it is of infinite importance whether the magnitude of the sum shall exceed, or fall short, of the balance of trade. Whether money so exported shall be applied to the payment of the British troops in Germany, for the foreign expenditure of fleets in the Mediterranean or Lisbon, or whether it shall be for an Imperial loan . . . is exactly the same to the country."

Here, as in other cases, the mistake lay in having undertaken an unjust and imprudent war. But, this mistake having been made, it was England's duty to secure Continental allies in the first instance, and then to retain them at all costs. This was the only way in which Great Britain with her insignificant army, could threaten the French frontiers; it was the only way in which she could keep the Republican army from her own coasts. Hence, although Pitt may be blamed for distributing several millions without adequate security for their proper use, I cannot in justice criticise him for trying by every means available to preserve his country from disaster.

SECTION II.

THE RATE AT WHICH THE LOANS WERE RAISED.

Mr. Newmarch in his apology, tries to prove that Pitt failed to raise loans at 5 per cent., not from any unwillingness to do so, but because he could find no one to lend money on such terms, since the public wanted to enjoy the

[1] *Op. cit.*, pp. 50-51. In the next chapter we give the sums expended abroad on behalf of the Government; they far exceed the money granted to the allied Governments. See Tooke, p. 208.

advantages of a high rate and to avoid the risk of conversion. Mr. Newmarch[1] supplies very convincing proofs in support of this theory. We will merely notice the most striking of these.

The first loan of £4,500,000, issued at 3 per cent., was raised at £72, that is, at an interest of £4 3s. 4d. per £100.[2] But according to Newmarch, Pitt, to judge by his own statement in the House (March 17, 1793), seems to have tried in vain to borrow at 4 or 5 per cent., and to have been forced, without option, to borrow at 3 per cent., although he realised that the conditions were more burdensome than he had expected. This fact is confirmed by J. J. Grellier, who states that Pitt did everything he could to excite competition, but without success.

The same thing is true for the subsequent loans. In November, 1796, a part of the floating debt which circulated in the form of Naval bills and Exchequer bills, was funded. The holders were offered a choice between stock bearing respectively 3, 4, and 5 per cent. interest. The offers were so arranged that in actual fact all the stock paid more than 5 per cent., and there was a bonus on that at 4 and 5 per cent. The first paid £5 5s., the second £5 10s., and the third £5 16s. per £100 of capital. But even this was not enough to attract the subscribers, who were alarmed at the possibility of conversion, and out of a total of £13,029,339 funded, 85 per cent. were subscribed at 3 per cent.

There remains another yet more characteristic fact. In 1796 England was in an isolated position and was threatened with an apparently inevitable invasion. The budget showed a deficit of 18 millions,[3] and as, under the circumstances, the yield from ordinary loans seemed insuffi-

[1] pp. 7-20.

[2] Mr. Gladstone laid great stress on the fact that to issue these loans nominally at 3 per cent. was a deception, and that Pitt borrowed first at £4 3s., then at £4 10s., then at £4 15s., and finally at £5 14s. and at £6 6s. 10d., which is the rate at which the loan in 1797 was raised. But this fact was perfectly clear to contemporaries and deceived no one.

[3] It was intended to raise fresh troops, viz., 15,000 foot, 20,000 irregular cavalry, and 60,000 militia.

cient, it was determined to raise a patriotic subscription, the Loyalty Loan.

Everyone who subscribed £100 was to receive £112 in 5 per cent stock. This loan was inconvertible until after all other 5 per cent. loans had been converted, and the shareholders were always to have the option of £100 in cash or £133 in 3 per cent. stock. In spite of all these advantages these shares, which were subscribed for amidst great patriotic enthusiasm,[1] fell so low that Pitt thought it advisable to help the shareholders by adding to the above conditions a long annuity of 7s. 6d. per share, hoping in this way to stop a fall which had already reached 14 per cent.[2]

To sum up: the accusations against Pitt as regards this second point do not seem to us well-founded; those made by Mr. Gladstone with respect to the continual appeal to loans are certainly more justifiable, without being wholly sound.

SECTION III.

LOAN *versus* TAX.

Mr. Gladstone's arguments will be remembered. Without disputing their correctness in principle, we may note that it has been said in reply: first, that in this particular case Pitt could not levy fresh taxes without risk of crushing the new-born English industries; and second, that those industries were not in a position to bear the burden of the war until after the naval victories had assured them a commercial monopoly; this, however, was not until 1798. It has been pointed out too, that the first years of the war were not only years of great commercial distress, as is proved by the number of failures, but also of agricultural distress due to the remarkable series of bad harvests. The conditions were thus very unsuited to the imposition of new taxes, and Pitt was well-advised not to impose any. This is true, but I am not convinced that Pitt gave any thought to the economic condition of the country and rather

[1] The loan was completely subscribed within 15 hours.

[2] Pitt's scheme only passed the House by 36 votes to 35, and consequently was not carried out.

believe with Gladstone that he was chiefly concerned to maintain his own popularity.

Mr. Gladstone's criticisms however only refer to the period 1793-1797; he has only praise to bestow on Pitt as regards the succeeding years. In 1797, he says,[1] Pitt made a first effort towards a more healthy policy "by proposing to raise £7,000,000 by assessed taxes.[2] The plan broke down . . . and he only got £4,000,000. In the year 1798, not daunted by that failure, he proposed to raise £10,000,000 by means of the income tax; and from that time onwards his career was one series of continued and almost convulsive efforts to . . . extricate the country from the frightful consequences of former laxity, and to provide against a recurrence of similar evils in future."

The revenues for the years 1799-1802 were, as we have said, 92 per cent. higher than those for 1793-1797. The peace of Amiens was of short duration. In 1803 the revenue was £38,600,000, in 1805 it was £50,900,000. In 1806 a further attempt was made to increase it. Lord Lansdowne increased the income tax to 10 per cent. The taxes brought in £59,300,000, that is, an increase of 15 per cent. From this date until 1816 the revenue never fell below 60 millions and sometimes exceeded 70.[3]

But from the breaking of the peace of Amiens until 1816 the national debt was only increased by £360,000,000; that is, a yearly increase of 25 millions. The period 1793-1802, though the expenses were much smaller,[4] had witnessed an increase in the debt of 30 millions a year. This comparatively satisfactory result was only obtained by a bold increase in taxation. Mr. Gladstone states that if the income tax had been imposed in time it would have saved the nation from these enormous loans, since the annual expenditure except for the interest on the debt, might have been

[1] p. 1474.

[2] These taxes afford an interesting study from the fiscal point of view. They were taxes on luxury, sumptuary taxes. Compare Stourm, *Systèmes Généraux d'impôts*, p. 95, and Leroy-Beaulieu, *Sciences des Finances*, Vol. I., p. 429.

[3] From 1793 to 1797 the yearly revenue averaged £17,500,000.

[4] The increased expenditure was mainly owing to the very expensive wars with Spain.

covered during the later years by the returns from taxation.

But even if we assume that all the excuses made for Pitt are justified;—if we admit, as we did at the outset, that Pitt was not wrong to send subsidies to the allies; if we admit that he could not issue loans under more favourable conditions than those forced upon him by circumstances; even if we admit, what is very doubtful, that Pitt could not have relied more than he did on taxation—he yet made three mistakes which are inexcusable. These are, the continuance of the Sinking Fund, his forecast as to the duration of the war, and his treatment of the Bank; and all three, especially the last, are unworthy of a great[1] statesman.

For the present we will confine ourselves to a consideration of the two first of these mistakes, the third will occupy the following chapter.

The Sinking Fund.[2] "The sinking fund established by Mr. Pitt," says Gladstone, "was another form of mischief. By means of the sinking fund you were continually buying up stock at 3, 4, or 5 per cent. below the rate at which you were simultaneously creating stock in order to find the money to make the purchase. You were buying stock to reduce it at 60, and creating it again sometimes as high as 68. Thus what the 'heaven-born policy' did was to re-establish the patient by putting a seton into the body; for this process was nothing but a perpetual drain upon the resources of the country."

Lord Grenville, Pitt's cousin, has tried to exonerate him[3] by pointing out that the nation accepted the sinking fund almost without consideration and with unlimited belief in what was regarded as an all-powerful remedy. This being so he concludes that "It can be no reproach to any individual to have partaken largely in these feelings, and least of all to that able and excellent statesman who carried

[1] We express our own firm conviction, but, as we have already pointed out, the subject is so difficult and involved that we do not maintain that our opinion is the right one.

[2] See also McCulloch and Rickards, *op. cit.*

[3] *Essay on the supposed advantages of a Sinking Fund* (1828). The author himself, however, condemns the policy.

through the Act of 1786." To which it may be replied that Pitt's mistake was not excused by the fact, if it be one, that he only believed in the sinking fund because the public looked upon it as a universal remedy.

Hamilton's criticisms[1] in 1813, and Ricardo's seven years[2] later, showed plainly the fallacies involved in this invention, and the sinking fund as a special institution was abandoned in 1829.[3]

False judgments as to the duration of the war and the strength of the enemy. Pitt was confronted by a vigorous though small Opposition, led by men who may indeed have made mistakes, and who, in my opinion, were too ready to remember that the government of their country was in the hands of their political opponents, but who exercised a real influence over the House by their eloquence and remarkable controversial skill. The Opposition speakers, whose names are preserved in history, pointed out untiringly that the war was unjust, that it would be long and unprofitable and that it would bring about the ruin of the country. The uninterrupted victories of the Republican armies and the disloyal behaviour of some of the allies provided them daily with fresh arguments. Pitt endeavoured not to disgust the country by increased taxation and to pacify the House by describing the war as necessarily of short duration, because France had exhausted her resources and was "on the verge, nay, in the gulf of bankruptcy."[4] This was one of his favourite arguments; he was always referring to the assignats and to the condition of the Republican finances.

[1] *Inquiry into the Rise and Progress, the Redemption and the Management of the National Debt.*

[2] *Essay on the Funding System.*

[3] The idea of paying off the debt did not however perish. Conversions and purchases in various forms have appreciably reduced the national debt under a wise, patriotic and far-sighted administration. Amongst the measures used, that of terminable annuities was imitated in France by M. Caillaux. When the South African War broke out (Autumn, 1899) the national debt had been reduced to 625 millions.

[4] This phrase served as a motto to a reply to Pitt's statements, written at Paris in 1696 by Tom Paine, and called *The Decline and Fall of the English System of Finance.*

It may be acknowledged that Pitt was sincere in what he said: and it is comprehensible that at first he may easily have flattered himself into the idea that the war would be short and that the chaotic state of the French Government would prevent its carrying on a vigorous campaign. But how long could he have kept up this illusion? How could a statesman such as he have cherished these ideas after the battle of Fleurus?[1] and when he could no longer reasonably believe them, was it loyal, in Fox's[2] picturesque phrase, to "amuse" the country "with his ideas on the finances of France," with calculations as to the *assignats* and the French bankruptcy, when he was himself leading the way to an inconvertible currency and to the verge of a similar bankruptcy.[3]

[1] Even in October, 1795, he wrote to Addington that peace would be made before Easter.

[2] See Fox's speech on the occasion of the suspension of cash payments, an analysis of which is given below. See also Sheridan's speech on the same occasion. "Surely it was not for want of warning. The Marquess of Lansdowne and several other enlightened senators in both Houses of Parliament predicted the approach of this melancholy event. Mr. Pitt was so busy on the calculation and depreciation of French *assignats* and *mandats* that he had not time, it is presumed, to attend to our own *immaculate* paper credit, as Lord Grenville, that luminous statesman, called it about two years ago." —(See *The History of the Bank of England,* etc., 1797, p. 105).

[3] Pitt's apologists (see Newmarch, p. 23), emphasise the fact that these illusions were shared by the majority of the nation and that traces of them are found in Burke's last work, *Letters on a Regicide Peace,* published at the end of 1796. As regards Burke, his opinion here is of little value. He had taken too important a part in the declaration of war against France to acknowledge his mistake openly, and, moreover, some doubts must have survived amidst the reasons which induced this champion of liberalism to write the *Reflections on the Revolution in France.* As to the fact that Pitt shared in a general delusion, it is of this especially that I complain. This "heaven-born minister"—to use the phrase quoted by Gladstone—had sufficient genius to enable him, in this matter as in that of the Sinking Fund, to form his own opinion; he ought not to have been reduced, like any ordinary politician, to accept the errors of his contemporaries.

CHAPTER III.

THE CRISES OF 1793 AND 1797.—THE BANK RESTRICTION ACT.—THE SUSPENSION OF CASH PAYMENTS BY THE BANK.

Crisis of 1793. Crisis of 1797. Pitt's unwise treatment of the Bank. Advances to Government forbidden by the Bank Charter. Modification of this. Incessant loans from 1793 to 1797. Exportation and drain of specie. Disturbances among the Country Banks, Panic due to the landing of a handful of French Troops. Policy of the Bank directors. Suspension of cash payments. Decision of the Privy Council. Message from the King to Parliament. Position of the Bank and parliamentary debates. The Bank Restriction Act.

A.—Crisis of 1793.

THE war began under gloomy auspices. The harvest in 1792 was very bad, as were most of the harvests between 1789 and 1802, the price of corn had risen 13s., and in addition to the agricultural distress, a serious economic crisis occurred just before the declaration of war.[1] This declaration, however much it may have been expected, gave the last blow to the tottering public credit. "In the month of November this year," says Macpherson,[2] "there were no fewer than *one hundred and five bankruptcies*. There were very few months in all the years preceding 1792 wherein the gazette . . . has exhibited above the half of that number." But this was only the beginning. On February 19, the Bank refused the paper of Lane, Son & Fraser, who suspended payment the next day, leaving a deficit of a million. This failure was followed by several others and the numbers continued to increase during the succeeding months.[3]

Failures among the country banks occurred almost simultaneously. The crisis began at Newcastle, where the

[1] Tooke (*History of Prices*, Vol. I., pp. 176-177) seems to me to minimise unduly the importance of the declaration of war. Baring, *op. cit.*, p. 19, gives a juster account.

[2] *Annals of Commerce*, Vol. IV., p. 254.

[3] There were 105 in March, 188 in April, 209 in May; then they declined to 158 in June and 108 in July.

banks stopped payment after an unexpected run although the shareholders had adequate resources to meet all demands.

The evil spread throughout the provinces, where credit facilities, as we have said, were very badly organised. The country banks mis-managed their issues, and although they were not all ruined, their credit was severely shaken. Distrust prevailed both in the capital and in the provinces; no money could be borrowed on the shares of industrial undertakings or canals and still less could loans be raised without security. The Bank itself gave way to alarms which Sir Francis Baring[1] condemns as ill-founded, contracted its issues, raised its rate of discount and looked on unmoved at the rapidly increasing number of failures going on around it.[2]

Matters became urgent, the more so because the evil had spread to Scotland and one of the directors of the Royal Bank of Scotland had come to London to request assistance, declaring that unless the Government gave immediate help there would be a general bankruptcy.

At the suggestion of Sir John Sinclair and after a meeting of the City merchants to consider the situation, Pitt agreed to advance £5,000,000 in Exchequer bills to the merchants upon the security of commodities of all kinds. The House passed the scheme, in spite of the somewhat short-sighted opposition of Fox[3] and Grey. The remedy was so effective that, as soon as the vote was known, £70,000 were sent to Manchester and Glasgow. This had excellent

[1] For all this crisis see Baring, *op. cit.*, pp. 15-35.

[2] According to Tooke (p. 193, note) the number of bankruptcies in 1793, compared with those in the two previous years, was as follows:—

1793—1,956 failures, of which 26 were country banks.
1792— 934 failures, of which 1 was a country bank.
1791— 769 failures, of which 1 was a country bank.

[3] Fox declared that the proceeding involved a violation of the Constitution (p. 757), and placed unsuitable and excessive powers in the hands of the executive (see his speech in *Parl. Hist.*, Vol. XXX., pp. 755-788). At bottom Fox's speeches are spoilt by his habit of condemning all measures, whether good or bad, which were proposed by the Government. A little more impartiality and a more serious study of the questions on hand would have improved his orations, which from many points of view were masterpieces. Fox's speeches were published in 1815 in six volumes, but this edition is incomplete and defective.

results in a crisis caused partly by lack of sufficient currency and partly by the general want of confidence. The feeling that credit could be obtained was enough to calm people's fears and to prevent many from actually asking for it. As Macpherson says: "The very first intimation of the intention of the legislature to support the merchants, operated all over the country like a charm, and in a degree superseded the necessity of the relief, by an almost instantaneous restoration of mercantile confidence."

It was not found actually necessary to advance the whole of the five millions voted by Parliament. There were 338 requests for £3,855,624; 238 of these were granted, the total amount advanced being £2,202,200. Of the other demands, 49 were refused and the rest were withdrawn by the applicants themselves. Far from losing by this transaction, the State made a net profit of £4,348; only two of the borrowers went bankrupt and some of the others repaid their debts before they fell due.

B.—Crisis of 1797.

Sir Francis Baring[1] and Mr. Tooke[2] are agreed that nothing could be more satisfactory than the economic condition of the country during 1794 and part of 1795. Both also recognise that the difficulties which ended in the catastrophe of 1797 began during the second half of 1795.

The quiet, the confidence and the general prosperity were, Baring states, so extraordinary during this period,

[1] p. 43.

[2] pp. 178-179 and 192-211. Tooke reckons the crisis as beginning rather earlier than Baring does. He considers that owing to the exceptionally hard winter of 1794-5, fears were felt even in the following spring with regard to the coming harvest, and prices rose very quickly. In the succeeding autumn the situation became so strained that the King drew the attention of Parliament to it in the following words: "I have observed for some time past with the greatest anxiety the very high price of grain, and that anxiety is increased by the apprehension that the produce of the wheat harvest in the present year may not have been such an effectual one to relieve my people from the difficulties with which they have to contend" (Speech of October 29, 1795).

Several remedies were suggested, the principal one being to offer bounties on importation until a certain quantity of corn had been brought in. Amongst minor proposals one is rather curious: the Members of Parliament agreed to reduce the consumption of wheat in their houses by one-third, and to urge all their friends to do the same.

that it was difficult to get 4 per cent. for money. The country was about to pass suddenly from abundance to scarcity, from scarcity to famine, and from famine to bankruptcy.

On February 27, 1797, the Bank stopped its cash payments. What were the causes of this suspension?

According to Baring[1] they were as follows:—

1.—Disorders among the country banks and in the paper circulation in the provinces, which produced a crisis similar to that of 1793.

2.—The general alarm due to a French invasion.

3.—The excessive exportation of bullion or coin to the Continent.

4.—The unwise influence of the Government.

Changing the order adopted by Baring, we will begin by studying together causes 3 and 4, which are closely connected. We shall then examine causes 1 and 2 in the same way.

SECTION I.[2]

THE UNWISE INFLUENCE OF THE GOVERNMENT.—PITT'S DISLOYAL BEHAVIOUR.—THE EXPORTATION AND DRAIN OF SPECIE.

"The enormous abuses," says Macleod,[3] "which might be perpetrated by an unscrupulous Government, and the dangerous power which so potent an engine as the Bank of England would confer upon them, had been clearly foreseen by its antagonists at the time of its foundation. We have seen that stringent precautions were taken in the first Act of 1694 to prevent the Bank making any advances to Government without the express permission of Parliament.[4] It had been the custom, however, time out of mind, to advance for the amount of such Treasury bills of exchange as were made payable at the Bank." These advances amounted to twenty or thirty thousand pounds; complaints were made if they reached fifty thousand. This limit was

[1] p. 65.
[2] For this Section see Macleod (5th edition), Vol. I., p. 516, *et seq.*
[3] Vol. I., p. 445. 5th edition, pp. 516, 517.
[4] See above, p. 69.

greatly exceeded during the American war, and sometimes £150,000 was advanced. The legality of these proceedings seemed doubtful to Bosanquet, the governor of the Bank, who discussed the matter with the directors; it was agreed to apply to the Government for a bill of indemnity for the past and for authority to continue these transactions in the future, but only on condition that they were kept within a fixed limit. This limit was to be £50,000—£100,000. Bosanquet went out of office at this time and could not continue the negotiations, but Pitt was too clever not to see at once what immense powers would be given to the Government by an Act of this kind. He therefore hurried the Bill through Parliament, but was careful to omit the limiting clause.[1]

No government had ever had such a formidable weapon placed in its hands. The Act allowed the Bank to be drawn upon without any restriction, for the directors dared not dishonour the Government drafts. Henceforward the Bank was completely at Pitt's mercy and he made large demands on the resources thus placed at his disposal.[2]

[1] Statute 1793, c. 32.

[2] See an analysis of the sums advanced to the Government according to the official documents laid before the House of Commons at the request of Tierney (*History of the Bank of England*, p. 110). *Bank of England, 9 March, 1797. An account of the amount of Money advanced for the public service by the Bank of England and outstanding on the 25th of February, 1797.*

Advances on the Land Tax—1794	£141,000
1795	312,000
1796	1,624,000
1797	2,000,000
Total	£4,077,000
On the Malt Tax—1794	£196,000
1795	158,000
1796	750,000
1797	750,000
Total	£1,854,000
Consols in 1796	1,323,000
Vote of credit for 2½ millions in 1796	821,400
Total	£2,144,400
General Total	£8,075,400

To this total of £8,075,400 must be added the advances without interest made on Exchequer Bills to the amount of £376,739, and on Treasury Bills to the amount of £1,512,274. This raises the total advanced by the Bank in four years to £9,964,413.

At about this time the English Government began to send subsidies to the Continental powers. And as we have explained, these were not the only sums remitted abroad. For various purposes £2,715,232 was exported in 1793; £8,335,592 in 1794; £11,040,236 in 1795. To which must be added £4,702,818 sent abroad for naval expenses.[1] These enormous payments had the effect of making the exchange adverse and caused great anxiety at the Bank. At the very time when this withdrawal of bullion was going on the Treasury bills were increased to an unheard-of extent, and the demands made by the commercial world were equally pressing.

On December 11, 1794, the directors, seeing that things were getting worse and worse, remonstrated with Pitt. In January, 1795, when they heard that a foreign loan and a home loan were about to be raised, they declared that the Treasury could not expect further assistance from them, and that in particular, they could not allow the advances on the Treasury bills to exceed £500,000. Pitt promised all they asked, then pretended that he had forgotten his promise in the stress of business, and finally, instead of keeping it, he asked in August for a fresh advance of 2 millions. He even began by demanding 2½ millions.

The exchange began to fall rapidly at the end of 1794, and in May, 1795, it was so unfavourable that specie point was reached.[2] The only way to counteract this adverse tendency would have been to reduce the issue of Bank notes. Instead of this, the Bank, worried by Pitt's demands, fell into the mistake of increasing the issue by issuing notes for £5, £10 having hitherto been the lowest value issued.

[1] Tooke, p. 208. In 1796 the exportations were £10,649,916; these figures are quoted by Tooke from the Appendices Nos. 23 and 27 of the Report to the House of Lords.

[2] Sir F. Baring (p. 49) shows that the profit on sending gold from London to Hamburg was 7½ per cent. in January, 1796, 6¼ per cent. in February, and 8¾ per cent. in March. After that, thanks to good harvests, the exchange was once more favourable until February, 1800.

On this question see Sir John Sinclair, *Letters written to the Governor and Directors of the Bank of England in September, 1796.* The author suggests four remedies:—

1.—An increase in the capital of the Bank. A remedy used on various occasions.

2.—The issue of £2 or £3 notes.

3.—The issue, with the authorisation of Government, of a million Bank notes, inconvertible for one year. These notes would circulate without dis-

In August, 1794, the total circulation did not exceed 10 millions; in February, 1795, it rose to 14 millions. The drain of coin began to take full effect in the autumn of 1795; the reserve declined more and more. The Bank directors saw that all their measures were unavailing and that they must choose between their own bankruptcy and that of the Government. Consequently in a resolution of December 31, 1795, it was announced that the sum to be employed in discounts should be fixed for each day in advance. Any excess in the demands was to be dealt with by returning "a *pro rata* proportion of such bills in each parcel as are not otherwise objectionable . . . without regard to the respectability of the party sending in the bills or the solidity of the bills themselves."[1]

count, in consequence of an agreement with the different merchants whose bills the Bank discounted.

These three measures would tend to increase the circulating medium.

4.—An alteration in the coinage: since "while we continue to make our gold coin so much finer than that of other nations, and almost give a bonus to the smelter by demanding nothing for the expence of the manufacture, it is impossible that our coin should not either be exported abroad or smelted down at home."

Sir John Sinclair proposed in fact to alter the coinage "by mixing a greater proportion of alloy," and this supplies the subject matter of the second of the two letters of which his pamphlet consists.

[1] See the text of the declaration in Tooke, p. 200, note. The policy of the Bank, combined with the restriction of issues and the high profits resulting from the export of precious metals, produced a great scarcity in the circulating medium and caused much protest in the commercial world. On April 2 there was a large gathering of merchants at the London Tavern; the meeting passed a resolution stating that the scarcity of coin was due to the increase of trade, and in particular, to the measures taken by the Bank. A committee was appointed to find a means of increasing the circulating medium without violating the Bank's charter. See for this incident Thornton, pp. 87-89, and especially a pamphlet by W. Boyd, the secretary to the committee, *Letter to the Honourable W. Pitt on the Influence of the Stoppage of Issues in Specie at the Bank of England* (1801), in particular pp. 86-102 of the edition of 1811, revised and corrected by the author. Mr. Boyd makes a long report, suggesting that Parliament should appoint a Board, consisting of 25 of its Members, authorised to issue notes payable at six months, bearing a daily interest of 1¼d. per £100, and exchangeable for gold or silver or for bills of exchange due in less than three months. This scheme was submitted to the Chancellor of the Exchequer. He replied that the Bank had already suggested a remedy, the consolidation of the floating debt, which would be tried before the proposal of the committee. Mr. Boyd adds (p. 102) that the floating debt was funded by means of a loan of £7,500,000 raised on very liberal terms, after the subscribers had been led to understand that there was going to be an entire change in the policy of the Bank. The distress in May, 1795, shows how this promise was kept.

Sir Francis Baring devotes a short pamphlet to a criticism of Boyd's scheme, *Observations on the Publication of W. Boyd, Esq., M.P.*

This resolution ought to have restrained the demands of the Government, but it proved insufficient to curb the Prime Minister's rapacity. Pitt had never carried out his repeated promises to reduce the advances on Treasury bills to £500,000; on June 14, 1796, the total of the advances was £1,232,649. He demanded £800,000 at the end of July and a like sum in August. The directors were induced to grant the first, but refused the second. Pitt said that the one was useless to him without the other and invited them to revoke their decision. This they did after indulging in some platonic remonstrances.

In November Pitt proffered a new request for £2,750,000 on the security of certain taxes. This was granted on condition that the advances on the Treasury bills, which now amounted to £1,513,345, should be repaid. Pitt secured the money, but was careful not to redeem the bills. Then he returned to the attack and asked for fresh advances, intended for San Domingo and Ireland. The sum needed for Ireland was at first to be only £200,000, but in the end it amounted to £1,750,000.

SECTION II.

THE DISORDERS AMONG THE COUNTRY BANKS AND THE SCARE OF A FRENCH INVASION WHICH LED TO AN ACTUAL PANIC.

Henry Thornton calculates that after the crisis of 1793, the issues of the provincial banks had been decreased by one-half, and he adds that the requirements of trade had attracted an enormous quantity of money to counteract this decrease. At the same time although the exchange was now favourable, the Bank of England continued to restrict its issues. During the three last months of 1796 they did not exceed those of 1782, although the total of commercial payments made was several times greater than the total in that year. The payments had to be made whatever happened and for want of paper money they were made in coin, so that calls were constantly made on the reserve, which fell from £2,972,000 in March, 1796, to £2,502,008 in December of the same year, when a serious withdrawal of bullion began.

At the beginning of 1797 the political situation was worse than ever. The country banks, scenting the storm, took precautions and tried to withdraw as much coin as possible from London. This helped still further to diminish the reserve.[1]

An occurrence of but small importance strategically produced a definite crisis. The landing of a handful of French troops, says Baring,[2] caused a general alarm, which showed itself chiefly in a demand for coined money, even bullion being refused. All ranks of society were seized with panic: traders, artisans and especially women and farmers, all wanted guineas merely in order to conceal them.

C.—The Bank Directors' share of responsibility in the Suspension of Cash Payments.

These, then, are the four causes enumerated by Baring as having led to the suspension of cash payments. Baring refrained from criticising the behaviour of the directors. What must be thought of this? The directors denied all share in the suspension and threw the whole responsibility on the Government, which had reduced them to this extremity by its excessive demands. They declared that if the Government had repaid them they would have had no hesitation in assisting the commercial world, and of this there seems to be no doubt. But many contemporary writers[3] allege that even the advances made to the Government should not have prevented the Bank from continuing its issues and helping commerce. Ultimately, then, it is upon this point that the matter turns, and good arguments are not wanting to those who adopt this adverse view. They point out that the undue restriction of issues caused an

[1] A very vivid description of the crisis of 1797, and in particular of its vicissitudes in Scotland, is given by Sir William Forbes in his *Memoirs of a Banking House.* These memoirs were not published until 1860 by Robert Chambers, although Sir William had died fifty years before and deserved the title given him by Stephens, p. 93, of the Evelyn of the Bank.

[2] Baring, pp. 45-54.

[3] See especially Thornton, Chap. iv., pp. 172-210 of McCulloch's reprint.

unusual demand for guineas, that in consequence, the provincial notes were discredited, and that the Bank took no steps to supply the gap left by the disappearance of the notes.[1]

Moreover this contraction had caused the forced sale and the consequent depreciation of the public stock, which would have been avoided if only the Bank had kept up its issues to the level of 1795. Finally, it was stated that when the exchange was most unfavourable and it was profitable to export gold, the directors had issued notes to the value of £14,000,000, and that, on the contrary, they had reduced their issues to £8,640,225 when the exchange had been favourable for several months. To put the matter briefly, the contraction of the issues had largely contributed to empty the coffers of the Bank during the autumn of 1796, when an extension of issue would have helped to replenish them.[2]

The Bullion Report adopted this opinion, which was in fact the development of the Expansive theory set forth by Bosanquet in 1783, and together with most of the contemporary authors, it condemned the Restrictive theory put into practice by the directors.

It thus seems evident that the Bank had a large share of responsibility in the crisis of 1797 and this was acknowledged by the directors themselves before the Committee of 1810. But, as Macleod[3] very clearly points out, it may be asked whether any administration, however wise and prudent, could have avoided the suspension of cash payments—a measure which Robert Peel in 1844 described as "fatal." Macleod is driven to believe that it was fortunate that the suspension occurred at this time, since later on the situation became still worse. The Irish rebellion and the naval mutiny joined with the permanent risk of an invasion to produce such an alarming combination, that a convertible paper currency would have had small chance of surviving. Finally, "the constant power of producing public em-

[1] See above, Chap. i., Part III., pp. 170 and 171, what we have said as to the bad organisation of provincial credit.

[2] Macleod, 3rd Edition, Vol. I., p. 461 (5th Edition, p. 533).

[3] pp. 461-463.

barrassment by demands for gold" would have been a powerful weapon in the hands of enemies who would have been supported in England by political sympathies.

The measure thus removed a perpetual source of alarm, and the extreme depreciation of the notes which took place some years later was in no sense a necessary result of the suspension, but was entirely due to a surprising want of foresight on the part of the Government and of the Bank directors. The suspension of payments was inevitable, and it was better for the country that it occurred before the great disasters.

D.—Suspension of Cash Payments.—The Act of Restriction.

The crisis began with the failure of the Newcastle banks on February 20th, 1797. The news quickly reached London and from this moment the events followed one another in rapid succession. The reserve of the Bank was reduced on February 25th to £1,272,000. The Bank had also considerably decreased its issues; they were reduced from £10,550,830 (January 21) to £8,640,000 (February 25). This only gives an inadequate idea of the decrease in the paper currency, for it must be remembered that the private banks were forced to imitate the Bank of England's example. Several of them were obliged to make enormous sacrifices to meet the demands on them, and to sell securities at a considerable loss. The 3 per cents. were at 51 and the other funds fell in a similar manner.

The fatal hour had come: the suspension of cash payments was not to be averted. The directors of the Bank applied to Pitt for advice and assistance. Pitt induced the King to preside at the council meeting summoned to consider the situation. The council unanimously agreed[1] that the Bank should be forbidden to make any payment in cash until Parliament should have decided on the policy to be adopted.

[1] See this order of Feb 26 in *Parl. Hist.*, Vol. XXXII., p. 1518.

The Bank, when it stopped cash payments on February 27, 1797, published[1] a statement that the satisfactory and prosperous condition of its affairs was such as might remove all doubts as to its solvency. At the same time, what was more important, a large meeting of well-known financiers and bankers passed a resolution undertaking to accept Bank notes in payment of sums due to them. This resolution was supported by four thousand signatures, including all the names of any importance in the City.

The King thought fit to announce the unprecedented event to the Commons in a Royal Message.[2] Pitt communicated this message to the House[3] and proposed that a committee should be appointed to inquire into the position of the Bank, although as he added, he felt no doubt of the solidity of the establishment. Fox replied in a rather dull speech[4] and Sheridan[5] in a violent oration, but neither opposed the nomination of the committee.

The discussion was resumed on the question of the reply to be given to the message and this gave Fox an opportunity to make a magnificent speech,[6] which, however, suggested no remedy except the speedy conclusion of peace.

In the House of Lords the speeches of Lord Grenville, Lord Bedford and Lord Lansdowne,[7] are worthy of mention. The latter remarked that his colleagues would do him the justice to remember that he had "foretold the present

[1] This notice is given in *History of the Bank of England* (1797), p. 43.

[2] See *The King's Message respecting the unusual demand for specie.*

[3] *Parl. Hist.*, pp. 1518-1519.

[4] *Parl. Hist.*, pp. 1519-1520.

[5] *Parl. Hist.*, pp. 1520-1522.

[6] pp. 1526-1538. The following are some extracts from its conclusion: "Let us see now what has been the conduct of the present minister in the course of this war, upon the subject of finance. Have any three months passed in which he has not produced some new expedient? And have they not, every one of them without a single exception, proved erroneous?" (see also *Fox's Speeches*, Vol. VI., p. 289), and again: "The minister has conducted the war upon the hope that we should be able to defeat the French by a contest of finance, and you now see the expedients to which we are driven." "Year after year the minister has been amusing us with his ideas of the finances of France—now on the verge, now in the gulf of bankruptcy! . . . But . . . while he was thus amusing us he has led us to the very same verge, aye, into the very same gulf."

[7] pp. 1564-1568.

exigency" since 1793. He compared public credit to the soul of England: everything had been done to ruin credit, in the first instance by "the inordinate increase of expense," then by the war and the subsidies sent abroad; now the death-blow was to be struck by decreeing an inconvertible currency. "Mark my prophecy, my lords," he exclaimed in conclusion,[1] "and do not disdain the counsel while yet in time. If you attempt to make bank notes a legal tender, their credit will perish. They may go on for a time, but the consequence is certain . . . We do not speak upon conjecture, the thing is matter of experience. A fever is as much a fever in London as in Paris or Amsterdam; and the consequences of a stoppage of payment must be the same in whatever country it shall happen."

On March 3rd, the Committee of the House of Commons presented its report. It stated that "the total amount of outstanding demands on the Bank on the 25th of February last . . . was £13,770,390; and that the total amount of the funds for discharging those demands (not including the permanent debt due from Government of £11,686,800, which bears an interest of 3 per cent.) was . . . £17,597,280; and that the result is that there was . . . a surplus . . . of £3,826,898."[2]

The situation thus seemed all that could be desired, but the committee omitted to mention that out of the £17,597,280 of funds, more than ten millions had been lent to the Government, which reduced the sum immediately available to seven millions. This fact was brought out very clearly by Sheridan.[3] The speaker began by remarking that the £11,686,800 of Government debt could not be regarded as capital, since the Bank could not demand its repayment. All that should be counted was the annuity of £130,000. Moreover, he continued, it appeared that besides these eleven millions, the Bank had advanced nearly ten millions for the public expenses. What was, then, its position?

[1] Vol. XXXII., p. 1567.

[2] See this report in *Parl. Hist.*, Vol. XXXIII., pp. 25-26, and the report presented in the name of the Committee of the House of Lords by the Earl of Chatham, Pitt's elder brother, which supports this conclusion, *Ibid.*, pp. 26-29.

[3] pp. 34-37, Vol. XXXIII.

Its debts amounted to only 13 millions, 10 millions of which stood to the account of a single debtor, and the debtor was most generously offering support. Suppose a merchant, owing in all £13,000, and with a sum of £10,000 due to him from one man, "would not that merchant think it very extraordinary conduct in that man if he should say, 'Sir, I understand that your affairs are in a ticklish way, let me make an inquiry into them, and if . . . I discover that you have wherewithal in due time to . . . discharge your debts, I will not say that I may not guarantee them for you.' . . . The gentleman would say, 'Why do you not pay me the money you owe me, . . . and then I may be able to satisfy every demand without your interference.'"

With regard to bankers, Sheridan inquired, "What are the bankers? The stewards and guardians of their constituents. What consolation will it be to those creditors to hear that those stewards lent this money to the minister, and that the minister lent a considerable portion of it to the emperor, and that the emperor gave it to his soldiers, and that these soldiers are killed off?"[1]

Warnings, Sheridan repeated, had not been wanting, but "Mr. Pitt, indeed, was so busy in the calculation and depreciation of French *assignats* and *mandats*, that he had not time, it is presumed, to attend to our own *immaculate* paper credit, as Lord Grenville, that luminous statesman, called it, about two years ago."[2]

These Parliamentary criticisms[3] were followed by a series of epigrams[4] and puns similar to those aimed at Law and the

[1] See *History of the Bank of England, etc.*, (1797), p. 106.

[2] *Loc. cit.*, p. 105.

[3] *The History of the Bank of England*, published in 1797, may be profitably consulted. This work, written directly after the suspension of cash payments by an ardent supporter of Fox and Sheridan, gives a good summary of the opinions of the Liberal Opposition on the crisis, with which it is almost entirely occupied.

[4] Lord Stanhope has preserved the following, which was much in vogue :—

"Of Augustus and Rome
The Poets still warble,
How he found it of brick
And left it of marble.
So of Pitt and England
Men say without vapour
That he found it of gold
And left it of paper."

According to the author of *The Life of Pitt*, this is only a rhyming version

assignats, and such as are the usual accompaniment of financial disasters.

But neither speeches nor epigrams prevented the passing on May 3 of the Bank Restriction Act, as it is generally called. Its chief provisions were as follows[1] :—

1.—A clause of indemnity was granted to the Bank and all persons connected with it, for anything done in pursuance of the Order in Council.

2.—The Bank was forbidden to make any payments in cash to any creditors, or to use cash for any payments except to the Army and Navy, or in pursuance of an order from the Privy Council.

3.—The Bank might make no advance above £600,000 for the public service, in cash or notes, during the restriction.

4.—If anyone deposited a sum not less than £500 in gold at the Bank, he might be repaid three-fourths of this amount.

5.—The payment of debts in Bank notes was to be deemed as payment in cash, if offered and accepted as such.

6.—No debtor could be held to special bail unless the affidavit stated that payment in bank notes had not been offered.

7.—Bank notes were to be received at par by all public offices in payment of taxes.

8.—The Act was to remain in force until the 24th of June following.

Finally, an Act dated May 1st and intended to remedy the scarcity of currency, suspended the Statute 1775, c. 51., which restricted the circulation of Bank notes of low values.

In a few days the Bank had arranged for the preparation and issue of £1 and £2 notes. To meet the demand for

of an epigram which had previously appeared in a Society journal.

These verses recall those written in France three or four years earlier :—

"Ah! le bon billet qu'a la Châtre!
Disait Ninon d'un air folâtre
Dans ses ébats
Gardez-vous, détracteurs frivoles,
D'appliquer jamais ces paroles
Aux assignats."

[1] See Macleod (5th edition), Vol. I., pp. 529, 530.

small money, the directors announced that they had obtained a large quantity of Spanish dollars valued at 4s. 6d.[1]

In short, it may be said that the Act of 1797 allowed the Bank not to cash its notes and gave these notes a highly privileged position, but did not make them legal tender and left people free to refuse payments not made in cash.

By a curious coincidence, at the very moment when the Bank Restriction Act was passed in England, the system of *assignats* collapsed in France, and the *mandats* which succeeded them were destined shortly to disappear also.

[1] It was discovered later that they were really worth 2d. more, and their current price was increased by 3d. This left a profit of 1d. per dollar, and the goldsmiths began to manufacture them; they issued dollars so like those of the Bank that the latter could not distinguish them and was obliged to accept both kinds.

In order to naturalise these coins, a little head of George III.,was stamped over the image of Ferdinand, King of Spain. This inspired the following severe but just lampoon :—

"The Bank to make their Spanish dollars current pass,
Stamped the head of a fool on the head of an ass."

—See Lawson, *History of Banking*, p. 104.

CHAPTER IV.

RESULTS OF THE BANK RESTRICTION ACT.

Results of the Act between 1797 and 1808. Pitt's caution. Prevailing errors on the subject. Increase in the issues and in the advances to Government. Results of the Act in reference to Economic theories. Parliamentary debates. Theory stated by Addington. Speeches of Fox and Lord King. The economists and the influence of excessive issues on the foreign exchanges and the price of gold. Crisis of 1800. State of public opinion. Theories of Walter Boyd, Thornton, Lord King and Ricardo on the depreciation of a paper currency. Monetary crisis in Ireland. Parliamentary inquiry. Opinion held by the Directors of the Bank of Ireland. Report of the Committee.

SUCH was the Bank Restriction Act. It has been credited with producing important and even extraordinary results.

It has been stated that England owed to it those immense resources which enabled it to carry on and to conclude successfully the greatest of modern wars; that it was owing to the paper currency that Pitt and his colleagues were able to raise those loans which amazed the world; that to the paper money, also, various other advantages must be attributed; that in short, by passing the Restriction Act the English Government had discovered the philosopher's stone for which the alchemists of the Middle Ages had searched in vain.

These opinions spread rapidly. The debates on the Bullion Report of 1810 will enable us to show that the majority in Parliament believed them firmly. Since then the doctrine has been continually revived, and even as late as 1861, after the Act of 1819, after the publications of Tooke and Macleod, an author of Lord Stanhope's reputation, in a book which is regarded in England as the standard life of Pitt,[1] could write as follows:[2]

"It must be observed, however, that so long as the war

[1] This appreciation is sufficiently accurate to give a somewhat depressing idea of the other books devoted to this subject and of the condition of historical study in England. It is much to be regretted that Lord Rosebery's work did not exceed the narrow limits of an essay.

[2] *Op. cit.*, Vol. III., p. 21.

continued, the system of inconvertible paper money did good service in England. Expanding precisely in proportion to the exigencies of the public service, and supported by an undeviating reliance on the national good faith, it enabled us, as certainly no other system could, to raise year by year loans of unparalleled amount; to transmit repeated subsidies to Foreign Powers in alliance with us; and to bear, without sinking beneath it, the burthen of accumulated taxes. It was, in short, a gigantic system of paper credit, giving us power to cope with no less gigantic foes."

In our sketch of the condition of England at the end of the 18th century we stated, basing our opinion upon undisputable authorities, that England's success in withstanding the onslaught of the revolutionary armies, and the final defeat of Napoleon were less due to the genius of her sailors, of Wellington and of Pitt, than to that of Brindley, Watt and Arkwright. It was owing to the remarkable stimulus given by these great men to her industry and commerce that Great Britain was able to raise such immense loans, to keep Europe in her pay, to maintain her armies and fleets and to endure steadfastly until it pleased fortune to favour her arms. We shall proceed to show that Pitt, who supported the Restriction Act from necessity alone,[1] did not make such use of it as his clumsy admirers have alleged; and that as soon as his successors began to follow this policy, and the Bank directors, with extraordinary blindness, took advantage of their exemption from cash payments to make over-issues, England, instead of reaping any benefit from their action, found herself involved in endless difficulties—difficulties which, had it not been for the Russian campaign, must have brought disaster on the United Kingdom, and from whose effects the public suffered long after the conclusion of peace.

Our study of the effects of the Restriction Act will be divided into two parts: the first including the last years of Pitt's ministry and extending, strictly speaking, up to

[1] Lord Grenville said during the discussion on the Stanhope Bill (1811), that the day when Pitt was forced to propose the restriction was one of the most painful in his life. See below, p. 236, note 3.

1809;[1] the second dealing with the period from 1809 to 1819.

During the first period the privilege conceded by the Act of 1797 was used by both the Government and the Bank with the utmost prudence. The inconveniences of the suspension of cash payments were not at first great, but they were beginning to make themselves felt and to attract the attention of able men, who from this time onwards tried to define the rules and conditions of a healthy paper currency.

The second period will show the effects of those over-issues to which some have attributed England's salvation. The disastrous results, of which warning signs could be detected as early as 1801, definitely drew public attention to the problem of the circulation. They gave rise to a discussion which was the first, and is still perhaps the most famous of the great monetary controversies in the 19th century. The study of this celebrated controversy, which centred round the Bullion Report, will form the subject of the next chapter. For the present we shall deal with the first period only.

When the Restriction Act was passed, the exchanges were so favourable that gold was being imported in considerable quantities. On May 30th, Mr. Manning informed the House of Commons that very large quantities of gold had come in to the Bank both from at home and abroad. The Government and the directors were however agreed that it would be unwise to resume cash payments just at the time when the Restriction Act expired, and the Act was accordingly continued until a month after the beginning of the next session.

Parliament met on November 2nd. On the 15th the House of Commons appointed a committee to consider the

[1] We may notice here three French books which appeared about this time, and which are, I believe, the first French works dealing with the Bank of England.

1.—J. H. Marnière (1801), *Essai sur le crédit commercial*. The author describes the Banks of Genoa and of England.

2.—*Considérations sur la facilité d'établir à Paris une banque égale à celle de Londres* (1802), by the same author.

3.—J. H. Lassale, *Des finances d'Angleterre* (1803). A consideration of the results of the Restriction Act, and a discussion on the burden of the taxes; the book is full of political discussion.

question, and the report of this committee, presented on the 17th, stated that on the 11th the total liabilities of the Bank amounted to £17,578,910, and the assets to £21,418,460, leaving a favourable balance of £3,839,550 without counting the Government debt of £11,686,800; that the advances made to the Government had been reduced to £4,258,140; whilst the stock of coin and bullion was five times greater than it had been on February 25th and much larger than it had been since September, 1795; and that the exchange on Hamburg was remarkably favourable and was to all appearances likely to continue so; that finally, and above all, the London bankers and merchants experienced no inconvenience from the Act, since, although the law allowed them to withdraw three-quarters of their deposits, they had actually withdrawn only one-sixteenth.

Notwithstanding all these statements and in spite of the directors' assertion that the Bank could resume cash payments without danger, the Government chose to keep things as they were, and a law was passed prolonging the Act until one month after a peace should be concluded.

The note issue was managed with great care: the issue in 1797 hardly exceeded by half a million that for 1796, which had been £11,030,110, and this in spite of the lack of coin for ordinary transactions.[1] In August, 1798,[2] the note circulation had increased to £10,649,550 in notes of £5 and upwards, and to £1,531,060 in notes of under £5, the total being £12,180,610.

Two years after the suspension (on February 25th, 1799), the issues amounted to £12,959,800. The metallic reserve had risen to £7,563,900; it exceeded one-third of the Bank's liabilities, which were only 21 millions, including 8 millions of deposits. This favourable state of things was maintained throughout the remainder of the year 1799.

The Charter was to expire in 1812. In 1800 the Bank secured a renewal for 21 years, reckoned from this date,

[1] The total of issues had been £13,539,160 in 1795.

[2] Tooke, p. 207. At this date the deposits amounted to £8,300,720, as against £4,891,530 in February, 1797.

i.e., until 1833, making in return a loan of 3 millions for three years without interest.[1] This sacrifice of 3 millions, drawn from the reserve, was a heavy one, in spite of the considerable profit which the Bank made from its right to a commission on the public loans subscribed at its offices. The Bank agreed to it nevertheless, because it was just then the object of vigorous attacks—made especially by Pulteney, who proposed the foundation of a national bank—and it was hence of particular importance to secure the renewal of its monopoly.

But to return to the question of the issues. On December 25th, 1799, there were £12,335,920 of notes over £5 in circulation. This total was not greatly superior to the total issues on the day of the suspension of cash payments.[2] At any rate an increase of two million pounds could have been very little use to Pitt for his European payments, and for meeting the expenses of a terrible war. The fact is that Pitt was fully conscious of the mistake he had made in misusing the Bank's credit; his was not a nature to be obstinate when once he had realised a mistake, nor to profit by the Restriction Act to obtain artificial resources. He knew too much of the disadvantages of paper money to indulge in excessive issues and thus convert the Bank of England notes into common *assignats*. Whatever his past mistakes may have been, from 1797 onwards his policy deserves nothing but praise; he made vigorous use of taxation, was not afraid of injuring his popularity by the introduction of the income tax, consolidated by successive loans a floating debt which had attained formidable proportions, and finally, arranged that the advances made by the Bank, so far from increasing after the Restriction Act, should on the contrary, be reduced.

He thus set an excellent example to his successors, and the wise policy of his later years was maintained even after

[1] At the end of this time the loan was continued for six years, but at an interest of 3 per cent.; finally the repayment was deferred until the conclusion of peace.

[2] It was actually less than the total for 1795.

his death. This was shown by Tooke in a work which has made a study of this period possible.

Tooke first of all[1] showed that after an almost negligible rise during 1802 and 1803,[2] the total issues declined again. The average for the five succeeding years was only £12,957,404, whilst from 1802 to 1803 it had been £13,450,727. The study of averages being somewhat deceptive, it is better to say that "the total of issues in 1808 was less than that in 1802,"[3] and Tooke could justly remark that the position of the Bank in February, 1808, was probably the same as if it had been paying in gold.[4]

But, what is better still, Tooke[5] showed the surprising moderation in the advances made by the Bank to the Treasury.

He proved, from some documents laid before Parliament at the repeated request of Mr. Grenfell, that the average of the Government deposits was £12,197,303[6] in 1806, and that this average varied between 11 and 12 millions for several years. But, during these same years, the average of the advances made by the Bank to the Government was rather less than 14½ millions. Hence the actual advances in cash, and likewise the actual sums employed by the Government in excess of its deposits did not much exceed 3 million pounds during the period 1804-1808.

[1] *Op. cit.*, p. 281.

[2] The years 1800 and 1801 witnessed a crisis with which we shall deal presently.

[3] The totals for the seven years are :—

1802, £13,917,977.
1803, £12,983,477.
1804, £12,621,348.
1805, £12,844,170.
1806, £12,697,352.
1807, £13,221,988.
1808, £13,402,160.

[4] Its assets were £35,239,550, of which £7,855,470 was metallic reserve; its liabilities were £30,150,820, of which £11,961,960 were deposits (Tooke, p. 281). Thus the totals of its metallic reserve and of its deposits exceeded those of 1799, although this was an exceptionally prosperous year. The metallic reserve fell to 5 millions in 1800, to 4 and 3½ millions from 1801 to 1803, then it increased again and was 6 millions in 1804, and £7,644,500 in 1805. It will be remembered that after the crisis in 1793 the reserve increased in 1794 to £6,770,000, but afterwards fell to £1,186,170 in February, 1797.

[5] pp. 286-287.

[6] In 1800 the average of deposits was £6,251,488; in 1806, £12,197,303; and during the ten years 1807-1817 it varied between 11 and 12 millions.

The advances to the Government, reckoned in yearly averages, exceeded the deposits of the Treasury:

From 1780-1784 by £4,841,000.
,, 1785-1789 ,, £2,335,000.
,, 1790-1796 ,, £5,664,000.
,, 1799-1803 ,, £5,364,009.
,, 1804-1810 ,, £4,146,000.

"This comparative smallness of the advances to Government," says Tooke,[1] "completely negatives the supposition, so commonly entertained and reasoned upon as a point beyond doubt, that the Bank was rendered, by the restriction, a mere engine in the hands of Government. . . . And whether this moderation in the amount of advances resulted exclusively from the forbearance of Government in not requiring, or from the firmness of the directors in refusing, such accommodation, it equally tends (especially when combined with the consideration of the large amount of treasure in possession of the Bank during the greater part of the restriction[2]) to strengthen the presumption that the Government and the directors of that period were sincere in the declaration that there constantly existed, on the part of both, a reference to the eventual resumption of cash payments."

It is evident how little foundation remains for the statements of those historians and economists who have tried to make out that Pitt was a more fortunate Law.

We shall soon see the results of the over-issues into which the Bank allowed itself to be drawn after this period. But first we must consider the economic theories which sprang from the Restriction Act. For notwithstanding the moderate use which the Government had made of this Act, it had had its influence upon the economic life of the country. The troubles due to it aroused the interest of the

[1] Vol. IV., p. 96. In this volume Tooke reconsiders the question rather more in detail.

[2] The amount of this reserve shows that the Bank intended to resume its cash payments, for what otherwise could have been the object of buying gold bullion at £4 the ounce, as was done during 1808?

intelligent public, and resulted in the discovery of truths whose existence had hitherto been only suspected.

Effects of the Restriction Act on economic theories. The theoretical side of the question came to be discussed in Parliament through an accidental circumstance which deserves notice. The Restriction Act should have expired in September, 1802; six months before that date the Peace of Amiens had been concluded, but although the Bank declared its readiness to resume cash payments, the Act was prolonged by the advice of Addington, the Chancellor of the Exchequer, until March, 1803. The arguments brought forward in support of this policy showed complete ignorance of the subject. Addington, in proposing the delay, based his view on the fact that the exchanges were unfavourable. He said[1]: "It cannot be necessary for me to inform the House that the rate of exchange between this country and foreign parts is disadvantageous to ourselves—that the export trade has been for some months at a stand, that while the rate of exchange is disadvantageous to us, an augmentation of the circulating cash would create a trade highly injurious to the commerce of this country. For several months past there has been a trade carried on for purchase of guineas with a view to exportation." These were the very reasons for which cash payments should have been resumed without delay. Guineas were being bought up on account of the excess of paper; the paper was declining in value compared with guineas and as a necessary result the guineas were being exported.

In spite of this the Act of Restriction was prolonged until March 1st, 1803. Naturally the exchanges did not improve in the interval, and arguing from the same principle, Addington proposed a further continuation. This he secured, and as the war broke out again shortly after, there was no further question of repealing the Act of 1797, which remained in force until 1819.

This time however the prolongation was not agreed to without discussion. Fox points out[2] that arguments of this

[1] *Parl. Hist.*, Vol. XXXVI., p. 540.
[2] See this speech in *Parl. Hist.*, Vol. XXXVI. (the last), pp. 1150-1153.

kind would logically establish it as an axiom that cash payments ought to be suspended whenever the exchanges were "so unfavourable as to leave no room to expect the importation of bullion." "Perhaps even," he went on, "it might happen that the unfavourable turn of the exchange against this country might be owing to the very restriction on the Bank. . . . In 1772, or 1773, when there was a great quantity of bad money in the country, the course of exchange was then also much against us; but when, in the room of this adulterated money good gold was substituted, the consequence was that the exchanges turned almost immediately in our favour. As long as our currency continued bad, the exchange was against us; so is it now, because paper is not much better than bad gold; or, it is attended with the same inconveniences. May it not therefore be expected, that as, in the former case, when our currency was ameliorated, the course of exchange turned in our favour, so also if the Bank now resumed its cash payments the same favourable circumstances might attend the change?"[1]

The theory thus suggested by Fox was expounded with much skill and clearness in the House of Lords by Lord King, who, a few months later,[2] gave an admirable exposition of the principles upon which a paper currency ought to be based. In his opinion,[3] "The natural and only true limit of every paper currency was the power of compelling payment in specie, . . . paper currency not convertible into specie had no rule or standard except the discretion of the persons by whom it was issued. To determine the quantity of currency necessary for circulation was in all cases a difficult and delicate problem. A very strict attention to the price of bullion, and the state of the foreign exchanges,

[1] p. 1153. This was the first time that the causes of unfavourable exchanges were set forth in the House of Commons. Fox has been much praised for his reference to the subject, and his biographers also make a point of the fact that it was he who first quoted Adam Smith in a Parliamentary debate. It is unfortunate that in the first case his statement of the truth was exceedingly hesitating, and that in the second he referred to a book which he afterwards confessed never to have read. For the second point see the *Dictionary of National Biography* under "Adam Smith."

[2] On December 13, 1803.

[3] See *Parl. Debates*, Vol. I., p. 1836.

was alone capable of affording a just criterion by which the quantity could be truly ascertained." In the present case it was evident from the derangement in the price of bullion and in the foreign exchanges that the directors had exceeded the proper limit.

The question discussed before Parliament had already attracted the notice of the public in the following way.

We know that the exchanges were favourable up to the end of 1799. The price of gold was maintained at £3 17s. 6d. an ounce. A bad harvest and some serious failures at Hamburg led to a great exportation of coin and entirely changed the situation. The price of bullion[1] rose to £4 5s. an ounce, and the exchange on Hamburg fell 14 per cent. below par, whilst the cost of transporting gold was not more than 7 per cent.

These phenomena were only to be explained by the depreciation of the currency; but at the time their cause entirely escaped the notice of the stupefied public. Macleod gives the following excellent analysis of the prevailing state of mind: "We have already seen that, in the great monetary crisis of 1696-97, it was universally acknowledged by Parliament and the most eminent merchants, that it was the bad state of the coinage which produced the great rise in the market price of bullion and the heavy fall in the foreign exchanges. . . . At that time Bank notes were not a legal tender, and the language invariably applied to them, when their current value differed from their nominal value, was that they were at a *discount*. . . . There is no trace of anyone having thought of saying that it was the notes that denoted the pound sterling, and that bullion had risen. . . . Adam Smith laid it down as a principle that any permanent difference between the market and the Mint price of bullion must be necessarily caused by the condition of the coinage itself; and Hume had observed that the exchange never could vary but little beyond the cost of the transportation of specie. . . . Such were the truths established, when a

[1] Since the export of gold coin was forbidden, gold bullion was the only means, except smuggling, of conducting transactions abroad, hence the true condition of the foreign exchanges must be estimated by its value.

metallic currency was the only one thought of, in estimating value. But at this time a new principle was introduced—there was what was substantially an inconvertible paper currency." What rules were to be applied to this new form of money?

The question did not at first arise, for "the general resolution of bankers and merchants to support the credit of the Bank, the determination of the Government to receive Bank notes in payment of taxes at their par value, and the great caution exercised by the directors during the first few years after the restriction," removed the apprehension which had been generally felt that as soon as the suspension took place the Bank notes would be depreciated, and for some time the notes circulated at par.

It was not until after the crisis of 1800 that the great truth was suspected, "that if a deterioration of the coinage produced a rise of the market price of bullion above the Mint price, and a fall in the foreign exchanges under a metallic currency, then that the opposite proposition was also necessarily true. That under a paper currency, which was only the representative of a metallic currency, if the market price of bullion . . . exceeded the Mint price, and the foreign exchanges fell beyond the cost of the transmission of specie, that excess could only arise from the depreciation of the representative of the metallic currency, and, therefore, when these circumstances occurred, they infallibly indicated that the paper currency was depreciated."[1]

It is not clear who ought to be credited with the discovery of this important truth. Walter Boyd, in his letter to Pitt,[2] was certainly the first to state it. Boyd guessed, from the effects of Pitt's policy, although the amount of the issues was kept secret, that the number of notes must have been increased; and, in actual fact, in 1801, when his pamphlet

[1] Macleod, 3rd Edition, Vol. II., pp. 2-4.

[2] *A letter to the Right Honourable W. Pitt on the influence of the stoppage of the issues in Specie*, etc., a work to which we have referred above.

appeared, this increase exceeded three millions.[1] Boyd's pamphlet served to call attention to the matter, and it was followed by the more complete works of Thornton and Lord King.[2]

A financial crisis in Ireland very soon afforded opportunity for defining and completing this theory.

Financial crisis in Ireland.[3] In spite of the fact that the exchanges were favourable to Ireland and that gold was plentiful there, the Bank of Ireland was ordered to suspend its cash payments by an Act passed by the Irish Parliament, which followed on the Act of 1797 and was prompted solely by a mania for uniformity.

The exchange at Dublin on London had always been favourable to Ireland, and this state of things continued until 1797. Then the situation suddenly changed, and a steady fall began, which was stated by Lord Archibald Hamilton[4] to coincide with an increase in the issues of the Bank of Ireland: these had been £600,000 in 1797, and were now £2,700,000.[5] Moreover there was a difference of 10 per cent. in the exchanges at Dublin and Belfast, which were only 100 miles apart, and the exchange on London was 20 per cent. against Dublin. At the same time, the price of gold rose, and guineas could only be bought at a premium of 2s. 6d.

A committee was appointed to inquire into the state of the Irish currency. It included the leading statesmen of the day and was the first committee appointed by the British Parliament to make an inquiry into the paper currency.

[1] The increase was not large, but the organisation of the currency was so delicate that the slightest shock was enough to disturb it.

[2] We have frequently referred to Thornton's *An Enquiry into the nature and effects of the paper credit.* Lord King's pamphlet only appeared in 1803, after his speeches: we shall discuss it presently.

[3] Mr. Bastable kindly called my attention to a work by John Leslie Foster, *Essay on the Principle of Commercial Exchanges, more particularly on the relations between England and Ireland* (1804). Unfortunately the British Museum, though possessing other works and speeches by Foster, has no copy of this. An analysis of it is given in the *Dictionary of Political Economy,* Vol. II., p. 121. Dillon's book (*History of Banking in Ireland*) contains nothing of interest about this crisis.

[4] See *Parl. Debates* for February 13, 1804, on the *Irish Restriction Bill,* pp. 1082-1098.

[5] p. 1083.

Opinions of the directors of the Bank of Ireland. Amongst the witnesses who gave evidence were Mr. Colville and Mr. D'Olier, directors of the Bank of Ireland. The former explained the increase in the issues by the adverse state of the exchange; the coin of the country was exported to pay the balances of the remittances and hence it was necessary to supplement the scarcity of gold by paper. He did not believe that the increase in the issues was a cause of the adverse exchange; on the contrary, the paper replaced the gold and allowed it to be exported, hence it was "a clear and decided cause" preventing the exchange from falling still lower.

His companion entirely agreed with him. As regards the depreciation of the notes, they were of opinion that "the circulation said to be depreciated must first be proved to have become burdensome to the holders, and bargains to have been made by unnecessary purchasers to get rid of that which they have found inconvenient, or were apprehensive to hold. The mere buying of gold at an advanced price beyond that of the Mint, is the effect, and not the cause, of the exchange, and, therefore, no proof of the depreciation of the paper itself." Both the directors considered that the sole cause of fluctuation in the exchange was an unfavourable balance of trade, in other words, the fact that Ireland owed more money than she could pay.

In reality the basis of their reasoning was entirely false. The inquiry held by the committee showed that the balance of trade, instead of being unfavourable to Ireland, was the opposite, and that in the only district in the country (Belfast) where paper money was tabooed, the exchange was unfavourable to Great Britain.

In short, a theory was beginning to be current in Ireland which was soon to prevail in England; it may be summed up thus:—It is inaccurate to speak of depreciated paper money; the paper is not depreciated but the price of gold has increased.[1]

[1] This theory was vigorously disputed by Mr. Marshall, the Inspector-General of Imports and Exports at Belfast. He pointed out that the Dublin exchangers were selling guineas at the rate of a paper guinea plus 2s. 2d., and that a bill of exchange on London for £100 could be obtained for £106

With regard to the regulation of the issues, the directors of the Bank of Ireland suggested the following theory, which was afterwards adopted by the directors of the Bank of England: "that the issues of a bank should be governed on totally different principles under a convertible and an inconvertible paper currency."[1] That in the first case the issues ought to be regulated according to the price of guineas and the rate of exchange on London, and that, supposing there to be an unusual demand for guineas, or an adverse exchange, the issues should be decreased in order to stop the withdrawal of coin.

But in the case of an inconvertible currency a different policy would be adopted. A bank, under prudent management, might issue notes in proportion to the demands made on it, and without taking into account the rate of exchange and the price of guineas; always provided that the notes were issued in exchange for real and convertible assets, such as commercial bills of undoubted solidity, payable at fixed dates, and based on actual commercial transactions.

After prolonged consideration the committee decided that the paper was depreciated and that the theory that gold had increased in value was absurd. The report added that normal fluctuations in the rate of exchange could not exceed those in the cost of transporting specie from one country to another, and hence that any increase in excess of this cost must be due to other causes. In reference to this the report pointed out the enormous increase in the Irish issues, which, since the Restriction Act, had not been restrained by the convertibility of the notes.

The committee after suggesting some minor remedies, in particular the assimilation of the English and Irish currencies,[2] advised the directors to regulate their

in gold or Bank of England notes, whilst it cost £116 in Irish paper money, and that this difference existed whatever the nature of the goods purchased. If this fall of 10 or 12 per cent. in prices were due to the increased value of gold the effect would necessarily be to attract gold from England, for the precious metal could not remain in a country where its value continued stationary. Moreover the Bank notes, which were issued at par with the coin, should have risen *pari passu* with it, so that one could be exchanged for the other. Since the contrary had happened, there had been a fall in the original value and thus depreciation.

[1] Macleod, 3rd Edition, Vol. II., p. 17.

[2] Also Irish Bank notes were to be payable in Bank of England notes and the Bank of Ireland was to keep a deposit account at London for this purpose.

issues in future upon the price of guineas and the foreign exchanges.

The presentation of the report on the Irish currency does not appear to have aroused much interest, and it had little effect. The issue of notes of a value below £1 was indeed forbidden in Ireland in 1805, but a proposal, made in 1809, by Mr. Parnell, to assimilate the English and Irish currencies, was rejected without discussion. Moreover the report itself was not printed until 1826. It must however have been communicated to the Bank of Ireland, and apparently had some influence upon it, since the directors reduced their issues from 3 to 2½ millions during the months of May, June, and July, 1804, and the exchanges were affected thereby; but the improvement was short-lived for in the succeeding months the directors relapsed into their former errors.

Some time afterwards, Fox took advantage of Addington's statement that the over-issue of notes led to their depreciation, to congratulate him[1] and to assert triumphantly that the House would never hear again the fantastical opinion that the paper was not depreciated but the value of gold increased.[2]

We shall see later how far this prophecy was fulfilled.

[1] It must be noted, however, that Addington continued to say that it was heresy to believe that the depreciation of the paper could influence the exchanges.

[2] With regard to the theories suggested by the Act of 1797 see Lord King's *Thoughts on the Restriction of Payments in Specie at the Banks of England and Ireland* (1803).

Lord King, writing of the Irish crisis, anticipates Ricardo in his statement of the true method of demonstrating the depreciation of a paper currency: "A rise of the market or Paper price of gold above the Mint price, and a fall in the foreign exchanges beyond the cost of sending bullion from one place to another, is the proof and the measure of the depreciation of the Paper money." (See Stephens, *Contribution to the Bibliography of the Bank of England*, p. 34, the account of King's pamphlet). Lord King's pamphlet is followed by a very useful appendix, giving the rates of the exchange with Hamburg, Paris, and Dublin, and the prices of standard silver since 1789.

This little work, which is superior to those of Boyd and Thornton, has since been thrown into the shade by Ricardo's pamphlet, *The high price of Bullion a proof of the depreciation of Bank notes* (1810). This was originally published in the form of letters in the *Morning Chronicle*. The first appeared on September 9, 1809. See McCulloch's one volume edition of Ricardo's works, pp. 261-290. See also another of Ricardo's writings on the subject which is published in the same edition, pp. 303-360, *A Reply to Mr. Bosanquet's Practical Observations*.

CHAPTER V.

THE BULLION COMMITTEE AND THE BULLION REPORT.

Appointment of the Bullion Committee. The Berlin Decree and the Spanish Wars. Speculation due to these events. Imprudent policy of the Bank. Crisis of 1809. Appointment of a Committee of Inquiry. The Bullion Report. Comparison with the Irish Crisis in 1804. The problem put before the Bullion Committee. Discussion on the depreciation of the notes. Discussion on the effects of increasing the note issue. Discussion on the effects of decreasing the note issue. Discussion on the policy to be adopted with regard to the Issues. Conclusions of the Bullion Report. Discussion of the Bullion Report in Parliament. Speeches of Horner, Roe, Thornton, Vansittart and Canning. Horner's resolutions thrown out, those of Vansittart passed.

A.—Appointment of the "Bullion Committee."

We have seen that the Bank of England avoided the folly of over-issue during the first years of the Restriction Act. The prudence of the directors, the moderation of the Government demands, the wisdom and patriotism of the commercial world, all combined to save the English notes from the fate of the Irish issues. The inconvertible Bank notes circulated at par, and the most celebrated of the French economists has justly remarked that this was one of the best experiments in political economy ever made. This admirable state of things continued even after Pitt's death, but did not long survive him; a succession of political events combined with a change in the policy of the Bank sufficed to transform everything.

The transformation began with the Berlin and Milan decrees. These had the effect of closing all European ports to England, with the exception of the Swedish. England responded by a series of similar measures, which served to prohibit the importation of a number of French products and of products of countries under the direct influence of France, such as Spanish wools and Italian silks, and hence encouraged speculation in all such goods. Moreover the blow given by these measures to the rights of neutrals nearly led to a war with America, and the possibility of this new war caused an artificial rise in the prices of American products, especially tobacco and cotton.

Speculation, favoured by the scarcity of commodities, was still further stimulated by the following facts: The invasion of Portugal, and later of Spain, by the French, gave practical independence to the colonies of these two countries and hence opened the South American ports to English products, which had hitherto been entirely excluded from them. This offered a wide field to speculation and the opportunity was seized without delay. Very soon there was a repetition of the events of 1720. Joint-stock companies of all kinds were formed to construct canals and bridges, to found breweries and insurance companies and to carry out undertakings of every kind imaginable. The Bank of England, instead of applying the curb, encouraged the prevailing fever to the full. Sir F. Baring stated in his evidence before the Bullion Committee, that he knew several clerks not worth £100, who, since the restriction, had set up as merchants, and to whom the Bank had granted credit accounts of 5 to 10 thousand pounds; these accounts had no connection with the real requirements of trade, and would never have been opened if it had not been for the suspension of cash payments.[1]

The value of the paper discounted by the Bank, which was £2,946,500 in 1795, was £15,475,700 in 1809, and £20,070,000 in 1810. Nor was this all. The speculative mania coincided with an increase of country banks, which, as in 1793, flooded the provinces with their notes. The number of these banks, which in 1797 had been reduced to 270, was 600 in 1808, and soon rose to 721. It stood at the latter figure two years later when the Bullion Committee was appointed. During this same year (1810) the Bank of England had issued notes to the value of £21,000,000, and the issues of the country banks appear, according to the best estimates, to have exceeded this figure and reached 30 millions.

This increase of paper currency, which had no legitimate

[1] See Macleod, 5th edition, Vol. II., p. 25.

basis, was accompanied by two phenomena already observed in Ireland in 1804—a rise in the price of gold, and a fall in the exchange. These two phenomena assumed disquieting proportions; the price of guineas rose to 26s. or 27s. On February 1st, 1810, Mr. Horner demanded explanations from the Government. At the conclusion of his speech, the House decided to make an inquiry into the causes of the rise in the price of bullion and the famous Bullion Committee was charged with this task.

The Bullion Committee included some of the most competent among the Members of Parliament, such as Messrs. Baring, Huskisson, Horner, and Foster, but it contained fewer political celebrities than the committee of 1804, with whom it had only two members in common, Mr. Sheridan and Mr. Foster.

B.—The Bullion Report.

The report of this committee, drawn up by Horner, Huskisson and Thornton, has become celebrated under the name of the "Bullion Report."[1]

Macleod[2] rightly points out that although the Bullion Report made a great stir, and threw into the shade the report of 1804, yet both deal with similar facts, state the same theories, and draw the same conclusions.

The greater success of the second of these two reports is probably due to the fact that it referred to matters of more general interest, and that it was drawn up more scientifically and in a more literary form. In addition to the points of likeness already noticed it may be remarked that a strong analogy existed between the evidence collected on the two occasions. In both cases the witnesses examined were drawn from four classes: (1) Bank directors, (2) private bankers, (3) merchants, (4) independent witnesses. Further, the evidences given by the English Bank directors and mer-

[1] For the Report and the Minutes of Evidence see *Parl. Debates*, Vol. XVII., Part VIII., p. ccii., *et seq.*

[2] See the masterly analysis of the *Bullion Report* given by this author, *op. cit.*, §§58-80.

chants[1] agreed with that of their Irish colleagues in 1804: they, too, maintained that the price of gold had risen and that the paper was not depreciated, and held the same theories as to the regulation of the issues and the various other points in the controversy.

The problem submitted to the Bullion Committee. What was the exact point of dispute which the committee had to decide?

It was as follows:[2] Three facts were agreed upon: (1) that whilst the Mint price of gold bullion ought to be £3 17s. 6d. an ounce, the market price had risen to £4 10s; (2) that the foreign exchanges had fallen below par, 14 per cent. in the case of Paris, 9 per cent. in that of Hamburg, and 7 per cent. in that of Amsterdam; (3) that whilst the note-issue was increasing, specie had disappeared from circulation. There was however no agreement as to the causes of these facts, and the controversy centred chiefly round four points which we shall consider in order:

1.—Whether the notes were depreciated, or whether, on the contrary, the price of gold had actually risen.

2.—Whether the increase in the issue had any influence upon the rate of the exchanges.

3.—What effect a restriction of the issues would have on the price of gold and the rate of the exchanges.

4.—What policy ought to be followed with regard to the regulation of the issues.

These are the four points which formed the object of the Bullion Committee's investigations and were dealt with in the conclusions of the Bullion Report.

§I.—*The depreciation of the notes.* The condition of England in 1810 was exactly like that of Ireland in 1804, with one exception. In Ireland the bank-notes were obviously depreciated: there were two prices in trade, the one in notes, the other in coin, and there existed shops in which guineas were sold for bank-notes at a higher nominal

[1] The merchants had something to gain from the victory of the directors' theory, for it was natural that they should wish to see their bills discounted in the largest numbers possible, and there were fewer facilities for this when the notes were convertible.

[2] Macleod, 5th edition, Vol. II., p. 29, *et seq.*

value. This was not the case in England,[1] partly because Bank notes were accepted at their face value, but mainly owing to the fact that it was a criminal offence to sell guineas at more than 21s. and the law in this matter was not a mere dead letter. About this time a man named Young[2] narrowly escaped the penalty imposed. Had it not been for this there would have been two prices for everything as there had been in Ireland. As it was no one paid for bullion in guineas, but only in paper.

Apart from this the problem was the same and the doctrine that the notes were not depreciated found numerous and determined supporters. One of these, Mr. Chambers, a well-known merchant, defended it with remarkable ability.[3]

Mr. Chambers was willing to recognise that forced currency affected the exchanges, but he did not conceive it possible that a currency which was not forced could be excessive: there was no forced currency so long as the paper was accepted willingly, which was only the case when the said paper was not depreciated. In the same way, although Mr. Chambers believed that an excessive increase in the metallic currency, such as might result, for instance, from the discovery of new mines, would raise the price of all commodities, he denied that a similar effect would follow an excessive increase of paper money. The latter would maintain its full value because paper money could not be increased beyond the needs of the public, who would otherwise refuse to exchange any article of value for a piece of paper.

Mr. Chambers, under pressure of questions, afterwards

[1] At least in general, but many instances to the contrary were supplied by Members of Parliament during the debates on the Bullion Report. See below, pp. 232 and 233.

[2] Some time afterwards the Court of Common Pleas annulled the sentence pronounced on Young and decided that it was not criminal to sell guineas at a premium. Moreover the only effect of reviving an obsolete law was to cause the guineas to be melted into bullion. This was illegal, but the profit was 12s. an ounce, and people preferred to incur a penalty rather than exchange their guineas for paper. Thus the guineas disappeared, and there was comparatively little opportunity to transgress the law by establishing two prices for commodities.

[3] *Parl. Deb.*, Vol. XVII., p. cccxc.

had to acknowledge that, according to the Mint standard, the price of a one-guinea note was 5-dwts. 3-grs., whilst on the market it was only 4-dwts. 8-grs., and hence that the Bank note was not exchangeable for the amount of gold it represented. But the witness, who was not to be embarrassed by so small a difficulty, added: "I do not conceive gold to be a fairer standard for Bank of England notes than indigo or broadcloth."

The reply might have been that a Bank note was a promise to pay a definite weight of gold of a certain standard, but that it could not be said to represent any given quantity of indigo; hence, as soon as it was not worth the 5-dwts. 3-grs. of standard gold, it was depreciated. Chambers' mistake, and that of all who agreed with him, was that he had come to believe that the paper money was the real measure of all commodities and that gold was only one of those commodities whose value is determined by reference to this invariable and universal standard.

This is the theory which Canning ridiculed with so much eloquence and whose untenability was sufficiently exposed in the Bullion Report. According to the report the notion that the market price of gold could exceed the Mint price was due to a misconception. Gold was the measure of value in this country. Commodities were thought to be cheap or dear according to the greater or lesser amount of gold for which they were exchangeable. "*But a given quantity of gold will never be exchanged for a greater or a less quantity of gold of the same standard fineness*"[1] except there be a slight difference depending on special causes.[2] An ounce

[1] p. ccix.

[2] The difference might for instance arise from the greater convenience of having coin rather than bullion. The Report also mentions other possible causes: the deterioration of the coinage, the delay involved in minting the coin, obstacles to exportation,—the two latter causes combined producing an actual difference of nearly 5½ per cent. None of these causes existed at Hamburg with regard to silver, the currency there being of a definitely fixed weight and of standard fineness and no opposition being made to exportation. In England, the Report concludes, the difference had never exceeded 5½ per cent. so long as the Bank paid in gold and the coin was of full weight. The difference might have been greater in countries where the Mint charged for the expenses of making the coin, but in England people only had to suffer a loss of interest for the time during which the coin was kept at the Mint.

of standard gold could never fetch more than £3 17s. 10½d. on the market unless £3 17s. 10½d. in our currency contained less than an ounce of gold.

Since the suspension of cash payments however, gold had partially ceased to be the measure of value, and the only standard was the circulating medium, issued partly by the Bank of England and partly by the country banks—a circulating medium whose value varied only in proportion to its quantity. It was most desirable that its value should correspond to that of the real and legal standard, gold.

Finally, the Bullion Report compared the state of things under a depreciated metallic coinage with that under an inconvertible and excessive credit currency and showed that the two produced the same effects, *i.e.*, a general rise in prices, including that of gold, and a fall in the exchanges on all countries except those which had an equally depreciated currency.

§II.—*The possible effects of an increase of the issues upon the rate of exchange.*[1] In order to discuss this the report began by stating, as an indisputable principle, that the difference of the exchange between two places cannot exceed the expenses of transport, that is, the charge for freight and insurance. Dangers in war time might, of course, increase these expenses. But the evidence collected showed that the total cost of sending bullion to Holland did not exceed 7 per cent., and that of sending it to Paris was still less. The depression of the exchange had, however, been 20 per cent., and the problem was to account for this fall of 13 per cent., which was independent of the cost of transport. It could only be explained by the depreciation of the currency.

It was said, indeed, that the difference was due to a demand for gold on the Continent. But if this were so, the price of the metal must have risen to a like degree on the Continental markets, and it was clear that no such rise had taken place.

One witness, who gave evidence on two occasions under

[1] pp. ccxv.-ccxxvii.

the name of "a Continental merchant,"[1] displayed a knowledge on this question of the effect of the issues on the exchanges which might well have been envied by his English colleagues. He considered that as the balance of trade was considerably in favour of England,[2] the fall in the exchange could only be accounted for by excessive issues. This effect of excessive issues, he remarks, is of constant occurrence; "we have seen a strong instance of it last summer" (*i.e.*, the summer of 1809), in Austria, when "a considerable additional issue became necessary, in consequence of which the exchange on that country fell an additional 50 per cent., and gold coin fetched from three to four times its nominal value there."

§III.—*The influence which a decrease in the issues may have on the price of gold and the rate of the exchange.* It is easy to see after what has been said, that in the opinion of the Bank directors such a decrease could have no influence whatever. Obviously if an increase of issues is thought to have no effect, a decrease must be equally fruitless.

At the same time it is clear that the decrease in the paper money would raise its value compared with all other commodities, including gold. And, since the market price of gold was determined entirely with reference to the price as paid in Bank notes, and not in guineas, evidently a reduction in the quantity of paper would have reduced the price of gold expressed in paper, and would have tended to make the real value of the notes correspond more closely to their nominal value. To raise in this way the value of the currency must, if the decrease was sufficiently large, raise the exchange to par, and bring back gold into circulation. In addition to these theoretical considerations, the Bullion Report, working out the analogy between a metallic currency and a paper currency when both are alike depreciated, instanced, amongst others, the historical example of the

[1] For his evidence see *Parl. Debates*, Vol. XVII., Part VIII., pp. cccxxxv. and cccliii.

[2] The following figures are given in the Bullion Report, p. ccxxiii. The balance of trade had been favourable to England:—

In 1805 by £6,616,000.
1806 ,, £10,437,000.
1807 ,, £5,866,000.
1808 by £12,481,000.
1809 ,, £14,834,000.

crisis of 1696-1697, when the restoration of the coinage had the effect of lowering the price of bullion and of restoring the rate of exchange to par.

§IV.—*The policy to be adopted in regulating the issues. In particular the question whether this policy ought to vary according to the convertibility or inconvertibility of the notes.*[1] According to the directors, there was no need after the restriction to regulate the issues by reference to the price of bullion and the foreign exchanges; the only criterion was the demand for discount. The directors[2] and some of the merchants were eager to establish a theory of whose truth they felt assured, *i.e.*, that an over-issue was impossible so long as the advances took the form of discounts of "paper of undoubted solidity arising out of actual commercial transactions, and payable at short and fixed periods."

The Bullion Committee set itself to refute this doctrine, which had already been supported by the directors of the Bank of Ireland. According to the report: "The fallacy upon which it is founded, lies in not distinguishing between advance of capital to merchants and an additional supply of currency to the general mass of circulating medium. If the advance of capital only is considered as made to those who are ready to employ it in judicious and productive undertakings, it is evident that there need be no other limit to the total amount of advances than what the means of the lender and his prudence in the selection of borrowers may impose. But, in the present situation . . . every advance . . . becomes an addition, also, to the mass of circulating medium. In the first instance, when the advance is made by notes paid in discount of a bill, it is undoubtedly so much capital, so much power of making purchases, placed in the hands of a merchant who receives the notes; and, if these hands are safe, the operation is so far, and in this, its first step, useful and productive to the public. But . . . as soon as the notes are exchanged by him for some other article which is capital, they fall into the channel of circula-

[1] Bullion Report, p. cccxxviii., *et seq.*

[2] See in particular the evidence of Mr. Whitmore, a former Governor of the Bank of England, and of Mr. Pearse, who was then Governor.

tion, as so much circulating medium, and form an addition to the mass of currency. The necessary effect of every such addition to the mass is to diminish the relative value of any given portion of that mass in exchange for commodities."[1] And, since the notes are inconvertible, they cannot be returned to the Bank by the free working of economic laws, and the increase continues in existence until the Bank is repaid the principal of the bills originally discounted. But before the notes are thus paid in, fresh issues will have already neutralised the good results which might have followed from their return. "Each successive advance repeats the same process. If the amount of discounts is progressively increasing, the amount of paper which remains out in circulation over and above what is wanted for the occasions of the public, will progressively increase also; and the money prices of commodities will progressively rise."[2]

The report then gives various statistics as to the quantity of notes in circulation at different periods. But it denies that the quantity of notes can be a test of over-issue or the reverse. Different commercial conditions require different quantities of notes. The state of public credit must also be taken into account, and various methods of economising the use of money may alter the quantity required appreciably. *The only real test is to be found in the state of the foreign exchanges and the price of bullion.*

Conclusions of the Bullion Report. Macleod sums up the general conclusions thus:[3] "That at that time there was an excessive paper currency, of which the most unequivocal symptom was the very high price of gold bullion, and next to that the very depressed state of the foreign exchanges. That the excess was to be attributed to the removal of all control on the issues of the Bank of England by the suspension of cash payment. It was greatly to be regretted, therefore, that this Act, which at best was only intended to be temporary, had been continued as a permanent war

[1] See Macleod, Vol. II., 5th edition, pp. 269, 270.

[2] Macleod, *loc. cit.*

[3] See Macleod, 3rd edition, Vol. II., pp. 45, 46.

measure." That the fatal results of the existing situation were too well known to need description, and it was more than likely that things would get worse; the integrity and honour of Parliament demanded, therefore, that an immediate remedy should be found.

"That the continuance of this state of matters held out a temptation to Parliament to have recourse to a depreciation of the gold coin by an alteration of the standard, which had been done by many governments under similar circumstances, and which might be the easiest remedy to the evil. But it would be a great breach of public faith and of the primary duty of the Government, to prefer the reduction of the coin down to the paper, rather than the restoration of the paper to the legal standard of the coin." Some had proposed to remedy the evil by a legal restriction of the Bank's issues, but such a measure would be fruitless, because the required proportion could never be determined, "and even if it were so, might very much aggravate the inconveniences of a temporary pressure"; in any case, such an interference would be incompatible with the rights of commercial property.

"The only true and proper remedy . . . was . . . a resumption of cash payments. That, however, was an operation of the greatest delicacy, and it must be left entirely to the discretion of the Bank. . . Parliament should merely fix the time, and leave it to them to carry out the details." In any case, the committee judged that an interval of two years would be necessary and sufficient to conclude the matter satisfactorily.

This, then, is the Bullion Report; it stimulated the publication of a complete economic literature,[1] and caused long

[1] This literature is most abundant, and it would be a considerable undertaking to study it in detail. It would be almost impossible to attempt here what we tried to do with regard to the literature advocating the foundation of the Bank. Neither is there anything new to be learnt from the pamphlets published about 1810; they only reproduce the well-known arguments. The most able criticism of the theories contained in the Bullion Report is that of Mr. Bosanquet, who has given an excellent summary of the doctrines which we have already described, in his *Practical Observations on the Report of the Bullion Committee*. This pamphlet is famous less for its own merits than on account of the crushing reply made to it by Ricardo. See *Reply to Mr. Bosanquet's Practical Observations*.

discussions in Parliament. These debates must be briefly considered. But we shall not attempt any detailed analysis of the speeches, and we shall only refer to those which raise points not already dealt with.

C.—Discussion of the Bullion Report in the House of Commons.

The report was presented by Horner on June 9, 1810. It was not formally considered until the 6th of May, 1811. The discussion was opened by Mr. Horner, who spoke at great length.[1] His speech may still be read with interest and pleasure; in it he stated the arguments which we have already sufficiently discussed, and concluded by moving a series of resolutions, of which we give the substance in a note,[2] and which embody in the main the conclusions of the Bullion Report.

Mr. Rose answered Mr. Horner in another long speech,[3] stating arguments on the opposite side which are also familiar to us.

The debate became more interesting when it was taken up by Mr. Henry Thornton, in the most original of the speeches[4] heard by the House on the subject. In his opinion the main point at issue was whether it was

[1] The speech lasted three hours. It will be found in *Parl. Debates,* Vol. XIX., pp. 799-832.

[2] See pp. 830-832. The first 7 resolutions referred to the legal standard of value in the country. 8.—"That the Promissory Notes of the Bank of England are stipulations to pay on demand the sum in Pounds Sterling respectively specified in each of the said Notes." 9.—That when Parliament passed the Restriction Act it did not intend that any alteration should take place in the value of such Notes. 10.—That it appears that they have for a considerable time been below their legal value. 11.—That this fall "has been occasioned by too abundant Issue of Paper Currency, both by the Bank of England and by the Country Banks." 12 and 13.—That the extraordinary depreciation of the foreign exchanges has been in a great measure occasioned by the depreciation of the currency of this country. 14.—That during the suspension "it is the duty of the Directors of the Bank of England to advert to the state of the Foreign Exchanges as well as to the price of Bullion with a view to regulate the amount of their issues." 15.—That the only method of preserving the paper currency at its proper value is to make it payable on demand. 16.—That cash payments ought to be resumed in a period of two years from that time. See Macleod, 5th edition, Vol. II., p. 48.

[3] See pp. 833-895.

[4] See pp. 895-919.

expedient that the Bank should regulate its issues with reference to the price of bullion and the state of the exchanges, and whether these were influenced by the quantity of paper. He set himself to prove the affirmative, firstly by stating in his turn the principles contained in the Bullion Report, and then by the help of a number of historical examples. In particular, he referred to the case of the Bank of France as remarkably to the point.[1] This bank was forbidden by its statutes to lend money to the Government, and the latter was obliged in 1805 when the war again broke out, to borrow from various "merchants and capitalists, who then contrived to fabricate among themselves, and proceeded to discount at the Bank, as many securities as were sufficient . . . so that the Bank was the true lender." The consequence of this transaction was a great increase in the paper of the Bank of France. "A drain of their cash followed; the diligences were found to be carrying off silver into the departments, which the bank . . . had continually to bring back, with much expense." It was obliged at length to stop payment, and its notes were at a discount of 10 per cent. Almost immediately there was a corresponding fall in the exchanges. The bank now, acting on the advice of Dupont de Nemours,[2] the secretary of a special commission, restricted its issues. In three months' time payments were resumed as usual and the exchanges became normal.

Another useful example of conditions analogous to those in England was supplied by the Bank of Sweden. Thornton[3] briefly described the Scandanavian banking

[1] See p. 907. For the causes of the crisis of 1805 see also the report of Dupont de Nemours, especially pp. 48-55, London edition, 1811. The more recent work of M. V. de Swarte should also be consulted: *Les vingt premières années de lá Banque de France*, p. 18, *et seq.* (author's note).

[2] The secretary's words were as follows: "The Bank should always draw in its discounts as soon as it perceives the existence of a more than ordinary disposition to exchange Bank paper for money. For what mean these applications for money? They imply that there are more Bank notes on the spot than the circumstances of the time demand. And how are you to provide against this evil? By diminishing their quantity through a reduction which shall exceed the new emissions."

The exact title of the Report is, *Sur la Banque de France et les causes de la crise qu'elle a éprouvée.*

[3] pp. 910, 911.

system and remarked that although the paper money was at a discount of nearly 70 per cent. after the suspension of cash payments, "the public in Sweden . . . were not fully persuaded of the depreciation of their paper; for many of their commodities, their iron in particular, had not risen in any proportion to the fall of their currency."

In Russia, too, although the rouble had fallen from its original value of 48 pence to that of 12 or 14 pence, and although it was known that the quantity of paper money had been largely increased, yet the Russian merchants and business men, amongst whom the speaker had lived for a long time, persisted in ascribing the fall to an unfavourable balance of trade, or to political events which were quite incapable of producing such a result. The same mistake was made by the American public with regard to the crisis of 1720, which was entirely due to the excessive issues of the American banks.[1]

Mr. Thornton compared the public to a man in a boat, "who seems to see the shore departing from him. . . . In consequence of a similar prejudice, we assume that the currency, which is in all our hands, and with which we ourselves are, as it were, identified, is fixed, and that the price of bullion moves." Then with regard to the balance of trade, which Mr. Rose believed unfavourable, Mr. Thornton refuted this opinion by a previous statement made by Mr. Rose himself, in which he declared how uncommonly favourable the balance of trade had been. And, in fact, according to the annual report of the Custom House, the balance in favour of England amounted to £16,000,000.

The second part of Mr. Thornton's speech dealt with the standard of the currency. He showed that a permanent currency of paper money was most dangerous in that it tended to swell the numbers of those who advocated a return to a metallic currency combined with a lowering of the standard. "The very argument of justice, after a certain time, passes over to the side of deterioration . . . if eight, ten, or even fifteen or twenty years, have passed since the paper fell, then it may be deemed unfair to restore the

[1] See Marshall, *History of Washington.*

ancient value of the circulating medium; for bargains will have been made, and loans supplied, under an expectation of the continuance of the existing depreciation."[1]

Mr. Vansittart, afterwards Lord Bexley, in moving the counter-resolution to Mr. Horner's, denied the principles set forth in the Bullion Report. In particular he appeared to believe, like most of his colleagues, that the Restriction Act had supplied the country with the enormous resources needed for the war. We have already discussed this theory, but it is well to recall it here since it was in the course of these debates that it was first stated as an indisputable fact.

Mr. Vansittart based his argument on the fact that there had never been any difference between prices in coin and those in paper and hence declared that the theories which had held as regards Ireland in 1804, were not applicable to the case in point. The two situations were not analogous; whilst in Ireland coin was openly sold at a premium, owing to the depreciation of Bank notes,[2] and two distinct prices were in force according to the form of payment, in England on the contrary, none of these things had occurred. Hence there was no depreciation. This was a cheap victory since the non-appearance of such phenomena in England was due to the severity of the laws which suppressed them. At this very time three men were committed for trial under an old statute of Edward VI., revived for the occasion. And besides, was it really true that prices did not vary according to the form of payment? This was strongly denied by several Members.

Mr. Sharpe, who was on the committee, showed[3] that the Government itself, though responsible for the laws, was obliged to break them and to acknowledge the very depreciation which it claimed to prevent. For instance, "it had been usual to send over specie to Guernsey to pay our troops there. Each guinea had recently been paid to

[1] See p. 917.

[2] Mr. Vansittart explains this depreciation, moreover, as due not to over-issue but to temporary political circumstances.

[3] *Parl. Debates*, p. 1062.

the soldiers at the rate of twenty-three shillings. . . Again, a person who inherited from a distant relation the sum of a thousand guineas, was lately paid in specie. He went to invest the money in the funds, and on asking the price of the 3 per cents., was told 64½. On inquiring, however, at what rate he could obtain the stock if he paid real money for it, he was told, after some consideration, that he might have it for cash at 60.'"[1]

Several other speeches were made before the close of the debate, and I cannot resist the temptation to give some extracts from that of one of the best and most able men ever born in England.

Lord Castlereagh had spoken of "a sense of value in reference to currency as compared with commodities." Canning seized the opportunity to crush utterly the theory opposed to that of the Bullion Report. This theory consisted simply in the doctrine that the pound sterling was nothing tangible; it was a creature of the imagination, which had no real existence, and might vary with the weather. It was a sense of value communicated mysteriously from one person to another. "A sense of value," exclaimed Canning, "but whose sense? with whom is it to originate? and how is it to be communicated to others: who is to promulgate, who is to acknowledge, or who is to enforce it? . . . What ingenuity shall calculate, or what authority control its fluctuations? . . . this wild and dangerous principle . . . would throw loose . . . all contracts and pecuniary bargains, by leaving them to be measured from day to day, and from hour to hour, by no other rule than that of the fancies and interests of each individual conflicting with the fancies and interests of his neighbour."

Notwithstanding the excellence of these speeches the House remained unconvinced of the truth of the principles maintained in the Bullion Report. Not only did it reject

[1] Sir Fr. Burdett also stated that in spite of the prohibitions he had himself been asked "far different prices" according as he paid in specie or in Bank paper.

Mr. Horner's resolutions,[1] it also passed, in spite of Canning's[2] protests, a series of counter-resolutions moved by Mr. Vansittart at the end of a second speech.[3] These resolutions, contained in sixteen articles, included such statements as that Bank notes "have hitherto been, and are at this time, held in public estimation to be equivalent to the legal coin of the realm."[4]

[1] The first resolution was thrown out by 152 votes to 75, and the remaining ones by increasing majorities, with which Robert Peel voted. See *Parl. Debates*, p. 1169.

[2] At the end of his speech (see *Parl. Debates*, Vol. XX., pp. 94-123) Canning proposed an amendment, which was rejected by 82 votes to 48. Canning's two speeches have been published under the title of *Substance of two Speeches delivered on the 8th and 13th of May*, 1811.

[3] See Mr. Vansittart's second speech, Vol. XX., pp. 1-74.

[4] See the 2nd and 3rd resolutions. The statements are contrary to all the evidence.

CHAPTER VI.

REPEAL OF THE RESTRICTION ACT.

Results of the rejection of the Bullion Report. Lord King's circular to his tenants. The Stanhope Act. The Act of 1819. Great drain of specie in 1818 and 1819. Appointment of Committees to consider the advisability of resuming cash payments. Reports of the Committees of both Houses. Proposals of Lord Lauderdale. Debates in Parliament: Robert Peel's Speech on the alteration of the standard. The Act of 1819, its chief provisions. Resumption of cash payments.

SECTION I.

Results of the Rejection of the Bullion Report.—Action of Lord King.—The Stanhope Act.

One inevitable result followed from the vote in Parliament, to wit, that the Bank was encouraged to issue as many notes as it wished; in this way it could make prices fluctuate continually, and the value of land and of everyone's income depended on its good pleasure.

As the depreciation of notes continued to increase, debtors had everything to gain by prolonging the existing state of things, but creditors were being ruined. Things reached such a pitch that Lord King, as much to protect his own interests as to decide a theoretical question, sent a circular to his farmers and tenants requesting to be paid for the future either in gold or "in guineas, in Portugal gold coin," or "in Bank notes of a sum sufficient to purchase at the present market price the weight of standard gold requisite to discharge the rent."[1] The reason for this action, which Lord King also stated in the circular, was that in 1807, when the farmers had agreed to pay "in good and lawful money of Great Britain," gold was worth £4 an ounce, but that its present value was £4 14s., which meant a difference of £17 10s. per £100.

[1] See the complete text of this circular given in Lord King's speech in the House of Lords.—*Parl. Debates, Vol.* XX., pp. 792-793.

This claim was perfectly legal, since the Act of 1797 while authorising the Bank to suspend cash payments, had not decreed a forced currency. It was moreover just, for besides the reasons given by Lord King, there is another very obvious one: the price of the farmers' crops was rising whilst they were continuing to pay the same rents in depreciated notes.

But however legal and however just the request might be, it nevertheless completely upset the theory which the House had just taken such pains to establish. Lord Stanhope[1] brought in a Bill forbidding all differences between payments in paper and in coin; he justified this by the assertion that 27s. had been asked for a guinea,[2] a statement which was confirmed by Lord Holland, who opposed the Bill, and which is an additional proof of the inaccuracy of Vansittart's assertions.

The Bill was opposed by Lord Grenville,[3] a member of the Cabinet which had brought in the Act of Restriction, and by the Marquess of Lansdowne, Lord Grey and Lord King, who spoke in explanation of his action in the matter of the circular.[4] It was easy enough for these speakers to show that since the inconvertibility of the notes had been authorised, such a measure as the present would inevitably lead the way to a forced currency.

As a matter of fact, the Restriction Act led on naturally to the passing of the new law and ultimately to a forced currency. This was ably demonstrated by Lord Eldon, who supported the Bill. He took as an illustration the case

[1] Scandal-mongers alleged that Lord Stanhope owed £100,000, and that when he pleaded so earnestly on behalf of debtors he was really pleading *pro domo*. But he himself made a formal denial of the accusations.—*Parl. Debates*, p. 762.

[2] Lord Stanhope thought that "there was no such thing in this country as a measure of value founded on a quantity of bullion of standard fineness. The legal coin was the money with the stamp upon it. . . . If Bank notes and gold bore a fixed proportional ratio to the pound sterling by law they were equal to one another, and to prove this he need go no further than the first book of Euclid, where it was laid down as an axiom that things equal to the same thing are equal to one another."

[3] It was on this occasion that Grenville said that the day on which Mr. Pitt and he had been forced to propose the Restriction Act was one of the most painful in their political life.

[4] See this speech, pp. 790-814.

of a young professional man who has to make his way in the world. Suppose that he has a private fortune of £3,000 on deposit at the Bank, which ought to yield him an annual income of £90. His landlord demands his rent in gold, while the Bank refuses to pay his interest in specie. He may reasonably ask whether it is just that the same law which forces him to accept the notes also forces him to pay his rent in gold, when he cannot obtain any and is hence reduced, if not to prison, at any rate to the sale of his property.

Whatever may be thought of these speeches, the Act was passed,[1] and though originally its effects were to cease on March 25, 1812, it was afterwards continued as long as the Act of Restriction was in force.

It is hardly necessary to add that things continued as before in spite of this Act, and the price of an ounce of gold rose to £5 10s. But the law had a bad effect on business. Creditors of long standing lost 30 or 40 per cent. of their outstanding debts, and in particular, those who had granted long leases received only two-thirds of their rent. The Bank did not restrict its issues, and country banks continued to be established, hence general prices went on rising: the price of corn indeed, reached a level hitherto unknown.

SECTION II.

THE ACT OF 1819.

The conclusion of the war, plentiful harvests and a great reduction in country bank issues[2] so improved the situation that the Bank began to consider the possibility of a return to cash payments. By November, 1816, the directors had collected so much gold that they announced

[1] The Act was passed in the House of Lords by 43 votes to 16, and in the Commons by 95 to 20. Its form differed somewhat from that at first proposed by Lord Stanhope, but it would be useless to give details which have only a retrospective interest.

[2] This reduction was chiefly due to the failure of 89 country banks of issue, which occurred between 1814 and 1815; as a result, and in proof of the truth of the principles of the Bullion Report, gold fell from £5 6s. the ounce to £3 18s. (1st October, 1816).

their readiness to redeem at once all notes issued before 1812, and in April, 1817, all those issued before January, 1816. People had however grown so accustomed to the notes that they did not present them at the Bank, and indeed in many cases they preferred them to gold. The partial resumption of cash payments was nevertheless quite successful and preparations were being made for a general resumption, when a steady demand for gold made its appearance. This withdrawal was mainly due to the big loans at high rates raised in England by the Continental States in order to replace their depreciated paper currencies; and also in part to a reduction in the interest paid on Exchequer bills, which caused these bills to lose some of their popularity.

The price of gold began to rise,[1] the Bank directors, far from reducing their issues, made an advance of 28 millions instead of 20 millions to the Government, and the country banks displayed even less intelligence. Matters became so serious that on February 3, 1819, the two Houses each appointed a committee to inquire into the position of the Bank.

The two committees examined a certain number of witnesses on the subject and the inquiry had a surprising result. Whereas in 1804 and 1810 the majority of the commercial world denied that the issues had any effect on the foreign exchanges or on the price of gold, in 1819 it was in entire agreement with the theories of the Bullion Committee. This may be seen from the evidence of most of the witnesses, even that of the governor, the deputy-governor and several other directors of the Bank. The general court of the Bank directors was alone in maintaining the opposite opinion in spite of everything, and on March 25th it passed an official resolution to give firm expression to its belief.[2]

The committees of both Houses agreed in recommending that after February the 1st, 1820, the Bank should be required to deliver gold of standard fineness in quantities

[1] It was £4 3s. an ounce in January, 1819.

[2] The Bank maintained this opinion for eight years. It was not until 1827 that this resolution was solemnly expunged from its books.

not less than 60 ounces, at £4 1s. an ounce; that after October the 1st, 1820, the rate should be reduced to £3 19s. 6d., and after May the 1st, 1821, to the Mint price of gold, viz., £3 17s. 10½d. This obligation to pay in bullion was to continue for not less than two and not more than three years after May 1st, 1821, when cash payments should be resumed.

The report was presented to the House of Lords on May 21st, 1819. Lord Harrowby very shortly afterwards brought forward, on behalf of the ministry, some proposals which embodied those of the report. These were discussed, but the debate was somewhat strangely diverted by a resolution moved by Lord Lauderdale to alter the Mint price of gold to correspond with the market price. Robert Peel, in a masterly speech, demonstrated (1) that it was essential to resume cash payments, (2) that the standard of the coin ought not to be lowered.[1]

With regard to the first point Peel freely acknowledged that his opinions had undergone a material change since 1811. Every sound writer agreed that the true standard of value consisted of a definite quantity of metal of an equally definite fineness, with an inscription stating the weight and fineness. No doubt the Bank was perfectly solvent, but it did not therefore follow that an over-issue of paper was an impossibility. If solvency alone was sufficient proof that there was no excess, Law's theory was just, and the land as well as the funds might be converted into a circulating medium.

Peel strenuously opposed any lowering of the standard. His arguments were as follows:—"There could be no inconvenience in compelling the Bank to pay in specie at the Mint Price. It had done so from 1776 to 1797,[2] and the price of gold had never risen above £3 17s. 6d. The fact that this price had since risen to £5 2s. did not therefore prove that the standard was variable. What had happened was that a substitute for gold had been intro-

[1] See *Parl. Debates*, pp. 676-705, for this speech, also Macleod, 3rd edition, Vol. II., p. 84, *et seq.*

[2] There had been a restoration of the coinage in 1774. See above, p. 158.

duced, and its price was considered in relation to that substitute. Let not the House be led away by any calculation to mistake the price for the value. When people talked of gold rising in price, were they prepared to show that it had risen in intrinsic value? So far from gold having risen in value during the last fifty years, it had actually fallen, partly from the greater abundance of the metal itself, partly from the substitutes that were used for it.[1]

A very prevalent theory was, that instead of regulating paper by the value of gold—gold should be regulated by the value of paper. This was nothing less than a fraud upon the public creditor. It was vain to think that foreign nations could be imposed upon by such a deception. The only result would be that after the public creditor had been cheated, the coin would be debased.

We ought to follow the example of our wisest and most distinguished ancestors, and return to the ancient standard of the coins. Three great reforms of the coinage had already been undertaken on these lines—in the reigns of Edward III., Elizabeth and William III.[2] In all three cases the difficulties were much greater than on the present occasion.

The idea that the country owed its glory and military honours to an inconvertible paper currency was ridiculous: there had been great military victories even before 1797. Peel believed that the true difference between England and

[1] This was also pointed out by Lord Liverpool in a speech in the House of Lords which deserves to be mentioned in connection with Peel's.

[2] With regard to the first of these reforms see Ruding, Vol. I., pp. 190-206. For the third see above, p. 90, the chapter entirely devoted to this subject. For the second see Ruding, Vol. I., pp. 332-343, and Froude, *History of England from the fall of Wolsey to the defeat of the Spanish Armada*, Vol. VII., pp. 453-460. Elizabeth found the coinage in an appalling state of depreciation. By the advice of Burleigh, the founder of the house of Cecil, she ordered a general re-coinage in spite of the enormous difficulties which such an undertaking involved. The operation was most successful, and the Crown made a profit of £14,079 out of it.

As Froude remarks (p. 453), no measure in Elizabeth's reign has received praises which were better merited. Sometimes, to be strictly accurate, the praises have exceeded the merits, for some historians have described the reform as carried out at the cost of the Crown.

Elizabeth was very proud of her reform. Official congratulations were offered by Parliament (see *Parl. Hist.*, Vol. IV., p. 214). She caused a medal to be struck in commemoration with the inscription, *Bene constituta re nummaria*, and her monumental inscription concludes thus: *Gallia domata, Belgium sustentum, Pax fondata et Moneta in justum valorem redacta.*

other States was that she always kept her faith inviolate. It was this feeling that enabled the country to resist adversity and to secure a final triumph. Now that they had reached the other shore in safety, let them not abandon the great principle which had supported them through the dismal voyage.

The rest of the discussion in the Commons threw no fresh light on the subject. Amongst the other speakers we may mention Canning, whose speech at the end of the next sitting seems to have had a brilliant reception,[1] and Ricardo,[2] who pointed out with considerable effect that the evidence given by the directors as individuals contradicted their resolution as a court; he concluded that in view of their past conduct, the only course open to the House was to deprive them of their extraordinary powers.

The Act (statute 1819, c. 49)[3] was passed unanimously after amendment by the House of Lords.[4]

Its chief provisions were as follows:—

I.—The Acts restraining cash payments were continued until May 1st, 1823, at which date they were to cease.

Temporary provisions adopted from the reports:

1.—Between February 1st and October 1st, 1820, the Bank was bound to pay all notes presented to them at the rate of £4 1s. an ounce.[5]

2.—Between October 1st and May 1st, 1821, the rate was to be £3 19s. 6d.

3.—Between May 1st, 1821, and May 1st, 1823, the rate of gold bullion was to be £3 17s. 10½d.

II.—The trade in bullion and coin was declared free.

III.—Moreover, a law of July 6th, 1819 (statute 1819, c. 76), forbade the Bank to make any advance to Government without the authority of Parliament. Supposing a request of this kind to be thought necessary, it was to be made in

[1] See *Parl. Debates*, p. 800. According to this journal, the conclusion of his very short speech was greeted with "Loud and Universal cries of hear, hear."

[2] See Ricardo's Speech, pp. 742-748.

[3] *Statutes of the Realm*, Vol. LIX., p. 156.

[4] See *Parl. Debates*, p. 1137.

[5] The bearers thus suffered a loss of 3s. 6d. an ounce.

writing and laid before both Houses of Parliament together with the answer made to it by the court of directors.

It was hoped that this would put a stop to a liberty which had rapidly degenerated into licence and which had resulted in this terrible crisis lasting 22 years.

Resumption of cash payments. The Act fixed May 1st, 1823, as the latest date for the resumption of cash payments. But this final date was anticipated, and on May 1st, 1821, the paper currency, established since 1797, was replaced by a currency on a metallic basis, of which the country had been deprived for 24 years and 2 months.

During this period the crisis had at times been very intense, and the scarcity of coin had caused a depreciation in the notes issued by the Bank. This depreciation, from being £8 7s. per £100 in 1801, had varied in the following manner:—

£7 5s. in 1802.	£25 3s. in 1814.
£2 3s. from 1803 to 1809.	£19 14s. in 1815.
£13 9s. in 1810.	£16 14s. in 1816.
£7 16s. in 1811.	£2 13s. from 1817 to 1818.
£20 14s. in 1812.	£4 9s. in 1819.
£22 18s. in 1813.	£2 12s. in 1820.

The depreciation continued until 1821, at which date the notes once more circulated at par.

END VOL. I.

VOLUME II. 1819—1903.

INTRODUCTORY CHAPTER.

Difference between Volume II. and Volume I. in respect to their subject matter. The possibility of omitting references to general history in Volume II. Necessity for dealing in one part of the present Volume with the working of the Bank under the existing system. The Act of 1826 regarded as one of the causes of the Act of 1844. Method adopted in examining the intention of Peel's Act.

THE first volume of this book dealt with the early history of the Bank of England,—the causes leading to its foundation, the foundation itself, and subsequent developments. In this volume we propose to examine the later history,—the system under which the Bank has carried on its business since 1844,—and a few introductory remarks on this subject may not be out of place.

The materials made use of in the present volume will be found to differ slightly from those studied in the preceding one.

In the first place, it has been possible to ignore the general history of England. The Government and the English public have learnt to understand better their own interests and the part that should be played by the Bank; hence this general history has become less and less closely connected with that of the Bank, or rather the connection has ceased except when absolutely unavoidable.

The ignorant hostility of one section of the nation, and the "runs," or worse still, the actual assaults to which it gave rise, have vanished. The Government, too, grown wiser by experience and helped by the remarkable increase of facilities for public credit, no longer applies to the Bank whenever it has need of money and hence does not now involve that institution in all its financial embarrassments.[1]

[1] On the other hand the normal connection between the Bank and the Treasury has become closer and closer as regards all that concerns the business of the Treasury account and the administration of the national debt, both floating and permanent; we have examined this subject at some length in an Appendix.

In the second place, a study of the actual working of the Act of 1844 has not seemed to us out of place in the history of the Bank, though we have reduced this study to comparatively modest proportions. A mere analysis of the Act followed by a description of the crises which the Bank has since experienced would not constitute a history; just as an analysis of the constitution of a country, accompanied by a description of the wars in which it has taken part, do not by themselves make up its history. The history of a country must include some study, however short, of its internal life; at the least it must point out the general lines of its development. Similarly in the case before us the section dealing with the working activities of the Bank is in all essentials an historical study. After an analysis of Robert Peel's Act as it appeared in 1844, we shall study the Bank as we find it after an existence of sixty years. During this interval we shall find that the Bank of England has undergone considerable change in several important particulars. For instance, the Act of 1844 contemplated that silver would play a considerable part in the reserve, but for a long time past the reserve has consisted entirely of gold. Again, in 1844 people were very far from anticipating what has actually been the case since 1893, viz., that the metallic reserve would exceed the paper currency. Nor was it realised that the Bank would cease to be a bank of discount and would become the guardian of the cash reserve for the commercial world, etc.

In this part of our work we shall have occasion, also, to discuss various questions of a more or less historical character, which it would have been difficult to deal with elsewhere; such matters, for example, as the increasing importance of cheques, of current accounts and of the bankers' reserve, and Mr. Lowe's scheme for reform in 1873, etc.

To pass to another point—it may seem strange that we have included in Part I., amongst the causes of the Act of 1844, the crisis of 1825 and the Act of 1826, which enforced those very regulations in opposition to which Peel's Act was passed. But a moment's thought will show that just because Peel's Act involved a reaction against the Act of 1826, we are justified in describing it as a consequence of this Act. In fact, especially in the mid 19th century, the conception of a monopoly could hardly have been arrived at without making preliminary trial of a system of freedom. The crisis of 1825 was generally attributed to the bad organisation of provincial credit; the remedy had been sought in the removal of those restrictions placed on the issue of notes in the provinces by the Act of 1742. Then, when this policy was found to be inadequate and was even regarded by some as the cause of the crisis of 1836-1839, it was judged necessary to centralise the control of the note issues and to take the management of them out of the hands of the Bank.[1] But the debates in Parliament and the contemporary pamphlets show clearly enough that such a policy would never have been adopted if people had not first experienced the effect of the opposite system.[2]

Finally, to gain a better understanding of the Act of 1844, we have traced the origin and development of its main provisions, first in the works of its chief promoters, Lord Overstone, Torrens and Norman, and then in the speeches and *Memorandum* of Sir Robert Peel, who presented it to Parliament and by whose name it is known. This plan seemed more satisfactory and more suited to an historical study like the present, than the alternative of giving a detailed criticism of each provision of the law.

[1] The Report of the Committee of 1832 brings out the theories according to which the Bank regulated, or at least was supposed to regulate, its issues.

[2] The Act of 1833, which forms the subject of our second chapter, by making Bank notes legal tender, by insisting on some degree of publicity for the Bank's balance sheets, though less, it is true, than is imposed to-day, and by granting official recognition to the joint-stock banks and to the employment of their cheques, gave to the existing system of English banking three of its most salient features. Consequently, this Act may be regarded as one of the causes of that of 1844, notwithstanding the great differences between the two.

PART I.

CAUSES AND ANALYSIS OF ROBERT PEEL'S ACT.

CHAPTER I.

THE CRISIS OF 1825 AND THE ACT OF 1826.

The Crisis of 1825. Effects of the resumption of cash payments. Renewal of speculative mania. Its causes. Speculations in South American and Foreign Loans. The crisis. Policy of the Bank during the crisis. The Responsibility of the Banks and the effect of over-issues on the crisis exaggerated. The Act of 1826. Meeting of Parliament: Speeches of Lord Liverpool, Peel and Huskisson. The Act of 1828, its two-fold object. Reorganisation of the provincial credit system. Suppression of the Bank of England's privileges in the Provinces. Abolition of small notes. Small notes continued in Scotland. Action of Sir Walter Scott.

A.—THE CRISIS OF 1825.

THE resumption of cash payments and the ease with which the Bank had anticipated the date fixed by the law of 1819[1] quickly restored public confidence. The harvests, which had been scanty during the last three years of what had been practically a forced currency, were plentiful for three seasons after 1821. According to Tooke the trade and industry of the country had never been in a more satisfactory condition than they were between 1821 and 1824. Indeed, at the end of the session of 1823, the King congratulated Parliament on the general prosperity, and he repeated his congratulations at the end of the following year and even at the beginning of the year 1825.

The Bank of England shared in the general prosperity and its bullion reserve rose to £14,200,000—an immense sum at that date.

At the same time an Act passed in April, 1822, empowered the Bank of England and the country banks to increase their

[1] The latest date fixed for the resumption of cash payments was May 1st, 1823, but the Bank had actually resumed them two years earlier.

issues. The result of this was a rise in prices, which enabled the Government to reduce the rate of interest on the National Debt from 5 to 4 and from 4 to 3½ per cent., with the help of an advance of £5,000,000 made to it by the Bank.

The conversion of the 5 per cents. affected stock to the value of 135 millions, while that of the 4 per cents. applied to 80 millions.

Such an important reduction[1] of the rate of interest on capital caused many of the holders of public securities, who could not be satisfied with a small income, to sell out as quickly as possible. There was, in fact, a proverb current in the financial world that "John Bull can stand many things but he cannot stand 2 per cent." When the price of money remains at a low level for any considerable period, people will turn to risky investments if no good ones offer themselves, and a crisis is the necessary result of such experiments.

This fact has been frequently noticed;[2] the period of which we write affords an illustration of it. Speculation of all kinds reappeared, but especially in the form of transactions with South America, which had already been a notable feature in 1809 and 1810. The South American Revolution had excited intense interest in England. As soon as the independence of the Republics had been recognised, their appeal was responded to with unreasoning eagerness by investors and traders, who subscribed indiscriminately to all the loans raised by these States, which generally proved quite incapable of meeting their liabilities. At the same time increased support was given to a number of other public loans.[3] The commercial world allowed itself to be deceived into a false estimate of the value of the new

[1] The reduction in the interest on the public funds was accompanied by a reduction in the half-yearly dividend of the Bank from 5 to 4 per cent. This caused a number of sales and the Bank stock fell 16 points.

[2] This fact is so obvious that after the crisis of 1866 William Newmarch suggested that a minimum limit should be fixed, below which the Bank might not lower its rate of discount. This limit was to be 4 per cent.

[3] The public loans raised between 1822 and 1825 are given in a well documented essay by Mr. Hyde Clarke in the *Journal of the Statistical Society*,

markets thus opened up, and especially in regard to the Colonial food stuffs.

Macleod[1] estimates that 150 millions were invested in various ways in Mexico and South America. Transactions of this kind, essentially speculative in nature, multiplied continually and the Lord Chancellor thought it necessary even at the beginning of 1825 to call the attention of Parliament to the prevailing mania, while seven weeks later Lord Lauderdale stated that £200,000,000 had been subscribed to companies of all kinds.

Very soon the situation recalled memories not only of 1810, but of 1720 and the time of the South Sea Bubble. Companies were formed with the most absurd objects,[2] and as the first subscriptions paid up did not often exceed 5 per cent. of the nominal value of the shares, persons of very modest fortunes were able to take part in the transactions. The number of companies formed rose to 624, involving a nominal capital of £372,173,100. This enormous sum represented £150 per head for the 13 million persons who

Vol. XLI., p. 313. The following list shows the amount of the loans raised in London and the prices at which they were issued :—

Year.		*Amount of Loan.*	*Price of Issue.*	*Year.*		*Amount of Loan.*	*Price of Issue.*
1822	Chili ...	£1,000,000	70 %	1824	Greece ...	£800,000	59 %
	Columbia ...	2,000,000	84 %		Mexico ...	3,200,000	58 %
	Denmark ...	2,000,000	77½ %		Naples ...	2,500,000	91½ %
	Peru ...	450,000	88 %		Peru ...	750,000	82 %
	Russia ...	3,500,000	81 %	1825	Brazil ...	4,000,000	85 %
1823	Austria ...	1,500,000	82 %		Denmark	3,500,000	75 %
	Portugal ...	1,500,000	87 %		Greece ...	2,000,000	56½ %
1824	Brazil ...	1,686,000	75 %		Guatemala	167,000	73 %
	Buenos Ayres	1,000,000	85 %		Mexico ...	3,200,000	89¼ %
	Columbia ...	4,750,000	88½ %		Peru ...	616,000	78 %

As regards these loans, the prices at which they were issued should be noticed, and it may also be remarked that, at any rate in the case of the Greek loans, only a small part of the sums paid in reached their intended destination in the hands of the Greek Government. The remainder was frittered away in the form of orders insisted on by the banking firms which undertook the issue. Thus the Greeks were forced to buy certain frigates which were never able to reach Gibraltar, and some fire-arms which exploded as soon as they were used. Probably much the same thing happened in the case of the other loans, and most likely a good deal of the money subscribed never went out of England.

[1] *Theory and Practice of Banking*, 3rd edition, Vol. II., p. 109.

[2] One company, which was able to secure subscribers, was promoted in order to drain the Red Sea with a view to recovering the treasure abandoned by the Egyptians after the crossing of the Jews. Juglar, *Les crises économiques*, p. 334.

then constituted the population of England, and was equivalent to a third of the total wealth of the country.[1]

The price of the shares in several of the new companies rose very quickly. Those of *The Anglo-Mexican Mining Company,* for instance, which were issued at £10, rose within a month from £43 to £150; and the shares of the *Real del Monte,* issued at £70, rose from £550 to £1,350.[2] A still more significant feature was that the prices of commodities were doubled and sometimes tripled in a few months. The inevitable reaction came. Prices began to fall at the beginning of the summer, and this was followed by a collapse in securities upon which no further payments could be obtained. At the end of November the failure of several large firms which speculated in cotton produced a general panic. The Bank of England thought fit to abandon the policy of 1797 and to increase its issues freely. Its reserve sank from £13,500,000 in January, 1824, to £11,400,000 in October, 1824. It persevered in this conduct in spite of an unfavourable exchange, and in April, 1825, its reserve was only £6,650,000, while its issues exceeded the total in circulation in January, 1824. The Bank only realised its mistake at the very height of the crisis, but on December 31st it raised its discount rate to 5 per cent. This did not prevent a further decline in the reserve from over 3 millions in November to £1,260,890 (December 31st), which threw the circulation into unheard-of confusion.[3]

[1] Conant, *A History of Modern Banks of Issue,* p. 446.

[2] The fluctuations in the share values of the different mining companies will be found in Palgrave, *Dictionary of Political Economy* (Vol. I., p. 458).

[3] The following table from Juglar (p. 337) will give an exact idea of the continued fall in the Bank reserve:—

	1824. £	1825. £
January	13,500,000	9,400,000
February	13,800,000	8,800,000
March	13,800,000	8,100,000
April	13,400,000	6,600,000
May	12,800,000	6,100,000
June	12,800,000	5,400,000
July	11,800,000	4,100,000
August	11,700,000	3,600,000
September	11,800,000	3,400,000
October	11,400,000	3,100,000
November	11,300,000	3,000,000
December	10,700,000	1,200,000

The scarcity of coin increased, notwithstanding the action of the Government which ordered the Mint to be kept working day and night; and this scarcity became a veritable famine after the failure of the London Bank, one of the leading banking firms, which dragged down with it sixty other financial companies.

The drain on the coin was so great that the Bank was obliged to put into circulation 600,000 one pound notes, which, although they had been created when the Restriction Act was passed, had lain for a long time forgotten in its safes. This measure was effective in saving the Bank of Norwich, but could not materially alter the unprecedented state of affairs. No one was willing to part with such money as he possessed, and according to Huskisson's statement in the House of Commons,[1] it was impossible during the greater part of December to realise even the best securities, such as Government stock and the shares of the Bank of England and the East India Company.

The general distress was increased by the failure of thirty-six country banks which the Bank could not assist in time; and several of the important London commercial firms were threatened with a like fate. The Bank, under pressure from the Government, decided finally to increase its issues; it granted new loans to the value of £400,000. This afforded substantial assistance to those firms which were solid enough to offer resistance to misfortune, and at length, when the weaker ones had all collapsed, things gradually improved and two years later money was being lent at 4 per cent.

These are the broad outlines of the crisis of 1825. The attempt has been made, and indeed is still made, to throw the whole responsibility for it upon the over-issues of the Bank of England and of the country banks.

On this point Macleod[2] very fairly remarks that:

[1] *Parliamentary Debates*, Vol. XIV., p. 230. See the whole of Huskisson's Speech, pp. 229-244.

[2] 3rd Edition, Vol. II., pp. 117, 118.

"Though it is indisputable that the Bank acted on the most unsound principles in not contracting its issues when the great drain of bullion for exportation was going on, it is a mere delusion for men to attribute the consequences of their own wild and extravagant mania to the Bank of England, or to any bank. The errors of all the banks put together were trivial compared to the outbreaks of speculative insanity which seized upon all classes. . . . Was it the issue of Bank notes that led a respectable book-selling firm to risk £100,000 on a speculation in hops? The Bank had committed many errors before, as serious as those of 1825, without leading to any such disaster."

B.—The Act of 1826.

When once the crisis had subsided, the time came to search for its causes and to find a remedy for them; this task devolved on Parliament when it assembled on February 3rd.

The King's Speech[1] specially drew the attention of Parliament to the question and neither House showed any disposition to neglect it.

The Prime Minister, Lord Liverpool, in a speech[2] of which we made use in studying the condition of provincial credit on the eve of the French Revolution, criticised severely both the system on which this credit was organised and also the Act of 1709, which limited the number of partners in a bank of issue to six, so that any small provincial tradesman, a fruiterer, a grocer or a butcher, might open a bank whilst the right of issue was refused to genuine companies, well deserving of confidence.[3]

Peel supported these views in the House of Commons[4] and contrasted the monopoly which existed in England with the free Scotch system. He pointed out that in England 100 banks had failed in 1793, 157 between 1810 and 1817,

[1] *Parl. Debates*, Vol. XIV., pp. 2-3.

[2] For this speech see *Parl. Debates*, pp. 454-463.

[3] p. 462.

[4] See the sitting of February 13, pp. 286-298.

and 76 during the recent crisis, and that, moreover, the numbers recorded would have been much greater had it not been for the different ways of making composition, and so on; whilst in Scotland, on the contrary, there was only a single bank failure on record, and even in that case the creditors had ultimately been paid in full.

Peel then described the terrible condition of country banking, and declared his conviction that a system of well-established joint-stock companies would supply a more secure basis for the circulation.

With reference to the small notes, which had just formed the subject of a strong speech by Huskisson,[1] Peel agreed with the latter in thinking that the £1 notes only served to drive out the sovereigns; that the over-issue of paper money was one of the worst evils from which the country suffered and that the present was an excellent opportunity of getting rid of it.

The Act of 1826 was passed by a very large majority.

This Act had a two-fold object, corresponding to the two-fold criticism brought against the previous legislation; it attempted (*a*) to reorganise country credit by abolishing the monopoly established by the laws of 1708 and 1742; (*b*) to suppress the small notes.

A.—*The Reorganisation of Country Credit.* We are already familiar with the organisation of country credit previous to 1826. We have seen its absurdity.[2] The situation was made still worse because the Bank, while insisting on its monopoly in the provinces and preventing the formation of banks of issue with more than six partners, yet made no attempt to secure the right of establishing branches. In other words, the Bank hindered the provision by others of any satisfactory form of paper currency, and at the same time refused to take the matter into its own hands. It played the part of the proverbial dog in the manger. The effect of this mistaken policy was the introduction of an absurd and dangerous system of provincial credit facil-

[1] The small notes were attacked with equal vigour in the course of the debate by Lord King, Baring and various other speakers.

[2] See above, p. 170, *et seq.*

ities, which allowed every small grocer to set up a bank and to issue notes which he was unable to honour.

The Statute 1826 (c. 46), in order to remedy this evil, authorised the establishment of banks 65 miles or more from London, having any number of partners and with power to issue notes. In this way encouragement was given to the creation of joint-stock banks of issue. The Bank of England was at the same time empowered to establish branches in any part of England.

B.—*The Suppression of the Small Notes.* The small notes were said to be of no use except to raise prices and encourage speculation. The Statute 1826 (c. 6) abolished Bank notes of values less than £5; the primary result of this was to force the Bank to redeem between 7 and 8 millions of notes.

This latter Act was to have been extended to Scotland. But the measure was strongly opposed in that country, where £1 notes were established by long custom, and it found a celebrated opponent in the person of Sir Walter Scott. Sir Walter, under the pseudonym of Malachi Malagrowther, published three letters containing a most amusing satire on the mania for uniformity.[1] These letters made a great stir and the Scotch were ultimately victorious. By an Act of 1828 (c. 65), however, the circulation of Scotch notes in England was forbidden.

[1] These three letters, which originally came out in the *Edinburgh Weekly Journal* in February and March, 1826, were soon afterwards published in one volume. They are also to be found among the complete works of W. Scott.—See *The Miscellaneous Prose Works of W. Scott* (3 vols., Edinburgh, 1854-56), Vol. I., pp. 725-756.

CHAPTER II.

THE COMMITTEE OF 1832 AND THE ACT OF 1833.

The Inquiry of 1832. Chief problems brought forward: (*a*) The regulation of the currency. Theory stated for the first time by Horsley Palmer, that a reserve equivalent to one-third of the liabilities guarantees a Bank from all risk. Application of this theory by legislation in various cases. Its worth. (*b*) Establishment of Joint-Stock Banks in London. History of this matter. Mr. Joplin's book. Legal aspect of the question. (*c*) Bank notes as legal tender. Advantages of making the notes legal tender as stated by Lord Althorp. Peel's opposition. Notes made legal tender. (*d*) The limitation of the rate of interest. Need for suspending the usury laws especially with reference to the Bank. (*e*) The publication of accounts. The Act of 1833. Its chief provisions. Fate of the Joint-Stock Banks.

THE period succeeding 1830 was a time of much political agitation in England; the country was on the eve of the Reform Bill of 1832. Disturbances were frequent in London, where the distress was as great as in the rest of the country. There was a run on the Bank, but as it was of a purely political character and was confined to London, it is of no importance as far as our subject is concerned; it is enough to mention it in passing.

The Bank's Charter was to expire in 1833. At the beginning of 1832 a Committee of Inquiry was appointed to consider the question of its renewal, but owing to the excitement aroused by the Reform Bill, its report was not presented until the end of the year.

The inquiry dealt with several important points:[1] (1) The regulation of the issues; (2) The possibility of establishing

[1] We have changed the order of the questions and have omitted some of them. For further details see an excellent Summary of the Inquiry of 1832, called, *A digest of the Evidence on the Bank charter taken before the Committee of* 1832 (London, 1833, edited by Ridgway). The extracts from the evidence are preceded by 121 pages dealing with the Bank of England and with previous crises. The work contains also some very useful tables on the coinage, on the note circulation of country banks, etc.

joint-stock banks in London; (3) The Bank notes as legal tender; (4) The Usury laws; (5) The publication of the accounts of the Bank.

I.—Regulation of the Issues.

As regards this question the inquiry of 1832 is of much interest. In the first place the directors of the Bank of England were unanimous in supporting the theories contained in the Bullion Report and recognised that a paper currency ought to be regulated according to the foreign exchanges and the price of bullion.[1]

Besides this, one of the directors, Mr. Horsley Palmer, stated for the first time a theory with regard to the note circulation, which has since been frequently repeated and has even formed a basis for legislation on various occasions.[2] He said that in principle only two-thirds of the assets ought to be invested in interest-bearing securities and *one-third ought to be kept as reserve in bullion.* This proportion would, in his opinion, prevent all risk.[3] Palmer's theory was supported by another director, Mr. G. W. Norman;[4] it served at the time to guide the issues of the Bank of England and it still finds some partisans. "It is," remarks M. Cauwès,[5] "an empirical formula which may

[1] The directors of the Bank had hitherto been misled by observing that in practice the foreign exchanges did not follow exactly the variations in the paper currency of the Bank. The difficulty was a serious one for those who were unwilling to look further. A little closer examination would, however, have shown, as M. Juglar justly observes (p. 341), that it was necessary to reckon in the paper currency not only the issues of the Bank but those of the whole country, which would include bills of exchange, commercial securities, drafts, warrants, etc.

[2] Compare the organisation of the Imperial Bank of Germany and that of the Bank of Algeria before 1880. We may note as conforming to this theory: the system under which the Bank of Belgium works, according to which the reserve should amount to one-third of the notes and deposits combined, but may fall to one-fourth with the authorisation of the Government; the Hungarian law of 1873; the very complicated Swedish law of 1874; the Swiss legislation, which fixes the amount of the reserve at 40 per cent. of the amount of the note issue, and which is, indeed, only a variation of the same principle.

[3] *A Digest of Evidence*, p. 7. See the whole of Palmer's evidence, pp. 4-24.

[4] *Digest*, p. 31.

[5] *Cours d'Économie Politique*, Vol. II., p. 316.

have some value as the result of experience; but it would be a mistake to suppose that the proportion one-third can have any absolute value as a safeguard. It has sometimes been found in a crisis that a reserve of more than one-third of the issues was insufficient."

M. Gide[1] also observes that if "the proportion is fixed at one-third, not only discounting but also the conversion of the notes may become impossible! Suppose that there is a reserve of 100 millions and notes to the value of 300 millions; the Bank has preserved the required proportion. But it has done this so exactly that at the moment it cannot cash a single note without breaking the rule and causing the reserve to fall below one-third of the value of the notes, *for* 99 *is not a third of* 299. Thus the precaution leads to the very danger it was intended to avoid.

II.—Establishment of Joint-Stock Banks in London.

This point requires some explanation; we have already briefly referred to it.[2] The Statute 1742 (c. 13-15), an Act often referred to in this work, gave to the Bank the monopoly of issue in "that part of Great Britain called England"; only banks formed by fewer than six persons were exempt from this monopoly. But the privileges conferred by this Act were limited to borrowing or owing money on notes payable at sight. The business of banking was really limited to this at that time. The clause was interpreted strictly and hence the use of cheques, which was borrowed from the Dutch, was not forbidden by the law. Thus there was no obstacle to prevent banking being carried on by the help of the cheque system. This custom spread little by little without giving Parliament any excuse for interference and by the time its existence was realised it had extended too widely for prohibition to be possible;

[1] *Principes d'Economie Politique*, p. 374, note. See also Wilfredo Pareto, *Cours d'Économie Politique professé à l'Université de Lausanne*, p. 386. "No rule can be laid down as to the amount of the reserve. The reserve is needed solely to insure the convertibility of the notes into gold, and for this purpose it has sometimes to be a large fraction and sometimes a small fraction of the paper circulation.

[2] See above, pp. 171, 172.

moreover a short time afterwards, Mr. Joplin pointed out for the first time that the establishment of these banks of deposit[1] and their transactions were absolutely legal.

This was the state of affairs when the Act of 1826 was passed authorising the foundation of joint-stock banks of issue outside the 65 mile limit.

This Act however said nothing as to the legality of similar institutions in London (of course, without the right of issue). The question thus remained unsolved. It was difficult to deny that from a legal point of view the right to form companies carrying on all kinds of banking transactions except that of note issue was absolutely established. Joplin's reasoning was irrefutable. The Bank of England tried in vain to dispute it and applied unsuccessfully to the Government for a modification of the law. The question was, however, brought before the Committee of 1832;[2] even those who supported the new banks realised that to avoid uncertainty it would be better to settle the matter by legislation.

III.—Bank Notes as Legal Tender.

The Bank of England notes had never been legal tender. Even under the regime of the Restriction Act, the notes, though inconvertible, were not legal money and it was this fact which enabled Lord King to write his famous circular to his tenants. The problem now was whether it was advisable to give them this legal character. This question was raised before the Committee of 1832 as well as before Parliament.

[1] Joplin, *Supplementary Observations to the third Edition of an Essay on Banking*, p. 84 (1823).

[2] It is interesting to note that the question was raised as a matter of theory, not of practice. In fact, notwithstanding Joplin's discovery, no joint-stock bank had been established in London, though the Government had obtained a decision from the Court of King's Bench in case such a difficult problem presented itself.

[3] Our readers will remember that the founders of the Bank and in particular Godfrey, so far from asking that the notes should be legal tender, asserted that the only thing which enabled notes to circulate was that the bearer could convert them into cash whenever he desired. See above, p. 83.

Lord Althorp[1] spoke in favour of the measure in the House of Commons. He explained very ably the advantages which would result if the notes were made legal tender. In ordinary times it was true the change would have little effect, for, now that the small notes were suppressed, gold and £5 notes would be able to circulate together; the directors would take care of that. But on the other hand, the proposed alteration would protect the Bank from any drain which was not due to the state of the exchanges. Under existing conditions, when a provincial bank feared a run on its reserve, it was forced to send for bullion from the Bank of England, not only for the amount immediately needed, but for that much larger sum which would be required if it had to meet all its liabilities. The Bank was thus liable to unexpected withdrawals for home use and suffered from the effects of every run on the provincial banks.

The proposal to make the notes legal tender was opposed by Sir Robert Peel during the sitting of July 1st,[2] as being contrary to the true principles of a paper currency. In Peel's opinion the matter resolved itself into a question of confidence and confidence could not be had to order. No doubt anything that tended to increase confidence and security in a country was a good thing, but this result could not be obtained by Act of Parliament.

IV.—Legal Limitation of the Rate of Interest.

This was another important question which came up for discussion in 1832. There were many general arguments to be given in favour of the repeal of the usury laws. In the case of the Bank there was a special reason, which was that these laws hindered the rate of discount from working freely enough to withstand an actual or impending crisis.

This particular disadvantage of limiting the rate of interest

[1] *Parliamentary Debates*, Vol. XVIII., p. 179. See the whole of the speech made by Lord Althorp in introducing the Act of 1833, pp. 169-187.

[2] *Parl. Debates*, pp. 1369-1370.

was felt in France also. There a special law had to be passed in 1857 authorising the Bank of France to raise its discount rate above 6 per cent.[1]

V.—Publication of the Accounts of the Bank of England.

The necessity for a publication of the accounts was fully recognised at this time.[2] There were no differences of opinion on the subject in Parliament; though there was some opposition before the Committee of Inquiry on the part of the directors of the Bank.[3] There was, however, no suggestion as yet of a weekly statement, it was merely a question of deciding between monthly and quarterly publications.

The Act of 1833.

The Act of 1833 (Statute 1833, c. 98) embodies the solutions generally accepted of the problems we have just considered. It made the Bank three concessions of appreciable value:[4]

1.—The Bank notes were made legal tender, which they had never been hitherto.[5]

2.—The Bank was exempted from the action of the usury laws so far as the discount of bills not having three months to run was concerned. It was thus enabled to raise its rate above 5 per cent.

3.—The Government repaid to the Bank one-fourth of its capital, which was thus reduced from £14,520,000 to

[1] Cauwès, p. 322. It will be remembered that 6 per cent. was then the maximum rate for commercial business.

[2] See Lord Althorp's speech, pp. 176-178.

[3] Palmer declared himself opposed to any publicity. See *Abstract*, p. 20. Norman, on the other hand, was willing to agree to a quarterly statement—see p. 44. Compare the very discreet evidence of Richards, a former Governor.

[4] The correspondence between the Chancellor of the Exchequer and the Bank of England at the time of this renewal of the charter was published by the Bank in 1858. See *A Copy of the Correspondence between the Chancellor of the Exchequer and the Bank of England relative to the renewal of the Charter in 1833*.

[5] This proposal, which, as we have seen, was opposed by Peel, was passed by 214 votes to 156.

£10,890,000. But in return the Treasury reduced by £120,000 the yearly sum paid to the Bank for the management of the public debt; this sum was now only £131,000.

On the other hand the Bank had to furnish the Chancellor of the Exchequer with exact accounts of the amount of its bullion, of the number of notes in circulation and of the total of its deposits. The *London Gazette* was to publish monthly the balance sheet for the previous quarter.

The Act of 1833 also affirmed the legality of joint-stock banks which issued cheques—a legality which the Bank had long contested in vain. And it was not long before the first joint-stock bank, the London & Westminster, was established in London. It was followed by many others. Amongst the most famous of these were the London Joint-Stock Bank in 1836, and the Union Bank and the London & County Bank in 1839.[1]

Finally, the Bank's charter was renewed until 1855, but the Government reserved the right to suspend it, under certain conditions, at the end of twelve years. It will be seen how the English Government was induced to make use of this power.

[1] The Bank of England was not to be deterred from its opposition and it took advantage of the wording of some of the laws to wage a violent war against the joint-stock banks. The latter having at their head such men as Gilbart and George Pollard, met this attack by the most ingenious devices and legal interference was again necessary in 1844. The struggle by which the joint-stock banks secured their independence would afford a most amusing subject of study.

CHAPTER III.

THE CRISIS OF 1836-1839.

Condition of public opinion from 1833 to 1836. Extensive speculations at home. Foreign Loans. The Bank's policy during this period. Rapid fall in the Bank reserve in 1836. Its causes: President Jackson's monetary reform in America: the crisis in Ireland. Refusal of Bank to re-discount paper already discounted by a joint-stock bank. Outbreak of the crisis in Lancashire. It spreads throughout England. Firm policy of the Bank, the crisis apparently over. Return of the crisis in 1838 on the Continent and in the United States. The Bank of Belgium suspends payment. Remarkable imprudence of the Directors of the Bank of England. Violence of the crisis on the London Market. The Bank on the verge of ruin. Assistance of the Bank of France. Painful and prolonged liquidation of the crisis.

THE three years which followed the Act of 1833 were a time of great prosperity. The harvests were remarkably abundant. Moreover the foundation of a number of joint-stock banks[1] in the provinces increased the facilities of credit and considerably lowered the rate of interest. Finally the success, as great as it was unexpected, of the first railway lines, encouraged the formation of numerous railway companies.[2]

All these things combined to make the English public forget the crisis of 1825 and plunge anew into a speculative mania which was only distinguished from those we have already described by the fact that this time the speculation

[1] Between 1833 and 1836, 72 joint-stock banks were founded in England and 13 in Ireland. See *The Causes and Consequences of the Pressure on the Money Market, with a statement of the action of the Bank of England from 1st October,* 1833 *to 27th December,* 1836, by J. H. Palmer, p. 10. Palmer's work is interesting reading; he states clearly enough the causes of the crisis of 1836, but he tries unsuccessfully to absolve the Bank of England, of which he was a director, from all responsibility. Palmer criticises most severely the joint-stock banks, whose continued existence he thinks incompatible with that of the Bank of England. His pamphlet gives in an appendix the correspondence between the Treasury and the Bank in 1826 with regard to the establishment of branches in the provinces. The work is best known through the reply made to it by S. J. Loyd, afterwards Lord Overstone.

[2] For the Railway Mania see Leroy-Beaulieu, *L'État moderne et ses fonctions,* p. 182, note.

was mainly in home enterprises.[1] This did not prevent an additional dabbling in certain foreign speculations nor subscriptions to the numerous foreign loans which were issued on the London market.[2]

How did the Bank of England act when confronted by such a situation?

The rule according to which it was supposed to conduct its business was as follows: the reserve kept, composed of bullion and securities, was to be equal to its liabilities; while the regulation of the note circulation was left to the public through the natural movement of the foreign exchanges, and meanwhile, whether the demands on the Bank came from at home or abroad, it was to maintain a metallic reserve equal to one-third of its liabilities. This

[1] These speculations led to the formation of a great many companies, of which some few were useful but the majority entirely futile. The following list of them is given by Levi, *The History of British Commerce*, p. 220, note:

Companies.	*Nominal Capital.*
	£
Railways	69,666,000
Mining Companies	7,035,200
Packet and Navigation Companies	3,533,000
Banking Companies	23,750,000
Conveyance Companies	500,000
Insurance Companies	7,600,000
Investment Companies	1,730,000
Newspaper Companies	350,000
Canal Companies	3,655,000
Gas Companies	890,000
Cemetery Companies	435,000
Miscellaneous Companies	16,104,500
	135,248,700

[2] Hyde Clarke, *loc. cit.*, gives the following list of these loans and the prices at which they were issued:—

	State.	*Amount.*	*Price of Issue.*
1832	Greece	£2,344,000	100 p.c.
	(Loan guaranteed by the three Powers protecting Greece).		

	State.	*Amount.*	*Price of Issue.*
1833	Portugal	£2,000,000	48 p.c.
—	Russia	3,000,000	—
—	Portugal	1,000,000	94 p.c.
1834	Spain (Cuba)	450,000	—
—	Spain	4,000,000	60 p.c.
1835	Portugal	6,000,000	70 p.c.
1836	Belgium	1,200,000	92 p.c.
—	Florida	200,000	—
—	Portugal	900,000	80 p.c.

supposed rule was not easy to keep inviolate and between 1833 and 1835 it was often broken.[1]

At the beginning of 1836 the reserve of the Bank was sufficiently large; it was over 8 millions. Towards the end of March it began to decline and fell to 6 millions in June, to 5 millions in October and to £3,640,000 at the end of November. The Bank's liabilities at this last date amounted to more than 30 millions.[2] A vain attempt had been made to stop this withdrawal of gold by raising the rate of discount, at first to 4½ per cent. and then to 5 per cent.

The drain was the result both of foreign and home demands.

As regards the former, President Jackson had determined not to renew the charter of the United States Bank and to give what he considered to be a more secure basis to the currency.[3] A large number of securities of all kinds were sold in England to obtain the gold needed for this reform; this transaction was made easier by the low rate of discount and by the multiplication of country banks.

In the autumn of 1836 there was another exportation of gold, this time to Ireland, where the failure of the Agricultural and Commercial Bank[4] made the other banks afraid of a run upon their reserves. They were only able to prevent this by importing 2 millions of gold, borrowed from the Bank of England.[5]

[1] On September 9, 1834, for instance, the reserve was £7,010,000, as against liabilities of £31,058,000, and in May, 1835, it was £5,951,000, as against liabilities of £29,417,000. For details see Levi, p. 221, note, and Macleod, *Theory of Credit*, p. 1011.

[2] Exactly £30,941,000.

[3] For an account of President Jackson's reform and of his famous Specie Circular of June 11, 1836, see Conant, *A History of Banks of Issue*, p. 481. The following may also be consulted with advantage as regards the reasons which led to this reform. Poor, *Money and its Laws*, pp. 489-537; Knox (J. J.), *United States Notes*, pp. 40-46, and in particular, *A History of Banking in all Nations*, Vol. I., pp. 191-335.

The United States Bank, which Jackson opposed, still exists, but is now only the Bank of Philadelphia.

[4] For the history of this bank and its charter see Dillon (Malcolm), *The History and Development of Banking in Ireland*, pp. 71-77. It is not however, too severe a criticism to say that this book of Dillon's is worthless.

[5] This enormous importation of gold confirmed Lord Althorp's theory, which was that so long as the notes of the Bank of England were not legal tender, the Bank would suffer for every run on a country bank. But it

The inevitable settlement after a period of speculation which had already lasted three years, began in Great Britain simultaneously with the crises in Ireland and America.

One of the most prevalent forms of speculation had been the re-discount of bills, which had been largely practised by the joint-stock banks. In August however, the Bank of England was not content with merely raising its discount rate to 5 per cent. but also refused flatly to discount any bill which had been already endorsed by a joint-stock bank. This was a fatal blow to most of the American securities, which had been bought by the joint-stock banks and put into circulation again after endorsement.

The actual crisis began in Lancashire, a county which had become deeply involved in American and Irish investments. As early as November the Northern and Central Bank of Manchester applied to the Bank of England for help. At first this was refused, but the failure of this establishment which had 39 branches in industrial districts, would have been so disastrous that the Bank was forced to consent to make advances, at first of £500,000 and ultimately of £1,370,000.

In January, 1837, similar difficulties were experienced in London: the American houses were in urgent need of assistance. It was found upon examination that these houses were actually solvent, although unable to meet the demands made upon them at the moment. Besides this, it was evident that to allow them to fail would produce a complete upset of credit. Under these circumstances the Bank determined on a bold step and advanced them 6 millions. It had no cause to regret its courage: not only was a terrible crash avoided, but the advances made were repaid almost in full and, since the previous liquidation had withdrawn a large quantity of paper from circulation, gold now flowed back into its safes.

This influx of gold continued throughout 1837; in De-

was a disputed point whether the Bank of England notes were legal tender in Ireland. Owing to this uncertainty, the Bank of Ireland had to import a much larger quantity of gold than it would otherwise have needed and the Bank of England felt the effects of the run upon the Bank of Ireland. During the crisis the Bank of England notes were depreciated 2½ per cent. in Ireland.

cember the metallic reserve was £10,500,800. In March, 1838, the desired proportion was again attained, the assets being £10,527,000 in coin and bullion and £21,046,000, while the liabilities were £31,573,000.

The crisis seemed to be over. In reality it was only just beginning.

The harvests, which had been excellent from 1833 to 1837, were very bad in 1838. Such scarcity had not been known since 1816; corn to the value of £10,000,000 had to be imported. The natural result was a great exportation of gold.

Other causes combined with this primary one to increase the drain of gold. During the preceding years there had been a great misuse of credit and of paper money in America, France and Belgium. This in itself, by attracting large quantities of gold to England, had helped the Bank to replenish its coffers more rapidly. But this extension of credit stopped suddenly, as was indeed to be expected, and towards the end of 1838 a general collapse came, the Bank of Belgium giving the signal for the crisis by suspending its payments. The Bank of France was obliged almost immediately to send to London for money in order to withstand a run upon it, whilst America, where the crisis was complicated by a currency reform, also helped to increase the drain on English gold.

During this time the Bank of England had been acting in a manner very far from prudent. Seeing that gold came in plentifully, it reduced its rate of discount from 5 to 4 per cent., and in November, 1838, even to 3½ per cent. Consequently, at this latter date, at the very moment when the collapse of the Bank of Belgium gave clear warning of the imminence of a serious drain, the Bank rate was lower than the market rate. By way of meeting the danger, and not content with increasing its discounts when it was evident that everyone was exporting gold to America, the Bank thought fit—in the face of an unfavourable exchange—to send a million to America on its own account! "Of all acts of mismanagement in the whole history of the Bank," says Macleod,[1] "this is probably the most astounding."

When the drain began the Bank did not at first change

[1] *Op. cit.*, p. 1016.

its policy and it was not until May 14th that it decided to raise its discount rate to 5 per cent. Its metallic reserve, which, according to the statements of the directors, ought always to equal one-third of its liabilities, was then £4,117,000, whilst the liabilities amounted to £25,711,000. After this matters got worse, and on July 16 the reserve had fallen to £2,987,000 and the Bank of England was face to face with bankruptcy.

Some expedient had to be devised to avoid the suspension of payments. At first an attempt was made to sell "dead weight" annuities, but no purchaser could be found at the price demanded: it was then decided to sell public securities to the value of £700,000 and later, in May, bills were drawn upon Paris for £600,000. But when these expired the Bank was quite unable to meet them and the foreign bankers, understanding the situation, hastened to realise their securities in London.

Things seemed desperate, and would actually have been so if the Bank of France had not come to the rescue of the Bank of England, as indeed it had to do on a second occasion, fifty years later. But since the Bank of England was not in the habit of drawing on foreign countries and the Bank of France was unaccustomed to make loans except by discounting bills of exchange or on public securities, it was arranged that Baring Brothers should draw bills of exchange on twelve Parisian bankers to the amount of £2,000,000, whilst the Bank of France undertook to discount these bills.[1] A similar transaction with Hamburg brought in £900,000.

These measures were gradually successful in stopping the drain of bullion. The reserve was at its lowest on September 2nd, 1839, when it amounted to £2,406,000; after this it slowly rose. Bankruptcy had been avoided, but at what cost! The liquidation went on until 1843 and during the crisis sixty-three country banks, of which twenty-nine issued notes, had had to suspend payments.[2]

[1] Compare Levi, p. 224.

[2] See Robert Peel, *Speeches*, Vol., IV., pp. 357-358.

CHAPTER IV.

THE BANKING PRINCIPLE AND THE CURRENCY PRINCIPLE.

Active movement for reform aroused by the crisis of 1836-1839. Numerous schemes proposed. Two main tendencies: (*a*) The Banking Principle: Its chief exponents, Tooke, Fullarton and Wilson. The essence of the Banking Principle, Current errors on this subject. Criticism and dangers of the theory. (*b*) The Currency Principle: Statement of the Currency Principle. The theoretical and practical errors involved. Success of the Currency Principle. Need to examine the practical form under which this theory presented itself in England.

THE experience of these three years was not lost upon England.[1] The most competent financiers and men of business were convinced that the intensity of the crisis was due to the fluctuations in the currency and that unlimited freedom of issue was a danger for a country exposed, by its exceptional position as commercial centre of the world, to the effects of the crises occurring on all the other markets of production and consumption.

It was pointed out on all sides that most of the banks of issue that had failed had not been on a satisfactory basis; that they had usually been founded in the hope of finding, through the issue of paper money, the means to negotiate big enterprises and hence to make large profits, and that of the twenty-nine institutions which had disappeared beween 1839 and 1843, seventeen had never paid any dividend. An epigram much in vogue at the time asserted that, "Free trade in banking is synonymous with free trade in swindling."

This being the prevailing state of mind, it was not surprising to find a number of pamphlets appearing and a thousand systems being proposed, each of which, according to its author, would prove a sovereign remedy.

[1] Noel, *Les Banques d'Émission en Europe*, p. 24

It would be impossible here to discuss all the plans suggested.[1] Moreover the various schemes quickly grouped themselves round two opposing theories—the Banking Principle and the Currency Principle. We propose to examine these two theories and seek to find out the partial truth contained in each, while briefly noticing the chief of the works in which they were originally stated.[2] Then we shall consider the practical form assumed by that one of the systems which ultimately won the day.

I.—The Banking Principle.

A.—*Statement of the Banking Principle.* The advocates of the Banking Principle were believers, not, as has often been wrongly asserted, in unlimited competition in the matter of issues, but in the absence of a definite limit imposed on the issues, which is quite a different thing.[3] They

[1] The chief of these have been very clearly stated in Gilbart's *Currency and Banking* (1851). See the works of this author in six volumes, Vol. IV., pp. 289-356.

[2] Apart from contemporary writings and the evidence, which is well worth study, given before the various Committees of Inquiry between 1840 and 1858, statements of the controversy between the Banking and the Currency Principles are given by J. T. Danson, *On the Account of the Bank of England under the operation of the Act 7 and 8 Vict., ch.* 32 (in the *Journal of the Statistical Society*, Vol. X.), by Roscher, *Nationalökonomik des Handels und Gewerbfleisses*, pp. 314-332, and in several other works on Political Economy or on Banking.

More recently the question has been summarised in a most able manner by Dr. N. G. Pierson, the well-known Dutch economist.—See *Principles of Economics*, English translation, by A. A. Wotzel, pp. 454-461.

[3] This is especially true of Tooke, who is the chief representative of the Banking Principle.—See *History of Prices*, Vol. III., pp. 201-208. Tooke, far from desiring competition in the issue of notes, lays down most strongly, as a principle, the right of the State to make regulations in such a matter. "I am here assuming," he says (p. 206), "as an undoubted right on the part of the State, the principle that banks of issue are properly subjects for regulation. As to free banking, in the sense in which it is sometimes contended for, I agree with an American writer, who observes that free trade in banking is synonymous with free trade in swindling." On the following page Tooke adds that there can be no question of free competition, since the issue of paper as a substitute for coin is not a branch of productive industry; it is a thing which ought to be regulated by the State and be included in the department of administration. Compare a similar statement in Tooke's other book, *An Inquiry*, p. 105.

The full exposition of Tooke's theories on banking will be found in his *History of Prices*, particularly in the 3rd volume, chapters iii. and v.; in his evidence before the Committees of Inquiry, of which a critical summary is given by Poor, *op. cit.*, pp. 313-317, and in a special work, *An Inquiry into*

had no objection whatever to legal measures taken with the object of guaranteeing the *quality* of the notes, but they were opposed to any which tended to restrict the *quantity* of the paper money issued. In fact, they maintained that an over-issue could involve no danger either for the issuing bank or for the public *so long as the notes remained convertible.* If the conversion of the notes into gold was not assured, the danger from an excessive issue was evident enough. But otherwise there was no risk whatever to be feared, because it was impossible that an over-issue should occur.[1]

For how could such an over-issue take place? In the first place the notes are only issued in the course of banking transactions, that is, in discounting or making advances on securities. The amount of the issue therefore depends, not on the wishes of the Bank, but on the needs of the public.[2] The number of notes issued by the Bank will depend on the amount of the bills presented for discount and this in its turn will depend on the activity of business.

the Currency Principle, the connection of the currency with prices, and the expediency of a separation of Issue from Banking.

Tooke's two most important supporters were J. Fullarton, *On the Regulation of Currencies and the working of the new Bank Act* (1844), and James Wilson, *Capital, Currency and Banking,* a collection of articles re-published from the *Economist,* 2nd edition, 1859. The latter has been translated into Italian.—See *Biblioteca dell' Economista,* 2nd series, Vol. VI.

All these writers have been answered at great length, if not with great ability, by Torrens. See *The Principles and Practical Operation of Sir Robert Peel's Act of 1844 explained and defended,* pp. 189-299. The 3rd edition, 1858, of this work also contains a refutation of J. S. Mill's theories on currency, and of the article by Danson to which we have just referred.

For the sake of completeness we may notice also a work by Charles Tennant called *The Bank of England and the organisation of Credit in England,* which contains, pp. 15-17, a refutation of the currency principle. But this lengthy (990 pp.) book is hardly worth the trouble of reading. The 3rd edition, 1867, contains a translation of the evidence of the brothers Pereire before the Committee of Inquiry in 1865 concerning the Bank of France, and a correspondence between Tennant and Wolowski.

[1] See especially Chapter V. in Fullarton's book, a chapter entitled, *Proof of the impossibility of Over-Issue.*

[2] "It is not," says Tooke, "in the power of Banks of Issue, including the Bank of England, to make any direct addition to the amount of notes circulating in their respective districts, however disposed they may be to do so."—See *Inquiry,* p. 123. Compare *History of Prices,* Vol. III., pp. 373-374.

M. Gide, *op. cit.,* p. 377, remarks that this is only true in theory, since an unscrupulous Banker, whose sole object is to attract customers, could always by lowering his rate of discount enough, unduly extend his business and hence also his issues.

In the second place, Bank notes only remain in circulation for a very limited time,[1] they return to the Bank a few weeks after issue. Hence, even if the Bank managed to issue notes in very large quantities, it could not keep them in circulation, for if too many notes are issued they necessarily become depreciated and the least depreciation will be enough to bring them all back to the Bank in a body.

To sum up, it is evident, say the advocates of the Banking Principle, that a bank can only circulate a certain quantity of notes, which quantity is determined by force of circumstances, and that any over-issue will return to the bank as if contracted by an iron law.

B.—*Criticism of the Banking Principle.* This is the theory known as the Banking Principle; it has often been refuted and Mr. Pierson has quite recently once again demonstrated its weakness. This able Dutch economist, while admitting that excessive issues are returned to the Bank, expresses surprise that this should be considered a safeguard, whereas it is precisely in this fact that the danger lies. "The amount of the circulation continues the same, it is true, but its components are no longer the same; 'uncovered' is substituted for 'covered' circulation and the relation between metallic reserve and note circulation becomes less favourable."

Mr. Pierson[2] gives the following illustration in support of his reasoning: Suppose that a bank has a note circulation amounting to £18,000,000 and a metallic reserve of £8,000,000. "It grants loans for a further £2,000,000, but the public does not require more than £18,000,000 in notes; the extra £2,000,000 put into circulation will therefore cause a redundancy of money. It now becomes advantageous to export coin or bullion and that coin or bullion is obtainable at the bank in exchange for notes." The extra 2 millions will now return to the bank and the circulation will be again

[1] This is true. As we shall see below (Part II., p. 298), it has been calculated that the average time during which each note remains in circulation is 70 days for £5 notes and from 58 to 9 days for notes of higher values; indeed, the £1,000 notes only circulate, on the average, for a single week.

[2] See *op. cit.*, pp. 458-460.

reduced to 18 millions. But against these 18 millions the bank's reserve will now be only 6 millions. "The bank may pursue this course for a long time. It may increase its loans up to £18,000,000, the amount of its note circulation remaining all the while at the old figure." But the whole reserve, that is, the guarantee of the convertibility of the notes, will have been exhausted.

II.—THE CURRENCY PRINCIPLE.

A.—*Statement of the Currency Principle.* According to the Banking Principle the business of the Bank was to extend its transactions as much as possible, provided of course, that these were sound in character, without any feeling that it had a special function to perform of greater importance than all its other functions and to which these must of necessity be sacrificed.[1] The Currency Principle embodied a totally different view of the position of the Bank of England. The primary function of the Bank was not the transaction of business, but the maintenance of a sufficient reserve on behalf of the nation to enable the latter to meet its liabilities with other countries.

The supporters[2] of the Currency Principle took up the following position as their starting point. There was, Lord Overstone repeatedly asserted, a certain quantity of gold in the world; each country naturally possesses that share of it to which it has a right. A country might certainly be

[1] Leroy-Beaulieu, *Cours d'Éc. Polit.*, Vol. III., p. 590.

[2] The inventor and the most important advocate of the Currency Principle is undoubtedly the London banker, S. J. Loyd, who was afterwards raised to the peerage as Lord Overstone. Between 1837 and 1848 Loyd wrote a series of pamphlets in support of his system. These pamphlets, together with the letters contributed by Lord Overstone to the *Times* between 1855 and 1857, on the state of the currency and his evidence before the Committees of 1840 and 1848, were collected and published in a volume by McCulloch in 1858, under the title of *Tracts and other Publications on Metallic and Paper Currency*.

Lord Overstone was vigorously supported by Colonel Torrens, see *A Letter to the Right Hon. Viscount Melbourne, on the causes of the recent derangement of the Money Market* (1837), and *The Principles and Practical Operation of Sir R. Peel's Act explained and defended* (3rd edition, 1858), and by Geo. Warde Norman, *Remarks on some prevalent errors with respect to currency and banking* (1838), and *A letter to C. Wood, Esq., on Money and the Means of Economising it* (1841).

Tooke has given a somewhat colourless summary of the Currency Principle in the first chapter of his *Inquiry*.

poor, but its capital would always include such a proportion of coined money as might be needful.[1]

In fact, *in the case of a country without any paper currency,* there could be no scarcity of metallic money. An unfavourable balance of trade could not cause the permanent exportation of the coin and bullion; for a scarcity of money increases its value, this produces a fall in prices and hence a decrease in imports and an increase in exports, which will continue until the country has once more an adequate supply of coin.

Things are different in the case of a country which has a mixed currency, that is, paper money combined with coined money. Here, if the balance of trade is unfavourable and gold is exported, there is no ground for hoping that its absence will be short; in actual fact the banks will increase their paper circulation and since the circulating medium is no scarcer, prices will not fall. It may even be feared that the situation, instead of improving, will become increasingly serious. The metallic money may even be entirely driven out without prices being at all reduced.

What is the remedy for such a state of things?

The supporters of the Currency Principle maintained that it was as follows:[2] A decrease in the circulation, of whatever kind, must never be replaced by paper. It ought to be illegal for banks to substitute paper for the gold exported, or better still, *the banks ought to be obliged to reduce their issues in proportion to the gold exported.*

[1] Compare Norman, *A letter to C. Wood, Esq.*, p. 17.

[2] See Torrens, *A Letter to Lord Melbourne*, p. 29; S. J. Loyd, *Further Reflections on the Currency*, p. 34.

Norman also, who is at times hesitating in his conclusions, seems to be quite decided upon this point. Before the Committee of Inquiry (Question 1749) he stated that notes are preferable to coin because they are cheaper and more convenient, but that they ought not to be preferred unless they also possess the other qualities of a metallic currency and in particular, unless they increase or diminish in the same way as a metallic currency would do. In his *Remarks*, Norman alleges that the existing paper circulation suffered from the following disadvantages, which were due to the fact that it was not regulated upon the metallic circulation :—

"1.—A tendency to vary in amount both as to excess or deficiency in an unnecessary degree and at unsuitable periods.

"2.—A liability to discredit . . . in a large proportion, if not the whole of it.

"3.—Insolvency on the part of many of the issuers."

B.—*Defects in the Currency Principle.* The defects in the Currency Principle have been set forth very clearly by Mr. Pierson.[1]

The first mistake made by the advocates of the Currency Principle was that of supposing "that a bank invariably does wrong when it supplies a deficiency in the monetary circulation by issuing notes." This view would oblige us to forego "one of the greatest advantages of a well-regulated banking system." In fact, in the case of a demand due to a panic or to a great exportation of bullion resulting from a bad harvest, it is the bank's duty to assist the public, lest, in order to obtain precious metal for which paper money might quite well be temporarily substituted, people are forced at an unfavourable moment to sell either securities, which may be excellent in themselves, or, in the case of farmers, machinery or cattle. It will be time enough for the bank gradually to restrict its issues and to refill its coffers when the crisis is past and the public have been helped.

The Currency Principle involves a second no less serious mistake. "It is not true that, in a country where no bank notes are in circulation, exportation of specie results in an immediate fall in prices and consequently in an alteration in the balance of payments. It would be so if bank *notes* were the only possible substitutes for specie; but bank deposits also serve as substitutes for specie." But "bank notes and bank deposits differ only in form, since both take the place of specie when they are not covered by a metallic reserve."

"Let the needful stock of media of payment," says Mr. Pierson in illustration,[2] "be represented by the figure 100, and suppose it to be made up of specie and bank deposits each to the extent of 50. If specie be now exported to the value of 10, but the banks at the same time grant credits to their depositors to the same amount, how is the fall in prices to take place? . . . A bank of circulation issues notes

[1] *Op. cit.*, pp. 456-458. In spite of the defects he points out, Mr. Pierson considers that the Currency Principle is less dangerous than the Banking Principle and agrees with Bagehot in preferring the mediocre rules imposed on the Bank directors by the Act of 1844, to those which they might have invented for themselves.—See p. 461.

[2] p. 457.

. . . with which people pay each other. A deposit bank credits its depositors' accounts, and the balances produced in this way also constitute a medium of payment."

The exponents of the Currency Principle refused to recognise this fact,[1] hence their theory has never been accepted by economists. As the *Dictionary of Political Economy*[2] puts it: "It marks the difference between those who regard bank notes as 'money,' and those who consider them, in the words of Huskisson, as 'circulating credit,' and a 'substitute for money.' . . . While insisting, and properly, on adequate security being given for the bank note, the Currency doctrine leaves out of sight the operation of all other instruments of credit, equally effective in their way, as bank notes, on price and the movements of commodities."

In excuse for Lord Overstone it has been pointed out that notes then formed the principal part of bankers' liabilities, deposits played only a secondary part. For instance, in February, 1820, the circulation of the Bank amounted to £23,000,000, while the deposits were £4,000,000; in February, 1890, they were respectively £23,500,000 and £35,000,000. But although the deposits were small in amount in 1820, their character, their advantages and the future before them were clearly understood by 1844. And Tooke, after pointing out that the deposits, thanks to the use of cheques, served the purpose of money as well or even better than Bank notes,[3] distinctly foretells the extension which this method of payment would undergo.

It is difficult to decide in favour of either one of these two

[1] Apparently Torrens must be included among those exponents of the Currency Principle who were unwilling to recognise this. Compare pp. 6-12 of his letter to Lord Melbourne, and pp. 6 and 9 of his *Principles and Practical Operations*. On p. 8 of this latter work Torrens finally says that a cheque is distinct from money, because it possesses a power of purchase but not of liquidating debt, since if it is not subsequently honoured the transaction comes to nothing.

[2] Vol. I., p. 473.

[3] Cheques, according to Tooke (*Inquiry*, Chap. v., *Deposits and Cheques*), possess the following advantages compared with bank notes: they save the worry of having to pay the fractions of the sum owed in coin and the risks of theft and fire; they do not necessitate a receipt, since the banker's books are sufficient proof of payment, etc., etc.

opposing principles. Apart from defects of theory, they both have their practical disadvantages, and in general it may be said, that as regards the regulation of issues, all systems risk one or other of two dangers: either the paper currency is unduly restricted or it is left so free as to endanger its security.

For the rest, the discussion of the merits and demerits of these two systems is not only, speaking generally, somewhat futile and very dull, but is also rather out of place in an historical work.

Whatever may in reality be the advantages of the Banking Principle (and it may be noted that as applied in a prudent manner in France its results are far from bad), it was very soon rejected in England. Hence it is more important to examine the practical form given by the exponents of the Currency Principle to their theory, and the methods by which they wished to enforce it.

For this purpose we judge it advisable to begin by analysing Lord Overstone's numerous pamphlets, and in so doing to compare his proposals with those of Torrens and Norman. This study will have the double advantage of giving a closer knowledge of the Currency Principle and of explaining beforehand the ideas which inspired the legislation of 1844.

CHAPTER V.

THE CURRENCY PRINCIPLE AND THE PROMOTERS OF THE LAW OF 1844

(LORD OVERSTONE, COLONEL TORRENS, G. W. NORMAN).

Lord Overstone, the chief promoter of the Act of 1844, his pamphlets and his theories. Analysis of the "*Reflections Suggested by Mr. Palmer's Pamphlet.*" Lord Overstone and the Bank of England: Criticism of the organisation of the Bank. Suggests two reforms: (*a*) Full publication of accounts, (*b*) Division of Bank into two departments. Colonel Torrens' plan. Bank obliged to purchase bullion at a fixed price. Lord Overstone and the country banks of issue: Numerous disadvantages in the multiplicity of banks of issue. Need for strengthening the central monopoly of issue—Summary of the proposals of the advocates of the Currency Principle.

THE Currency Principle was expounded for the first time in a pamphlet by S. J. Loyd, published in 1837 and entitled, *Reflections suggested by a perusal of Mr. J. Horsley Palmer's pamphlet on the causes and consequences of the pressure on the Money Market,* which is a reply to a work of Palmer's already referred to, on the crisis of 1836.

This pamphlet, the first which Loyd wrote,[1] merits careful study for it contains in germ the Act of 1844. It recommends, indeed, as much the reform of the Bank of England as the reform of English banks. The author begins by an examination of the rules which govern the Bank of Eng-

[1] He wrote many others afterwards; McCulloch's edition, to which all our references are made, contains the following:—

I.—*Remarks on the Management and the Circulation, and on the conditions and conduction of the Bank of England and of the country issues during the year* 1839 (1840).

II.—*A Letter to J. B. Smith, Esq., President of the Manchester Chamber of Commerce.*

III.—*Effects of the Administration of the Bank of England.—A second letter to J. B. Smith, Esq.* (1840).

IV.—*Thoughts on the Separation of the departments of the Bank of England* (1844).

V.—*The petition of the Merchants, Bankers and Traders of London against the Bank Charter Act, with comments on each clause.* In collaboration with Torrens, 1847.

land and after pointing out their absurdity, suggests two remedies: (*a*) the publication of the accounts in full, (*b*) the separation of the Bank into two departments. Loyd then passes on to consider the system of country banking, finds numerous defects in it, criticises the system of joint-stock banks and the confusion between banks of issue and banks of deposit and finally suggests as a remedy the extension of the monopoly of central issue.

We shall proceed to discuss these various points.

I.—Lord Overstone and the Bank of England.

According to Lord Overstone the Bank "acts in two capacities":—

1.—"As a manager of the circulation."

2.—"As a body performing the ordinary functions of a banking concern."

These two functions are in themselves entirely distinct. Unfortunately this distinction has not been sufficiently regarded in the principles laid down by the Bank for its own guidance.

Lord Overstone[1] proceeds to describe this principle as formulated by Mr. Palmer as follows: that "against the amount of notes out it shall hold at its disposal securities and specie, that the amount of securities shall be invariable, and that consequently all fluctuations in the amount of notes out shall be met by a corresponding fluctuation in the amount of specie in deposit; thus the public, and not the Bank, will be made the regulators of the amount of the circulation, and that amount will by this principle be made to fluctuate precisely as it would have fluctuated had the currency been purely metallic."

Lord Overstone goes on to point out that this rule is only accurate in reference to the Bank as a manager of the circulation; it is quite unworkable in regard to the Bank of England considered as an ordinary banking concern. For "it is in the nature of banking business that the amount of its deposits should vary with a variety of circumstances;

[1] pp. 5-7 in McCulloch's edition.

and as its amount of deposits varies, the amount of that in which those deposits are invested (viz., the securities) must vary also." Hence it is absurd to expect the Bank of England, as a banking concern, to keep the amount of its securities invariable, any more than this is done by any other banking establishment.

The rule as stated by the Bank's directors is therefore false. What method should be adopted to secure a circulation which will fluctuate as though it were metallic?

The methods are two: (1) The publication of simple, full and intelligible accounts. (2) The separation of the Bank into two departments.

1.—"The rule ought to be, That the variations in the amount of circulation shall correspond to the variations in the amount of bullion, and the adherence of the Bank to this rule ought to be obvious upon the face of the published accounts. By this means, and by this means only, can we obtain a paper circulation varying in amount exactly as the circulation would have varied had it been metallic; and, in addition to the establishment of this only sound principle of currency, we shall obtain a simple and intelligible account, requiring no further explanation, nor the production of any information not at the command of the public."[1]

2.—Were the management of the currency, Lord Overstone continues, "entrusted to a body established exclusively for that purpose, this is the rule by which such body must govern its operations. . . . The importance of a rigid adherence to this rule cannot be over-estimated; and if it be incompatible, as is alleged by some, with the mixed functions of the Bank of England, it seems to become a very serious question whether it is not better to separate altogether the business of banking from that of regulating the currency, rather than suffer so essential a rule to be in any degree compromised. . . . ."

Moreover it is difficult to see any insurmountable obstacles to this separation. "In proportion as these two functions are kept distinct will each be rendered more

[1] pp. 10, 11.

effectual for its purpose. The two branches of the business of the Bank thus divided" suggest "those animals described by naturalists, whose peculiar property it is that, when cut into two parts, they move off in opposite directions, each half equally full of life and energy."

Torrens, in his letter to Lord Melbourne, had suggested a scheme for the division of the Bank into two departments. This scheme, which was much more detailed than that just described by Loyd, was imitated in the Act of 1844; it must therefore be briefly noticed.[1]

The issue department, or the department of circulation as Torrens called it, was to confine itself to exchanging gold for notes, and notes for gold. It was also to be subject to the following regulations:—

1.—It was to be free to buy or sell silver to the value of 2 or 3 million pounds. 2.—It was to be obliged to buy foreign gold in bullion at a fixed price of £3 17s. 6d. the ounce, with permission to sell it at £3 17s. 9d. 3.—It was to be authorised to lend notes on coin or bullion at a very low rate, say 1 per cent., so as to give facilities to trade without disturbing the circulation.

The accounts were to be published in full.

II.—Lord Overstone and the Country Banks of Issue.

After criticising the rules according to which the Bank of England was managed and pointing out the changes which he thought were needed, Lord Overstone goes on to criticise the organisation of provincial facilities for credit.

The existing system, he says,[2] combines and confuses two

[1] Torrens' scheme was ably summarised by G. W. Norman, who was in the main also an advocate of the separation into two departments. See *Remarks*, pp. 98 and 105.

[2] p. 13. In the author's opinion these criticisms applied as much to the Bank of England as to the country banks. Hence he suggested a little further on, p. 38, that the issue department should be controlled by a committee on which a representative of the Government should sit. For a similar proposal see Torrens, p. 64; he advocates the appointment of a committee chosen by the Government and Parliament.

absolutely distinct functions. Moreover the persons who exercise the right of issue are "not a body of individuals qualified (by their total separation from all such interests) to exercise a dispassionate and disinterested judgment; but, on the contrary, men the most largely engaged in mercantile and monied operations, and, therefore, more than any other class exposed in their private interests to the immediate effects of any action upon the currency.

"Again, with respect to joint-stock banks, we create by law large and powerful establishments, to which is given the right to issue paper money without any absolute restriction; and even that knowledge of the action of the Bank which is essential to enable them to take a just view of the condition of the currency and of their corresponding duty, is afforded to them only through . . . imperfect and delusive accounts.'"[1]

Besides this, Loyd continues a little further on,[2] banks of issue are confused with banks of discount, whereas the objects of the two are entirely different. "The sole duty of the former . . . is to take efficient means for issuing its paper money upon good security and regulating the amount of it by one fixed rule. The principal object and business of the latter . . . is to obtain the command of as large a proportion as possible of the existing circulating medium and to distribute it in such a manner as shall combine security for repayment with the highest rate of profit."

Loyd concluded that it was necessary to strengthen the central monopoly of issue.[3]

He explains[4] that "when prices are rising, profits increasing, and every merchant . . . is desirous of extending his operations," and demands credit for this purpose, the banker's position is difficult. His relations with trade are intimate and it is unpleasant for him to refuse the credit, however much it may be his duty to do so. "If under these

[1] p. 13. [2] p. 31.

[3] Norman, who arrived at the same conclusion, points out, pp. 33-34, the abuses in the management of the issues and the resemblance between the right of issue and that of coining money as possessed by powerful subjects in barbaric times.

[4] pp. 32, 33.

circumstances the banker, in addition to what may be properly called his ordinary and legitimate resources, is also entrusted with the power of issuing paper money *ad libitum;* is it not inevitable that he should abuse that power? Can we expect that under such circumstances, whilst all his other resources are strained to the utmost for the accommodation of his customers, he will still keep a firm and unyielding restraint over the amount of his issues? Will he under such temptation in no respect confound or compromise his respective duties as a Banker of Issue and a Banker of Deposit and Discount?"

A knowledge of human nature and experience, combined with a study of the Bank returns, prove that he will not resist, and that the result will be a confusion of and a compromise between the two functions. "The effect . . . of such an application by the Banker of his power to issue will be to give a further stimulus to the existing tendencies of the trading world, and ultimately to aggravate the convulsion to which they must lead."

This is the outline of the practical application of the Currency Principle put forward by the chief exponents of the theory. The plan may be summarised, as far as concerns the Bank of England, under three heads:—

1.—The regulation of the paper circulation according to the fluctuations it would have undergone had it been coined money.

2.—The separation of the Bank into two departments, and the regular publication of clear and full balance sheets.

3.—The obligation imposed on the Bank to buy gold at a fixed price.

As regards country banks, the multiplication of banks of issue was opposed and the extension of the central monopoly of issue was demanded, so that the indirect control exercised over the provincial issues might be more powerful and more efficient.

CHAPTER VI.

SIR ROBERT PEEL AND THE ACT OF 1844.

(*a*)—INTERVENTION OF SIR ROBERT PEEL; (*b*)—THE ACT OF 1844; (*c*)—THE ACT OF 1844 AND RICARDO'S PLAN FOR A NATIONAL BANK.

Action of Sir Robert Peel. Peel's theories on banking. His two Speeches in the House of Commons. His *Memorandum* to the Cabinet. Peel's rejection of free competition as regards note issue. Argument from reason. Argument from experience; disastrous part played by country banks. Necessity for a central bank of issue: Reasons why this should be the Bank of England. The Act of 1844 passed without opposition. Chief provisions of the Act. As regards the Bank of England. As regards the country banks of issue. Limitation and gradual loss of the right of issue. Ricardo's plan for a National Bank. Points of likeness to Robert Peel's Act. Its uselessness.

THE dispute between the advocates of the Currency and of the Banking Principles might have gone on for a long time. The Committees of Inquiry had been sitting for five years, and had asked more than 14,000 questions[1] without reaching any definite conclusion; indeed, without even presenting a report. Fortunately there was then at the head of affairs a man whose intelligence was equal to his high character, and who, with Canning and Gladstone,[2] ranks among the most eminent English statesmen in the 19th century.

Robert Peel, for it is to him that we refer, had been a Conservative all his life, but a Conservative of that English type which does not confuse conservatism with reaction and never shrinks from a necessary reform. He considered that

[1] That is, 3,000 questions in 1836; 4,570 in 1837; 1,700 in 1838; 3,859 in 1840; and nearly 1,000 in 1841. See Peel's speech on December 3, 1847, *Parl. Debates*, Vol. XCV., p. 655.

[2] Were it not for my national feeling I should rank Peel even above Canning and Gladstone; he was placed in more difficult circumstances than the former and showed himself equally courageous but less nervous than the latter. It must also be noted that Gladstone owed some of his greatest financial successes to the apprenticeship which he served under Peel.

it was time to have done with theoretical discussions and to come to the actual reform for which everyone wished, but as to whose exact form no one could agree. Peel took advantage of a clause in the law of 1833 which empowered the Government to suspend the Bank's charter in 1845, and after careful reflection he brought in the Bill which was to become the Bank Charter Act of 1844.

This Bill is obviously inspired by the writings of the exponents of the Currency Principle. We shall examine presently the reasons which decided Peel in their favour, but it may be noticed at the outset that Peel did not come to the study of banking problems with an absolutely open mind. He had been so strongly impressed by the evils of over-issue, the most dangerous of the abuses to which banking is liable, which had displayed themselves with extraordinary violence between 1836 and 1839, that he became almost blind to any other consideration.[1]

(*a*)—Sir Robert Peel's Opinions on Banking.

Although the banking question finds no place in the *Memoirs*[2] of the great English statesman, Sir Robert Peel's views on the matter are fully stated in a *Memorandum* which he laid before the Cabinet[3] and in two speeches, remarkable

[1] It is interesting to notice that the misuse of paper money always produces a demand for remedies of extraordinary severity and an entire forgetfulness of the possible uses of this paper. Macleod (Vol. I., p. 267), quotes a Chinese author, who, writing in 1309, at a time when the Chinese currency had been thrown into extreme disorder by over-issues, regretted former days in the following words: "Then it was ordered that at the offices of the rich merchants who managed the enterprise, when notes were paid in the money came out, when the bills came out the money went in. The money was the mother, the note was the son. The son and the mother were reciprocally exchanged for each other."

"This doctrine," adds Macleod, "put forth in the year 1309 by a Chinese writer, is the *Currency Principle*." (*Theory and Practice of Banking*, 3rd edition).

[2] See *Memoirs*, published by Lord Stanhope and Lord Cardwell. These memoirs are divided into three parts: (1) The Roman Catholic Question; (2) The New Government, 1834-5; (3) Repeal of the Corn Laws, 1845-6.

[3] This *Memorandum* has been recently published in a work by Charles Stuart Parker, *Sir Robert Peel from his Private Papers*, Vol. III., p. 134, *et seq.* Lord Rosebery published an analysis of Parker's book in the *Anglo-Saxon Review;* this analysis, which is in fact a brilliant essay, has been issued in a volume entitled *Sir Robert Peel.*

alike for high purpose and closeness of reasoning, made on May 6 and May 20 in the House of Commons, and which supplied the explanation and justification of the law of 1844.[1]

After inquiring, " What is the signification of that word 'a pound,' " and answering that it is "a quantity of the precious metals of certain weight and certain fineness," Peel proceeded to deduce from this definition the various consequences implied in it.[2] He then pointed out the distinction between bank notes and other forms of paper credit and tried to show that the convertibility of the note did not afford sufficient guarantee against the dangers of excessive issue. He rejected the doctrine of free competition in the matter of issue from grounds both of reason and experience.

(a)—*Argument from Reason.*

"We should infer, certainly, from reasoning," says Peel,[3] " that free competition in the supply of any given article will probably ensure us the most abundant supply of that article at the cheapest rate. But we do not want an abundant supply of cheap promissory paper. We want only . . . just such a quantity of paper . . . as shall be equivalent in point of value to the coin which it represents. . . . That system, therefore, which provides a constant supply of paper equal in value to coin, and so varying in amount as to ensure at all times immediate convertibility into coin, together with perfect confidence in the solvency of the issuers of paper, is the system which ought to be preferred." Quality, not

[1] For Peel's two speeches see *The Speeches of the Right Hon. Sir R. Peel, delivered in the House of Commons*, Vol. IV., pp. 349-366 and 374-385 respectively and, *A Corner in Gold*, Appendix, p. 113. A translation of them has been published in the *Journal des Économistes*, Vol. III., pp. 251 and 357. William Taylor gives a summary of them in *Life and Times of Sir R. Peel*, Vol. III., pp. 259-276. Taylor's work, in three volumes, is unfinished; a fourth volume has been added by Ch. Mackay, and contains an account of Peel's life from his retirement until his death. The whole work is of little value.

[2] *Speeches*, Vol. IV., p. 351.

[3] p. 357.

cheapness, is required, and this quality cannot be regulated by an unlimited competition. "Unless the issuers of paper conform to certain principles, unless they vigilantly observe the causes which influence the influx or efflux of coin, and regulate their issues of paper accordingly, there is danger that the value of the paper will not correspond with the value of the coin." That is, there will be an excessive issue.

(b)—*Argument from Experience.*

Peel[1] goes on to discuss the arguments which he deduces from the history of the country banks of issue. Competition among the country banks is determined by the feeling which makes each issuer say, "naturally enough, 'It is vain for me individually to contract my issues when others will not do the same. I shall suffer by doing so. My efforts will produce no effect on the aggregate, while some competitor will take that share of the circulation which I may withdraw.' And thus, each refusing to make the individual sacrifice, . . . the crisis comes."

The principle of free competition had exposed the Bank of England to great danger Peel thought, on four occasions, owing to the unwillingness or inability of the country banks to contract their issues. The history of the country[2] banks, in spite of the value of their services, was not in their favour. Between 1839 and 1843, 82 banks, of which 29 were banks of issue,[3] failed; 240 suspended payment between 1814 and 1816 and similar disasters occurred from 1825 to 1840. The great losses resulting from these failures ought to be considered and it must be remembered that the worst suffering fell upon those who were least able to resist it; the situation of the victims, artisans, small farmers and so on, deserved the more pity because they could not choose between several

[1] For what follows see *Speeches*, pp. 357-358.

[2] See p. 381.

[3] Out of these 29, 17 had paid no dividend.

banks, but were forced to make use of the one in their own neighbourhood.

Peel concluded his criticism of the existing system by citing in addition to the example of the English country banks, that of the American banks, an illustration which appears somewhat ill-chosen; then he passed on to explain the system whose adoption he recommended.

In brief the new system consisted in this: that a central bank of issue should possess the right to control the provincial banks.

With respect to the central bank, Peel remarks that this single bank could no doubt be specially established, but "the true policy in this country is to work, so far as it be possible, with the instruments you have ready to your hand —to avail yourselves of that advantage which they possess from having been in use, from being familiar from constituting a part of the habits and usages of society. They will probably work more smoothly than perfectly novel instruments of greater theoretical perfection.[1] . . . We think it the wisest course to select the Bank of England as that controlling and central body."

So much for the theories which inspired the legislation of 1844;[2] it remains to examine Peel's Act in detail.

(*b*)—The Act of 1844.

The Act of 1844 was passed by the House of Commons with hardly any opposition by 185 votes to 30. In the House of Lords things went even more smoothly and after a single protest from Lord Radnor, it was passed without a division.

[1] See p. 360. In his *Memorandum* Peel rejects the idea of a special board of issue, independent of the Government but responsible to Parliament (see pp. 135-137). Amongst other disadvantages, he thinks that it would be inconvenient to impose a uniform system upon each of the three divisions of the United Kingdom, when, as things are, each has a differently organised currency. Compare, *contra*, Ricardo's *Plan*, p. 73.

[2] Peel, in speaking of the regular publication of accounts (p. 360), says that "nothing will more conduce to the credit of the Bank itself and to the prevention of needless alarm."

Chief Provisions of the Act of 1844.

The chief provisions of the new law can be grouped under two heads: those which concern the Bank of England and those which concern the country banks. We shall discuss each in turn.

I.—*Provisions Concerning the Bank of England.*

1.—After August 31st, 1844, the Bank of England was to be divided into two departments, the issue department and the banking department.

On the same day the Governor and Company of the Bank of England must transfer to the issue department securities to the value of £14,000,000, of which the Government debt to the bank (say £11,000,000) was to form a part, and also all the gold coin and gold and silver bullion not needed in the banking department.

The silver in the Issue Department, it should be noted, was never to exceed one-fourth of the gold.[1]

In return the issue department was to hand over to the banking department an amount of notes equal to the securities, coin and bullion, so transferred to it.

In other words the Bank might issue notes against securities to the amount of 14 *millions, but beyond this sum it could not issue a single note except against coin or bullion.*

2.—If any banker who had retained the right of issue ceased to exercise this privilege, the Bank of England might increase the amount of the securities in the issue department by a sum not exceeding two-thirds of the notes withdrawn from circulation.

In this way the Bank gradually inherited the rights of

[1] This proportion has never actually been reached, but the Bank has at times held a considerable quantity of silver bullion. The maximum was attained on October 3rd, 1846, when the Bank had a reserve of £2,727,000 in silver and £12,632,000 in gold. Since August 20th, 1853, the balance sheet of the Bank has ceased to quote the stock of silver except during the very short interval between November 28th, 1860, and July 3rd, 1861, when the Bank held some silver bullion, though no great amount. For the stock of silver bullion held by the Bank of England see Palgrave, *The Bank Rate and the Money Market,* Table I., p. 80.

issue of those country banks which resigned their privilege or which ceased to exist. We shall see that, thanks to this clause in the law, the Bank of England has extended its right of issue considerably, *i.e.*, from £14,000,000 to £18,450,000.[1]

3.—The Bank was exempted from all stamp duty on its notes, but in return for the privileges granted to it the annual sum paid to the Government was increased from £120,000 to £180,000.

4.—Anyone was entitled to demand notes from the Bank in exchange for standard gold at the rate of £3 17s. 9d. per ounce.

In other words, the Bank is forced to buy at a fixed price all the gold offered to it.

5.—Weekly accounts in a specified form were to be sent to the Government and published in the *London Gazette.*

The importance of this last reform will be understood from a comparison of the balance sheets of the Bank before and after the law of 1844.

Weekly Return of the Bank of England, week ending September 7th, 1844 (*New form*):—

Issue Department.

Notes issued	£28,351,295	Government Debt	£11,015,100
		Other securities	2,984,900
		Gold coin and bullion	12,657,208
		Silver bullion	1,694,087
	£28,351,295		£28,351,295

Banking Department.

Proprietors' Capital	£14,553,000	Government securities, (including the dead-weight annuity[2]	£14,554,834
Rest	3,564,729	Other securities	7,835,616
Public deposits	3,630,809	Notes	8,175,025
Other deposits	8,644,348	Gold and silver coin	857,765
Seven-day and other bills	1,030,354		
	£31,423,240		£31,423,240

M. MARSHALL, (*Chief Cashier*).

[1] For further details see below, p. 299.

[2] The dead-weight annuity was a yearly payment of £588,740 made by the Government in return for an advance of £13,000,000, granted in 1823 for the Waterloo pensions, etc. This annuity expired in 1867.

The same Return, before the law of 1844, would have appeared in the following form :—

Circulation.	
London	£14,802,000
Country	6,405,000
	£21,207,000
Deposits, Public, viz.:	
Exchequer Account .	£2,198,000
For Payment of Dividends	315,000
Savings Banks, etc. .	501,000
Other Public Accounts	617,000
	£3,631,000
Deposits, Private, viz.:	
Railways	£30,000
London Bankers . .	963,000
East India Co. . .	636,000
Banks of Ireland and Scotland, etc. . .	175,000
Other deposits . . .	5,631,000
Deposits at Branches .	1,209,000
	£8,644,000
Total Liabilities .	£33,482,000

Public Securities.	
Advances on Exchequer Bills—	
Deficiency Bills . .	—
Other Exchequer Bills	£870,000
Exchequer Bills purchased	311,000
Stock and Annuities .	12,821,000
	£14,002,000
Private Securities.	
Bills discounted—	
London	£113,000
Country	2,003,000
	£2,116,000
Bonds.	
East India Bonds . .	£198,000
City Bonds	3,357,000
Mortgages	620,000
Advances.	
Bills of Exchange . .	883,000
Exchequer Bills . . .	661,000
	£5,719,000
Total	£21,837,000
Bullion	15,299,000
Total Assets . . .	£37,046,000

The difference between the liabilities and the assets is explained by the omission of the Rest, which was £3,564,000 and which when added to the liabilities made the total £37,046,000.

It will be noticed that the Proprietors' Capital of £14,553,000 and the public securities corresponding to it are omitted in the old form of Return.

It will also be remembered that before 1844 the balance sheets were not published weekly, but that according to the Act of 1833, the *London Gazette* had to publish every month the balance sheet for the previous quarter.[1]

[1] See above, p. 261.

II.—*The Act of 1844 and the Country Banks.*

The Act provides that the right of issuing notes shall be confined to those bankers who possessed this privilege before 1844. Even in their case the right of issue was regulated as follows:—

The right of issue of each country bank was not to exceed the average issue of the twelve weeks preceding April 27th, 1844.

Any banker who became bankrupt was to forfeit his right of issue. If two or more banks afterwards became united they might not issue notes should the number of partners exceed six.

The notes issued by country banks were not to be legal tender.[1]

It is evident that the whole tendency of the Act of 1844 was to eliminate by degrees all notes except those of the Bank of England.

Such are the leading provisions of the Act of 1844.

Its complicated nature is obvious, as are also the numerous precautions with which it hedged in the right of issue. Wagner[2] might well speak of Peel's Act as a "strait waistcoat."

But laws, like men, cannot be judged by appearances, and in order to judge of the value of legislation, its practical results and the degree to which it has attained its object[3] must be examined.

A banking system must moreover be studied both in ordinary times and in periods of crisis if a just appreciation of its influence is to be formed. We propose to do this with regard to the system of the Bank of England. But first we must say a word or two concerning a scheme which re-

[1] For the practical results of this clause see below, p. 299.

[2] In his article on *Kredit und Banken* in Schönberg (*Handbuch d. Pol. Oekon.*). See the Italian translation, *Biblioteca dell' Economista*, 3rd series, Vol. XII., p. 953.

[3] We may remark at once that if the framers of the law of 1844 intended through it to secure a strict application of the Currency Principle, *i.e.*, to restrict the home circulation in exact proportion to the exportation of bullion, they were the victims of illusion. See below, the discussion, p. 333, on the crisis of 1847 and the Bank of England.

tains a certain interest from the name of its author and which undoubtedly attracted Peel's notice. The scheme in question is Ricardo's plan for a National Bank.[1]

(c)—Comparison between Peel's Act and Ricardo's Plan for a National Bank.

Ricardo had previously recognised that the Bank of England had two distinct functions, (1) the issue of notes, (2) the business of banking properly so called. He wished to create a special body, a State bank, to which he would have entrusted the duties imposed by the Act of 1844 on the issue department, but not those of the banking department.

In short, Ricardo's National Bank was a State Treasury which issued notes. The notes were all to be issued against gold, with the exception of a quantity, not to exceed 25 millions in value, which the Bank might issue uncovered. Of these 25 millions, 15 millions would have sufficed to repay to the Bank of England the capital lent to the Government, and the 10 millions remaining would have served on the one hand to buy bullion, and on the other to redeem the Government debt to the Bank, which took the form of Exchequer bills.[2]

"At first sight," says Courcelle-Seneuil,[3] "Ricardo's plan of a bank appears very different from the system established in England by Sir Robert Peel's Act. Ricardo, in fact, wished to have only a single bank of issue for the United Kingdom, whereas several such banks still continue to exist in Great Britain. He suggested a State bank, while in actual fact the Bank of England has been maintained. But these two points are only secondary details in the plan of the great economist. The originality of his scheme lies in the definite restriction of the paper circulation, the prohibition of the issue of notes payable to bearer in excess of a certain amount, except when secured

[1] See Ricardo's posthumous work, *Plan for a National Bank* (1824).

[2] See articles 2 and 3 of the scheme. A French translation of the *Plan* is given at the end of M. Courcelle Seneuil's book, appendix No. 2.

[3] *Loc. cit.*

by gold. This feature is also the distinctive characteristic of the system established by Robert Peel."

Ricardo's plan was answered as early as 1831 by McCulloch,[1] and quite recently it has been again condemned by M. Leroy-Beaulieu.[2] According to the latter,[3] the only profit which the State could derive from Ricardo's bank would be that resulting from the issue of notes in excess of the reserve. If it happened, as is the case to-day, that the metallic reserve exceeded the issues, the State would actually lose.

[1] See Chap. III. of his *Historical Sketch of the Bank of England*, headed *The Bank of England in connection with the Government and the Public.* This little work was published anonymously, but McCulloch acknowledged the authorship of it by placing it under his name in his *Literature of Political Economy.*

[2] See the analysis and refutation of Ricardo's plan, *op. cit.*, Vol. IV., pp. 639-645; see also above, p. 288, and note Sir Robert Peel's criticisms, especially *Memorandum*, pp. 135-137.

[3] p. 642.

PART II.

THE BANK OF ENGLAND IN ORDINARY TIMES.

INTRODUCTION.

THE BALANCE SHEET OF THE BANK OF ENGLAND.

The weekly Bank Return. The works of Clare and Raffalovich. Outward form of the Return. Comparison with a French balance sheet. The separation of the Bank into two departments; the issue department and the banking department. The plan both dangerous and artificial.

The amount of the issue and the part played by cheques. The issue of notes from an administrative standpoint. Manufacture of the notes. Destruction of all notes returned to the Bank. Average circulation of the notes. The issue of notes from a legal standpoint. Rules governing the issue: Except for a fixed amount, the issue to be against gold. Rights of issue held by certain country banks. Present position of the question. Authorised issue much reduced since 1844, the actual issue much less than the authorised issue. Statistics. The issue and circulation. Quantity of notes in circulation less during the last ten years than the metallic reserve of the Bank. Explanation of the fact. The function of cheques. The Clearing Houses in London and the provinces. Consideration of the English system of note issue. The English system indefensible from a theoretical standpoint. The practical aspect of the question. Comparison between the Act of 1844 and the German Laws of 1875 and 1899.

The Banking Department of the Bank of England is like any other bank except that it must publish a weekly balance sheet. This balance sheet, like all others, states the liabilities and the assets. The liabilities of the banking department. Proprietors' Capital and the Rest. Amount of the Capital; Comparison with that of the Banks of France and of Germany. The Rest and its amount. Public Deposits. Amount and fluctuations of these. Other Deposits. The current account of the bankers. Advantage of publishing a separate statement of this account, discontinued in 1877. Seven Day and other Bills. The assets of the Banking Department. The four headings under which the assets are divided are: (*a*) Government Securities, (*b*) Other Securities, (*c*) Notes, (*d*) Gold and Silver Coin. The two first constitute the investments of the Bank, and the two last its reserve.

THERE is no better guide to a study of the working of the Bank of England than one of the Returns which the Bank issues weekly.

Since 1844 the Bank's balance sheet has been remarkably clear and an examination of it, besides being of interest for its own sake, will help us greatly in our study of the questions now before us.[1]

By way of illustration we give the Bank Return for the week ending September 16th, 1903:—

Issue Department.

Notes issued	£50,654,500	Government Debt	£11,015,100
		Other securities	7,434,900
		Gold coin and bullion	32,204,500
	£50,654,500		£50,654,500

Banking Department.

Proprietors' Capital	£14,553,000	Government securities	£16,950,841
Rest	3,753,869	Other securities	21,655,875
Public deposits	7,117,298	Notes	22,011,110
Other deposits	37,184,730	Gold and silver coin	2,109,573
Seven-day and other bills	118,502		
	£62,727,399		£62,727,399

The same balance sheet in the form which, according to M. Noel,[2] is generally used in France, would appear thus:—

Assets.		*Liabilities.*	
Specie (gold and silver coin and bullion)	£34,314,073	Notes payable at sight in circulation	£28,643,390
Securities	21,655,875	Warrants and seven-day bills	118,502
Government securities, advances, and other marketable securities	16,950,841	Current account with Treasury	7,117,298
Government debt and other non-marketable securities	18,450,000	Current accounts and deposit accounts	37,184,730
		Dividends unpaid	3,753,869
		Shareholders' capital	14,553,000
	£91,360,789		£91,360,789

The study of the Bank of England's balance sheet naturally falls into two sections:

Section I. The Issue Department.

Section II. The Banking Department.

But we may remark at the outset that this division of the Bank into two absolutely separate departments,—into two watertight compartments which are entirely disconnected,—

[1] For this examination consult Clare (George), *A Money Market Primer and Key to the Exchanges.* The first part of this excellent work deals with the Returns of the Bank of England. A complete analysis of it has been given by M. Raffalovich, *Bilan de la Banque d'Angleterre,* in the *Journal des Économistes* for June, 1893.

[2] *Op. cit.*, p. 44.

is not only very artificial and also unnecessary, but may sometimes be actually harmful.

M. Wolowski, one of the advocates of the Act of 1844, criticises it as follows :—[1]

"The expedient of separating the Bank into two departments does not seem to us to possess that high degree of importance which has been attributed to it; a good system of accounts, like that of the Bank of France, is enough to enable people to judge of the various factors in the balance sheets periodically issued. It would be easy, were it thought necessary, to impose a definite limit to the issue of notes, without having recourse to the public parade of a division of functions between two branches of the same establishment."

From another point of view, Mr. Palgrave, in a recent and most valuable book to which we have already referred,[2] expressly condemns the division of the Bank into two departments and attributes to it a considerable share in producing those variations in the discount rate which are so frequent in England.

In fact, the division of the Bank into two departments involves the separation of its resources into two very unequal parts, upon the smaller of which all the demands fall, —demands which in England are naturally very large and may be unexpected. The Bank has thus to guard against a continual danger which would be far less formidable if a less artificial plan had been adopted.

SECTION I.

The Issue Department.

(a)—*The amount of the issues and the part played by cheques.*

The Return of the issue department shows the following figures for September 16th, 1903 :—

Notes issued	£50,654,500	Government Debt . .	£11,015,100
		Other securities . . .	7,434,900
		Gold coin and bullion .	32,204,500
	£50,654,500		£50,654,500

[1] *La Question des Banques*, p. 362.
[2] *The Bank Rate and the Money Market*, p. 198.

Thus the notes issued amount to £50,654,000 and the total issued not "covered" by gold is £18,450,000. The issue of notes is subject to certain interesting administrative regulations and also to certain legislative provisions, which latter it is essential to understand.

From the administrative point of view the issue of notes is subjected to the following regulations:—

Every note issued[1] is entered in the registers of the issue department with its proper number and date, and these registers are duly made up at the end of each day, when the notes remaining over are returned to the cashier, whose accounts must thus show the number of notes issued in the course of the year.

At the Bank of England the notes cashed by the issue department are never returned into circulation—a practice contrary to that adopted by most European banks. Such notes are first cancelled and then, after they have been submitted to the test of a special system of book-keeping, they are put away in the strong boxes, where they remain for seven years before being destroyed.[2]

The number of notes cashed each day varies roughly from 25,000 to 60,000. It has been calculated that the average time during which each note stays in circulation is 70 days for £5 notes, 58 days for £10 notes, 27 days for £20, £50, and £100 notes, 9 days for £200, £300, and £500 notes, and 7 days only for £1,000 notes.

From the legislative point of view:

The notes are bound to be issued against gold, except that notes to a certain fixed amount are issued against securities of which the greater part represent the Government debt to the Bank.

According to the Act of 1844 the "uncovered" issue amounted to 14 millions, of which 11 millions represented the Government debt. How has this amount come to be

[1] With regard to the preparation of the Bank notes see Hankey (4th edition), p. 106, and a most interesting lecture by Mr. Henry Bradbury *On the Security and Manufacture of Bank Notes*; compare also as a curiosity, Barlow, *On a Bank of England Note*, of which a summary is given by Lawson, *History of Banking*, pp. 149-150.

[2] Noël, p. 46.

increased to £18,450,000? This increase is due to the loss of rights of issue possessed by country banks, of which rights, it will be remembered, the Bank of England inherits two-thirds.

The Act of 1844 recognised:

207 Private Banks with a right of issue amounting to	£5,153,417
72 Joint Stock Banks	3,478,230
	£8,631,647

In January, 1901, the position was as follows:—[1]

	Authorised Issue.	*Actual Issue.*
33 Private Banks	£1,120,588	£344,760
27 Joint Stock Banks	1,541,735	825,009

The reduction in the rights of issue possessed by the country banks was one of the objects of the law of 1844 and this object has evidently been attained most successfully.[2] Moreover, the notes of the country banks are not legal tender and hence the bankers shrink from the risks involved in the issue of notes payable to bearer at sight and keep well within the legal limit. It is on this account that their actual issues are so much below their authorised issues.

[1] *Encyc. Brit.*, supplement, Vol. I., p. 113.

[2] The following table from the *Quarterly Journal of Economics* (Vol. XIV., p. 561, number for August, 1900) shows the various dates at which the Bank of England's right of issue has been increased and the amounts of the respective increases:

Years.	*Amount of Increase.* £
1855	475,000
1861	175,000
1866	350,000
1881	750,000
1887	450,000
1890	250,000
1894	350,000
1900	975,000
Total	£3,775,000

To this must be added the original sum of £14,000,000, making a fresh total of £17,775,000 for 1900. There has thus been a further increase of £675,000 since this date.

Many country banks have lost their right of issue through amalgamation with other firms.

We must now consider the amount of the issues from another and a very important point of view.

The note issue in England is smaller than in the other great European countries, but notwithstanding this it would be quite wrong to suppose that the whole of this issue passes into circulation; the greater part of it is kept at the Bank as "reserve." For the last ten years the value of the notes in circulation has been less than the value of the gold in the issue department.

Thus on September 16, 1903, out of £50,654,500 of notes issued, £22,011,110 were in the banking department, which reduces the total of notes in circulation to £28,643,390, against which a gold reserve of £32,204,500 was held. Thus we get a curious application of Vico's theory on spiral progression and are carried back to the banking systems at the end of the Renaissance; bank notes, in fact, have once more become certificates of deposit, but resting on better security than did the original ones.

And more even than this, a considerable portion of the 28 millions, *i.e.*, more than 4 millions,[2] is not actually in circulation, but locked up in safes, and forms the reserve of banks and bankers.

[1] Before 1893 the value of the circulation exceeded that of the metallic reserve; since then it may be seen from the following figures, taken from a recent paper by Mr. Jackson (Table I.), that the opposite has been the case.

Years.	*Metallic Reserve.*	*Circulation.*
	£	£
1893	26.425	25.858
1894	34.414	25.262
1895	38.951	25.815
1896	44.319	26.474
1897	35.551	27.198
1898	33.567	27.448
1899	32.268	27.878
1900	33.321	29.396
1901	35.831	29.559
1902	35.644	29.404
Average	£35.030	£27.429

Thus for the last ten years the proportion of the metallic reserve to the circulation has been 128 per cent.; it was only 91 per cent. for the ten preceding years, during which the average metallic reserve was £22,595,000, as compared with a circulation of £24,884,000.

[2] According to Wilfredo Pareto.

The question then arises, how, with a paper circulation of 28 millions[1] (of which, we repeat, at most 24 millions are actually in the hands of the public), and a metallic currency much scantier than that of France,[2] England is able to carry on more transactions than the latter country? The explanation of this must be sought in the fact that in England notes and coin are merely a subsidiary means of making payments. The latter are made through bills and, above all, through cheques, thanks to that admirable institution known as the Clearing House.

The Clearing House system is familiar to all who have an interest, however slight, in banking transactions, and a study of this institution would be misplaced here. We may content ourselves with saying that it developed rapidly in London[3] and that payments made there in paper and coined money have very quickly been reduced to a mere fraction of the whole.

Thus in 1864 and 1881 payments were made in London in the following proportions:—[4]

	1864.	*1881.*
Coin	.6	.728
Notes	2.6	2.039
Cheques and Bills ...	96.8	97.223
	100.	100.

and since then the change of method has been still more noticeable.

[1] About 700 million francs; the average paper circulation in France during the last ten years has been 3,768,200,000 francs, and in Germany 1,384,300,000 francs (see Jackson, Table I.).

[2] According to M. Leroy-Beaulieu, Vol. III., p. 609, the English stock of metal is hardly equal to 40 per cent. of the French; it is £131,600,000 (3,290,000,000 francs), of which 110 millions are in gold and £21,600,000 in silver, as compared to a French stock of about £320,000,000 (8,000 million of francs), of which 180 millions are in gold and 140 millions in silver.

[3] As early as 1858, according to Courcelle-Seneuil (p. 336), out of a million pounds, the methods of payment were in the following proportions:—

Bills	£422,948
Cheques at sight	510,694
Bank notes	45,649
Coin and Postal Orders	20,709
	£1,000,000

[4] Pownall, *The insufficiency of our cash reserves and of our central stock of gold*, in the *Economic Journal*, Vol. II., p. 535.

In the country the development has been slower, but still sufficiently marked; thus in the case of Manchester, Mr. Pownall[1] gives the following figures for the cash payments (coin and notes). They formed:

In 1859	about	53	per cent. of the total turnover.
" 1864	"	42	" " "
" 1871	"	32	" " "
" 1881	"	20	" " "

The transactions of the Manchester Clearing House have increased from a total of 72 millions in 1873 to a total of 163 millions in 1891.

The movement may be more vividly realised from the following detail: the number of impressed stamps, which are principally used for cheques, was 13 millions in 1857, in 1891 it was more than 152 millions.

And since 1891 the employment of cheques in the country has increased more and more. In the ten years from 1892-1902, the deposits at country banks have risen from 184 millions to 334½ millions, that is an increase of 81½ per cent., and this increase is due to the increase in the branches established by the country banks. These were 1,271 in 1892, as compared with 2,578 in 1902.[2]

(b)—*Merits and Demerits of the English System of Note Issue.*[3]

Leaving on one side the question whether the tendency of the country banks of issue to disappear should not be resisted,[4] and, *a fortiori*, also the question whether it would not be better to return to freedom of issue and the system existing before 1844, it may be asked, to refer only to the Bank of England, *what judgment must be pronounced on the organisation of the issue department?*

[1] *Loc. cit.*

[2] See Jackson, p. 9.

[3] We give only an outline of the matter here. It will be discussed in more detail in the last chapter of this volume.

[4] This is the opinion of M. Leroy-Beaulieu, (Vol. III., pp. 595 and 606), and of many other eminent economists.

From a theoretical point of view it can only be condemned. The amount of the "uncovered" issue was fixed at 14 millions in 1844 because the Government debt and the public securities held by the Bank amounted to that sum! A curious method of determining the amount of the paper currency! If the Government debt had been twice this amount, would the uncovered circulation have been doubled? or, forsooth, if the debt had not existed, would there have been no issues except those covered by gold?

Moreover, a Government debt and particularly a permanent debt, cannot afford a guarantee or a basis for the issue of notes. If every Government debt could be used to create an equivalent sum of money, the conclusion would inevitably follow "that the way to create money is for a government to borrow it," and we should have far outdistanced all the Laws and Chamberlains in creation.

To this it may be replied, from a practical standpoint, that however unfortunate these mistakes may be, they are not dangerous on a small scale and that in the present instance the total uncovered issue was not fixed at 14 millions solely because this was the amount of the Government debt, but also because the requirements of the English public had been estimated at this figure.

This answer, however, only suggests another and more serious criticism of the existing system. If we grant that the needs of society were limited to 14 millions in 1844, we are led to inquire why this limit has been preserved intact when the needs of society and, above all, the actual population, have increased so greatly?

It is difficult to find an answer to this criticism, all the more because the principle of a fixed issue is in itself open to attack, for as has already been pointed out,[1] at certain times a larger issue is justified, whilst at others the limit fixed would itself be too high.[2]

[1] See especially Cauwès, *op.* and *loc. cit.*, pp. 317-318.

[2] In Holland an attempt has been made to avoid the disadvantages of a fixed issue by leaving the amount of the paper circulation to be fixed from time to time by royal decree.—Pierson, p. 498.

For all these reasons the attempt has been made to discover a system which combines the currency principle with a greater degree of elasticity. Such a system has been adopted by the German Empire and we must therefore consider how the German plan differs from the English.

Comparison between the Note Issue in England and in Germany. The law of 1875, which created the Imperial Bank, and the more recent law of 1899, subjected the issue of bank notes in Germany to the following rules:

The amount of the uncovered circulation, as in the case of England, is fixed beforehand—it is at present £22,500,000.[1] Out of this total only £4,438,550 is contributed by banks of issue other than the Imperial Bank.

Moreover the law of 1875, like the English law of 1844, tends towards centralisation, and both aim at the suppression of the plural system of issue.

The banks of issue in Germany, apart from the Imperial Bank, originally numbered 33, but are now reduced to 6,[2] and their position has been made so much worse by the law of 1899[3] that it is a question whether these banks and in particular the Bank of Frankfurt, will not choose to give up their rights of issue.

So far the two systems, the English and the German, only show points of resemblance; the great distinction from the point of view of the note issue[4] is that the Imperial Bank may exceed the limit fixed for uncovered issues by paying a tax of 5 per cent. Since this tax is added to the rate of

[1] Before 1899 the amount had been first £12,500,000 and then £14,811,450.

[2] The Banks of Frankfurt, of Saxony, of Bavaria, of Wurtemburg, of Baden and of Southern Germany.

[3] In order to protect the reserve of the Reichsbank, the law of 1899 forbids other banks of issue (1) to discount below the rate of the Reichsbank when this rate is 4 per cent. or higher, (2) to discount more than ¼ per cent. below the rate of the Reichsbank in other cases.

[4] There are many other differences between the two banks; for instance, the metallic reserve of the Bank of Germany must equal at least one-third of the amount of notes in circulation, while the remaining two-thirds must consist of bills of exchange not having more than three months to run; again, the German system has a highly-developed fiscal side, which would probably be objectionable to English ideas and which has been made still more prominent by the law of 1899. But we are not concerned with all this, for a comparison between the Bank of England and the other European banks does not fall within our province.

discount, which would be already high in times of crisis, there is no danger that the Bank will use its power rashly and thus indirectly encourage speculation.[1]

SECTION II.

THE BANKING DEPARTMENT.

The banking department is a bank like other banks with this difference, that it is obliged to publish a weekly return of its transactions.

This balance sheet, like that of other banks, shows liabilities and assets. The examination of these in turn will occupy the two parts of our second section.

The liabilities fall under five heads: (1) Proprietors' Capital; (2) Rest; (3) Public Deposits; (4) Other Deposits; (5) Seven-day and other bills.

The assets fall under four heads only: (1) Government Securities; (2) Other Securities; (3) Notes; (4) Gold and Silver Coin.

PART I.

THE LIABILITIES OF THE BANKING DEPARTMENT.

Nos. 1 and 2.—*Proprietors' Capital and Rest.*

The capital of the Bank of England is £14,553,000; it is larger than that of the Bank of France or that of the Bank of Germany, although the latter has lately (1899) been increased by one-half and raised from 6 to 9 millions. But —and this distinguishes it from other systems—the capital of the Bank is all sunk in Government debt and hence constitutes a guarantee capital.

The *rest* or reserve fund was only formed, as we have seen, in 1722. The directors have agreed never to let this fund fall below 3 millions and on September 16, 1903, it was £3,753,869.

The principal object of the capital is to afford security to

[1] The Bank of Germany has however recently been accused of misusing its supplementary issues, which reached a total of £6,800,000 in 1899. See *Encyc. Brit., loc. cit.*, p. 117.

the depositors and these enjoy complete safety at the Bank of England. The capital, combined with the *rest*, represents nearly 40 per cent. of the total deposits and more than 45 per cent. of the private deposits.[1] But the magnitude of the capital has its disadvantages, since, according to Clare,[2] its earnings, in spite of the fact that the total profits are 1½ millions, only amount to 10 per cent., *i.e.*, a dividend of £2 18s. on shares at £342. The other important English and Scotch banks pay dividends varying from 3¾ to 4¼ per cent.

No. 3.—*Public Deposits.*[3]

These form the largest account in the Bank's books and "the largest probably that any bank has ever possessed."[4] The daily receipts from the Customs and Excise are paid in at the branches of the Bank of England, and, moreover, the payments made by the Treasury for the Army, Navy and Civil Service, are effected by cheques on the Bank; the latter also undertakes the administration of the Public Debt, but for this it receives a special payment.[5]

The balance kept by the Treasury at the Bank amounts on an average to about 3 millions. In addition to this sum, the Public Deposits include the balances credited to the Secretary of State for India and to the National Debt Commissioners. At the beginning of the year the Public Deposits shrink on account of the dividends paid on the National Debt, but from the middle of January until the end of March the sums paid in exceed by 6 or 7 millions those paid out. This is due to the fact that the greater part of the direct taxes (income tax, house duty and land tax) are collected during the first quarter. At the same time the

[1] The average of the total deposits for the last ten years is £48,610,000, and the average of the private deposits £39,482,000.—See Jackson, Table I.

[2] See Clare, p. 25, and Raffalovich, p. 364. For everything relating to the liabilities of the banking department, we have found Clare and his commentator invaluable.

[3] Clare, pp. 25-28.

[4] The total value of this account has increased from £5,231,000 in 1844 to £9,285,000 in 1900.—Palgrave, p. 13.

[5] See below, Appendix, the section specially devoted to this question.

payments made by the Government are deferred till the end of March, which marks the close of the financial year. During the first days of April the Public Deposits fall again by about 4 millions and the balance returns to what it was in January.[1] The result of this payment of taxes is an appreciable decrease in the circulation of notes and coin, amounting to 3 millions for gold and 1½ millions for notes. The reserve of the Bank reaches its maximum at the end of March.

The transfer to the Bank of a considerable sum, drawn mainly from the resources of the joint-stock and private banks, narrows the margin between the official rate of discount and the market rate. The difference between the two is sometimes reduced from £1 3s. per cent. to 10s. per cent. This is the time when the Bank discounts least. After some unimportant fluctuations, the Public Deposits reach their minimum about November. Preparation then has to be made for the payments falling due in January and if the Exchequer has but a small balance, advances are made to it on bills[2] which it repays out of the January revenues.

No. 4.—*Other Deposits.*[3]

The Bank's liabilities to private individuals, which fall under this head, correspond closely enough to the current accounts of other banks.

The balance of the sums standing to the credit of the Bank's customers serves as a kind of measure of the supply of available capital. If the total rises above the average there is an excess of such capital and *vice versa*.

The Bank of England is in fact the bankers' bank, the central reservoir which contains not only the balances of

[1] For the fluctuations in the public deposits at the Bank of England see Clare, Table III.

[2] These bills used to be known as deficiency bills, but have since been replaced by deficiency advances. See in the Appendix on the Relations between the Bank of England and the Treasury, the section dealing with the floating debt.

[3] Clare, pp. 28-31. The total of these private deposits has increased from £8,069,000 in 1844 to £40,602,000 in 1900 (Palgrave, p. 12), *i.e.*, an increase of 503 per cent.

the great merchants and the big limited companies, but also those of numerous country banks and of all the London bankers belonging to the Clearing House. Each of the 18 clearing banks has an account at the Bank and differences are paid by means of transfers in its books. These transfers sometimes amount on Settlement days to a total of 50 millions.

Besides this, the London bankers keep at the Bank the reserves which they hold in case of emergency. "*The Bank has therefore the responsibility of looking after what is really the ultimate banking reserve of the whole country,*"[1] and should difficulties arise it is to it that appeal will be made. This state of things necessarily carries with it serious dangers.[2]

Up to 1877 the Bank specified in its Returns what proportion of the deposits belonged to bankers. At this date there was a balance of 13 millions credited to customers who were not bankers, and one of £9,500,000 to bankers.[3] One of the most desirable reforms in the Bank's administration is the resumption of this statement.[4]

In normal times the total of the private deposits fluctuates regularly enough,[5] but during a crisis it has been frequently observed that this total increases appreciably. This is partly because the banks feel it necessary to strengthen their reserves and partly because the public are eager to be rid of all doubtful investments and to entrust their money to the institution which they believe, and not without reason, to be the safest in the world, *i.e.*, to the Bank of England.

One other point remains to be considered with reference to the current account of the bankers.[6]

When there is a drain of gold, which normally occurs in the autumn, the only defence which the Bank can make is to raise the discount rate so as to attract capital to England.

[1] Clare, p. 30.

[2] As regards this point, see below the chapter on the Reserve, p. 323, *The reserve of the Bank and the reserve of the bankers.*

[3] See Palgrave, pp. 12, 13. In 1876 the current account of the bankers was £11,851,000 out of a total of £23,493,000; the proportion was thus greater.

[4] On this point compare the last chapter of the present volume.

[5] Clare, Table IV.

[6] Clare, pp. 37-40; Raffalovich, p. 367.

Foreign bankers are thus induced to buy bills on London, a proceeding which reacts on the exchanges.

The success of this policy depends on the support given to the Bank of England by the outside market. If the latter is well supplied, it will not follow the Bank's lead; hence it is possible to judge from the state of the current accounts whether this policy will be successful or not.

The Bank has also an indirect method of clearing the market of its surplus capital : it sells Consols for "money," and buys them back for the "account." The purchasers pay in cheques on their bankers and the balance to the credit of the latter is decreased.

It has been suggested, says M. Raffalovich, that the Bank should secure command of the situation by paying interest on deposits. Since a large proportion of the money deposited with private banks is placed there for security, there is no doubt that in view of the prestige of the Bank of England, a very low rate of interest would serve to attract considerable sums and when once it had adopted this policy, a slight increase in the rate paid would be sufficient to deplete the market. There are, however, very serious objections to this course; for one thing it would be contrary to the Bank's traditional policy, which is to sacrifice profit to absolute security; and besides, by entering into competition with other bankers, the central institution would certainly incur enmity and it would lose the profit which it makes from the balances of the current accounts on which no interest is paid. Finally by increasing the total of its deposits, the Bank would find it difficult to maintain the proportion between its reserve and its liabilities, which is now 50 per cent.[1]

The liabilities of the banking department conclude with the heading No. 5, *Seven-day and other bills,* as regards which no comment is needed.

[1] The average for the last ten years: from 1882 to 1892 the average was only 42 per cent. The maximum was reached in 1894, when the proportion was 63 per cent.; since then the tendency has been towards a decline. See Jackson, Table I.

PART II.

THE ASSETS OF THE BANKING DEPARTMENT.

We have said that the assets of the banking department fall under four heads:

(1) Government Securities; (2) Other Securities; (3) Notes; (4) Gold and Silver Coin.

In actual fact, however, the first two groups, Government securities and other securities, represent the Bank's investments, while the two last groups, notes and gold and silver coin, form the stock of money best known as the *reserve*. Hence instead of discussing each group separately, it will be convenient to combine them under two heads, which will supply matter for the following chapters.

Chapter I. The investments of the Bank. The Bank of England and the rate of discount.

Chapter II. The reserve.

CHAPTER I.

THE INVESTMENTS OF THE BANK.

THE BANK OF ENGLAND AND THE DISCOUNT RATE.

(*a*) Government Securities. Their nature; (*b*) Other Securities. Hankey's theory as to the proper nature of these. Uncertainty as to their actual character.

The average Bank Rate. Its fluctuations. Average since 1844 and variations. Periodic fluctuations. The Autumnal Drain. The Bank Rate and the Market Rate. The Bank Rate before 1844. Competition between the Bank and the market between 1844 and 1878. Since 1878 the Bank Rate in London has always been above the Market Rate. Position different in the Provinces. Frequent fluctuations in the Bank Rate. Comparison with the chief European Banks. Bad effect of the fluctuations in the discount rate upon trade. Explanation of the fluctuations of the English Bank Rate. Special character of the London Market. Artificial character of the Act of 1844. Lack of fluidity in the securities held by the Bank of England.

(*a*)—GOVERNMENT SECURITIES.

THE Government securities are those securities which yield an income guaranteed by the State (Consols, Treasury bills, etc.). Little importance is attached to variations in the amount of the Government securities. At the end of the quarter the total increases because the Government borrows on the security of bills, which it redeems in the course of a few weeks.

When the Bank does not renew the Treasury bills which it holds the result is a tightness on the money market.

(*b*)—OTHER SECURITIES.

Thomas Hankey, at one time Governor of the Bank of England, in his book on *The Principles of Banking*,[1] discusses the nature of the securities which ought to be held by a bank. He distinguishes short loans and bills of exchange, which are based on commercial transactions, and

[1] p. 26, *et seq*. Hankey was a director of the Bank of England for more than fifty years; the full title of his book is, *The Principles of Banking, its Utility and Economy, with Remarks on the Working and Management of the Bank of England*. 1st edition, 1867; 4th edition, revised by C. Wigram, 1887.

are readily and naturally converted into money, from other securities, such as mortgages, and business securities of a similar character, which, although they offer suitable openings for an investor, are not the kind of securities which a bank should hold, because they cannot be easily realised.

The Bank of England follows Hankey's advice closely enough. Its securities consist of Indian stock, railway debenture stock, discounted commercial bills, and advances on security.

We can only speak on supposition, however, for since 1875 the details of the Bank's investments have not been published. Before this date a return was supplied to Parliament, which distinguished the discounts, the loans, and the other assets. The discontinuance of this return is much to be regretted.

Moreover, the discounts have decreased considerably owing to the competition of the outside market. Paper is only brought to the Bank under exceptional circumstances, when the market is ill-supplied with money and it is feared that the official rate may be raised.

Even before 1875, however, the total of the bills discounted was exceedingly variable;[1] it was very high when the market was stringent, as in 1836, 1847, 1857, and from 1864-1867, it sank very low when the pressure was removed.[2]

Since this very difficult question of the Bank of England and the discount rate has been touched upon, it will be advisable to study it fully once for all, and, indeed, the matter is as much and perhaps more in place here than elsewhere.

The Bank of England and the Discount Rate.

This important question[3] can be best discussed under three heads, viz.:—I., The average rate of the Bank of England and its periodical fluctuations. II., A comparison

[1] Compare Palgrave, p. 14.

[2] Thus discounted bills made up more than half (56 per cent.) of the securities held by the Bank in 1847, and they were 46 per cent. in 1857, and 42 per cent. from 1864 to 1866, but they only made up 28 per cent. of the total securities in 1844, and only 23 per cent. in 1875.

[3] The very difficult question of the English Bank rate cannot be examined without a preliminary study of Mr. Palgrave's recent book, *Bank Rate and the Money Market* (1903). Mr. Palgrave has written no less than three

between the Bank rate and the market rate. III., A comparison between the discount rates of the Bank of England and those of the Banks of France and Germany. The great fluctuations in the Bank of England rate; the results and the explanation of this phenomenon.

I.—*The Average Discount Rate of the Bank of England.—Its Periodical Fluctuations.—The Autumnal Drain.*

The average rate of the Bank is relatively low in comparison with the usual rates of the Continental banks; it exceeds that of the Bank of France only.[1]

It has been pointed out that the rate, after displaying a tendency to increase between 1854 and 1866, has shown a constant tendency to fall since this period.

The period 1844-1900, if divided into six groups, corresponds to the following average rates :—[2]

	£	s.	d.
"1845-54	3	8	5
1855-64	4	12	9
1865-74	3	16	1
1875-84	3	3	11
1885-94	3	3	2
1895-1900	3	0	4

"*The average for the whole period* 1845-1900 *is* £3 12s."

The rate of discount is subject to periodical fluctuations in the course of each year; it is generally higher in the winter half as compared with the summer half. In autumn and early winter money is needed to meet the expenses of the home harvest, the cost of holidays and travelling, and,

works on this subject, in 1874, 1880, and 1892; his last book revises and completes the earlier ones, which were in themselves standard works on this question. M. Paul Loubet's essay on *La Banque de France et l'Escompte* may also be consulted with pleasure as well as profit; this book, like Mr. Palgrave's, contains a mass of comparative statistics. Mr. F. E. Steele has also published an essay on the subject, entitled, *On the Changes in the Bank Rate; First their Causes, and Secondly their Effect.* This study originally came out in the *Journal of the Institute of Bankers.*

[1] This may be seen from the table given by M. Paul Loubet (p. 103) of the average discount rate in the principal European capitals from 1885 to 1900. Between 1883 and 1902 the average rate was $2\frac{4}{5}$ per. cent. for the Bank of France, $3\frac{1}{5}$ per cent. for the Bank of England, and $3\frac{3}{5}$ per cent. for the Bank of Germany.

[2] Palgrave, p. 107.

above all, for the imports of corn and cotton. These causes combined with others[1] produce a phenomenon also observed in several other countries and known in England as the *Autumnal Drain*.[2] This withdrawal of money is important. Clare[3] calculates that the average rate of discount is $1\frac{1}{10}$ per cent. higher from October to March than from April to September.

II.—*The Bank Rate and the Market Rate.*

The Bank's policy as regards its discount rate has varied considerably. For a long time, indeed almost up to 1844, the Bank kept its rate fixed at from 4 to 5 per cent. When the market rate was high the Bank discounted, but when it was low—and it was sometimes from $1\frac{3}{4}$ to 2 per cent. lower than the Bank rate—the Bank of necessity ceased to discount, since no one was stupid enough to apply to it.

After 1844 the Bank began to compete with the other banks of discount, sometimes leading and sometimes following the market. Then by degrees its discounts, which had been very considerable,[4] declined, and in 1878 it even made an official statement to the effect that it did not feel bound to keep to the published minimum rate.

As a matter of fact, from 1872 until the present time, the market rate has always been less than the Bank rate. Between 1845 and 1872, on the contrary, there were ten years during which it was higher.[5] It should be observed that in the provinces the current rate is sometimes higher than the Bank rate and, strange to say, this causes discontent

[1] In particular the periodic increase in the paper currency in Scotland, which causes an immediate demand for gold from the Bank of England. For further details on this point see Palgrave, pp. 107-110.

[2] For the *Autumnal Drain* see Stanley Jevons, *Investigations in Currency and Finance*, pp. 160-193. This chapter in Jevons' posthumous work had appeared in June, 1866, in the *Journal of the Statistical Society*. The phenomenon had previously been pointed out and described by Mr. William Langton before the Manchester Statistical Society.

[3] *Op. cit.*, p. 9.

[4] See the whole of the Inquiry of 1848. Mr. James Morris estimated that the discounts of the Bank at this date were one half of the total discounts.

[5] For details see the table given by Palgrave, p. 33.

among the local bankers who have their deposits at the Bank and who complain that the latter is using their own capital as a means of competing with them.

III.—*Frequent Fluctuations in the English Bank Rate; Comparison with other European Banks in this respect. Effects and Explanation of this Phenomenon.*

(*a*) The most noticeable feature about the Bank of England rate is its lack of stability and this is yet more remarkable when we compare it in this respect with the rates of the Banks of France and of Germany.

To take the period from 1875-1900[1] alone; during this interval the English Bank rate was altered 167 times, whilst only 84 changes are recorded in the German rate and only 25 in that of the Bank of France.[2]

Thus the average duration of the same rate is 365 days for the Bank of France, 108 days for the Bank of Germany and 54 days for the Bank of England.

If instead of taking averages the movements of the rate are examined year by year, it is found that between 1844 and 1900, *i.e.*, during 57 years, there are only two years (1851 and 1897) during which the English Bank rate was unaltered, as compared with nine in the case of Germany and twenty in the case of France.[3]

What is still more serious is that the fluctuations in the English Bank rate are not only very frequent, but are also very great. The Bank of England is the only bank at which

[1] Paul Loubet, Appendix E.

[2] The discount rate at the Bank of France was only altered 124 times during the whole of the 19th century, so that in 25 years the English rate has changed 43 times more than the French in a period four times as long. Compare Paul Loubet, p. 104. Between 1866 and 1900 the Bank of England made 400 changes in its rate, the Bank of Germany 161, the Bank of Belgium (established in 1851) 173, the Bank of Holland 173 and the Bank of France 111. See Palgrave, Tables 37, 38 and 39, pp. 196-198. The statistics given by Mr. Palgrave with regard to the fluctuations in the discount rate are exceedingly complete and full; they begin in 1844 and relate to the five banks of issue just mentioned.

[3] Palgrave, p. 211, Table 43. This Table is inconsistent in some points with Table 39, given by the same author.

the range of fluctuation during the same year has on three occasions amounted to 5½, 6 and 6½ per cent.[1]

Nowhere else, except on one occasion in Germany, have the fluctuations during a single year reached 4 and 5 per cent., as a rule they have not been more than 1 or 2 per cent.[2]

(*b*) *What are the results of this fact?* These constant and large fluctuations have very injurious effects on trade.[3] This may be better understood by considering the great advantages of a moderate and a relatively stable rate.

With respect to the moderation of the rate in the first place, anyone who discounts paper at a bank, that is in fact, every trader, naturally wishes to borrow at as low a rate as possible, since otherwise he cannot as a rule find such a use for the capital lent him as will repay him for the expenses of the transaction and one of the main objects of the banking system will have disappeared.

With respect to the stability of the rate, it may be said that a certain fixity is an essential. This enables the trader to reckon beforehand, at least approximately, the amounts that he will have to pay his banker; the stability is thus a guarantee of the safety of his transactions.

The English commercial world does not enjoy these advantages and guarantees[4] to the extent which it has a right to expect. It remains to discover the explanation of this fact.

(*c*) *Explanation of the Fluctuations in the Bank Rate of Discount.* These fluctuations are due to several causes. We shall deal first with those about which everyone is agreed and then pass on to those which are only partially accepted.

[1] See the years 1858, 1873 and 1866 respectively.

[2] Palgrave, Table 38, p. 127.

[3] Compare Steele, pp. 19 and 20. For the effect of the variations in the discount rate on the Stock Exchange see Steele, pp. 20-25. For the important question of the relations between the discount rate and prices see Giffen's second essay in his *Essays in Finance (second series)*, pp. 37-89.

[4] These advantages are so great that Professor Foxwell has observed that, "The true test of sound economic, as distinguished from merely solvent banking, is the moderation of the average rate of discount."—*Economic Journal,* March, 1892, p. 154.

1.—*The Peculiar Character of the London Market.*

The London market is distinguished from the other European markets by its importance. Nearly all the trade of the world is connected with London, and it has justly been said that London is the "*clearing house for the international exchanges.*"[1] Unfortunately, this privileged position has its disadvantages; it subjects the London market to the risks of sudden and large demands.

The London market is also distinguished from the other European markets by the fact, to which, indeed, much of its importance is due: that *London is the only free market for gold in the world.* In France the Bank charges a premium, varying from 2½ to 6 per mille, on gold for export purposes; in Germany, according to the witty remark of Mr. F. H. Jackson,[2] there exists the equally formidable deterrent of the *Imperial displeasure.* In England there is nothing of this kind, the trade in gold is absolutely free; perhaps it is this which makes London the financial capital of the world, but in return, it leaves only one means of resisting a demand for gold,—that is an increase in the value of the capital lent, or in other words, a rise in the rate of discount. England thus subjects herself to fluctuations in the discount rates, but she does it only because she finds that the advantages of possessing a free market for gold fully counter-balance the disadvantages, and at any rate she acts with her eyes open.[3]

2.—*The Artificial Nature of the Act of* 1844.

Has the system established by the legislation of 1844 any influence on the discount rate? Some have answered this in the affirmative.

[1] Edmond Théry, *Europe et États Unis d'Amérique,* p. 111. London has also been called the *Rome of finance for civilised countries.*

[2] Jackson, *op. cit.,* p. 6.

[3] Professor Foxwell justly quotes in this connection Mr. Pownall's observation, "*Our money market is sensitive because we choose that it shall be so.*" *Art. cit.,* p. 155.

Mr. Palgrave,[1] for instance, observes in the first place that the division of the Bank of England into two parts also "divides the resources of the Bank artificially into two parts, and causes the demand to fall on the smaller of them." In England the demands are naturally very large and may be sudden. The division into two departments, which has the advantage of "directing immediate attention to the amount of free resources which the Bank has at its disposal, nevertheless tends to render the amount actually available to meet any sudden demand smaller than it would be if this artificial arrangement were not followed."

Moreover, the Bank is obliged by the Act of 1844 to buy standard gold to any amount at a fixed price, whether it needs it or not, and hence it is forced to replenish its reserves at the will of the importers and not at the wish of its directors. Hence there is at times a useless accumulation of gold, which sometimes leads to a low Bank rate, and sometimes, when the accumulations produce a tightness on the market, to the opposite result, neither of these movements in the rate having any connection with the needs of trade.[2]

3.—*Lack of Fluidity in the Composition of the Securities held by the Bank of England.*

It has been remarked that the exact nature of the securities held by the Bank is not known, but all the evidence goes to make it probable that short loans only acquire importance under exceptional conditions and that the number of discounted bills is very limited. In an ordinary way, indeed, the Bank of England does not compete with the other banks of discount. It does not discount at the market rate except for its own customers and as this is generally lower than the Bank rate (the average difference during the last twenty years has been $\frac{5}{8}$ per cent. per annum), evidently it can hold only a very small number of commercial bills.

[1] Palgrave, pp. 198, 199.
[2] Palgrave, p. 199.

On the other hand, as Mr. Jackson[1] points out, apparently with regret that things are not the same in England, the Banks of France and of Germany usually hold a large number of bills of exchange. These Banks also are habitual purchasers of commercial securities—the Bank of France because it is obliged to be so by its constitution; the Bank of Germany because it must hold bills to the value of two-thirds of its issues.

If we examine, as Mr. Palgrave[2] does, some recent balance sheets, we find that the Bank of France held securities at Paris and the branches to the value of £54,000,000 (1,375,000,000 francs), of which £31,000,000 was in bills for short periods and £24,000,000 in short loans. At the Bank of Germany, out of securities worth £64,000,000, nearly £50,000,000 was in bills, £2,100,000 of these being English paper, while £8,000,000 was in the form of short loans.[3]

The large quantity of specie held in reserve, combined with the readily available and fluid character of the securities, enables the Continental banks to control the market and always to have an easy command of ready money.

The Bank of England cannot secure this control of the market except when circumstances force the latter to apply to it for discount, hence if in ordinary times the Bank wishes to obtain money quickly, it can only do so by selling Consols,[4] and it does not hold any considerable quantity of securities which by maturing rapidly will provide it with cash without forcing it to disturb the home market. Consequently the Bank has to determine its discount rate very carefully and must often vary it in order to protect its reserve.

[1] p. 6.

[2] pp. 206 and 207.

[3] The average of bills discounted during the last ten years was 27 millions (675 millions of francs) for France and 35 millions for the Bank of Germany. For further details on the total discounts of the Banks of France and Germany between 1883 and 1902 compare Jackson, Table I.

[4] And this has obvious disadvantages.

It may be added, and the remark is worth making at the risk of its appearing irrelevant, that this characteristic feature of the Bank of England securities is analogous to a characteristic which may be observed in English finance as a whole.

Whilst other countries hold numerous bills of exchange on England, and an appreciable number of English Treasury bills, the English public, which possesses an enormous quantity of Continental securities, State loans, railway shares, industrial securities, etc.—the English public, I repeat, holds very little foreign commercial paper and seems to consider it of small importance.

No doubt the possession of foreign shares is a good thing, it serves at need to pay a debt abroad and thus to avoid a drain of English bullion. But it is no less true, on the other hand, that supposing a rise in the value of money on the European market or some danger of political trouble, a very considerable drain of English bullion may be produced through the bills of exchange and the Treasury bills which are held abroad. Some writers, in particular Mr. Palgrave,[1] think that the situation is made more serious by the fact that the imports increase more rapidly than the exports and that the amount of "international securities" held in England tends to decrease, suggesting that "the country may have been living above its income."[2]

[1] p. 213, *et seq.* [2] p. 215.

CHAPTER II.

THE RESERVE.

Nature of the reserve. What is meant by the term. The reserve as the keystone of English credit. The bank reserve and the reserve of the bankers. Amount of the reserve. Its normal fluctuations. The reserve in time of crisis. Question whether the suspension of the limit of issue was foreseen by Peel in 1844. Obscurity of the debates in Parliament. A letter of Peel. Mr. Lowe's scheme for reform (1873).

THE Reserve, as we have said, consists almost entirely of notes, which are retained in the banking department, and only to a very small extent of gold and silver coin.

The Reserve forms the essential point, the "vital" point, as Clare calls it, of the Bank Return. "On the maintenance of a sufficient store of actual cash to satisfy the claims of depositors depends the very existence of the Bank, for the whole of the Deposits are practically debts payable in gold on demand and the Bank must either fulfil its obligation to repay when called upon, or close its doors."[1]

We shall study this delicate subject under five heads:

1.—The nature of the Reserve.

2.—In what way is the Reserve the keystone of all English credit?

3.—The Reserve of the Bank and the bankers' reserve.

4.—The amount of the Reserve; its fluctuations.

5.—The Reserve during a crisis.—Did the author of the Act of 1844 foresee the suspension, at such times, of the limit fixed for the uncovered issue? Mr. Lowe's scheme for reform.

I.—THE NATURE OF THE RESERVE.

Mr. Clare's remarks on this subject are exceedingly well judged and should be read carefully by everyone who wishes to obtain a clear understanding of the matter.

[1] Clare, *op. cit.*, p. 45.

It is sometimes thought, he observes,[1] "that the Reserve secures the note-holder as well as the depositor and that an export of gold is bad for the country, because it must impair the ability of the Bank to cash its notes on presentation." This is a misconception. The convertibility of the note has nothing to do with the banking department. The Reserve is solely a banking reserve.

This misconception is due to a confusion between "the banking department's cash reserve against deposits," and "the issue department's stock of gold appropriated to the service of the note." It may be connected with the fact that the Reserve is commonly spoken of as gold, while in reality the principal stock of gold is deposited in the Issue Department as security for the notes.

"It is obvious, too, on examining the Return, that a withdrawal of bullion must diminish the stock in the issue department." Why should it also affect the cash at the banking department?

This is readily understood if we consider the method used to withdraw gold from the Bank.

"The usual course is to obtain credit with a London banker by discounting bills or selling securities, etc., to make use of this credit by asking for Bank of England Notes, and to convert the notes into gold at the Issue Department. The gold, it is true, is actually paid out by the Issue Department, but the notes, which give power to demand that gold, are bound to come out of the Reserve of the Banking Department." This explains why a withdrawal of gold may weaken both the stock in the issue department and also the Reserve properly so called.

II.—Why May it be Said that "If the Reserve were Lost, the Whole English Nation would go Bankrupt?"

The issue department works automatically in giving out gold in exchange for notes. The result of a drain is to weaken the Reserve and hence the position of the Bank. The importance of variations in the Reserve depends on the

[1] p. 45, *et seq.*

fact that in England gold is the only metal which is unlimited legal tender; silver is only legal tender for sums not exceeding forty shillings.

Under ordinary circumstances payments are made by cheque, but the very basis of credit is "the principle that debts are payable in gold."[1] Yet the liabilities of bankers to their depositors exceed by hundreds of millions the stock of gold actually in the country and this involves an obvious danger.

The total of the deposits, which Mr. Newmarch estimated in 1851 at 250 millions, amounted in 1901 to £888,100,000; it is thus seven or eight times larger than the whole stock of gold in the country.[2] Besides this, the Bank of England Reserve in 1901 was only £24,046,000, *i.e.*, 2.71 per cent. of the total liabilities of the banks.[3] This 2.71 per cent. is thus all that the banks have to depend upon to meet possible demands.

The terrible responsibility which rests on the Bank of England is evident, as is also the manner in which the Bank is the keystone of the whole system of English credit. In fact, as Mr. Clare remarks, "if the Reserve were lost, this 'nation of shopkeepers' would have to put its shutters up."

III.—The Reserve of the Bank and the Bankers' Reserve.

In the United States a deposit bank is obliged to keep 25 per cent. of its deposits in cash. In England, on the contrary, the banker is under no restriction whatever,

[1] Clare, p. 48.

[2] The exact value of the English coined money is not known; Mr. Goschen and others have estimated it at 73 millions, but it was shown in the *Economist* for January 3rd, 1892, that this estimate is too small. According to this journal, the coin in circulation amounts to 86 millions, while the authorities of the Mint go still further and reckon it at 100 millions.

[3] Formerly the proportion was still smaller; in 1872 the Reserve was only £12,100,000 as against 584 millions of deposits, *i.e.*, the proportion was 2.06 per cent.—Palgrave, p. 104. Mr. Pownall declared (*Economic Journal*, Vol. II., p. 532) that: "If the system did not exist, the man who suggested its introduction would be branded madman." See the whole article, *The Insufficiency of our Cash Reserves and of our Central Stock of Gold*, pp. 530-543.

although, as we have seen, the total liabilities of the banks exceed the total metallic stock of the country. It is true that people sometimes speak of the bankers' reserve. But the word is not here used in its exact sense; there is no reference here to a special fund set aside for use in emergencies, but merely to the till-money, the cash required by the bankers for their ordinary business. "The reserve, properly so called, of a Provincial Banker consists of readily convertible securities, such as Consols, etc., of money payable 'at call' with the London brokers, of a credit balance in the books of his London Agent, and in some cases of a balance at the Bank of England as well. The same is true of the London banker. His actual reserve consists, not of a store of cash locked up in his strong-room, but of money at call, a balance at the Bank, and a bundle of securities."[1]

These reserves are sufficient in ordinary times, but they are not coin and the banks have undertaken to pay in coin[2] very large sums. Thus they all depend, directly or indirectly, on the Bank of England, and not one of them is prepared to meet an unusual demand *out of his own resources*. This state of things is, it cannot be too often repeated, very serious, and may some day cause an unpleasant surprise.

It may be well to refer at this point, when opportunity offers, to a question which has aroused endless discussion: *The question of the bankers' deposits at the Bank of England.*

What is the value of these deposits? Since 1876 no special information on this point has been given in the Bank Returns—a most regrettable fact—but we know that in 1876 they amounted to 11½ millions out of a total of 23 millions.

Mr. Foxwell[3] notes that between 1844 and 1877 there were 61 occasions when the Bank Reserve was "not sufficient to meet the London bankers' balances." Even in 1876, when the Reserve was 40 per cent. above the average, the bankers' deposits amounted to 75 per cent. of this reserve.

[1] Clare, pp. 49-50.

[2] This fact, says Mr. Pownall, is only clearly realised in time of crisis (p. 536).

[3] *Loc. cit.*, p. 150. For further details compare Palgrave, pp. 23, 27.

Hence it has several times been suggested[1] that the Bank of England should keep unemployed the whole or a part of the bankers' deposits. The Bank itself[2] has always protested vigorously against such a theory and it has been pointed out that since these banks themselves only exist by using their customers' deposits, they cannot expect to impose a different policy upon the Bank of England.

Moreover the Bank has never hitherto acknowledged that it felt bound to keep a metallic reserve for the whole country; it contents itself with a consideration of its own liabilities. But this latent responsibility is shown in the extreme care and promptitude with which it defends itself against the dangers of a foreign drain. The position involves a conflict of interests. On the one hand, the shareholders would like to see the unemployed capital, upon which they make no profit, reduced to a minimum; on the other hand, the public, remembering that the Bank pays no interest on its deposits, is of opinion that it might well keep a larger reserve.

Private bankers who belong to the Clearing House have often been advised to form an association and to keep their own reserve.

Peel himself considered[3] that the joint-stock banks ought to be obliged to share in the expenses necessary to keep up a gold reserve and this opinion has in more recent times received the support of Mr. Goschen[4] and Mr. Lidderdale.[5]

[1] This theory was first put forward in the *Economist* for November 18th, 1872.

[2] See Hankey, preface to the second edition of his *Principles of Banking,* and Jackson, pp. 11 and 12.

With regard to the proportion of the bankers' deposits that the Bank of England ought to keep intact, see the correspondence between Mr. H. H. Gibbs and Professor Bonamy Price, which has been published at the end of Price's *Chapters on Practical Political Economy.* This correspondence deals with a number of questions of interest. Mr. Gibbs was a director of the Bank of England for more than fifty years; he was raised to the peerage with the title of Lord Aldenham.

[3] See his speech on December 3rd, 1847, *Parliamentary Debates,* Vol. XCV., p. 669.

[4] "*It is a false and dangerous system,*" says Lord Goschen, "*to rely simply upon the aid the Bank of England can give in a crisis. I hold that the great banking institutions are bound to take their share.*"

[5] "*I feel,*" said Mr. Lidderdale, in a speech at the Mansion House, "*that the one thing needful is the concern, in their various degrees, of all banks, and not merely the Bank of England.*"

But the bankers have always refused to do anything of the kind, being convinced that *in case of need the Government would always intervene to save the Bank of England.*[1] Indeed, apart from considerations of general interest, which would necessarily have immense weight since the Bank is the keystone of the national credit, it is thought with reason that the Government would be forced to interfere, for the Treasury is the Bank's greatest customer and any misfortune which affected the Bank would completely upset the business of the State.

IV.—The Amount of the Reserve.

Between 1895 and 1900 the average amount of the Reserve was £25,791,000; during this same period the Reserve varied from 23 to 28 millions. This is a great improvement, mainly due to the lesson learnt from the crisis of 1890. Between 1880 and 1890 the average Reserve was only 13 millions and the actual amount varied from 19 to 9 millions.

If we compare the amount of the Reserve with that of the liabilities, we find here also a satisfactory increase: the Reserve, which was formerly only 46 per cent. on the average, of the total liabilities, is now equal to more than 50 per cent. of the liabilities.

Normal Fluctuations in the Reserve.

The Reserve increases during the first quarter and reaches its maximum at the end of March; it then falls, but increases again at the end of June.[2]

The influences which affect the Reserve are both home and foreign.

[1] Clare, p. 53. In 1866 the directors of the Bank protested vigorously against the idea, which was afterwards supported by Bagehot (p. 170), that the private banks had a right to count on assistance from the Bank of England during a crisis. Twenty-six years later the fact that the bankers relied on the Bank was so obvious that Lord Goschen, in his speech before the London Chamber of Commerce on December 2nd, 1891, did not even trouble to discuss it. He condemns, however, as likely to encourage speculation, the feeling that, at the worst, a letter from the Treasury will supply an easy remedy.

[2] Thus the average reserve for March was £14,364,000 between 1845 and 1900, as compared with £12,747,000 for May.

An increase of trade, the payment of wages, the fear of a crisis, cause a withdrawal of gold or notes from the Bank. There is also a home drain in May and in the autumn[1] for the half-yearly payments in Scotland and an influx of 3 millions of sovereigns in March after the collection of the income tax.

The normal and expected fluctuations in the Reserve do not affect the discount rate when they merely involve a withdrawal of gold for home uses; but the case is quite different when it becomes a question of abnormal movements or of a foreign drain.

V.—The Reserve During a Crisis.

When credit is good experience shows that money will only be used for current needs; the gold and notes drawn from the Bank will be returned to it as soon as they have fulfilled their purpose, but "when credit is bad . . . there is no knowing how much additional currency the country may suddenly ask for, nor how long it may keep it. If it asks for too much there will be a panic."[2] The chief defect in the constitution of the Bank is that it is unfitted to meet a sudden and excessive demand. "The Reserve may melt away before the measures taken to relieve it have had time to act."

In fact, the importation of gold from abroad, which is the only way to increase the currency, is still a tardy remedy, notwithstanding the improvements in methods of communication.

On the other hand, a rise in the discount rate under such circumstances does not produce a decrease in the demands, since the people who have immediate liabilities to meet will pay whatever they are asked.

[1] The average reserve for October was £11,904,000 between 1845 and 1900.

[2] Clare, p. 58; this is also J. S. Mill's opinion. Mill is very doubtful in pronouncing judgment on the Act of 1844; as he says himself, he is far from believing that in a problem so new and difficult we can learn nothing from discussion and experience. No doubt Mill realises perfectly well the dangers of the Banking Principle, but at the same time he declares (*Principles*, Bk. III., Chap. xxiv., §4) that, whatever may be the advantages of the Act of 1844, they are purchased at the cost of forbidding a certain extension of credit in time of crisis, when a temporary deficiency needs to be met.

Hence in such a case the Reserve is in danger of disappearing and it is usual—the thing has happened three times, in 1847, in 1857 and in 1866—for the Government to take the responsibility of authorising the Bank to break the law.

We shall presently see, when we study the crises through which the Bank of England has passed, the way in which these permissions have been given and what their effects have been.

For the present, to conclude this chapter, I wish briefly to discuss a question which has never been definitely cleared up. I wish to consider whether these authorisations to exceed the legal limit were foreseen by Peel in framing the Act of 1844.

The question is worth discussing, since, if these repeated transgressions of the legal limit for the uncovered issues were foreseen by Peel, he did actually provide a kind of second reserve for times of crisis—that second reserve about which so much was said in 1891.

Besides this, the question possesses historical interest and hence deserves examination in a work like the present. Unfortunately the answer is not easy to find.

First as regards the text of the law. The Act of 1844, after fixing the amount up to which the Bank might issue notes against securities at 14 millions, adds that an authorisation from the Government will be required for any additional issue.

Unfortunately, this clause refers to the succession to the rights of issue of a provincial bank. The law itself, then, throws no light on our question. S. J. Loyd, Torrens and the other promoters of the Act are also silent on this point; it may be that they did not realise the possibility of any such event.

Peel, who in his speeches in 1844 was purposely vague, said in his answer to Baring,[1] "The Bank would supply the void, with the consent of the Privy Council, by an issue beyond the £14,000,000." But the context shows that these words also refer to the possible inheritance of the rights of issue of provincial banks.

[1] During the sitting of May 20th.—Vol. IV., p. 384, of the *Speeches*.

On the other hand, in his speech on December 3rd, 1847, Peel congratulated the Government on their action in authorising the suspension of the Act of 1844[1] and Parker[2] quotes a letter from Peel to Cotton which shows that as early as June 4th, 1844, Peel acknowledged the possibility of suspending the Act in question.

The wording of this letter, written by Peel to the Governor of the Bank, and in particular the concluding sentence, leaves no room for doubt in the matter.[3]

But whatever Peel may have thought in the first instance, it is clear that at the present day the possibility of suspending the Act in case of a crisis is a recognised part of the English legal regulation of the issue of Bank notes, and Mr. (afterwards Lord) Goschen made it clear that the commercial world relied absolutely on a measure of this kind.

As a rule the mere suspension of the Act has proved sufficient to calm the severity of the crisis. This has been laid to the credit of English legislation; but in reality it is the best proof of a weakness in the system that the uneasiness caused by the Act of 1844 should be allayed by the mere announcement that the restriction imposed by the said Act can be ignored.

Mr. Lowe's Scheme for Reform in 1873.

Only one *official*[4] proposal for reform in the matter before us has been brought forward. This was the scheme suggested in 1873 by Mr. Lowe, that Liberal Chancellor of the Exchequer whose cutting freedom of speech often did more

[1] *Parl. Debates*, Vol. XCV., p. 668.

[2] Vol. III., p. 139.

[3] The letter runs as follows: "My confidence is unshaken, that we are taking all the precautions which legislation can prudently take against the recurrence of a monetary crisis. It *may* recur in spite of our precautions, and if it does, *and if it be necessary* to assume a grave responsibility for the purpose of meeting it, I daresay men will be found willing to assume such a responsibility."

And Peel concludes: "I would rather trust to this than impair the efficacy and probable success of those measures by which one hopes to control evil tendencies in their beginning, and to diminish the risk that extraordinary measures may be necessary."

[4] For Mr. Goschen's project and the reform movement which followed the crisis of 1890 see below, Part IV., Chap. i., p. 370.

harm to his own party than to his opponents, and who, under the title of Lord Sherbrooke, "was extinguished in the House of Lords like a rocket in a fish-pond."[1]

Mr. Robert Lowe[2] proposed that the Bank of England should be allowed to exceed the authorised limit of its issues under three conditions: (1) That the rate of discount was not less than 12 per cent.; (2) That the foreign exchanges were favourable to England; (3) That the situation was one of internal panic.

The Bill was not well received and soon passed into oblivion. Its failure was deserved. It is, indeed, difficult to imagine a case in which Mr. Lowe's three conditions would be satisfied and if they were satisfied, it would mean that the country was already suffering from those disadvantages which it is the object of a good system of banking to prevent.

[1] Augustin Filon, *Profils Anglais.*

[2] The text of this Bill is given by Palgrave, p. 93.

PART III.

PEEL'S ACT IN TIMES OF CRISIS.

CHAPTER I.

THE CRISIS OF 1847.

Causes of the crisis: Failure of the harvests made necessary a large importation of grain and hence a large exportation of specie. Extensive speculation. The railway mania. The crisis of 1847 and the Bank of England. Unfortunate effect of the Act of 1844; useless pressure on the Money Market; luckily the object of its promoters not attained as regards the restriction of the interior circulation in exact proportion to the export of bullion. Unwise policy of the Bank: its reserves reduced to £2,558,000. The crisis, allayed for a time, renewed with violence. Large number of failures. Bank refuses to make advances on Government securities. Panic produced by this policy, hoarding of notes and coin, increase in failures. Bank forced to choose between complete Refusal to Discount and Suspension of Act of 1844. Suspension of Act of 1844. End of the crisis. Delay of Government to suspend Act until situation desperate. Letter from the Chancellor of the Exchequer to Governor of the Bank. Conditions under which the suspension granted. Magical effect of the suspension. The knowledge that notes could be obtained removed the desire to have them. End of the crisis. Great services of the Bank to the public during the crisis. Results of the crisis. Parliamentary Debates. Speech of Sir Robert Peel; his opinion of the effects of the Act; degree in which its object attained; modifications to be made in the Act; the joint-stock banks and the metallic reserve. The Inquiry of 1848. Report of the Committee of the House of Commons. Remarkable Report of the Lords' Committee.

(*a*)—Causes of the Crisis.

The crisis of 1847 was due to bad harvests and in particular to the failure of the potato crops in Ireland,[1] which made it necessary to purchase foreign grain in large quantities. The importations of grain increased as follows:—[2]

Years ...	*1845.*	*1846.*	*1847.*
Wheat	3,777,410 cwts.	6,207,894 cwts.	11,511,305 cwts.
Wheat Meal and Flour	945,864 ,,	3,190,429 ,,	6,329,058 ,,
Maize	241,667 ,,	3,024,883 ,,	15,464,194 ,,

[1] The crisis produced in Ireland by the failure of the potato crops in 1845 and 1847 recalls the famines of the darkest ages of humanity. The peasants literally died of hunger in such large numbers that in some districts it was impossible to provide coffins. Famine and emigration combined reduced the population of the country from 8 to 6 millions. More than 700,000 Irish emigrated to the United States alone. A touching description of this crisis will be found in a most interesting and fairly impartial book by an Irish Member of Parliament, Mr. Justin MacCarthy: *A History of our Own Times, from the accession of Queen Victoria to the General Election of* 1880, Vol. I., pp. 299-304.

[2] Levi, p. 310.

Since the price of corn had risen to a corresponding extent, it is not surprising that these importations produced a great demand for gold and were the immediate cause of the crisis of 1847.[1]

Combined with this immediate cause were others more deeply rooted and dating further back—to wit, speculation, and in particular, speculation in railways. It must be admitted too, that the effects of the export of gold were intensified by the over-rigid provisions of the Act of 1844 and by the imprudent conduct of the Bank of England.[2]

The Railway Mania. Some brief remarks must be made with respect to the "railway mania" which spread persistently throughout Great Britain. The sums annually invested in railway enterprises increased in the following proportions:—[3]

Yearly average from 1826 to 1829	...	£817,000
" " " 1830 to 1833	...	2,157,000
" " " 1834 to 1837	...	10,880,000
" " " 1838 to 1841	...	3,614,000
" " " 1842 to 1843	...	4,586,000
Total for the year 1844	...	£17,870,000
" " " 1845	...	60,824,000
" " " 1847	...	132,096,000

The other European countries followed England's example as regards excessive construction.[4] The movement

[1] The crisis, which was so disastrous for England and other European countries, brought unusual prosperity to the United States. The American exports in 1847 exceeded by 40 per cent. those of the preceding year, and by 34,317,249 dollars the imports for 1847. It was 29 years before such favourable conditions occurred again. See Conant, p. 487.

[2] For these two causes see D. Morier Evans, *The Commercial Crisis* 1847-1848, pp. 1-52 and 53-108 respectively.

[3] See Porter (G.), *The Progress of the Nation in its Social and Commercial Relations*, p. 327. Porter was Ricardo's brother-in-law.

According to Tooke (Vol. IV., p. 314) the expenses of labour and material alone, reached the following sums:—

1841	£1,176,000	1844	£4,880,000
1842	£2,384,000	1845	£11,280,000
1843	£3,548,000	1846	£29,188,000

1847 (first six months) £20,560,000

[4] "In 1845 Belgium had already 343 miles of railways at a cost of £5,872,000; France 552 miles, at a cost of £10,232,000, with projects and authority for 1,900 miles more, involving an expenditure of £30,000,000 additional; Germany had 2,000 miles of railway, made at a cost of

lasted in England throughout the first part of 1847, and then suddenly stopped after a specially intense outburst. There were thus two equally objectionable features about the railway mania: (1) It involved a sudden absorption of the savings of the nation in enterprises of a single kind. (2) It ended in a still more sudden stoppage in the development of the undertakings in which this capital was invested. These characteristics were rendered still more objectionable by a burst of speculation in railway shares.

At the same time it must be acknowledged that the railway mania was the least harmful of the causes of the crisis of 1847, since the evil was in some degree only a temporary one and the extension of the railway system laid a foundation for future prosperity.[1]

(*b*)—The Crisis of 1847 and the Bank of England.

The Act of 1844 was intended by its authors to restrict the interior note circulation in exact proportion to the export of bullion. If this end had been attained the results would have been even more disastrous than they actually were;[2] all that the Act did produce was a useless pressure on the money market and a sudden contraction in the discounts at a time when it was too late to arrest speculation. The policy of the Bank of England was, on the whole, most unwise.[3]

The harvests in 1842, 1843 and 1844 had been very plentiful and the improvement in means of communication

£15,500,000, and 2,300 miles more were authorised; and the United States of America had completed 3,688 miles, at an expenditure of £17,702,000, and in construction 5,624 miles, involving an expenditure of £26,995,000."—Levi, pp. 303-304. See also Conant, p. 488.

[1] For a statement of this point of view see Sir Robert Peel's speech in *Parl. Debates*, 3rd series, Vol. XCV., pp. 666-667.

[2] How little the end at which Lord Overstone and his supporters aimed was actually attained is shown by the following figures: On August 29, 1846, the notes in the hands of the public amounted to £20,426,000 and the bullion to £16,366,000. On January 30 in the following year the bullion had decreased to £12,902,000, whilst the notes amounted to £20,469,000. By April 10 the bullion had dwindled to £9,867,000, the amount of the notes remaining practically the same, viz., £20,243,000. This state of things much perplexed F. T. Baring, ex-Chancellor of the Exchequer, who had believed in the "mechanical" action of the Act of 1844. See Baring's speech, *Parl. Debates*, Vol. XCV., p. 615.

[3] See Sir Robert Peel's speech, p. 657.

now made superfluous an accumulation of commodities such as had formerly been necessary, hence money flowed into the Bank of England and the discount rate was lowered to 1¾ per cent. and after some fluctuations, remained at 3 per cent. from August, 1846, till January, 1847.

The failure of the potato crop in 1845, followed by the still more disastrous crop of 1846, made it necessary, as we have seen, to export large quantities of bullion for the purchase of foreign corn. Notwithstanding the continuous drain the Bank maintained the same rate of discount from the middle of September, 1846, until the following January; it was not until its stock of bullion, already reduced to £15,163,000 in December, 1846, had fallen to £13,940,000, that it raised the rate to 3½ per cent. on January 16th. This proved absurdly inadequate, for the bullion continued to disappear, and it was decided to raise the rate gradually until on April 10th it reached 5 per cent. At this date the bullion in the Bank was reduced to £9,367,000, whilst the Reserve had fallen from £8,869,000 to £2,558,000 during the period we have just described.

In face of such a situation the market was seized with panic and severe measures had to be taken to stop the demand for notes. The directors decided to keep the discount rate at 5 per cent., but only to discount short paper, and to limit the number of bills discounted, however good they might be. This policy caused the discount rate of the private banks to rise to 10 or 12 per cent., which rise naturally stopped the drain of bullion, and a sum of £100,000, which had been shipped to go to America, was hastily re-landed.

The crisis was appeased for the time; the bullion at the Bank increased to £10,526,000 and the Reserve to £5,625,000. Unfortunately the improvement was only temporary.

The high prices of grain had induced many merchants to speculate on its importation. But the large quantities of goods imported, joined to the prospects of a good harvest both for corn and potatoes, led to an enormous fall in cereals,[1] which fall was disastrous to the speculators. A series of failures occurred between August and October, involving total liabilities of £15,000,000,[2] and upset the market once again.

The firm of Saunderson & Co., one of the principal bill-broking establishments, which was in close connection with the most important corn dealers, stopped payment in the middle of September. Nearly all the firms engaged in trade with the Mauritius followed suit. These disasters were combined with other important failures in connection with East India trade, in which credit was generally allowed for very long periods on account of the distance. Finally, the collapse was made absolute by the results of the insane speculation in railways to which we have referred above.

The directors of the Bank of England recognised that the time had come for heroic measures; in fact, the bullion had declined to £8,365,000 and the banking reserve had fallen once more to £3,409,000. On October 2nd, 1847, it was therefore announced that the discount rate would be raised to 5½ per cent. and that for the time, no advance would be made on public stock or on Exchequer bills. This last measure caused a panic on the Stock Exchange,[3] and led to a fall in Consols[4] and to the accumulation of notes and coin in private strong boxes.[5] Moreover the banks, which had hitherto held their own[6] in the midst of so many other failures, now began to give way. On October 13th Knapp & Co. of Abingdon, stopped payment. On October

[1] The price of wheat, which at the end of May had been 131s., had fallen to 49s. 6d.

[2] Amongst the firms which went bankrupt the following may be mentioned: Leslie, Alexander & Co., with liabilities of £50,000; King, Melville & Co., with liabilities of £200,000; Coventry & Sheppard, also with liabilities of £200,000; Robinson & Co., whose senior partner was one of the directors of the Bank of England, etc., etc.

[3] For the effect of this announcement see the *Economist* for October 9, 1847.

[4] Consols were at 84½, on October 5th they fell to 77¾. Exchequer Bills also fell 35 per cent.

[5] Samuel Gurney, in his evidence before the Committee, estimated at 4 or 5 millions the value of the notes hoarded on account of the terror people felt of being left without any.

[6] Before October 13 only one bank, Messrs. Cockburns & Co., of Whitehall, had failed.—See *Dictionary of Political Economy,* Vol. I., p. 460.

18th the Royal Bank of Liverpool failed, and before the 23rd of October large numbers of banks in Liverpool, Manchester, Newcastle and the West of England had followed its example.

The Bank of England had to choose between the utter ruin of English trade by an absolute refusal to discount, and the violation of the Act of 1844.[1]

(c)—Suspension of the Act of 1844.

The Government persisted in hoping that the crisis would pass like that in April and waited until things were desperate[2] before they suspended the Act.[3] It was not until October 23rd, when the banking reserve was £1,176,000, that the Government decided to inform the Bank unofficially that they would propose a Bill of Indemnity to Parliament should notes be issued in excess of the limit fixed by the Act of 1844, provided that the discount charged was not less than 8 per cent. The official letter was actually sent to the Governor of the Bank two days later; it authorised an increase in the discounts and loans at a minimum rate of 8 per cent. According to the terms of the letter these transactions were to be kept within reasonable limits and a Bill of Indemnity was promised should this policy lead to an infringement of the law. In order that the Bank might not gain by the situation and so be tempted to prolong it, the letter added that all profits resulting from the additional issues were to go to the Treasury.

The publication of the Chancellor of the Exchequer's letter had a magical effect. The certainty that money could be got took away all desire to have it.[4] The Bank prepared

[1] Compare Tooke's evidence before the House of Lords' Committee. See *Extraits des Enquêtes Anglaises*, p. 251.

[2] It was not unlikely that the Bank would have to suspend payment, although it had 6 millions in the Issue Department.—*Dict. of Pol. Econ.*, p. 461.

[3] The Chancellor of the Exchequer, Sir Charles Wood, afterwards Lord Halifax, refused several times to agree to such a measure.

[4] During the debate on November 30, Sir Charles Wood repeated the following words, characteristic of those who demanded the suspension of the Act of 1844: "Let us have notes . . . We don't mean, indeed, to take the notes, because we shall not want them; only tell us that we can get them, and this will at once restore confidence." See *Parl. Debates*, Vol. XCV., p. 399.

£400,000 of additional notes, but there was no need to use them. Notes which had been hoarded under the impression that the limit fixed by the Act of 1844 would shortly be reached and that the Bank would be unable to assist the commercial world, were brought out in a mass from their hiding-places;[1] the same thing happened with regard to gold, so that both the bullion and the reserve of the Bank rapidly increased to adequate amounts.

Aid Given by the Bank of England during the Crisis.

The mistakes made in the management of the Bank must not make us forget the immense services which it rendered. Between September 15th and November 15th the Bank assisted different important financial and trading establishments and through them the whole of English commerce, in the following ways:—[2]

"1.—It advanced £150,000 to a large firm in London . . . on security of debentures of the Governor and Company of the Copper Miners of England," and prevented a failure with liabilities of several millions.

"2.—It advanced £50,000 to a country banker on the security of real property."

"3.—It advanced £120,000 to the Governor and Company of the Copper Miners, which prevented them stopping payment."

"4.—It advanced £300,000 to the Royal Bank of Liverpool." Unfortunately, this sum, large though it was, proved insufficient to save the Royal Bank.

"5.—It advanced £100,000 to another joint-stock bank in the country."

"6.—It advanced £130,000 on real property to a large mercantile house in London."

"7.—It advanced £50,000 to another mercantile house."

[1] See Wood's speech, *loc. cit.*

[2] See Macleod, *Theory of Credit*, p. 1031, and *Theory and Practice of Banking*, Vol. II., p. 168. These two works are almost identical: towards the end of his life Macleod deceived himself into a belief that he was working by re-publishing his previous books under different titles.

"8.—It advanced £50,000 on bills of exchange to a joint-stock bank of issue, which soon after stopped payment."

9.—It saved a bank in Liverpool from failing by not insisting on the immediate payment of £100,000 which was due to it.

"10.—It assisted another very large joint-stock bank in the country by an advance of £800,000 beyond its usual discount limit."

11.—It advanced £300,000 to two Scotch banks.

Besides these advances it made many others in addition, both in London and in the provinces, but it would be tedious to specify them. We must, however, note the well-deserved tribute paid to the Bank by the Chancellor of the Exchequer during the debate in the Commons on November 30th. "The Bank of England," said Sir Charles Wood,[1] "was pressed directly for assistance from all parts of the country, and indirectly through the London bankers, who were called upon to support their country correspondents. . . . Two bill-brokers had stopped, and the operations of two others were nearly paralysed. The whole demand for discount was thrown upon the hands of the Bank of England. Notwithstanding this . . . the Bank never refused a bill which it would have discounted at another time, but still, the large mass of bills which, under ordinary circumstances, are discounted by bill-brokers, could not be negotiated."

(*d*)—Results of the Crisis of 1847.

There was a General Election in the autumn of 1847, and when Parliament met[2] the first proceeding of the Ministry was to propose the appointment of a Committee of Inquiry "into the causes of the recent commercial distress, and how far it has been affected by the Laws for regulating the Issue of Bank Notes payable on Demand."

The Parliamentary debate on this motion lasted three

[1] *Parl. Debates, loc. cit.*, p. 398.

[2] The Queen's Speech (*Parl. Debates*, Vol. XCV., pp. 11-14) dealt at some length with the Bank of England and stated that happily the authorisation granted to the Bank had not led to an infringement of the law.

days. The principal speakers were Messrs. Wilson, Molesworth, Ellice, Newdegate, Baring, the Chancellor of the Exchequer and Sir Robert Peel. We have already referred to the speeches of Baring and Sir Charles Wood, and now propose to give a rather more detailed analysis of that of Sir Robert Peel, partly because the speaker was mainly responsible for the Act of 1844, which had claimed to be a preventive against crises, but also because his speech is in itself worth recording.[1]

Peel, after denying the statement that the Act of 1844 had been passed without sufficient preliminary inquiry,[2] proceeded to consider the triple object of the law in question.[3]

"Its first object was . . . to prevent, by early and gradual, severe and sudden contraction, and the panic and confusion inseparable from it." In this object Peel admitted that the Act had failed, for the Bank had not been forced to take early precautions to prevent the withdrawal of its treasure. He remarked, however, that: "If the Bank had possessed the resolution to meet the coming danger by a contraction of its issues, by raising the rate of discount, . . . if they had been firm and determined in the adoption of those precautions, the necessity for extrinsic interference might have been prevented, it might not then have been necessary for the Government to authorise a violation of the Act of 1844."[4]

But, besides this first object which had not been attained, the Bill had "two other objects of equal importance: (1) 'to maintain and guarantee the convertibility of the paper currency'; (2) 'to prevent the difficulties which arise at all times from undue speculation being aggravated by the abuse of paper credit in the form of promissory notes.'"

In these two objects Peel believed that the Bill had completely succeeded. There had been no shadow of doubt cast on the convertibility of the paper currency and the power of making unlimited issues had been wisely checked with respect both to the Bank of England and to the country banks.

[1] See Peel's speech in *Parl. Debates, loc. cit.*, pp. 650-672.

[2] p. 655.

[3] p. 657.

[4] p. 657.

After this discussion of the objects of the Act of 1844, Sir Robert Peel described the history of the crisis of 1847, beginning by an inquiry into its causes.[1] He explicitly approved the policy of the Government both in sending the letter and in their choice of the moment for sending it. He approved the policy in principle, because "when there occurs a state of panic—a state which cannot be foreseen or provided against by law—which cannot be reasoned with, the Government must assume a power to prevent the consequences which may occur."[2]

Finally, in reference to the advisability of making some modification in the Act of 1844, Peel declared himself "in favour of the maintenance of the great principles of that measure." He believed[3] that the *joint-stock banks ought to be required "to bear some share of the expense of keeping in reserve a stock of gold."* As to the Bank of England, if the identical restrictions now imposed were removed, others would have to take their place. "Some restrictions you must impose, for after the experience of 1826, 1836 and 1839, I, for one, am not content to leave the regulation of the monetary concerns of this country to the uncontrolled discretion of the Bank. In 1844 the general conviction was that it ought not to be so left; and I, for one, know no better mode of imposing restriction than that which was devised by the Act of 1844."

After Sir Robert Peel's speech the proposal to appoint a Committee of Inquiry was agreed to.

The Inquiry of 1848.

This inquiry is of interest from many points of view and supplies valuable information, without which the causes and the history of the crisis of 1847 could not be understood.[4] One of its most interesting features is perhaps that it shows plainly that the supporters of Peel's Act were in

[1] See what has been said above on this point.

[2] p. 668.

[3] p. 669.

[4] See the *Extraits des Enquêtes Anglaises* by MM. Coullet and Juglar; all references are to this edition.

no way discouraged by the crisis which was just over,—they upheld the law more zealously than the author of it himself.

Consider, in the first place, the evidence of the Governor and the Deputy-Governor of the Bank of England, Mr. Morris and Mr. Prescott.[1] They declared their full approval of the Act of 1844. The Act had attained its main object, which was to ensure the convertibility of the notes; further than this, it had made the crisis less severe, although it had perhaps hastened its arrival. It must be recognised, they said, that the commercial distress was inevitable and that it was independent of the Act of 1844. But the great merit of the Act in their opinion was that owing to it the Bank possessed a stock of bullion amounting to £8,000,000, when the pressure came, whereas if the Bank had been free it would have adopted the policy of dangerous liberality which had done so much harm on previous occasions.

Hence the Governors of the Bank naturally deprecated any modification of the Act of 1844 and the same conclusion was reached by Mr. G. W. Norman[2] and Mr. S. J. Loyd.[3] The brief and strongly worded Report of the Committee of the House of Commons came to the same decision.[4]

The Report of the House of Lords, however, embodied different conclusions. Its purport can be judged by the following quotation from M. Courcelle-Seneuil:—[5]

"Those who had believed that the Act of 1844 would prevent the periodical recurrence of over-excitement followed by a commercial crisis must have been sadly disappointed by the events of 1846 and 1847.[6] Those who hoped that the

[1] See *Enquête de la Chambre des Lords,* pp. 1-81, and *Enquête de la Chambre des Communes,* pp. 5-81.

[2] p. 218, *Enquête des Lords.*

[3] For the evidence of these two see *Enquête des Lords,* pp. 119-195.

[4] A French version of this report is given in the *Extraits de l'Enquête de la Chambre des Communes,* pp. 1-4.

[5] *Traité théorique et pratique des Opérations de Banque,* p. 324.

[6] It is only fair to point out that the authors of the law of 1844 never imagined such absurdities. Loyd, for instance, in a pamphlet entitled *Thoughts on the Separation of the Departments of the Bank of England,* which is reprinted in the *Tracts,* pp. 249-283, states definitely (pp. 240-241)

Act would discourage rash speculation could hardly have been less disappointed, for, according to the evidence of the Governor of the Bank of England, speculation had never been so rife as from 1846 to 1847. Those who thought that the Act would secure the market from violent fluctuations in the value of money, were undeceived when they found that the difference between the maximum and minimum rates of discount, which had varied from 2¼ to 2¾ per cent. during the disastrous years of 1837 and 1839, rose to 6¾ per cent. in 1847. Those who thought that in future the bankruptcies would be less frequent and less serious were conclusively answered when the Governor of the Bank described how in London alone thirty-three important firms had failed, with a total liability of £8,129,000, etc."

Two suggestions "had been made before the Committee of the House of Lords; the one advised the absolute repeal of the Act of 1844, the other proposed that the Act should be maintained, but accompanied by a wider relaxing power." The Report decided in favour of the latter suggestion.[1]

that the reform will not prevent crises from occurring, but he adds, "We can prevent an additional stimulus being given to a rise of prices and undue speculations by the influence of an ill-regulated currency." It must be acknowledged after an interval of sixty years that even this limited object has not been completely attained.

[1] Compare also the last chapter of this volume.

CHAPTER II.

THE CRISIS OF 1857.

Sudden outbreak of the crisis of 1857: a contrast to the preceding one. Cautious policy of the Bank during the Crimean War. Condition of the market during 1856 and more than half 1857. The crisis of 1857 in America. The three causes of the American crisis. Their influence felt also in Europe. (*a*) The great discoveries of gold, (*b*) The extension of railways, (*c*) The development of banking and the abuse of credit facilities. Extraordinary number of failures in America. The ruin of American banks led to that of a number of English banks. The Bank of England the only source of discount in the United Kingdom. Reduction of the Bank Reserve on November 12, to £384,114. Assistance given by the Bank to commerce in anticipation of the suspension of the Act. The suspension of the Act. Letter of the Chancellor of the Exchequer: text of this letter. Bank issues £2,000,000 notes in excess of the statutory limit, the maximum put into circulation only £928,000. Comparison between the crisis of 1857 and the crises of 1847 and 1866 with reference to the suspension of the Act of 1844. A Bill of Indemnity had to be passed. The Inquiry of 1858 and the causes of the crisis of 1857: (1) Unprecedented extension of International Trade, (2) Excessive importation of precious metals, (3) Remarkable development of banks of credit.

THE crisis of 1857 differs in several respects from that of 1847. It was not the result of a bad harvest, but was in the main the after effect of a crisis produced in America by unbounded speculation. The distinctive feature of this crisis in 1857 was that, although the panic accompanying it was less intense than that of ten years earlier, the pressure on the money market was more severe and more prolonged; it was also the only crisis in which the Bank of England was obliged to violate the Act of 1844 by exceeding the statutory limit.

The crisis began with great suddenness. There were, no doubt, signs of stringency on the money market even before 1857. Bad harvests and a decline in foreign investments had caused pressure on the European markets as early as 1853. But the Crimean War had increased people's timidity and had thus made the business world more prudent and delayed the crisis. On this occasion moreover, the conduct of the Bank of England deserved all praise;[1] its policy was analogous to that followed quite recently during the South African War. It raised its rate of discount unhesitatingly in spite of the violence and bitterness of the protests raised. The rate was very high throughout 1855 and even reached 7 per cent.[2] and when the war came to an end without producing the anticipated disaster, people were forced to acknowledge that the Bank of England deserved well of the country.

In spite of everything the market continued very uneasy during 1856; the discount rate was high and the situation continued somewhat strained until September, 1857, without, however, arousing any suspicion of what was to follow. According to the evidence of the Governor of the Bank, S. Neave,[3] "things were then pretty stationary," but the harvests promised well and except for "certain more far-seeing persons,"[4] the public were well content with the condition of affairs.

The Bank felt so confident that on August 17th, when the stock of bullion amounted to £10,000,000 and the Reserve of notes was £6,296,000, negotiations were opened with the East India Company to export a million in specie to the East.[5] A week later the crisis had burst out in America.

The Crisis of 1857 in America.

The American crisis was the result of a series of events which, indeed, had also affected Europe. These were: (1) The great discoveries of gold; (2) The extension of railways; (3) The development of banking and of speculation.

[1] See Weguelin's evidence, *Extraits des Enquêtes*, 1857, p. 101.

[2] It fell as low as 3½ per cent. only for a very short time during the summer.

[3] See p. xv. of the Report.

[4] These far-seeing persons had observed that the great stimulus given to business by the war expenditure could only be temporary and that nevertheless, merchants were continuing their purchases in anticipation of a continuance of the high prices.

[5] Juglar, p. 367.

1.—*The Great Discoveries of Gold.*

Towards the middle of the 19th century the discovery of a large number of gold mines caused an economic revolution, which recalled that due to the discovery of the treasures of Peru and Mexico four centuries earlier. The average annual production between 1493 and 1850 had been estimated at £1,800,000; between 1851 and 1860 it increased to a yearly average of £26,600,000.[1] President Buchanan[2] calculated that the production of the United States alone during the eight years 1850-1857, was £80,000,000.

Prices did not increase proportionately to the increase in metallic money, but "enterprises of all kinds received a stimulus unheard of in the history of the world."[3]

2.—*The Extension of Railways.*

In 1856, 3,642 miles of railway were constructed in the United States, and the construction from 1849 to 1857 had been 21,000 miles. This total, which amounted to seven-ninths of the railway system in the whole country, had absorbed capital to the amount of £140,000,000, mainly foreign. The steady increase of immigration, added to the normal growth of the population and the immense progress made in districts which had hitherto been undeveloped, intoxicated the nation. As Von Holst[4] remarks: "It was more and more lost sight of, that even in the age of steam, time must remain an essential factor in every process of development," and the American people were led "to mould the reality in their minds in accordance with what imagination pictured to them."

[1] According to Conant, p. 493, Professor Soetbeer estimates the total production of gold between 1493 and 1850 as 173,258,000,000 marks, and between 1851 and 1885 at 17,810,000,000 marks. Between 1885 and 1895 the production was £275,000,000, according to the *Encyclopædia Britannica* (Supplement Vol. XIX., p. 18), and between 1895 and 1899 it apparently increased by two-fifths.

[2] Conant, p. 493.

[3] Conant, *loc. cit.*

[4] *The Constitutional History of the United States.* Lalor's English translation, Vol. IV., p. 104.

England and the Continent had witnessed a similar extension in their railway systems. In England alone more than 4,000 miles had been constructed since 1850, the existing lines being thus doubled.[1]

And in Europe, as in America, speculation in railways had been encouraged by the payment of dividends out of capital.

3.—*The Development of Banking and the Abuse of Credit.*

The number of banks in America increased very rapidly; in 1847 there were 715, in 1857 there were 1,416. And what was worse, the discounts increased in like proportion and rose from 310,382,945 dollars to 684,456,887—more than double the previous amount. The circulation increased in an analogous manner from 105,519,766 dollars to 214,778,822 dollars. M. Juglar[2] remarks that this was not actually due to over-issue, since owing to the strictness of the regulations, the issues did not often exceed the metallic reserve; but the bankers got over this difficulty by attracting deposits by high interest and lending them on similar terms to reckless speculators.

M. Juglar[3] enumerates the evils of the position as follows: the increase of banks having an insufficient capital; too many deposits; an excess of currency doubled by an exaggerated extension of discounting.

Nevertheless foreign capital steadily flowed into the United States. "Conditions were ripe both in Europe and America for a crash when the impulse came on August 24th, 1857, from the failure of the Ohio Life Insurance and Trust Co., of Cincinnati and New York, with reported liabilities of 7,000,000 dollars. A panic followed on the New York Stock Exchange, stocks fell, money was hoarded to be

[1] For further details see James Ford Rhodes, *History of the United States from the Compromise of* 1850, Vol. III., p. 53. The author gives a full analysis of this crisis in America as well as some details with regard to Europe.

[2] p. 268. [3] p. 269.

loaned only at extravagant rates, deposits began to disappear from the banks, and late in September a run began on the banks of Philadelphia. They were compelled to suspend specie payments on September 26th."[1]

During the beginning of October the Illinois Central Railway, the New York and Erie and the Michigan Central all failed, as well as 150 banks in Pennsylvania, Virginia and Maryland. At the same time the New York banks shared the fate of those at Philadelphia. They had contracted their discounts very suddenly, reducing them from 122,000,000 dollars to 97,200,000 between August 8th and October 17th. But this contraction, says D. Morier Evans,[2] "by causing much damage to the country banks and the commercial interest, had awakened a feeling of jealousy in addition to the general alarm, and on the 13th (of October) a preconcerted run took place. The stoppage of eighteen banks was the immediate consequence of the pressure. The remaining establishments put themselves under the protection of the law."[3]

Out of the sixty-three banks in New York only one managed to avoid suspending its payments and the importance of this crisis of 1857 in America may be realised from the fact that there were 5,123 failures in the United States and Canada, with liabilities amounting to 291,801,000 dollars.[4]

The Crisis of 1857 in England.

Money was already dear in England and complaints were being raised against the Bank, when the news of the failure of the Ohio Life Insurance Co. caused intense alarm on account of the £80,000,000 which were reported to be invested in American stock. The operations of a syndicate

[1] Conant, p. 496.

[2] *The History of the Commercial Crisis*, 1858-59, p. 34.

[3] Sumner, *A History of American Currency*, p. 184, says that the constitution of the State of New York forbade the suspension of specie payments directly or indirectly, but on this occasion the judges of the Supreme Court met and agreed not to grant any injunction unless the Bank appeared to be really insolvent or guilty of fraud.

[4] Morier Evans, p. 34.

of bears, *i.e.*, speculators for a fall, increased the anxiety,[1] although the high rate of interest in New York attracted considerable sums. The Bank of France lost 25,000,000 francs in one week and the bullion in the Bank of England fell to £8,991,000 on October 19th.

On November 7th the firm of Dennistoun stopped payment, with liabilities of nearly 2 millions. The Western Bank closed its doors on the 9th of November, the City of Glasgow Bank soon did likewise and a number of failures occurred. The Bank of England had to send more than a million to Scotland, besides meeting important demands for gold in Ireland. It was the only source of discount during a crisis which paralysed everyone's courage; in a single day its discounts amounted to £2,373,000. The consequence was that on Wednesday, November 11th, its entire reserve, including what was held at the branch establishments, only amounted to £1,462,153, of which £957,710 was in notes and the next evening the reserve in the banking department had fallen to £384,914, consisting of £68,035 in notes, £274,953 in gold and £42,106 in silver.[2] The Bank could not have gone on for another day under the regime of the Act of 1844[3] and its stoppage would have meant the entire collapse of the London market.

Nevertheless, as we have seen, it had continued its discounts when everyone else had contracted theirs. This policy evidently implied a feeling of certainty that the Act would be suspended; this was actually done at the last moment, by a letter from the Chancellor of the Exchequer to the Governors of the Bank—a letter modelled on the

[1] Gilbart, Vol. II., p. 302. In Stock Exchange parlance *bears* are speculators for a fall, *bulls* speculators for a rise.

[2] Macleod, *Theory of Credit*, p. 1056.

[3] See the statement made by the Governor of the Bank before the Committee of Inquiry. Question 132: Supposing that the letter from the Chancellor had not been issued on that day, would the Bank on the morning of the 13th (November) have been in a condition to continue its discounts? "No, certainly not." See *Extraits des Enquêtes Anglaises. Enquête de* 1858, p. 18. Compare p. 30.

analogous one of October 25th, 1847, whose contents we have described.[1]

As in 1847, the public alarm was at once abated, but this time the demands for discount continued to be very numerous for more than a fortnight. The Bank issued £2,000,000 of notes in excess of the statutory limit; the maximum of additional notes actually in circulation did not however exceed £928,000 (on November 20th), the remainder were added to the reserve.[2]

[1] The text of the letter of November 12, 1857, is as follows:—

"Gentlemen, Downing Street, 12 November, 1857.

"Her Majesty's Government have observed with great concern the serious consequences which have ensued from the recent failure of certain joint-stock banks in England and Scotland, as well as of certain large mercantile firms, chiefly connected with the American trade. The discredit and distrust which have resulted from these events, and the withdrawal of a large amount of the paper circulation authorised by the existing Bank Acts, appear to Her Majesty's Government to render it necessary for them to inform the directors of the Bank of England that if they should be unable in the present emergency to meet the demands for discounts and advances upon approved securities without exceeding the limits of their circulation prescribed by the Act of 1844, the Government will be prepared to propose to Parliament, upon its meeting, a Bill of Indemnity for any excess so issued.

"In order to prevent this temporary relaxation of the law being extended beyond the actual necessities of the occasion, Her Majesty's Government are of opinion that the Bank terms of discount should not be reduced below their present rate.

"Her Majesty's Government reserve for future consideration the appropriation of any profits which may arise upon issues in excess of the statutory amount.

"Her Majesty's Government are fully impressed with the importance of maintaining the letter of the law, even in a time of considerable mercantile difficulty; but they believe that, for the removal of apprehensions which have checked the course of monetary transactions, such a measure as is now contemplated has become necessary, and they rely upon the discretion and prudence of the directors for confining its operation within the strict limits of the exigencies of the case.

"We have, etc., (Signed) "PALMERSTON.
"G. C. LEWIS."

We quote this letter from the report of the Committee of 1857, *Report from the Select Committee on the Bank Acts*, p. xl. (French version by M. Emile Jouveaux, see p. xix. of the *Extraits des Enquêtes sur la législation des banques*, 1857 *et* 1858).

[2] The following were the amounts by which the statutory limit was exceeded from November 13th to 30th. *Report*, p. xli. Compare *Rapport Commission d'Enquête*, p. xxi.

Date	Amount	Date	Amount
Nov. 13	£186,000	Nov. 23	£397,000
,, 14	622,000	,, 24	317,000
,, 16	860,000	,, 25	81,000
,, 17	836,000	,, 26	243,000
,, 18	852,000	,, 27	342,000
,, 19	896,000	,, 28	184,000
,, 20	998,000	,, 30	15,000
,, 21	617,000		

Comparison between the Crisis of 1857 and those of 1847 and 1866 with regard to the Suspension of the Act of 1844.

Although the amount by which the statutory limit was exceeded in 1857, was comparatively small, the mere fact that the limit was exceeded was unprecedented and has remained unique in the history of the Bank down to the present day. It is true that the Bank had been authorised in 1847 to exceed the limit fixed by the Act of 1844 and, as we shall see, it received a like authorisation in 1866, but neither in 1847 nor in 1866 did it make use of the permission given; hence there was no need either in 1847 or in 1866 for Parliament to ratify the authorisation granted by the Government. In 1857 the case was different. The intervention of Parliament was a necessity on this occasion. It will be remembered, indeed, that the Chancellor of the Exchequer does not actually authorise the Bank to violate the Act of 1844, this would be beyond his powers; all that he can do is to inform the directors that if they find themselves obliged, in the interests of commerce, to exceed the statutory limit, the Government is prepared to propose a Bill of Indemnity to Parliament. In 1847 and 1866 the Chancellor's letter proved sufficient to allay anxiety, the statutory limit was not exceeded, and there was no need for a Bill of Indemnity. In 1857, when Parliament met, the Government brought in and passed an Act sanctioning the additional issues which had been made, and temporarily suspending, (until February 1st, 1858), the Act of 1844, on condition that the directors did not reduce the rate of discount below 10 per cent. On December 24th however the Bank lowered its rate to 8 per cent. This proceeding automatically set the Act of 1844 in force again. It had actually been suspended for forty-three days, from November 13th to December 24th, but in theory and legally the suspension had only lasted twelve days, since the Act of Indemnity (21 Vict., c. i.) was not passed until December 12th.[1]

[1] The text of this Act is given by Palgrave, pp. 91-93.

Comparison between the Crises of 1847 and 1857 with Regard to their Severity.

As regards this point it is probable that the panic was less violent in 1857 than in 1847, but that, on the other hand, the real suffering was more widespread. This view is borne out by the fact that the total of loans, discounts and advances upon stock made by the Bank of England was £12,645,000 between November 12th and December 1st.[1] It is noticeable, too, that great care was taken not to reduce the rate of discount too quickly; it was maintained at 5 per cent. until the stock of bullion had risen to £15,000,000.

The Inquiry of 1858 and the Causes of the Crisis of 1857.

According to the wise English custom, the crisis of 1857 was followed by an inquiry. It is impossible to give an analysis of it here,[2] but we may, at any rate, summarise its conclusions as to the causes of the crisis.

As classified by the Select Committee,[3] the chief causes of the crisis of 1857 were three: (1) An unprecedented extension of foreign trade. (2) An excessive importation of gold and silver. (3) A remarkable development of banks and of credit.

(1) With regard to the first cause, it was shown that, owing especially to the reform of the tariff, the imports had increased from 71 to 124 millions and that the exports, which until 1848 had never exceeded £60,110,000, had reached £112,155,000 in 1857.

(2) With regard to the increase of bullion, it was stated that £107,500,000 of gold was added to the European stock, whilst £26,800,000 was exported, leaving a total increase of £80,700,000. There was naturally a corresponding increase in the circulating medium, the paper currency not represented by bullion being £31,600,000 and the gold coins amounting to 50 millions.

[1] Levi, p. 404.
[2] For this subject see *Extraits des Enquêtes* by Coullet and Juglar.
[3] *Report*, p. v. (*Extraits*, especially p. xii.); see also D. M. Evans, *op. cit.*, p. 32.

(3) The increased facilities for credit were a natural result of the extension of trade and of the increase in currency. The deposits at the joint-stock banks in London alone, which had amounted to £8,800,000 in 1847, were £43,100,724 in 1857, and there was a proportional increase in the other deposits, both at the private and the country banks. The result was a great extension of credit facilities. Mr. Fowler makes some apt remarks on this point:[1]

"It is not," he says, "very easy to define how far credit may extend safely, but it is very clear that during the years 1855 and 1856 the extension of credit was enormous and dangerous. It has been sometimes asserted, though there is no way of testing the truth of the assertion, that during the years in question there were as many bills offered for discount in Lombard Street as there are now (1890), though the real volume of trade has vastly increased since 1857, the total of imports and of exports being unitedly £311,764,000 in 1856, and £748,944,000 in 1890. In those times it was a common thing for banks in manufacturing districts to send great masses of bills to London for re-discount. . . .The amount of this business in 1856 and 1857 was enormous, and even after the panic of that year, when many bills came to an end by failures of traders and of bankers, the amount of re-discount by banks continued to be very large. But, at this moment, that business has almost come to an end."

[1] *Dict. of Political Economy*, Vol. I., p. 462.

CHAPTER III.

THE CRISIS OF 1866.

Economic results of the Civil War in the U.S.A. Influx of gold into Europe. Disturbance of the cotton trade. Immediate causes of the crisis of 1866, (1) The rage for limited companies, (2) The practice of financing, (3) Bad customs adopted by certain banks with regard to deposits. The crisis of 1866. The crisis of 1864 and the crisis of 1866. A retarded liquidation. The failure of Overend and Gurney. Black Friday. Remarks on the firm of Overend and Gurney and the causes of its collapse. Unprecedented panic resulting from the failure of this firm. Advances amounting to four millions made by the Bank in a single day (Friday, May 11). Suspension of the Act of 1844. End of the crisis. Part played by the Bank. The Act suspended on the evening of Friday, May 11. Announcement of suspension allayed panic, fresh outbreak a few days later, flow of deposits to the Bank, no additional issue required. Great services rendered by the Bank, Advances amounting to £12,225,000 made in five days. Results of the crisis of 1866. Excitement aroused by the crisis outside England. Lord Clarendon's circular. Heavy losses at home. Some good effects of the crisis.

(a)—ECONOMIC EFFECTS OF THE WAR OF SECESSION.

THE years which followed the outbreak of the Civil War in America were years of financial difficulty in Europe as well as in America. These difficulties were in part due to the war and in part to causes distinct from but intensified by it. The influx of gold into Europe and the disturbance of the cotton trade must be ranked among the most important of the direct consequences of the war.

Influx of gold into Europe. The system of inconvertible paper currency established in the United States in 1861 caused gold to flow into Europe in considerable quantities. An American author to whom frequent reference has been made in the course of this work, Mr. Conant,[1] estimates the gold exported from America at 21,532,891 dollars in 1862; 56,642,200 dollars in 1863; 89,484,865 dollars in 1864; and 51,882,805 dollars in 1865.

[1] p. 500.

This influx of currency only raised prices slightly, hardly 10 per cent., but it stimulated business considerably.[1]

Disturbance of the Cotton Trade. The blockade of the ports in the Southern States forced England to seek her cotton supply elsewhere. The quantity imported in 1855 was collected with some difficulty from all parts of the world, but the price of cotton was tripled. Moreover, though successful in obtaining supplies from India, Egypt, China and Brazil, England could not at once pay in merchandise for these unexpected imports; payment had to be made in cash, and as regards India in particular, in silver.[2] Hence the cotton crisis upset both the industrial centres and the money market.

(*b*)—Causes of the Crisis of 1866.

The disorganisation of the cotton trade, the confusion due to the export of gold, the fall in the rate of interest and the accumulation of capital resulting from the extension in the use of machinery, very soon gave a feverish and speculative character to the English money market, recalling the conditions prevailing in 1825 and 1847.

The speculative tendency showed itself especially in a craze for limited liability companies and in the practice of financing.

I.—*The Mania for Limited Liability Companies.*

Companies of this kind were originally only created under special charters; their promotion did not become easy until after the amendment of the Company Law in 1862.[3]

At the outset the hope of unlimited profit combined with limited risk aroused much enthusiasm. In a short time three

[1] Stanley Jevons: *Investigations in Currency and Finance*, p. 58.

[2] Between 1862 and 1866 the net imports of silver into India were 54,094,337 tens of rupees (the ten of rupees was about equal to £1), whilst the bills on India sold by the English Government were only 29,409,469 tens of rupees (Conant, p. 501, note).

France felt the indirect effects of this disturbance, since its silver pieces which were at a premium, vanished as if by magic.

[3] For this Act, 25 and 26 Vict., c. 139, see Lyon-Caen and Renault, *Traité des Societés Commerciales*, p. 478, *et seq.*

hundred limited companies were founded with a nominal capital of £504,000,000. In 1863 alone the shares issued, which in France amounted to £32,000,000, had reached the sum of £145,000,000 in England, and during the first four months of 1864 securities to the value of £75,400,000 were placed upon the English market.[1] It has been estimated that 90 per cent. of these limited companies founded between 1862 and 1865 ultimately failed. The abuses committed even made people forget for the time the advantages of the limited company system, and one distinguished writer[2] goes so far as to speak of the "pestilential principle" of limited liability.

II.—*The Practice of Financing.*

Owing to the excessive number issued, the shares became unsaleable. Since credit was lacking, people resorted to financing and to finance bills. These terms demand some explanation.[3]

Suppose that a railway contractor wanted £50,000; he applied to a company, offering as security shares in the line he was constructing. The company agreed to lend him the amount, not in cash, but by an acceptance made out in his favour; this acceptance the contractor could then discount, and thus obtain the money required. In this way profit was made by the loan of a signature only. The transaction was not analogous to the discount of a bill of exchange, for there were no goods delivered and sold and requiring only an interval before being consumed; hence the distaste which bankers felt to accepting and circulating such paper.

It must, however, be acknowledged that the new method "was legitimate within the limits of the strength of the guaranteeing companies and the prospects of the new enterprises." By its means enterprises which might prove of great value could be set going without delay. Unfor-

[1] Juglar, p. 378.

[2] Mr. James Sterling.

[3] On the subject of financing see Juglar, p. 380, and Levi, p. 462. The system was indeed not unknown in France; in fact, this country was ahead of England in this respect, thanks chiefly to the *Société de Crédit Mobilier.*

tunately the system was employed "without wisdom and sometimes without honesty,"[1] and it soon brought about a terrible crash.

Amongst the firms which turned their attention to financing one of the best known was that of Messrs. Overend, Gurney & Co., of which we shall have more to say later.

Combined with the limited companies and the practice of financing, bad habits in relation to deposits began to make their appearance. Hitherto respectable banks had only paid interest on their deposit accounts, which the depositors could only withdraw after due notice and in a lump sum, but had not allowed interest on current or drawing accounts, on which English depositors draw cheques and which can thus be withdrawn at will. The new banks, especially the Colonial banks, neglected these wise practices and began to pay interest even on drawing accounts, at first at low rates, but afterwards at fairly high rates.

This policy had the effect of attracting large supplies of capital; the deposits at joint-stock banks increased from £43,000,000 in 1860 to £91,000,000 in 1864, and the deposits at private and country banks increased by 20 millions[2] during the same period. But the system ended in the ruin both of the depositors and of the bankers.

(c)—The Crisis of 1866.

I.—*The Crisis of* 1864 *and the Crisis of* 1866.

There were two crises in 1864: the first ending in the liquidation of the smaller tradesmen, the second affecting the large capitalist. In both cases the liquidation on the Continent was completed in 1864; its effects were felt even in Brazil and Australia.

In England events took a somewhat different course. This country, like the rest of Europe, suffered great uneasiness. The foreign exchanges turned against it towards

[1] See Conant, p. 502.

[2] A large proportion of these deposits, about a quarter in fact, consisted of acceptances (see Juglar, p. 385).

the end of 1863 and during 1864 the Bank of England was twice obliged to raise its rate of discount to 9 per cent. For the time the collapse was successfully averted. Unfortunately it was only delayed a couple of years and England gained nothing by waiting. The crisis of 1866 was, in fact, the most serious that has been experienced in modern times.

The proof, as M. Juglar[1] observes, that the crisis of 1866 was not independent, but was the violent and inevitable completion of that of 1864, though somewhat delayed, is that other countries had no share in it. Their crash had occurred in 1864.

II.—*The Failure of Overend & Gurney.—Black Friday.*

The year 1866 opened with gloomy prospects. Abroad everything pointed to a European war; at home a commercial crisis soon appeared imminent. The first warning of it was given in February by the failure of the Joint-Stock Discount Company, and this was followed by the stoppage of Barned's Bank at Liverpool, with liabilities of £3,500,000.[2]

The situation obviously grew worse from day to day; the rate of discount at the Bank of England, which had fallen to 6 per cent., was raised early in May to 7, 8, 9 and finally, on May 11th, to 10 per cent. Towards evening of May 10th the news spread of the greatest failure which had hitherto occurred in England, that of Overend, Gurney and Co. The firm of Overend & Gurney was one of the most respected in the City. It enjoyed a European reputation; one of the partners, S. Gurney, had played an important part in the crisis of 1847 and the subsequent inquiry, and in addition it held deposits to the amount of 8 millions. Unfortunately, after 1860 this firm had become involved in a series of risky speculations and was actually insolvent without anyone suspecting it. An opportunity was taken in August, 1865, to reconstruct it as a limited liability com-

[1] p. 387.
[2] Gilbart, *op. cit.*, Vol. II., p. 308.

pany, with a capital of 5 millions in 100,000 £50 shares, of which £15 were paid up. £500,000 was paid for the goodwill of the old firm, whose position we have seen. The shares of the new company were at first sold at a premium of £10. Some months later Overend, Gurney and Company failed under the following circumstances:

An action was pending before the law courts against the Mid-Wales Railway to recover the value of securities amounting to £60,000 which had been accepted by the company, and which were held by Overend & Gurney and two other firms. Judgment was delivered on May 9th to the effect that the railway company had no authority to accept the securities. This decision, combined with rumours about Overend & Gurney which had been current for some little time, caused a run upon the firm. The directors tried to avert disaster by asking for help from the Bank of England to the amount of £400,000; but the security offered was insufficient, the loan was refused,[1] and the firm of Overend, Gurney & Company stopped payment with liabilities of £18,727,917.[2]

The next day (Friday, May 11th) will long be known in the annals of the City as "Black Friday."[3] The prevailing excitement is indescribable; Lombard Street was impassable, it seemed that demands for accommodaton must increase to an extraordinary extent, and doubt was thrown upon the position of the most respected houses.

"It might have been thought," exclaims Wolowski,[4] "that the ships carrying England and her fortune had suddenly sprung a terrible leak and that the wrecked persons

[1] Not without regret, for the Bank recognised the danger.

[2] The liquidation of the firm of Overend & Gurney lasted 27 years and cost £188,953. The final report of the liquidators was presented on November 18, 1893. For further details see the *Bankers' Magazine* for December, 1893.

[3] The same name had been given to Friday, December 6, 1745, when the advance of the Pretender struck terror into the London commercial world. See above, p. 150.

[4] See the beginning of an article by Wolowski which appeared in the *Revue des Deux Mondes* (August 15, 1866), under the title of *Le Noir Vendredi*. This article was reprinted with others by the same author in a book bearing the somewhat inadequate title of *La Banque d'Angleterre et les Banques d'Écosse*.

were clutching madly at the spars and fragments in search of a means of safety."

On this one day alone the Bank of England made advances to the value of nearly 4 millions; and its reserve, which had been £5,727,000 in the morning, was reduced to about 3 millions.[1]

III.—*Suspension of the Act of* 1844.—*End of the Crisis.—Part Played by the Bank of England.*

On the evening of this same Friday the Chancellor of the Exchequer described the situation to the House of Commons and stated that the Government had written to the Bank promising to introduce a Bill of Indemnity in case it was obliged to exceed the statutory limit of its issues.[2]

The news of the suspension of the Act of 1844 was received with applause from both sides of the House and was enthusiastically welcomed by the commercial world. The anxiety of the latter was so intense[3] that, as the authorisation for the additional issues was not announced before midnight, a deputation of bankers waited on the Chancellor of the Exchequer at the House itself. It is said that one of the representatives of the joint-stock banks remarked to the representative of the Bank of England, "I can draw a couple of cheques to-morrow morning which will shut you up at once."[4]

The suspension of the Act of 1844 had such an effect that the next day the crisis seemed to be at an end. The pressure on the banks ceased temporarily, and, as in 1847, the Bank of England was not obliged to exceed the legal limits of its issues. The demand for discounts continued to be considerable, but it was met by the deposits which flowed into

[1] These figures are taken from the letter of the Governor of the Bank, L. Holland, to Gladstone, who was then Chancellor of the Exchequer.

[2] The letter of the Chancellor of the Exchequer was modelled on the similar letters sent in 1847 and 1857. The text of this letter is given by Wolowski, pp. 102-103.

[3] On this same Friday (May 11) the great railway contractors, Morton, Peto & Betts, whose liabilities amounted to 4 millions, suspended payment.

[4] Gilbart, *op. cit.*, Vol. II., p. 319.

the Bank[1] as soon as it was known that a sufficiency of notes would be issued. Unfortunately during the following week a number of failures took place; these alarmed the depositors of the other banks and produced fresh disasters. The London Bank was obliged to stop payment with liabilities of £4,333,877, after paying 50 per cent. of its deposits. The Consolidated Bank tried to assist it but collapsed in its turn. The Agra and Masterman's Bank, which then occupied a most important position in the East, failed also, with liabilities of £15,582,002. These banks all possessed sufficient assets, but they had not time to convert them into cash.

The important part played by the Bank of England at this time is evident from a statement made by Mr. Gladstone in the House of Commons on May 17th.[2]

According to this statement, the advances made by the Bank of England on Government securities on Friday, the day of the panic, amounted to £929,000, on the following day to £747,000, and during the three succeeding days they made up the total of £2,874,000. With regard to commerce in general, "the best measure that can be given of the manner in which the Bank has exercised its functions is shown in this: that it has made advances upon bills and has discounted bills to the extent of £9,350,000, making a total of advances and discounts in five days of £12,225,000."

(*d*)—Results of the Crisis of 1866.

The crisis was not appeased in a single day. The discount rate of 10 per cent. was maintained by the Bank from May 11th until August 6th, for the distrust of English investments was so great that even this high rate failed to attract capital from countries where, as in France, the rate continued to be less than 4 per cent.

This distrust on the part of the foreigner, which at one time it was feared would persist, made people imagine that

[1] The deposits at the Bank, which were 13½ millions on May 10th, had increased to 16 millions by the 17th.

[2] In answer to a question by Captain Grindley.

London was going to lose its predominance in the world's money market. Sir Stafford Northcote is supposed to have remarked that there was "a run upon England."[1]

The circular issued at this time by the Earl of Clarendon,[2] in which it was stated that "Her Majesty's Government have no reason to apprehend that there is any general want of soundness in the ordinary trade of this country which can give reasonable ground for anxiety or alarm either in this country or abroad," only served to increase the distrust felt by foreigners.[3]

At home there was no lack of confidence so far as the Bank of England was concerned; its metallic reserve, which had never fallen below £11,800,000, rose to £19,200,000 in December, 1866. But the losses in commerce and of savings were enormous. It was estimated that the various failures involved liabilities amounting to 50 millions,[4] and it may be supposed that the losses which were not published and which therefore cannot be calculated exactly, must have been very great.[5] Railway shares were much depreciated and Consols fell to 85.

The crisis of 1866 had, however, some good results.

The weaker banks and the doubtful companies disappeared in the struggle, but the well-established banks emerged from it yet further strengthened and extended their good influence over a wider area. The practices of financing and of giving accommodation bills were replaced by sounder commercial methods, and finally, as a result of all this, there was no fresh crisis for twenty-three years.

[1] Wolowski, p. 133.

[2] Levi, p. 471.

[3] Sidney Buxton, *Finance and Politics*, Vol. II., p. 21.

[4] Macleod, *Theory of Credit*, p. 1063.

[5] Certain banks doing business with the East published the extent of their losses. The Bank of Hindustan, China and Japan, for instance, stated its profits at £23,485 and its losses at £87,796, to which must be added a further expected loss of £70,000; The Asiatic Bank lost £142,000, whilst its profits were £61,491, etc.—Macleod, *op. cit.* and *loc. cit.*

CHAPTER IV.

THE CRISIS OF 1890, OR THE BARING CRISIS.

The Bank between 1866 and 1890. Causes of the crisis. Formation of numerous limited companies. Extensive speculation, especially in the Argentine Republic. The Argentine Land Banks and the cedulas. The Bank rate of discount. Reprehensible policy of the joint-stock banks. Incidents of the crisis. Failure of the Barings. Intervention of the Bank. The guarantee fund. Firm and successful policy of the Governor, Lidderdale. Importation of foreign gold. Assistance given by the Bank of France. Fate of the firm of Baring. Comparison between the crisis of 1890 and the preceding crises. Important differences. The Bank Reserve during the various crises. The crisis of 1890 stopped in time, the others were not. The public knew nothing of the crisis of 1890 until it was over.

THE crisis of 1866 was followed by a long interval of quiet prosperity. The theory which held that crises recurred every ten years received a striking refutation. Even the failure in 1878 of two important banks, the City of Glasgow and the West of England, which, considering the circumstances, might well have caused a panic, only raised a slight alarm. Twenty-four years passed before another crisis occurred, that of 1890, better known as the Baring crisis.[1]

In 1890 there was, indeed, an economic crisis which might have proved very serious, and which involved the failure of the house of Baring Brothers. The unexpected collapse of this celebrated firm made such an impression on the public mind that at first the cause was mistaken for the effect and it was thought that the crisis only occurred because Baring Brothers had got into difficulties, whereas in actual fact their difficulties were due to the general situation, which was such that a crisis was bound to come sooner or later. More-

[1] For this chapter I have made frequent use of an article on the crisis of 1890 which appeared in the *Economic Journal* for March, 1891. I have also used an article published in the *Journal of the Institute of Bankers* for January, 1891, and Palgrave's *Dictionary*, Vol. I., especially pp. 462-466. Readers may also consult an article by M. Raffalovich, *Les Marchés Financiers en* 1890, in the *Journal des Économistes* for January, 1891.

over many other firms besides Baring Brothers had incurred liabilities which to a greater or less degree exceeded the limits of prudence.

It is, besides, easy to show that this crisis, like all the preceding ones, was the result of a series of earlier mistakes.

(*a*)—The Causes of the Crisis.

Both 1888 and 1889 had been years of extensive speculation. This was probably due to the recent conversion of Consols, which made the public look out for investments with higher profits than 2¾ per cent. At any rate a great many companies of a more or less speculative character were formed, such as American mining companies and brewery companies, whilst many commercial and banking firms were reconstructed as joint-stock companies. "The Returns of the Registrar of Joint-Stock Companies show that the total amount of capital registered during 1888 was £353,781,594, and in 1889, £241,277,460."[1]

Many of the newly-registered companies were founded for enterprises abroad, especially in the Argentine Republic, a country which was particularly attractive to English savings. The money lent to the South American Republic during 1888 and 1889 was £36,102,766 and £29,223,341, according to a table given in the *Statist*.[2]

The Stock Exchange was deeply interested in certain institutions for the mortgage of land in South America, which recall in a surprising manner the projects of Dr. Hugh Chamberlain two centuries before. "The British public also became interested to a very serious extent in the land mortgage bonds of certain Argentine banks known as cédulas, in connection with which it has since been ascertained that grave irregularities . . . have occurred. These cédulas were introduced in Europe by one or two respectable London houses without any regular prospectus, and

[1] *Jour. Inst. of Bankers, loc. cit.*, p. 1.

[2] *Jour. Inst. of Bankers, loc. cit.*

were bought by investors who trusted the firms in question."[1]

Towards the end of 1889 prudent people began to feel that the financial situation in Argentina, combined with the enormous amount of English capital involved in speculations of all kinds and the rash conduct of some of the most important firms, would prove a source of danger to England.[2] There was a fall in the best securities.

The Bank of England shared these anxieties and the directors, seeing that Consols were falling and that the reserve of the Bank declined also, wisely determined to raise their rate of discount to 6 per cent.

They maintained this comparatively high rate for seven weeks with a praiseworthy resolution, considering the strong opposition of the City bankers whose proceedings were thereby hindered. Unfortunately the joint-stock banks did not support the Bank of England in its prudent policy and the market rate of discount never rose above 4½ per cent.; in addition, the well-known arguments on the futility of amassing a reserve to meet a crisis which would most probably never occur, were heard and read on every side. Hence towards the end of February the Bank had to reduce its rate to 5 per cent., although it had not succeeded in attracting an effective stock of gold.

The *Economic Journal*[3] criticises very severely the behaviour of the joint-stock banks on this occasion. "It is a great pity," it remarks, "that the joint-stock banks did not take a wiser view of the situation, for if they had, and if the Bank had been allowed to strengthen itself in the early part of 1890, it would probably have been unnecessary to

[1] *The Econ. Journal*, Vol. I., p. 192.

[2] I may refer here to a personal recollection. A Greek financier from London, now dead, M. K——, spent the winter 1889-1890 in my native country of Corfu. He often discussed the new customs of the Stock Exchange with one of my relatives and complained that the English public were involving themselves in absurd speculation. "The evil," he remarked, "is worse than people think, many important English firms are entangled, and even the Barings have turned out of the straight path."

[3] p. 193.

apply to foreign countries . . . when the crisis occurred in the autumn. The banks have got thoroughly into the habit of regarding the amount of the reserve of the Bank of England as of no importance, although it is the sole fund in existence to enable them to meet their liabilities *if called upon*. They fully believe that, if the worst comes to the worst, the Bank will not be allowed to fail, as an ordinary bank would fail if the whole of its cash were gone,[1] and the experience of more than one commercial crisis has shown that this calculation is a safe one, and has consequently encouraged the banks to adhere to their present dangerous practice."

(*b*)—Incidents of the Crisis in November, 1890.

The autumn of 1890 began badly. The usual inconveniences of the autumnal drain were intensified by various issues of new shares and by a revolution in the country so closely connected with English trade and finance, the Argentine Republic.

The Bank rate fell in a short time to 4 per cent., then quickly rose to 5 per cent., and on November 7th, after an unexpected demand for gold for Spain,[2] it was raised to 6 per cent. The next day the firm of Baring Brothers collapsed.

The causes of the failure of this famous and much respected house, which was at one time called the sixth European Power, date back some way to the loss due to the attempt to issue the shares of the Buenos Ayres Water Works Company, which it had undertaken; Messrs. Baring had been obliged to keep the shares which they had "underwritten." Other misfortunes were soon added to this; the firm had several undertakings on its hands at once, and it has been justly observed:[3] "The chief of the firm appears

[1] Compare the passage often quoted from Lord Goschen's speech.

[2] £90,000 of gold were exported,making part of a much larger sum required for a Spanish loan.

[3] *Econ. Journal*, p. 192.

to have thought that their command of money was so great that there was no need for the ordinary calculations and precautions."

Although people began to suspect danger from so many uncertain undertakings, yet the firm of Baring appeared so firmly established, its branches were so extensive, and the services it had rendered to trade and to the State were so great,[1] that these first suspicions did not develop into alarm.[2]

It was not until Saturday, November 8th, that two or three prominent persons were told the true state of the case, and on the following Monday an eminent banker and a member of the Treasury Committee of the Bank of England were instructed to inquire into the affairs of Messrs. Baring.

Nothing definite was known by the general public, but a feeling of anxiety—increased by the numerous sales of Consols, the price of which had already fallen to 93¾—began to prevail in the City; and the next day, when it was heard on the one hand that £3,500,000 of gold was to be imported,[3] and on the other that the sale of Consols was continuing, everyone felt that they were confronted by a danger of the first magnitude. This feeling of vague alarm grew more intense in the course of Wednesday, on which day £750,000 of Consols were sold at once, and it became a panic on Friday,[4] when the position of Barings at length became known and people heard that there was a meeting at the Bank of England of the representatives of the leading banks and commercial firms.

That same evening, in view of the public interests at stake, and of the fact that it was impossible for the Barings to meet their liabilities—although they were actually solvent—the meeting decided to come to their help, and conse-

[1] It may be recollected that it was a Sir Francis Baring who wrote in 1797 one of the best studies that we possess on the Bank of England.

[2] *Jour. Inst. of Bankers*, p. 2.

[3] £4,500,000 were actually imported.

[4] On this day Consols fell to 93½.

quently it was agreed that the Bank of England should provide for their obligations, and should be secured from risk of ultimate loss by a guarantee fund which was to be maintained for three years.[1]

This fund, which at first amounted to 5 or 6 millions, rose to 10 millions the next day—when the announcement of what had happened calmed the public and arrested the panic.[2]

The fact that the settlement of Messrs. Barings' difficulties was known almost as soon as the existence of these difficulties, caused great satisfaction in the City. Congratulations were heard on all sides and everyone sung the praises of the Bank of England and of its Governor, Mr. Lidderdale, who had displayed so much resolution and courage.[3]

These praises were indeed fully deserved; the firm attitude of the Governor of the Bank in 1890 offers a curious contrast to the shifting policy of his predecessors in similar circumstances. Mr. Lidderdale's plan may be summarised as follows:

(1) Creation of a guarantee fund to last for three years.

(2) Importation of gold from abroad and maintenance of the Bank rate at the high but not exaggerated level of 6 per cent.[4]

Gold was imported chiefly from France. This was the second occasion during the 19th century on which the assistance of the Bank of France enabled the Bank of England to escape from a difficult position; and it must be acknowledged to the credit of the Bank of France that in 1890, as

[1] The text of the guarantee is given in the *Journal of the Institute of Bankers*, p. 5.

[2] The fund rose as high as 18 millions; many people, when once all danger was over, thought it good form to share in a measure taken for the public interest.

[3] On December 30 a deputation from the Stock Exchange officially presented an address of thanks to the Bank of England. For the text of this address and the reply made by the Governor Lidderdale, see the *Jour. Inst. of Bankers*, pp. 9-10.

[4] In spite of this the advances made increased from £25,100,000 to £32,000,000 in a single week.—Pierson, p. 473.

in 1839, it gave evidence of a friendly feeling towards the Bank of England which cannot be too much praised.[1]

(3) No suspension of the Act of 1844. The situation was such that a letter from the Treasury would have intensified rather than allayed the panic.

However praiseworthy Mr. Lidderdale's policy, as thus described, may be, we must nevertheless point out that the creation of a guarantee fund is a quite exceptional proceeding, which could not, whatever may be said of it, pass into general use, since there is theoretically no reason why it should not be applied to every case, for all securities and all investments may be regarded as virtually good and hence ultimately may be sold for a satisfactory price.

What was the fate of the firm of Baring Brothers?

The liabilities of the house amounted to £21,000,000. Those who had been charged with the investigation of its affairs estimated that, taking the value of the private property of the partners as £1,000,000, the assets of the firm, calculated at the very low prices of Friday, November 7th, exceeded the liabilities by 3 millions. After the events which we have just described, Baring Brothers was reconstructed as a joint-stock company under the name of Baring Brothers & Co., Limited, with a capital of one million. Mr T. C. Baring, who had retired from business in 1883, disinterestedly placed his entire fortune at the disposal of the new company, of which he consented to become a director. In 1894 the guarantors were relieved from all further responsibility and all subsequent payments devolved upon the company of Baring Brothers & Co., which has quickly restored the name of Baring to its former eminence.

(c)—Comparison between the Crisis of 1890 and the Preceding Crises.

The comparison is all in favour of the crisis of 1890, which differs greatly from its predecessors. "In former times alarm was diffused over the whole kingdom, London

[1] For the manner in which the remittance of the gold was accomplished see *The Political Science Quarterly*, March, 1894, p. 23. This review is edited by the Faculty of Political Science of Columbia College, Boston.

was drained of its reserves to fill up the wants of the country,[1] and the imprudencies of banks, having caused or aggravated alarms, there was a general uneasiness in the banking world and a consequent . . . indisposition to grant assistance to the trading world. But on this last occasion there was no general alarm in the country. Banks outside London were hardly sensible of the crisis, and even in London there was no panic except in Capel Court. No bank failed in town or country, and no suspicion of danger to banks seems to have existed amongst their customers. Some great issuing houses lost their position and narrowly escaped suspension. Enormous losses fell on the public, but not on banks except indirectly. It was not a panic causing general alarm amongst the public, but a crisis of a special kind, which might easily have been extended so as to have caused such a panic as never yet has occurred in any country. The danger was prodigious, but it was averted.

"In former crises the danger was not averted and things were allowed to drift, so that great houses and banks failed, and general alarm ensued." In 1890 on the contrary, "it may fairly be said that, for all practical purposes, nothing was known of the crisis in the country at large until all was over."[2]

[1] This will be better realised from a comparison of the Bank reserve in 1890 and during the earlier crises.

1857—October 3	......£6,014,000	1866—May 25	...... £830,000
10	 4,606,000	June 1	 415,000
17	 4,024,000	8	 2,167,000
24	 3,217,000	22	 4,067,000
31	 3,485,000	July 6	 3,335,000
November 7	 2,115,000	26	 2,498,000
14	 957,000	August 3	 2,412,000
21	 1,448,000	17	 3,611,000
28	 1,918,000	31	 5,833,000
December 5	 2,268,000	1890—October 16	 10,275,000
12	 3,900,000	30	 10,600,000
19	 5,757,000	November 13	 10,024,000
26	 7,426,000	20	 13,378,000
1866—April 13	 6,317,000	27	 15,309,000
27	 5,844,000	December 11	 15,904,000
May 11	 4,950,000	18	 15,797,000
18	 730,000	25	 14,205,000

[2] *Dict. Pol. Econ., loc. cit.*

PART IV.

GENERAL CONSIDERATIONS WITH REGARD TO THE ACT OF 1844.—PRESENT POSITION OF THE QUESTION.—SCHEMES FOR REFORM.

CHAPTER I.

SCHEMES FOR REFORM AND MR. GOSCHEN'S PROPOSAL.

Opposition to Act of 1844 re-awakened by the crisis of 1890. Numerous schemes for reform. Proposal of Mr. Goschen, then Chancellor of the Exchequer. Analysis of Mr. Goschen's speeches. Criticism of existing system, (1) Insufficiency of central stock of gold, (2) Absence of elasticity in time of crisis. Plan for reform. Drawbacks to and advantages of Mr. Goschen's plan, (1) The plan too complicated, (2) No conditions specified subject to which the second reserve to be available. Advantages of the scheme. Increase of the central stock of gold through the introduction of a new and convenient form of paper currency, and without resorting to the international gold market. Fate and results of Mr. Goschen's scheme. Doubtful welcome given to his proposals. Little justification for opposition to £1 notes. The situation in 1825 and at present. Mr. Goschen's proposals never drafted in the form of a Bill, but had the good effect of increasing the central stock of gold

THE crisis of 1890 re-awakened the opposition to the Act of 1844.

During the year 1891 numerous pamphlets drew the attention of the public to the need for a reform of the charter, and advocated the most varied remedies.[1]

[1] Amongst the most important of the works and articles which appeared about this time and at the beginning of 1892, the following may be noted :—

Stanley Cobb, *Banks' Cash Reserves*, especially Chaps. vi. and vii. ; and *Metallic Reserves and the Meeting of Parliament*.

Gardiner (Charles), President of the Institute of Bankers in Scotland, *Mr. Goschen's Scheme for Reform of the Bank Acts*.

Mavor (James), *The Call for Currency Reform and Mr. Goschen's Response*.

Bosanquet (B. Tindal), *Our Banking System*.

Moxon (T. B.), *Our Banking System and its effect upon Commerce*.

Gillett (W.), *A letter to the Chancellor of the Exchequer*.

In some of the works mentioned above the discussion of the Act of 1844 is combined with that of the bimetallist controversy, which was then raging.

We thought at one time of giving an analysis here of the chief proposals made at this time and had even prepared such a study, but this preparation determined us to abandon the idea. In the first place, the great majority of these schemes are now, after ten years' interval, completely forgotten, and some have been abandoned even by their authors. In the second place, in the critical portion of their work, which is generally the only one of any value, most of the reforms emphasise certain disadvantages in the English banking system, such as the insufficiency of the metallic reserve, the great fluctuations in the rate of discount, the necessity for suspending the Act of 1844 in time of crisis and other points with which we have already sufficiently dealt. Finally, and above all, among the chorus of reformers one voice was heard more clearly and effectively than the others, that of Mr. Goschen, who was then Chancellor of the Exchequer and the general attention and all the discussions soon centred round his proposals.

Hence the best method of studying the reform movement in 1891 is to examine the speeches delivered and the letters written by Mr. (afterwards Lord) Goschen.[1] This statesman has indeed summarised with moderation and ability all the serious criticisms which can be brought against the Act of 1844, and, in addition, has put forward practical suggestions for a reform, which afford a solid basis for discussion.[2]

Mr. Goschen began his speech on December 2nd before

[1] See (1) the speech at Leeds on January 28, 1891, *On the insufficiency of our cash reserves and of our central stock of gold;* (2) a speech before the London Chamber of Commerce on December 2, *On the Metallic Reserve.* The latter speech has been published as a pamphlet, together with a *Letter to the Governor of the Bank of England,* dated December 3, 1891, and a *Letter to Mr. Samuel Montagu, M.P.*, now Lord Swaythling, dated January 20, 1892

Mr. Goschen's proposals formed the subject of an excellent study by Professor Foxwell, the economist to whom we owe the very complete bibliography on the question of the "Right to the whole produce of labour." See *Mr. Goschen's Currency Proposals* in the *Economic Journal,* March, 1892. M. François also has examined Mr. Goschen's proposals in the *Journal des Économistes* for January, 1892.

[2] It must be acknowledged that, in addition to Lord Goschen's scheme, certain other proposals were made which would have repaid discussion, *e.g.*, those of Messrs. Stanley Cobb, Pownall, and Gairdiner. We have been unable to examine them owing to lack of time and space. See, however, with reference to these schemes, Foxwell, pp. 148-149, and Goschen, Speech on December 2, pp. 25-26.

the London Chamber of Commerce by repeating what he had already said at the commencement of his speech at Leeds, viz., that no form of regulation could prevent panics and failures resulting from imprudence and over-speculation, but that legislation might perhaps do something to prevent the spread of these panics.

He then proceeded to criticise the system existing in England and attacked it mainly on two grounds: (1) The insufficiency of the central stock of gold and (2) The want of elasticity in times of crisis which characterised the system imposed upon the Bank.

I.—Insufficiency of the Central Stock of Gold.

At the time of Mr. Goschen's speech the average amount of the metallic reserve in England was from 21 to 22 millions, as compared with 95 millions (gold and silver) in France, and 40 millions (gold and silver) in Germany. The United States held in the Treasury and in the National Banks, a metallic reserve (gold and silver) of 142 millions.

The inferiority of England in this respect was dangerous owing to the difficulty of *rapidly attracting gold.* Gold could always be obtained, but time was necessary. This fact had not been sufficiently foreseen and was what made the situation dangerous, especially " in these days when combinations are so easy, . . . when syndicates are so common " that an attack on the English stock of bullion would be a most simple matter.

II.—Want of Elasticity in Time of Crisis.

The method used for the suspension of the charter was inadequate. In actual fact, the situation had to be very serious and many disasters must already have occurred, before the Chancellor of the Exchequer could decide to write his letter. " There are certain authorities who hold that the very uncertainty as to whether the Chancellor of the Exchequer's letter will or will not be given is in itself a preventive to over-speculation." But experience has, unfortunately, proved the contrary, and it may be said that "in the City, gentlemen calculate with pretty considerable certainty that the Chancellor of the Exchequer's letter will be forthcoming if the alarm is great enough and the panic is great enough."

After these remarks, Mr. Goschen declared that it was not his intention to criticise the Act of 1844,[1] that he only desired to modify as little as possible a law which had, "on the whole," worked "extremely well." But after a lapse of fifty years circumstances had changed enormously; "the Bank of England has not that command over the money market which it used to have," and for changed conditions fresh legislation was necessary.

What are the Legislative Provisions Suggested by Mr. Goschen?

We have seen that Mr. Goschen had two objects—to increase the central stock of gold, and to give greater elasticity to the issues in time of crisis. These two reforms had already been indicated by others, but the originality of Mr. Goschen's plan consisted in his combining them, thanks chiefly to the issue of £1 notes.

The details of this scheme are very clearly summarised in the letter written by the proposer himself to the Governor of the Bank of England.

"The Bank of England," wrote Mr. Goschen, "is at present authorised to issue £16,450,000 on securities. Beyond that all notes must be represented by gold. The average amount of gold in the issue department for the years 1881-90 may be taken as . . . £21,550,000, which, if added to the £16,450,000—the authorised amount of the fiduciary issue—would give a total of £38,000,000, representing the average total issue under the provisions of the Act of 1844. I would disturb nothing up to this point beyond authorising the issue of £1 notes under precisely

[1] "I have been and am a Bank Charter Act man." See p. 8 of the Speech on December 2nd. Mr. Goschen's respect for Robert Peel's Act is shared by all the reformers; time has, in fact, raised the empirical measure passed in 1844 into an institution, which shares in the veneration enjoyed by every national institution in England.

the same conditions as those under which notes of higher denominations are issued at present. But beyond this limit of £38,000,000, I would authorise the issue of notes under the conditions which I have sketched—namely, £4 on gold to £1 on securities."

These proposals may be explained more vividly by means of an example. Suppose that the stock of gold in the issue department stands at £21,550,000. Suppose that "an additional sum of £25,000,000 were issued in the proportion of £4 on gold to £1 on securities, the addition to the stock of gold would be £20,000,000, bringing the total up to £41,550,000, and the position would be as follows:—

Total Notes—		
Old average	£38,000,000	
Additional issue	25,000,000	
		£63,000,000

"This total would be issued against gold and securities respectively, in the following proportions:—

Total stock of gold—		
Under the old provisions	£21,550,000	
Add four-fifths of £25,000,000 under the new provisions ...	20,000,000	
Notes issued against gold		£41,550,000
Notes issued against securities—		
Previous amount	£16,450,000	
Add one-fifth of £25,000,000 ...	5,000,000	
Total notes issued against securities		£21,450,000
Total notes as above ...		£63,000,000

"The contrast between the new and the old situation would be this:

"We should have £41,550,000 of gold at the Bank instead of £21,550,000, and the increase in the fiduciary issue would be only £5,000,000; and that increase would be due to the introduction of £1 notes, which if once acclimatized, would be far less likely to be presented for payment than £5 notes."[1]

Mr. Goschen completes his scheme as follows: "If the addition to the stock of gold through the issue of £1 notes should bring the total stock up to £30,000,000, a point which would be reached by the issue of £10,000,000 under the new conditions, I should be prepared to give certain additional powers of issue in times of emergency. . . . I would authorise the Bank to strengthen the reserve in the banking department by the issue of additional notes against securities, on paying to the Government a high rate of interest, to be fixed by law. . . . The rate of interest must be neither so high as to make the permission inoperative, nor so low as to encourage people to speculate up to it.

"This additional authority to the Bank is intended to take the place of and prevent the necessity for the Treasury letter, by which the Bank Charter Act has been several times suspended."

Advantages and Disadvantages of Mr. Goschen's Plan.

Mr. Goschen's plan, like all human proposals, has its advantages and its disadvantages. We will first consider the latter, which will enable us the better to explain the former.

Disadvantages of the Scheme.

The scheme has two main disadvantages: on the one hand, it is unnecessarily complicated and on the other hand it leaves undetermined a point of fundamental importance—it does not specify the conditions under which the second reserve is to be available.

[1] Mr. Goschen adds that "if contrary to my expectation, the additional issue under the new terms should reach £50,000,000, I should be prepared to require any further issues beyond that sum to be covered in full by gold. Such a provision would meet the objection that an indefinite amount of gold might be lost to the country under my plan."

These disadvantages were pointed out and clearly expounded by Mr. Foxwell.[1]

1.—The scheme is too complicated.

"Why, for instance, should he stipulate that there must be no fiduciary issue of £1 notes until £38 million notes are issued upon the old footing?" Especially as this limitation might lead to confusion in the working of the issue.

"Again, why are the new powers of relief issue not to be available until the stock of gold in the Issue Department amounts to £30 millions? This again seems an unnecessary precaution, and . . . might prevent the operation of the new powers exactly when it was most required. It would, for instance, have made the scheme inoperative in 1857, even if 25 millions of £1 notes had then been in circulation."

Why, in fact, not allow the issue of £1 notes, as the *Economist*[2] suggests, on the present basis? And why make any distinction between the issue of the two kinds of notes?

"It would seem," observes Mr. Foxwell,[3] "that Mr. Goschen has been led to complicate his proposals by an unnecessary tenderness for Peel's Act and a desire to represent his scheme as an addition to that Act rather than a modification of it. But surely the Act of 1844 is from its very nature one which no statesman need hesitate to amend. Its empirical basis shows that it was drafted to meet the special requirements of its own day, and cannot consequently be perfectly adapted to the greatly altered conditions of the present time."

2.—The conditions under which the second reserve is available are not sufficiently specified.

By not specifying these conditions, Mr. Goschen has omitted to specify the exact nature of the second reserve.

"Is it to be strictly a panic reserve, only available at times of absolute crisis," at times such as formerly have made it necessary to suspend the Act of 1844? "Or is it to

[1] p. 152. [2] No. 23, January, 1892. [3] p. 153.

be generally available to prevent injurious monetary strains? In other words, is the rate fixed for access to the reserve to be a comparatively low rate, fixed by the point at which the difficulty of obtaining accommodation becomes a serious obstacle to the ordinary business of the country; or is it to be a high rate, and are we aiming merely at relieving strains which threaten the entire collapse of the credit system?"

Mr. Goschen said that the discount rate must neither be so high as to prevent the use of the second reserve nor so low as to encourage speculation. But what is this rate? "Are we to follow the lines of Mr. Lowe's proposal in 1873,[1] fixing the minimum rate at 10 per cent. or even higher; or shall we follow the example of Germany, where relief begins at a 5 per cent. rate?"

This question is unsettled, and this want of definiteness makes it impossible to understand and consequently impossible to judge, the exact bearing of the scheme in this respect.

Advantages of Mr. Goschen's Plan.

Apart from these disadvantages, which could be easily remedied, it must be acknowledged that Mr. Goschen's scheme has obvious merits. "It would undoubtedly increase the central stock of gold, while at the same time providing us with a new and convenient form of currency, and this by a costless operation which would not make any fresh demands on the international gold market, or in any way unfavourably affect prices."[2] This latter combination, it should be noted, is one deserving of high praise, and one which is not a feature of the other projects. It is true that, in so far as the issue was fiduciary, gold would doubtless leave the country, but the quantity thus lost would not be large and would be fully compensated for by the increased power given to the Bank from the centralisation of a sum four times as great as that exported. As Mr. Goschen remarked, "£40,000,000 at the centre" was to be preferred to "£50,000,000 in the pocket of the people."

[1] For Lowe's scheme see above, p. 329. [2] Foxwell, p. 142.

As regards the issue of notes the new position of the Bank would obviously be much stronger than the old one. "The £1 notes would be much less likely to be presented for conversion than the larger ones, and therefore the circulation as a whole would require a smaller proportionate reserve; but the actual percentage of bullion held against it would be increased. With the issue department thus strengthened, it becomes safe to make its reserve available in certain emergencies for the purposes of the banking department."

THE FATE AND THE CONSEQUENCES OF MR. GOSCHEN'S PROPOSALS.

It must be confessed that Mr. Goschen's plan was not very favourably received by the public. The theorists, probably owing to the complicated and rather vague nature of the proposed reform, expressed very doubtful opinions, and the judgment of the commercial world was almost hostile.[1]

In particular, the introduction of £1 notes aroused much opposition. This opposition was ill-judged: these small notes, which have worked excellently in Scotland and in America, are convenient and very cheap, and are presented for payment much less often than notes of higher value. Their one disadvantage, as was pointed out by G. W. Norman more than sixty years ago,[2] is the risk of forgery, but Mr. Goschen showed conclusively[3] that this could be avoided. Hence the only argument that can be brought against £1 notes (an argument very frequently used), is based on the memory of the crisis of 1825; but it really shows a complete ignorance of the causes of this crisis to try to compare the new notes as suggested with those then existing. There can be no analogy between £1 notes issued

[1] See the outcome of a meeting held at Salters' Hall on January 21, 1892, to express the opinion of the City. Compare the *Economist, loc. cit.*, and Stanley Cobb, *Metallic Reserves*.

[2] *Op. cit.*, p. 67. M. Henri Germain made an interesting statement with regard to notes of low values before the *Académie des Sciences Morales et Politiques* at a meeting on July 9, 1892.

[3] Speech on December 2, pp. 22-23.

by the Bank of England and those issued by any chance grocer or cheese-monger.

The example of the crisis of 1825 is, in fact, the one and constant objection brought forward by those who reject all idea of modifying the Act of 1844; I was more than a little surprised to find it used even by a director of the Bank of England.[1] But it cannot be too often insisted upon that the crisis of 1825 was not due to the absence of a limit to the fiduciary issue of the Bank of England, but to the absurd system of country banking and in particular, to the fact that the Bank of England had not yet learnt that the paper circulation ought to be regulated by the foreign exchanges and the price of bullion.

Whatever may be thought of the merits of the discussion and in spite of the many advantages of Mr. Goschen's proposals, they were never embodied in a Bill.

It is, however, some consolation to know that the efforts of this statesman were not entirely wasted and that to make up for the elasticity which was still lacking in the Act of 1844, the central stock of gold was much increased.

From £21,820,000 in 1890, it rose to £24,377,000 in 1891, £25,524,000 in 1892, £34,414,000 in 1894, £38,951,000 in 1895, and reached a maximum of £44,319,000 in 1896. Since then the stock has slightly decreased, but has always been maintained at a sufficiently respectable level[2] and in 1902 was still £35,644,000.

At this same date the stock of gold at the Bank of France was £101,932,000 and that at the Bank of Germany £36,273,000. But it must be remembered that these two Banks have a much larger quantity of notes in circulation than the Bank of England and if we consider the situation during the last decade, we find that the proportion of gold to notes in England was 128 per cent., in France 54 per

[1] Mr. Jackson, *op. cit.*, p. 15.

[2] £35,551,000 in 1897; £33,567,000 in 1898; £32,268,000 in 1899; £33,321,000 in 1900; £35,831,000 in 1901.

cent. and in Germany 56 per cent.[1] If the silver reserve is also taken into account, though from an international point of view this is not comparable in importance to the gold reserve, the metallic stock at the Bank of France amounted to 86 per cent. of the notes in circulation and that at the Bank of Germany to 81 per cent. only.

In this respect clearly, the position of the Bank of England, though inferior in some other ways, remains superior to that of either the Bank of France or the Bank of Germany.

[1] From 1892 to 1902 the average of notes in circulation was—in England, £27,249,000; in France, £150,278,000; and in Germany, £55,372,000, as compared with stocks of gold of £35,030,000, £81,187,000, and £30,803,000, respectively. See Jackson, Table I.

CHAPTER II.

GENERAL REMARKS ON THE PRESENT POSITION OF THE BANK OF ENGLAND.

Change in public opinion as regards the Act of 1844. Opinion of the English economists. The Foreign economists. Opinions and observations of M. Paul Leroy-Beaulieu. Desirable reforms. Danger of a sudden withdrawal of large quantities of gold. Reforms suggested in the administration of the Bank. Report of the Lords' Committee of 1848.

THE Act has for a long time been the object of violent attack.

Courcelle-Seneuil has given a forcible summary of most of the criticisms of it.

"The Bank of England," he says,[1] "cannot regulate the circulation; it could only do so if it had a monopoly of the business of discounting and could stop any tendency to speculation in trade by the refusal of credit. But it is precisely at these times that trade has no need of the Bank of England; it can obtain credit more cheaply elsewhere. People only apply to the Bank when the ordinary sources of credit begin to be exhausted; is this a suitable moment to refuse discount? When the reactionary movement has actually begun, ought the Bank to fill the cup to overflowing and hasten the disaster, as in 1825?

"The Bill of 1844 was based on several errors of fact. It supposed that banks could increase their circulation at will, which is inexact; that commerce always requires the same quantity of money, which is inexact; and, finally, that a metallic currency is safer and less variable than a paper currency, which is equally inexact. Thus the Bill was framed in opposition to the natural laws which guide

[1] *Op. cit.*, p. 323-324. Compare the analogous judgment expressed by M. Courtois on the Act of 1844, p. 235, note, and pp. 251-252 of the *Histoire des Banques en France*, 2nd edition (1881).

the real movements of commerce, and as soon as it was put to the test of experience the inadequacy and danger of its effects became evident."

Although these criticisms are apparently unanswerable, nothing further has been heard in England, since 1892, of modifying the Act of 1844.

I even noticed, at a meeting of the Political Economy Club on the 12th of June last, at which the question was discussed, a marked disinclination to make changes which seemed useless and might be dangerous. As far as I could judge, the *quieta non movere* was apparently the motto of English economists as far as the Bank of England was concerned, a state of mind which would be of merely relative importance were it confined to England. For the English public, naturally conservative, only demands changes when disturbed by a violent crisis, and the Old Lady of Threadneedle Street, who is the Panglosse of the English commercial world, has adopted by turns with equal conviction, the most contradictory opinions.

This superstitious adherence, this *tabooism*, is the more childish when applied to Robert Peel's Act, considering the fundamentally empirical character of this measure and the fact that its authors themselves looked upon it as temporary.

But, what is more important, a tendency to respect the old charter of 1844 is observable even outside England. Whether it be that its success, at first partial, but since 1867 practically complete, has disarmed some of its critics; whether it be that theoretical discussions are somewhat out of fashion, and that nowadays people are inclined to admit the possible existence of several equally good systems as regards banks of issue; or whether it be for some other reason, the fact remains that the writers who have discussed the subject during the last ten years have concerned themselves less to criticise the Act of 1844 than to explain it. It might be supposed that after careful consideration it has been found less bad in reality than in appearance.

This is, in the main, the conclusion reached by M. Wilfredo-Pareto and by Mr. Pierson. The latter agrees with Bagehot that the indifferent rules which the Act of 1844 imposed upon the directors of the Bank were at any rate preferable to those which the directors might have framed for themselves.[1]

Even the *Société d'économie politique* in Paris, which has always been fascinated by the idea of freedom, was apparently not much affected by the numerous disadvantages which M. Sayous, following Mr. Pownall, pointed out in the working of the London money market during a crisis, disadvantages which in the main he attributed to the organisation of the Bank of England.

And finally, M. Leroy Beaulieu, an economist who combines immense learning with a sound, practical sense, and (what is nowadays growing more and more rare) a wide business experience, defends the Act with ability and moderation as follows:—[2]

"From 1870 to the present day England and the Bank of England—which have become the centre of the trade and finance of the world, which have in a measure to regulate all the exchanges and all the business affairs of the universe, and which act almost as the ultimate repository of the world's reserve—have succeeded in playing their part without a suspension of the Act of 1844, and this during a quarter of a century characterised by the activity of business and by financial and commercial crises. The Bank has always been able, in fact, to supply gold to those who demanded it, not only to settle extraordinary purchases of cereals and commodities, but for foreign loans and investments. All that it has done has been to charge more highly for this gold at certain times.

"Under the influence of general conditions and also of the Act of 1844, the position of the Bank of England has become much more definite. Strictly speaking, it does not supply credit facilities. Its function is to be the general repository for the cash reserve of British trade and finance and even ultimately of the trade and finance of the world.

[1] *Op. cit.*, p. 461.

[2] Vol. III., pp. 601-606 of his *Traité d'Éc. Politique.*

In particular it is the Bank's business to procure gold for international settlements, and yet it only keeps a limited supply. . . .

"Thus the 'Banking Principle' is entirely abandoned. The Bank of England, carrying out Ricardo's wish, if not his actual scheme, is the keeper of the gold reserve of Great Britain, while at the same time it provides the gold needed for international payments. . . ."

M. Leroy Beaulieu remarks that the loans on securities made by the Bank of England are even more limited than those of the Bank of France—which latter also is tending to become the repository of commercial cash—and observes that the Bank of England is thus returning to the system of banking which prevailed in ancient times and in the Middle Ages.

"Credit," he goes on,[1] "is actually obtained in England from the private bankers, from the joint-stock banks, which are hardly ever banks of issue, and also from the bill-brokers, who may be called the 'beaters' or purveyors of the large companies. . . . These large joint-stock companies only keep as much reserve in notes and coin as is required for their current needs; they deposit the rest at the Bank of England, which thus holds the reserve for all the banks in the country.

"*Delicate though this system appears, it has given rise to no danger since* 1871.

"Methods of attracting gold have multiplied during the last twenty-five years. International securities, negotiable on a large number of different markets, the use of the telegraph for assignments and transfers of money and of railways and steam-boats for its actual transport, have produced a new state of things, in which a comparatively small reserve can be increased with much greater ease, and consequently tends to be exhausted much less rapidly than formerly. . . .

"New habits are tending to reduce not only the quantity of gold but also the quantity of notes available. . . .

[1] p. 604.

"*The Bank of England is not perfection, but the tool does its work well on the whole.*

"The English banking system, artificial though it be, is less so than the French system. Since the privileged Bank practically undertakes none of the business connected with credit, there is more equality betwen the other banks.

"*Should the Act of 1844 be repealed?*[1] It would be better to modify it in respect to the regulation of note issue; the tendency for the notes not to exceed the cash reserve increases daily and may be looked upon as permanent. . . . To repeal the portion of the Act dealing with this matter would be attended by no inconvenience, but also by no particular gain, and any legislative change in a matter of this sort which is not obviously useful, may have moral disadvantages."

The matter could not be better expressed, and we have thought it of interest to give these full extracts from M. Leroy-Beaulieu's work, not only as supplying an appreciation of the Act of 1844, but as giving an excellent summary of the working of the English banking system. At the same time, while recognising that much current criticism is unduly violent, we must avoid falling into the exaggerated optimism of thinking that, in reference to the Bank of England, all is for the best in the best possible world, and that there remains nothing for the future to fear or to improve.

In the first place, the fact that important financial institutions, and even important foreign countries, have considerable gold deposits at London, has given rise to the fear of a possible sudden withdrawal of a quantity of gold. It is difficult to say whether any such danger actually exists. Mr. Jackson had tried to prove that a withdrawal of this kind is neither possible nor probable:[2] in any case,

[1] p. 606.

[2] For in the first place the foreign institution must already have the money in question in England. This money cannot be idle, it must have been employed or invested in one way or another. But long before the securities into which it has been converted, were sold, or the money withdrawn from the market, the effect of the withdrawal on the prices of the securities or of the money would be such that the foreign institution would abandon its scheme on account of the loss involved in carrying it out. In any case, there would be time to attract gold from abroad into England. *Op. cit.*, p. 14.

he considers that the attempt would be criminal and would hardly prove successful. But Mr. Palgrave[1] shows much anxiety as regards this matter, and various other people whose opinion I have asked, have seemed to be afraid that, in this age of trusts and gigantic combines, the danger is more serious than ever. They believe that it is of the utmost importance to strengthen the reserve and to give greater elasticity to the note issue in order to meet the difficulty should it arise.

Leaving on one side a problem which experience alone can solve—and hitherto no such attempt has ever been made—we must pass on to consider whether the present organisation of the Bank of England does not possess other drawbacks.

Some such drawbacks are already familiar to the reader, since we have dealt at length with the artificial nature of the Act of 1844. By separating the Bank into two departments it tends to increase the fluctuations in the discount rate. The same result follows from the clause obliging the Bank to buy all the gold offered to it. This latter provision indeed, leads to unforeseen accumulations of bullion and to abnormal reductions in the Bank rate. We have also pointed out how much it is to be regretted that a separate statement of the bankers' current accounts is no longer published, and have referred to the justice of the arguments in favour of making these bankers responsible for the expense of maintaining some portion of the reserve. Finally, in the course of our study we have made no secret of our lack of sympathy with the "strait jacket" imposed upon the note issue by Peel's Act.[2] No doubt, so far as the metallic reserve tends to exceed the notes in circulation, a reform such as we demand would have merely a speculative interest, but, after all, it is not certain, but only probable, that the present policy will be persisted in, and there is no

[1] *Op. cit.*, p. 215.

[2] The bad effects of the Act in this respect are due to the fact that it hinders the extension of the circulation at the very times when it would be most valuable, and this is so true that the mere suspension of the Act of 1844 has been sufficient on several occasions to allay public anxiety.

guarantee that a crisis analogous to that of 1866 will never occur again. In 1890 this was only averted by the prudence and courage of Mr. Lidderdale.

In addition to these drawbacks which have already been examined, others have been pointed out from an administrative point of view. The administration of the Bank is, it is alleged, somewhat costly, and its management might with advantage be more permanent.[1]

The management of the Bank of England is entrusted to a body of directors chosen from amongst the principal bankers and financiers of the City. This body, whose composition varies but slightly from year to year, has at its head a Governor who is appointed for two years only. This system has been criticised, as we have said, for its lack of continuity[2] and it has sometimes been suggested that a permanent Governor would be in a better position to manage the affairs of the Bank.

This idea has been frequently put forward, and even Bagehot thought that the appointment of a permanent Deputy-Governor "would give the decisions of the Bank that foresight, that quickness and that consistency in which those decisions are undeniably now deficient."[3] It is more curious to find the same view expressed in the Report of the Committee of Inquiry of the House of Lords in 1848.[4] "The objections," so the Report runs, "which have been often urged against the Bank, . . are a Want of Permanence and of Consistency derived from its system of periodical Elections of Governors and Deputy-Governers—the evil Consequences of filling these high and important Offices . . by a mere Rotation of Seniority—and the intimate Connection subsisting between the Directors and the Commercial World of London, which may cast on them a Degree of Pressure difficult at Times to be resisted. It appears further to be apparent from the Evidence that the immediate

[1] For the latter point see Palgrave, pp. 57-60.

[2] Thus it is risky if one governor authorises advances upon Consols in times of difficulty, while another governor adopts a different policy.

[3] Bagehot, *Lombard Street*, p. 239 (edition 1906).

[4] See Palgrave, p. 60.

pecuniary Interest of the Proprietors . . . may at Times supersede or control larger and higher Considerations. This ought not to be. . . ."

We have felt obliged as impartial historians, to state these criticisms, which condemn somewhat severely the lack of continuity in the management of the Bank resulting from the system of appointment by election. It is difficult for a foreigner to decide what exact degree of truth there is in these accusations. But it is evident that the mere fact that they are thus reproduced after an interval of nearly sixty years by competent persons and well-known writers gives them a certain weight.

APPENDIX.

HISTORY OF THE RELATIONS BETWEEN THE BANK OF ENGLAND AND THE TREASURY.

THE RELATIONS OF CHARTERED BANKS OF ISSUE TO NATIONAL FINANCE.

Relations of chartered banks of issue and the Public Finances. Various ways in which such banks pay for their privileges. Advantages gained by the English Government from the privileges granted to the Bank. Summary of these advantages: Business connected with the Treasury and the public money, the administration of the national debt. Management of the revenues: (*a*) The management of the revenues before the Act of 1834, (*b*) The Act of 1834, (*c*) Modifications made in the Act of 1834. Present position. Management of the expenditure. The Act of 1848. The Paymaster General. Simple and practical management of the accounts. The administration of the national debt. The Bank and the administration of the permanent debt. The Act of 1751. The Act of 1834. Deficiency bills and deficiency advances. The Bank undertakes not only the payment of interest, but also the administration of the national debt. The Bank and the administration of the floating debt (issue, circulation, redemption of exchequer bills and bonds and of treasury bills). The Act of 1709 and those of 1834 and 1866. The exchequer bills and bonds and the treasury bills. Indemnity paid to the Bank in return for the administration of the permanent and floating debts.

A CHARTERED bank of issue as a general rule must pay the State for the privilege accorded to it. This payment assumes various forms: a loan, a tax, a share in the profits, the undertaking of certain duties connected with the cash account of the Treasury, most generally the administration of the floating or permanent debt.[1]

We have already observed that a loan,[2] often a loan without interest, is the usual return made for the privilege of issuing notes and that the negotiation of a loan was the primary cause explaining the establishment of the principal European banks of issue, and in particular of the Bank of England.

[1] Leroy-Beaulieu, *Science des Finances,* pp. 106-107.

[2] See above, p. 80. Compare du Hays du Gassart *Des prêts consentis aux États par les Banques de Circulation,* pp. 1-43.

A tax on the circulation is another form of payment: it corresponds in theory to a stamp duty on commercial bills, the application of which to bank notes has certain drawbacks and from which the bank is usually exempted, either entirely, as in France, or in return for a definitely fixed yearly payment, as in England. Sometimes a compound system is adopted, the note circulation is exempt from taxation up to a fixed total issue, but if this total is exceeded a tax, and frequently a very heavy tax, has to be paid. This is the system in Germany and Belgium.

A share in the profits may take two forms: it may be either a share in the normal profits, or a share in extraordinary profits resulting, for instance, from an abnormal increase in the discount rate.

Finally, the State may secure an indirect return by entrusting the bank of issue with certain duties connected with financial administration or the Treasury.

The Profit which the English Government derives from the Privileges of Issue granted to the Bank of England.

These profits are relatively small when compared with those which some other European States obtain in return for the concession of similar privileges,[1] and this is a matter on which English legislation is deserving of the highest praise. If a monopoly of issue is granted, it should be because the Government considers this system to be for the public welfare, and especially because it involves least risk. The public interest is the only justification nowadays for a monopoly of this kind; hence the State ought to endeavour to lessen the drawbacks which inevitably attend any monopoly, instead of increasing them by appropriating

[1] In France these profits amounted to 8,785,269 francs in 1900, and to 6,977,345 in 1901, *i.e.*, respectively 18 and 20 per cent. of the net proceeds.

In Germany for the same years these profits were 25,859,799 and 12,770,445 marks, *i.e.*, 76 and 49 per cent. of the net proceeds.

In Belgium they were 6,615,336 and 4,969,590 francs, *i.e.*, 63 and 51 per cent. of the net proceeds.

Hence both France and England may be classed among the States which do not make undue profits out of the concession of a monopoly of issue.

profits which must ultimately be paid by the public, for whose benefit the monopoly was established.

In actual fact the advantages which the Treasury derives from the Bank of England are the following :—

(*a*) It is exempt from paying interest on its debt to the Bank so long as the charter of the latter is continued.

(*b*) It receives an annual payment of £180,000.

(*c*) Should the Bank be authorised to exceed the statutory limit of its issues, it is usually stipulated that its discount rate should be raised and that the profits resulting from the additional issue, deducting the amount required to cover expenses and risks, should go to the Treasury.

(*d*) Certain duties connected with public finance are entrusted to the Bank, such as the administration of the national debt, for which however payment is made.

Enough has already been said with regard to the first three points; it is only necessary to recollect that the annuity of £180,000 is partly paid in return for exemption from the stamp tax, and that the arrangement by which the State shares in any profits made from supplementary issues was not inspired by a desire for gain, but was made lest the Bank, tempted by high profits, should acquiesce in useless and dangerous issues.

Thus the only profit made by the State from the concession of the Bank charter is, so far, the non-payment of interest on a capital of about £11,000,000.[1] This, at the existing rate of 2½ per cent., is equivalent to an annual sum of £275,000, and it may be remarked, by the way, that this portion of the law of 1844 has been severely criticised by many English writers.

We now come to the last point, which is the only one that is really interesting and characteristic. It relates to the connection between the Bank and the Treasury and the way in which the Bank assists and even replaces the latter.

We are here faced by one of those gradual processes of evolution which are so characteristic of English nature, as in fact, they are characteristic of Nature in general. We can see an organism—the ancient Exchequer—gradu-

[1] **Corrigendum. The State actually pays 2½ per cent. on this sum.**

ally and without any sudden break, eliminated and replaced almost entirely by another—the Bank. This somewhat peculiar process has played as important a part in the history of the Bank of England as the Act of 1844 itself; the two together have completely modified the character of the institution. Considering the importance of this process and the difficulty of describing it piecemeal each time in the course of the years that a stage in its evolution has been reached, we have decided to deal with it separately by making it the subject of this Appendix. We hope in this way, if we cannot avoid the risk of confusing the question of the issues of the Bank with that of its duties in regard to the Treasury, at any rate to escape the introduction of further complications into a book to which it has already proved difficult enough to give some degree of unity.

The question of the relations between the Bank and the Treasury when thus limited and defined, divides itself naturally into two parts:

(*a*) The duties connected with the Treasury and the public money.

(*b*) The duties connected with the national debt.

We propose to describe these duties in succession and to complete our study by a few short comments.[1]

[1] As might be expected, there is no book in English on this important question. Two Italian works may however be consulted with advantage: Martinuzzi (Pietro), *La banca d' Inghilterra nei riguardi del servizio del tesoro;* and C. Perazzi, *Memorie intorno alla contabilita dello stato in Inghiltera*, a supplement to the Sella scheme. Sella, the famous Italian financier, wished, like many of his countrymen, to introduce the English system into Italy. Several analogous attempts have been made in France: under the July monarchy projects with this object were brought forward by Benoît Fould and Mauguin, while under the third Republic complete schemes were drawn up by MM. Hervé de Saisy, in 1873, and C. Dreyfus, in 1885; a superintendent of direct taxes even wrote a work embodying a scheme in no less than 113 articles. See *Réforme des Services de Tresorerie*, by R. Lemercier de Jauvelle.

With regard to the question as raised in France and Germany see an essay by M. Dartiguenave, *Relations de la Banque de France avec le Trésor*, and a publication of the Inspector-General of Finance, *Mission en Allemagne, Organisation et fonctionnement de la Banque de l'Empire allemand.*

Finally, with regard to Belgium, where (in 1850) a system very similar to the English one was introduced, see Noël, *Banques d'émission*, etc., pp. 546-567. For the Belgian Law of 1900, which was later than Noël's book, see Dartiguenave, pp. 179-180.

(a)—Duties Connected with the Treasury and the Public Money.[1]

I.—The Management of the Revenue.

It is customary in England to entrust the administration of the various receipts to special commissioners, who undertake all the business of assessing the different taxes; when this is done the taxes are paid to local receivers, who hand them over to the Receivers-General, by whom they are paid into the Bank of England; whereas formerly they used to be paid into the Exchequer, which was until 1834 the State Treasury.

(a)—*The Management of the Revenue before the Act of 1834.*

When, owing to the Act of Restriction,[2] Bank notes were accepted at par in payment of taxes, the Bank had to send a representative to the Exchequer to examine and take away the notes which were paid in there.

Shortly afterwards, by a series of Acts passed in George III.'s reign,[3] it was enacted that the Bank's representatives must take the notes direct from the various receivers, of the Customs, of the Excise, of the Stamp Duties, etc., and enter them to the credit of those receivers as though the payments had been made straight to the Bank in coin. In addition, it gradually grew into a custom for the Bank to take charge through its representatives at the Exchequer, not only of the revenues fixed by special laws, but of all the sums paid to the Government from whatever source. The general use of paper money had made this plan necessary; the notes presented at the Exchequer had to be verified in order that the latter might safely take the responsibility of accepting them in payment of the taxes.

[1] For what follows see also in Boucard and Jèze, *Éléments de Science de Finances et de Législation Financière française,* the part dealing with the Exchequer account at the Banks of England and Ireland, p. 1185.

[2] See above, Vol. I., p. 187.

[3] Lawson, *op. cit.*, p. 169.

The payments were actually made at the Exchequer, but the Bank took an increasingly important share in the management of these payments.

Besides this, since 1725 the Bank had held on deposit and been answerable for certain funds which, although belonging to private individuals, are yet under the control of the Court of Chancery, such as the securities belonging to the suitors of this Court. In 1786, as soon as the Commission for the reduction of the national debt, or in other words the Sinking Fund, was constituted, the Bank had to take charge of the sums resulting from the annuity which was granted with a view to the redemption. In 1802 the money produced by the redemption or purchase of the land taxes was entrusted to the Bank, and in 1828 it likewise took charge of the funds belonging to the Savings Bank, and subsequently of many other funds of a similar kind.

To all this was added the business connected with the national debt, which the Bank had long carried on, and the extra work due to the Act of 1827 (7 and 8 George IV., c. 53), in consequence of which the Receiver-General had to pay the receipts from the Excise into the Bank, where they were entered as a special account called "The account of the public money of the Receiver-General of the Excise."[1]

The gradual transfer of all this business to the Bank suggested to the Government the advisability of reorganising the old Court of the Exchequer and prepared the way for the Act of 1834.

(b)—*The Act of* 1834 (4 *William IV., c.* 15).

This Act reorganised the Exchequer and established the office of the Comptroller-General of the receipt and issue of his Majesty's Exchequer, to which were transferred the

[1] The Act of 1841 (4 and 5 Vict., c. 20) concerning the Excise made practically no alteration in the method of dealing with the receipts or in the administration of the tax.

In 1847 (10-11 Vict., c. 42) the duties on horses, carriages, etc., were transferred from the Commissioners of Stamps and Taxes to those of Excise and were administered like the latter; and in 1849 (12-13 Vict., c. 1) the two Boards of Excise were amalgamated into the single Board of Commissioners of Inland Revenue. The receipts forming the Inland Revenue are entered by the Bank to the account of the Receiver-General of the Inland Revenue and are transferred thence day by day to the general account of the Exchequer.

powers belonging to the different offices abolished.[1] The Commissioners of the Treasury were to "establish and direct" what books, etc., should be used in the Exchequer, and "the forms thereof, as well as the forms of all warrants . . . and other documents" in use.

An important change was made by this Act of May 22nd, 1834, in providing that, after the 11th of June following, all Exchequer bills, notes, security for money, etc, which had hitherto been entrusted to the four tellers, should be paid in to the Bank of England, where they were credited to the "account of his Majesty's Exchequer." At the same time, and this was still more important, all public moneys which had hitherto been payable at the Exchequer were in future to be paid to the Bank and entered by it to the credit of the Exchequer. At the end of each day the Bank was to send to the Comptroller-General a summary of all the amounts paid in and entered to the Government account.

All sums thus entered to the account of the Exchequer were to be regarded as constituting a fund for the payment of the various expenses arising out of the public service. The Comptroller-General was empowered by the Commissioners of the Treasury to authorise the Bank to open accounts with the officials.

A circular issued by the Commissioners of the Treasury, dated September 26th, 1834, formed the supplement to this law. This document repeated what we have just said, viz., that all public receipts, from whatever source, must be sent as soon as received to the respective Receivers-General in London, who must pay the money each day to the Bank of England. The Bank must at once enter these sums to the credit of the accounts of the receivers and also of the account of the Exchequer. In this way the latter account ultimately includes the whole of the revenue of the United Kingdom.

[1] Those of the Auditor of the Exchequer, of the Tellers of the Exchequer and of the Clerk of the Pells. The officials holding these posts received unduly large salaries and the posts themselves, which had become mere sinecures, were of no use except as a provision for the relatives of ministers (Sir William Anson, *The Law and Custom of the Constitution,* Vol. II., pp. 330-331).

Such is the outline of the Act of 1834. This Act was the outcome of a series of events, such as the granting of the status of legal tender to Bank of England notes in 1833, the persistent increase in the taxes, which rendered necessary a more complicated system of control, and so on.

It must be noted in particular, that when the Act was passed many of its provisions were already in force and that in the main it only co-ordinated and united into a single Act various earlier measures.

(c)—*Modifications made in the Act of* 1834.—*Present Position of the Matter.*

The Act of 1834 was modified by that of 1866 (29-30 Vict., c. 39), which in the first place established the office of the Comptroller and Auditor-General of his Majesty's Exchequer, which official took the place of the old Comptroller-General and of the Commissioners for auditing the public accounts. It also provided that the Commissioners of the Customs[1] and of the Inland Revenue and the Postmaster-General should pay in to the Bank their respective receipts, and that the Bank should enter them to the account of the Exchequer. These payments were to be notified daily to the Comptroller-General.

All the money thus credited to the Exchequer must be regarded as a general fund out of which the Comptroller and Auditor-General can order transfers to enable accounts to be opened with the various officials, whose business it is to make payments in connection with the public offices.

Four times a year the Treasury draws up a scheme of the receipts forming the "consolidated fund"[2] for the following

[1] For the Customs see also Statute 1876, c. 36.

[2] What is the exact explanation of the term "Consolidated Fund"? Since 1786 the English Budget has been divided into two parts, the one consisting of what may be called the permanent grants, the due payment of which is authorised by Parliament from time to time, but which are entirely in the hands of the Chancellor of the Exchequer as regards all details of time and method of collection; this first section of the Budget forms the "Consolidated Fund." The other part consists, on the contrary, of payments voted annually and thus remaining under the direct periodical control of Parliament; this section is known as the Annual Supply. See Alphæus Todd, *Parliamentary Government of England*, Vol. I., pp. 733-737.

quarter and the expenses to be paid out of these funds during the same period. If the receipts are insufficient to cover the expenses, the Comptroller and Auditor-General notifies the amount of the deficit to the Bank, which is authorised to make advances up to the sum indicated at the request of the Treasury. The principal and interest of these advances are paid out of the receipts forming the consolidated funds for the next quarter.

II.—The Management of the Expenditure.

The administration of the expenditure was definitely organised in 1848, but as early as 1817 certain payments were undertaken by the Bank of England.

The Act of 1848[1] (11 and 12 Vict., c. 55) abolished the various officials hitherto entrusted with the paying out of money, and substituted a single official, his Majesty's Paymaster-General.

As regards the Bank, it was decided that the different sums entered to the accounts of the officials thus suppressed should be transferred to the recently opened account of the Paymaster-General. In order to ensure complete control, it is provided that the person making a payment to the Bank must first be authorised to do so by the Paymaster-General.

All the accounts held by the Bank in the name of the Paymaster-General must be regarded, as has been already stated with regard to the Exchequer account, as a general fund to be used in the payment of current expenses.

The Paymaster-General has also to send to the Commissioners of the Treasury a weekly statement of the condition of his account with the Bank, and each month he must submit detailed accounts to them.

In order that its dealings with the Paymaster-General may be as clear as possible, the Bank keeps two supply accounts, in which it enters all sums which have to be placed to the credit of the Paymaster.

The first of these is called the Exchequer credit account,

[1] This law was supplemented by a circular issued by the Commissioners of the Treasury, dated December 22, 1848.

and represents all the credits granted to the Paymaster-General out of the account of the Comptroller-General of the Exchequer. The second is called the Paymaster-General's cash account and in this are entered all other sums credited to the Paymaster-General by the Bank.

No cheque or order for payment can be drawn on these accounts; such payments are managed by daily transfers of sums to two so-called "working accounts," viz., the "drawing account," or the current account for cheques, and the "bills account," or the current account for bills. This transfer of sums to the "working accounts" is made through orders from the Paymaster-General. The amount of such transfers must not exceed that of the payments for the day.

The control of expenditure is as important as that of the receipts. The Comptroller-General exercises a checking control: by comparing the accounts of the Paymaster-General stating the various transfers that he orders, with the daily returns made by the Bank of its own transfers, the progress of the expenditure can be continually supervised. Subsequent control is carried on by verification of the warrants, cheques and bills which have run out and by the examination of the various returns. In addition, it should be noted that a clear distinction is made between the supplying of the funds to be used in the payment of the various public expenses and the actual employment of these funds.

(*b*)—The Management of the National Debt.

A national debt consists of two portions, the permanent and the floating debt. We will consider these in turn.

I.—*The Bank of England and the Administration of the Permanent Debt.*

Before the English debt was consolidated in 1751, the interest was paid by the Exchequer; at that date the Bank first undertook the administration of the national debt.[1]

[1] See above, p. 153.

After the reorganisation of the Exchequer[1] the payment of the expenses connected with the debt were managed by the Commissioners for the reduction of the national debt. The interest is paid out of the consolidated fund. When it happened that this account was not large enough for the purpose, the difference was met by the issue of special Exchequer bills called deficiency bills. In 1866 an analogous but simpler plan was adopted and deficiency advances were substituted for these bills, which advances must be refunded in the following quarter.

The Bank is not only entrusted with the payment of the interest on the debt, it also acts as intermediary between the Treasury and the public with respect to the business of actual administration of the national debt. Thus it receives payments direct from the subscribers and enters their names in the "*Journal*" and opens special accounts to their credit in the "*Grand Livre*" of the national debt. Subsequently it manages the various formalities of transfer which may be required through stock-brokers and bill-brokers. To these different transactions, M. Noel[2] remarks, it devotes an enormous area containing about 1,700,000 registers, which are kept up to date by more than 400 clerks.

What is paid for all these services? Since 1892[3] the Bank has received from the Government as indemnity for the expenses of administering the national debt: (1) £325 a year on every million pounds up to £500,000,000; (2) £100 a year only for every million in excess of this sum. Thus the total indemnity amounts to about £160,000. Formerly

[1] For further details as to the administration of the debt before 1834 see Lawson, p. 184, and Martinuzzi, p. 130.

[2] *Op. cit.*, p. 39.

[3] Before this date the Bank was paid a much larger sum. At first the indemnity was £340 per million up to £600,000,000; beyond this amount the commission was only £300. Afterwards it was lowered on a similar plan to £300 and £150 respectively.—*Bulletin de statistique et de Législation comparée*, 1892, Vol. XXXII.

The Act of 1892 provided for a fresh reduction of the indemnity paid for the administration of the national debt, but, on the other hand, this Act increased the commission which the Bank received for the issue of Treasury bills. See below, p. 401.

it came to not less than £200,000, and even, in still earlier times, £250,000.

In France the English system was formerly imitated. The Bank of France was entrusted with the payment of the interest on the national debt and with the management of the business connected with its redemption; for this it received a commission of 1½ per cent. It was considered with reason that this commission was too high, and, after largely reducing it and converting it into a fixed rent, the management of the national debt was finally restored to the Government.[1]

II.—*The Bank of England and the Administration of the Floating Debt (Issue, Circulation and Redemption of Exchequer Bills and Bonds and of Treasury Bills).*

One of the most important of the services rendered by the Bank of England to the Government has been the circulation of Exchequer bills.[2]

An account of the manner in which this used to be done is given in the evidence of Abraham Newland, the chief cashier of the Bank of England, before the Committee of Secrecy on March 28th, 1797.[3]

When the Exchequer was re-constituted in 1834, a Comptroller-General was appointed, as we have seen, and the duty of preparing, issuing and numbering the Exchequer bills devolved on him. But the Act of 1866, which consolidated

[1] Dartiguenave, pp. 157-158. In 1897 M. Guillemet proposed to hand over this business to the Bank once more, but this time without payment. It was rightly thought that such a heavy charge could not be imposed on the Bank without indemnity and that if, on the other hand, it was necessary to pay an indemnity, it would be better to leave the matter in the hands of the Government, which had organised it economically enough. We may note, however, that in consequence of an Act of 1897 (art. 8 and 9), the Bank of France has to cash gratuitously for the benefit of the Treasury, both in Paris and in the provinces, the bearer coupons of the French *Rentes* and the bills of the French Treasury. The Bank of France also helps gratuitously in the issue of treasury bills.

[2] The Bank undertook this circulation in 1709 (see above, p. 122). It will be remembered that the first Exchequer Bills were issued by Montague in 1696.

[3] Compare Lawson, p. 167. With regard to the somewhat original personality of Newland see Stephens' notice at the end of his *Bibliography*, pp. 167-173.

and amended all the earlier laws on this matter, provided that in future all Exchequer bills and bonds should be prepared and paid at the Bank.

The Act of 1866 distinguishes exchequer bills and exchequer bonds. The difference between the two is the following: the Exchequer bonds, which were first introduced by Gladstone in 1853, are issued for a definite period of time, generally for three years, and bear interest at a fixed rate, whilst the interest on the Exchequer bills, which is determined and published every quarter by the Treasury, varies according to the rate of interest prevailing on the market at the time.

In addition to Exchequer bills and Exchequer bonds, there are also Treasury bills, issued for the first time in 1877. These new bills only differ from Exchequer bills—which they are gradually tending to replace entirely—in that they are issued for a maximum period of twelve months, and generally for a much shorter time.

The business of the Bank is the same with regard to all these different securities. Consequently it receives a uniform payment: for the issue, circulation and redemption of the various bills and bonds it is paid at the rate of £200[1] for every million pounds in bills or bonds in existence on the first of December in each year, on which day the payment in question is calculated.

[1] This sum was increased from £100 to £200 by the Act of 1892, which reduced the indemnity received by the Bank for the administration of the national debt.

In France, since the Act passed in 1897 (art. 8), the Bank shares in the business of issuing Treasury bills, but this service is unpaid. This arrangement, moreover, does not seem to be a very useful one; the expenses of issue are not diminished thereby, because the Bank only serves as intermediary and in actual fact the bills can easily be floated without its assistance. In 1901, when bills to the value of 589,342,266 francs were issued by the Treasury, the Bank of France only received 13,647,000 francs in subscriptions (Dartiguenave, p. 152).

CONCLUSION.

THE history of the Bank of England, the relation of which has occupied these two volumes, has been admirably summarised in a few lines, which we ask leave to quote here.[1]

"The Bank of England, which is now the most celebrated bank in the world, did not make its first appearance, like a second Minerva, invincible and completely armed. Its birth was heralded by long-continued misfortunes and its history is marked by romantic incidents and dramatic adventures, intimately connected with the political history of England. In this respect the development of the Bank is in no way different from the evolution and completion of all other social and political institutions in England. Their foundations have been laid piece by piece at the dictates of practical needs, instead of being planned as a whole according to abstract principles. And on these foundations the buildings themselves have been practically raised, curious in form, no doubt, and irregular, but remarkable in their solidity, imposing in their appearance and excellent in their practical working."

The accuracy and insight of these observations are easily demonstrated by the account of the circumstances under which the Bank was founded and a recollection of the slight degree of resemblance which, from the outset, existed between it and other modern national banks.

In the first place, the Bank of England, founded by a Scotchman, Paterson, under the patronage of a foreign prince, William III., had no monopoly of issue. Its

[1] These lines, whose force and vividness is much weakened by translation, are quoted from an article published in the Greek paper, *Néa Himéra* (No. for September 8/21, 1901), at the time of the publication of the first edition of a portion of the present work. The article was written by an eminent authority, whose identity will be easily recognised by many in spite of his anonymity.

original charter merely allowed it to circulate notes up to the value of its capital, which capital was lent in a lump sum to the Government. Not only then had the Bank no monopoly, but the holders of its notes had none of the modern guarantees of conversion, such, in particular, as the existence of a metallic reserve representing a fixed proportion of the issue.

The first notes issued were much more analogous to treasury bills than to the present bank notes. They were not legal tender, but, on the other hand, they bore interest which made them circulate more easily, though it led to fluctuations in their value.

Gradually the Bank secured a monopoly of issue, at first limited to London and its neighbourhood, then extended in 1844 to the whole of England; by degrees, too, its notes acquired their modern form; they were not made legal tender until 1833.

Compared with that of the Bank of France, the existence of the Bank of England has been remarkably agitated. Hated by some, passionately supported by others, developing in a country still hardly ripe for public freedom, whose inhabitants were thrown by the thirst for gain into the maddest of speculations, the "Old Lady of Threadneedle Street" passed a stormy youth, literally crammed with romantic adventures and dramatic experiences. Her maturity was hardly more peaceful and it is only in recent years that she has known tranquillity.

From 1694 to 1870 twenty-five years have never passed without some serious danger threatening the Bank of England. Twice over (in 1696 and 1797) the Bank was forced to suspend cash payments—on the first occasion owing to the confusion in the metallic currency, on the second owing to that in the paper currency. At other times there were "runs," often produced by political troubles or commercial crises resulting from insane speculation, which shook the institution to its very foundations. It will be remembered that it was at the conclusion of one of these crises, a crisis which lasted for three years, and during which the Bank of England had to seek assistance from the Bank of France, that the Act of 1844 was passed—that Act which largely modified the character of the Bank, deprived it of its discretionary powers in the matter of issue and reduced it, by the formation of an issue department working automatically, to the position of a great banking house, with the Government for its principal customer and the other banks for practically its only other customers.

What explanation can be given, considering that their positions are now very similar, of the widely differing histories of the Banks of France and of England?

In the first place it will be said that the contrast is owing to the dates of their respective foundations. The Bank of France had the benefit of the experience gained in the past. At the beginning of the last century the principles of political economy were beginning to be recognised, Governments were better instructed and hence less likely to be attracted by the deceptive dreams of a Hugh Chamberlain or of a Law.[1]

No doubt; but, unfortunately, this explanation, however true it may be with regard to the periods when the Banks were founded, will not serve to account for the events of the 19th century, during which the Bank of France was able to withstand the most serious revolutions and the most cruel national disasters, whilst from 1819 to 1870 the Bank of England came to the verge of bankruptcy every ten years. Another explanation must be sought, and I believe that it will be found rather in the different characteristics of the two nations than in the different organisations of the two Banks.

The French nation is prudent and economical, the English nation is enterprising and speculative; the one grows rich through saving, the other through business. What is true of the individuals is true also of the commercial communities. When interest goes down the English commercial world, unable to reduce its mode of life, deserts its usual business in favour of more profitable, but, on that very

[1] Besides this, it must not be forgotten that the *Caisse d'Escompte*, founded in 1776, collapsed during the financial troubles of the Revolution, and that the *Banque Générale* founded by Law in 1716, only survived for four years.

account, more risky undertakings. If the decline in the rate of interest is great and seems likely to continue, John Bull, who according to that old saying which we have already quoted, "can stand many things, but he cannot stand 2 per cent.," rushes into speculation. But in England, as elsewhere, speculation leads to disaster and ultimately to crises, the brunt of which must in the end be borne by the central bank. This has been the history of all the great crises which have occurred during the century that is just completed.

These crises might, it would seem, have been averted by the accumulation of a very large stock of specie. For, as Lord Goschen has remarked, the thing needed above everything in a crisis is cash. But to amass money and to forego its use in ordinary times involves a heavy expense; and the occasional risks of a crisis have been found preferable. Even nowadays the tendency to prefer the pursuit of a gain which, while involving some risks, is yet immediate, to a troublesome prudence, has not altogether disappeared. It is true that such a tendency is no longer to be traced in the administration of the Bank of England, but when it was proposed with entire justice, that the joint-stock banks should share in the formation of a metallic reserve, the prompt reply was, that however wise such a policy might be, it must mean a decrease in the shareholders' dividends, and this answer was sufficient to put a stop to further discussion.

Another characteristic feature is that in England no attempt is made to prevent or even to regulate the export of gold. This exposes the country to obvious dangers, but, on the other hand, it has made London, the only free market for gold, into the financial capital of the world. The English consider that this advantage fully makes up for the risks to which they are exposed, whilst the other European nations envy without daring to imitate them.

In conclusion, it may be said that to write the history of the Bank of England is, in some degree, to attempt to write the commercial and financial history of the English nation. For a foreigner this is not the least of the difficulties involved in the undertaking; as we observed at the outset,[1] this necessity of following the history of England, besides demanding studies of a sufficiently complicated kind, adds many confusions to the narrative of the events which concern the Bank of England. Under these circumstances, to give to our account that quality of unity so essentially desirable, demanded historical qualifications which we do not possess, whilst the second volume has needed a practical knowledge of business which also we do not possess. For want of this it has been difficult to arrive at definite conclusions and we have been obliged to give somewhat hesitating answers to the questions which we felt bound to raise.[2]

This is a fact which we did not realise at the outset, but only later on, when we had already thrown ourselves into the task with an eagerness which so often goes with inexperience, and when the work was already far advanced. The kindly reader will think more of the trouble taken than of the result obtained, and will perhaps consider that, in spite of its defects, this work has at least the merit of having prepared the ground and made the way easy for studies which shall be really worthy of the great institution whose history it has been our honour to write.

[1] See above, pp. 10-12.

[2] We are somewhat comforted by finding similar hesitation persisting among many persons whose theoretical training and practical knowledge of business were all that could be desired. Often during the past four years we have asked English economists and bankers for their opinions on Robert Peel's Act and on the reforms in it which had been proposed. It has been but seldom that we have received a decisive answer. One of those questioned, bolder than the rest, ultimately confessed that he thought the Act of 1844 "a bit clumsy"—a truth which we had already partly suspected.

On the other hand, I have frequently heard foreigners solve the problem without any hesitation. Unfortunately I have also noticed that this excess of certainty has not always proceeded from an excess of knowledge.

SUPPLEMENT I.

MEMORANDUM ON BANKING SUBMITTED TO THE CABINET BY SIR ROBERT PEEL.

Reprinted from "Sir Robert Peel from his private papers," by Charles Stuart Parker. 3 vols., 1891-99. By permission of the Publisher, Mr. John Murray.

THE chief legislative measure of 1844 was the well-known Act which after more than half a century still governs our currency and banking.

In 1819 Sir Robert Peel had passed a Bill establishing the principle that all bank notes should be payable on demand in gold. But five-and-twenty years' experience had proved that in commercial crises legal obligation to pay did not ensure actual payment in gold. County banks had failed to cash their notes, and even the Bank of England "had been exposed to great danger" in 1825, and again in 1839. On this account the House of Commons had appointed in 1840, and in 1841, Committees which had taken important evidence, but as yet with no result. Sir Robert Peel now took the work in hand. In a paper submitted to the Cabinet he shows that there are "three courses open for consideration," and presents "a general outline of the arguments for and against each of them."

CABINET MEMORANDUM (EXTRACT).

I.—Maintenance of the leading principles of the present system.

For this course it may be contended that we may safely calculate upon the success of a proposal to that effect. Many interests and many prejudices would be in favour of it; sufficient probably to command a large Parliamentary majority.

Against the course it would be argued that the system is a dangerous one; that the Bank of England has very imperfect control over the issues of paper: that the nominal convertibility of paper into gold, where there is unlimited competition as to issue, does not ensure the value and practical convertibility of the paper; that the Bank has more than once been exposed to great danger in respect to the exhaustion of its treasures, and for the purpose of averting it has been compelled to make sudden and violent contractions of the currency; that the effect even of such contractions has not immediately told upon other issuers of paper; that they have occasionally increased their circulation at the time when the Bank was taking measures for the reduction of its own, and by such counteraction of the views and measures of the Bank have aggravated the ultimate pressure upon the country.

It will be strongly contended in argument that it is discreditable for the Executive Government, with the experience of the past before it, to rely upon mere numerical majorities, upon the prejudices and interests of their supporters, and sanction and advise for another ten years the continuance of a system which they cannot in argument defend.

II.—The next course is the opposite extreme, the prohibition for the future of all issues of paper payable to bearer on demand, by the Bank of England and every other bank whatever.

That course proceeds upon the assumption that the issue of money is a prerogative of Sovereignty; that paper convertible into gold at the standard price at the will of the holder partakes of all the properties of coin, is equally the measure of value, and the common instrument of exchange; that it is the duty of the Sovereign to protect the holders of such paper from the injurious consequences of its discredit; and that any profit which may be derived from the issue of such paper justly belongs to the State.

The effect of the adoption of this course would be to make a complete separation between the various departments of banking and the department for the issue of money. By money I mean coin, and notes payable to bearer, convertible on demand into coin.

A Board would be constituted independent of the Government but responsible to Parliament, charged with the issue of paper, convertible into gold, to be a legal tender. There would be no necessary interference with banks, excepting so far as regards the power of issue. Government paper would be supplied by the public department of issue to the Bank of England and to other banks, and they would use this paper in purely banking transactions, in the same way in which they use their own paper.

In favour of this plan it would be contended that it is in conformity with strict principle; that it deals impartially with all interests, and is capable of application to all parts of the United Kingdom; that it shows no favour to any one powerful corporation like the Bank of England; that, if it interferes with private interests, it interferes with all in an equal degree, and on the broad intelligible principle of interference for the public good. If compensation to such private interests be due, it may be made more equitably and more easily under this plan than under any other, by giving to the existing issuers of paper an advantage over others in respect to the terms on which an amount of Government paper equal to the average amount of their past issues should be supplied to them.

If we were about to establish in a new state of society a new system of currency, it would be very difficult to contest theoretically the principles on which this plan is founded or the equity of the practical application of them.

The chief arguments against the plan are the risk of applying at once to three constituent parts of a great Empire, in each of which there is a different system of currency, any unbending uniform rule; the impolicy of disregarding altogether the feelings and habits that long prescription has interwoven with the modes of transacting business, and of rejecting the use of every instrument which is ready made to your hand; the presumption of concluding in a matter of so much uncertainty as this that you can infallibly command the public confidence for a perfectly novel and exclusive paper currency, and the tremendous hazard you incur in the event of failure. It will be contended, and not without reason, that however safe for commercial purposes such a system of currency may be, yet that a paper circulation resting altogether on Government security—a purely Government paper—is much more likely in times of political danger to be distrusted and discredited than that paper for which it would be the substitute.

Of this second method of solving the difficulties of the question it may, I think, be justly observed that many persons who, if they were responsible for the conduct of public affairs, would shrink from the proposal of it as a practical measure, will make abundant use of it in argument, in contrast with any other measure, for the purpose of showing its superior merit, on account of its conformity with strict principle, and the impartiality of its application to all interests which it may affect.

III.—The third and remaining course is an intermediate one between complete acquiescence in the present system and radical subversion of it. It would consist in enactments of which the following is an outline:—

Prohibit for the future the establishment in any part of the United Kingdom of any new bank of issue.

Separate the department of issue of the Bank of England from every other department.

Keep a separate account of the profits of issue. Let it be understood that the whole of these profits shall be accounted for to the Government; that they shall be applied in the first instance to the substitution generally of Bank of England paper, by holding out inducements to existing banks of issue to transact their banking business with this paper in preference to their own.

Require constant publicity of all accounts connected with the department of issue; the quantity of bullion, the amount of notes, the amount of securities.

Permit the continuance of existing banks, either permanently or for a definite period of years; but claim the right, if they are banks of issue, of subjecting them equally with the Bank of England to strict regulations as to the exercise of their privilege of issue.

Insist upon publicity of their transactions in such a form as shall enable the public to judge of the confidence which may be placed in them.

Deal in the first instance with England only, excepting in so far as relates to prohibiting new banks of issue.

Assume that the probable effect of regulations of this kind will be to encourage existing banks of issue in England to make voluntary arrangements for the substitution of Bank of England paper for their own; and that the ultimate effect will be such a degree of control by the Bank over the general issues of the country as to enable it to regulate the currency by gradual contraction and gradual expansion according to the state of the exchange.

The argument in favour of this plan it that it violates no existing right; that it takes precautions against future abuses; that it ensures by gradual means the establishment of a safe system of currency.

It is impossible not to foresee that it will be encountered by a formidable combination. It will be resisted by those who are for the rigid application of sound principle without reference to times or circumstances, and who think that all paper issues should proceed directly and exclusively from the Government; by those of the opposite opinion, who think there ought to be unlimited competition as to issue, provided there be the security of the immediate convertibility into gold; by those who charge the Bank of England with being the chief cause of the past derangements of the currency and consider that on that account it is entitled to no favour; by the country bankers and those whom the country banks can influence.

The Cabinet must weigh deliberately the several considerations which present themselves. My advice is that they should determine to propose the course which they may conscientiously believe to reconcile in the greatest degree the qualities of being consistent with sound principle and suited to the present condition of society, and should encounter the risk which it is impossible not to foresee must attend any proposal for guarding against eventual dangers at the expense of personal interests and in disregard of private feelings.

The Cabinet adopted, as Peel intended, the third course, in 1844 for England and Wales, and in 1845 for Scotland and Ireland. There was no serious opposition. His own speech in introducing his Bill has been well called "the Parliamentary foundation of all sound thinking upon the subject, and the most authoritative exposition of the true principles of the national currency."

SUPPLEMENT II.

THE BANK CHARTER ACT, 1844.

7 & 8 VICTORIA, CAP. XXXII.

An Act to regulate the Issue of Bank Notes, and for giving to the Governor and Company of the Bank of England certain Privileges for a limited Period. [19th July 1844.]

. . . . I.—That from and after the Thirty-first Day of August One thousand eight hundred and forty-four the Issue of Promissory Notes of the Governor and Company of the Bank of England, payable on Demand, shall be separated and thenceforth kept wholly distinct from the General Banking Business of the said Governor and Company; and the Business of and relating to such Issue shall be thenceforth conducted and carried on by the said Governor and Company in a separate Department to be called "The Issue Department of the Bank of England," subject to the Rules and Regulations hereinafter contained; and it shall be lawful for the Court of Directors of the said Governor and Company, if they shall think fit, to appoint a Committee or Committees of Directors for the Conduct and Management of such Issue Department of the Bank of England, and from Time to Time to remove the Members, and define, alter, and regulate the Constitution and Powers of such Committee, as they shall think fit, subject to any Byelaws, Rules, or Regulations which may be made for that Purpose: Provided nevertheless, that the said Issue Department shall always be kept separate and distinct from the Banking Department of the said Governor and Company.

II.—There shall be transferred, appropriated, and set apart by the said Governor and Company to the Issue Department of the Bank of England Securities to the Value of Fourteen million Pounds, whereof the Debt due by the Public to the said Governor and Company shall be and be deemed a Part; and there shall also at the same Time be transferred, appropriated, and set apart by the said Governor and Company to the said Issue Department so much of the Gold Coin and Gold and Silver Bullion then held by the Bank of England as shall not be required by the Banking Department thereof; and thereupon there shall be delivered out of the said Issue Department into the said Banking Department of the Bank of England such an Amount of

Bank of England Notes as, together with the Bank of England Notes then in circulation, shall be equal to the aggregate Amount of the Securities, Coin, and Bullion so transferred to the said Issue Department of the Bank of England; and the whole Amount of Bank of England Notes then in circulation, including those delivered to the Banking Department of the Bank of England as aforesaid, shall be deemed to be issued on the Credit of such Securities, Coin, and Bullion so appropriated and set apart to the said Issue Department; and from thenceforth it shall not be lawful for the said Governor and Company to increase the Amount of Securities for the Time being in the said Issue Department, save as herein-after is mentioned, but it shall be lawful for the said Governor and Company to diminish the Amount of such Securities, and again to increase the same to any Sum not exceeding in the whole the Sum of Fourteen million Pounds, and so from Time to Time as they shall see Occasion; and from and after such Transfer and Appropriation to the said Issue Department as aforesaid it shall not be lawful for the said Governor and Company to issue Bank of England Notes, either into the Banking Department of the Bank of England, or to any Persons or Person whatsoever, save in exchange for other Bank of England Notes, or for Gold Coin or for Gold or Silver Bullion received or purchased for the said Issue Department under the Provisions of this Act, or in exchange for Securities acquired and taken in the said Issue Department under the Provisions herein contained: Provided always, that it shall be lawful for the said Governor and Company in their Banking Department to issue all such Bank of England Notes as they shall at any Time receive from the said Issue Department or otherwise, in the same Manner in all respects as such Issue would be lawful to any other Person or Persons.

III.—It shall not be lawful for the Bank of England to retain in the Issue Department of the said Bank at any One Time an Amount of Silver Bullion exceeding One Fourth Part of the Gold Coin and Bullion at such Time held by the Bank of England in the Issue Department.

IV.—All Persons shall be entitled to demand from the Issue Department of the Bank of England Bank of England Notes in exchange for Gold Bullion, at the Rate of Three Pounds Seventeen Shillings and Ninepence per Ounce of Standard Gold: Provided always, that the said Governor and Company shall in all Cases be entitled to require such Gold Bullion to be melted and assayed by Persons approved by the said Governor and Company, at the Expense of the Parties tendering such Gold Bullion.

V.—Provided always, That if any Banker who on the Sixth Day of May One thousand eight hundred and forty-four was issuing his own Bank Notes shall cease to issue his own Bank

Notes, it shall be lawful for Her Majesty in Council, at any Time after the Cessation of such Issue, upon the Application of the said Governor and Company, to authorize and empower the said Governor and Company to increase the Amount of Securities in the said Issue Department beyond the total Sum or Value of Fourteen million Pounds, and thereupon to issue additional Bank of England Notes to an Amount not exceeding such increased Amount of Securities specified in such Order in Council, and so from Time to Time: Provided always, that such increased Amount of Securities specified in such Order in Council shall in no Case exceed the Proportion of Two Thirds the Amount of Bank Notes which the Banker so ceasing to issue may have been authorized to issue under the Provision of this Act; and every such Order in Council shall be published in the next succeeding London Gazette.

VI.—An Account of the Amount of Bank of England Notes issued by the Issue Department of the Bank of England, and of Gold Coin and of Gold and Silver Bullion respectively, and of Securities in the said Issue Department, and also an Account of the Capital Stock, and the Deposits, and of the Money and Securities belonging to the said Governor and Company in the Banking Department of the Bank of England, on some Day in every Week to be fixed by the Commissioners of Stamps and Taxes, shall be transmitted by the said Governor and Company weekly to the said Commissioners in the Form prescribed . . . . and shall be published by the said Commissioners in the next succeeding London Gazette in which the same may be conveniently inserted.

VII.—The Bank of England shall be released and discharged from the Payment of any Stamp Duty, or Composition in respect of Stamp Duty, upon or in respect of their Promissory Notes payable to Bearer on Demand, and all such Notes shall thenceforth be and continue free and wholly exempt from all Liability to any Stamp Duty whatsoever.

VIII.—Requiring the Bank to allow to the public £180,000 per annum, repealed by 37 and 38 Victoria, cap. 96.

IX.—In case, under the Provisions herein-before contained, the Securities held in the said Issue Department of the Bank of England shall at any Time be increased beyond the total Amount of Fourteen million Pounds, then and in each and every Year in which the same shall happen, and so long as such Increase shall continue, the said Governor and Company shall, in addition to the said annual Sum of One hundred and eighty thousand Pounds, make a further Payment or Allowance to the Public, equal in Amount to the net Profit derived in the said Issue Department during the current Year from such additional Securities, after deducting the Amount of the Expenses occasioned by the additional Issue during the same Period, which

Expenses shall include the Amount of any and every Composition or Payment to be made by the said Governor and Company to any Banker in consideration of the Discontinuance at any Time hereafter of the Issue of Bank Notes by such Banker; . . . . .

X.—No Person other than a Banker who on the Sixth Day of May One thousand eight hundred and forty-four was lawfully issuing his own Bank Notes shall make or issue Bank Notes in any Part of the United Kingdom.

XI.—It shall not be lawful for any Banker to draw, accept, make, or issue in England or Wales, any Bill of Exchange or Promissory Note or Engagement for the Payment of Money payable to Bearer on Demand, or to borrow, owe, or take up, in England or Wales, any Sums or Sum of Money on the Bills or Notes of such Banker payable to Bearer on Demand, save and except that it shall be lawful for any Banker who was on the Sixth Day of May One thousand eight hundred and forty-four carrying on the Business of a Banker in England or Wales, and was then lawfully issuing, in England or Wales, his own Bank Notes, under the Authority of a Licence to that Effect, to continue to issue such Notes to the Extent and under the Conditions herein-after mentioned, but not further or otherwise; and the Right of any Company or Partnership to continue to issue such Notes shall not be in any Manner prejudiced or affected by any Change which may hereafter take place in the personal Composition of such Company or Partnership, either by the Transfer of any Shares or Share therein, or by the Admission of any new Partner or Member thereto, or by the Retirement of any present Partner or Member therefrom: Provided always, that it shall not be lawful for any Company or Partnership now consisting of only Six or less than Six Persons to issue Bank Notes at any Time after the Number of Partners therein shall exceed Six in the whole.

XII.—If any Banker in any Part of the United Kingdom who after the passing of this Act shall be entitled to issue Bank Notes shall become bankrupt, or shall cease to carry on the Business of a Banker, or shall discontinue the Issue of Bank Notes, either by Agreement with the Governor and Company of the Bank of England or otherwise, it shall not be lawful for such Banker at any Time thereafter to issue any such Notes.

XIII.—Every Banker claiming under this Act to continue to issue Bank Notes in England or Wales shall, ... give Notice in Writing to the Commissioners of Stamps and Taxes at their Head Office in London of such Claim, ... then the said Commissioners shall proceed to ascertain the average Amount of the Bank Notes of such Banker which were in circulation during the said Period of Twelve Weeks preceding the Twenty-seventh Day of April last; . . . . and it shall be lawful for every such Banker to continue to issue his own Bank Notes after the passing of this Act: Provided nevertheless, that such Banker shall not at any Time after the Tenth Day of October One thousand eight hundred and forty-four have in circulation upon the Average of a Period of Four Weeks, to be ascertained as herein-after mentioned, a greater Amount of Notes than the Amount so certified.

XIV.—Provided always, and be it enacted, that if it shall be made to appear to the Commissioners of Stamps and Taxes that any Two or more Banks have, by written Contract or Agreement . . . . become united within the Twelve Weeks next preceding such Twenty-seventh Day of April as aforesaid, it shall be lawful for the said Commissioners to ascertain the average Amount of the Notes of each such Bank in the Manner herein-before directed, and to certify the average Amount of the Notes of the Two or more Banks so united as the Amount which the united Bank shall thereafter be authorized to issue, subject to the Regulations of this Act.

XV.—The Commissioners of Stamps and Taxes shall, at the Time of certifying to any Banker such Particulars as they are herein-before required to certify, also publish a Duplicate of their Certificate thereof in the next succeeding London Gazette. . . . .

XVI.—In case it shall be made to appear to the Commissioners of Stamps and Taxes, at any Time hereafter, that any two or more Banks . . . . have, by written Contract or Agreement . . . . become united subsequently to the passing of this Act, it shall be lawful to the said Commissioners, upon the Application of such united Bank, to certify, in manner herein-before mentioned, the aggregate of the Amounts of Bank Notes which such separate Banks were previously authorized to issue, and so from Time to Time; and every such Certificate shall be published in manner herein-before directed; and from and after such Publication the Amount therein stated shall be and be deemed to be the Limit of the Amount of Bank Notes which such united Bank may have in circulation: Provided always, that it shall not be lawful for any such united Bank to issue Bank Notes at any Time after the Number of Partners therein shall exceed Six in the whole.

Sections 17, 18, 19, 20, 21, 22 state the administrative conditions which must be fulfilled by all private banks continuing to issue notes. Sections 23, 24, 25, 26 state the conditions under which the right to issue notes may be taken over by the Bank.

XXVII.—The Bank of England shall have and enjoy such exclusive Privilege of Banking as is given by this Act, upon such Terms and Conditions, and subject to the Termination thereof at such Time and in such Manner, as is by this Act provided and specified; . . . . subject nevertheless to Redemption upon the Terms and Conditions following; (that is to say,) at any Time upon Twelve Months Notice to be given after the First Day of August One thousand eight hundred and fifty-five, and upon Repayment by Parliament to the said Governor and Company or their Successors of the Sum of Eleven million fifteen thousand and one hundred Pounds, being the Debt now due from the Public to the said Governor and Company, without any Deduction, Discount, or Abatement whatsoever, ... then and in such Case, and not till then, the said exclusive Privileges of Banking granted by this Act shall cease and determine at the Expiration of such Notice of Twelve Months; and any Vote or Resolution of the House of Commons, signified under the Hand of the Speaker of the said House in Writing, and delivered at the public Office of the said Governor and Company, shall be deemed and adjudged to be a sufficient Notice.

SUPPLEMENT III.

PLAN FOR THE ESTABLISHMENT OF A NATIONAL BANK.

By DAVID RICARDO, M.P. 1824.

THE Bank of England performs two operations of banking which are quite distinct and have no necessary connection with each other: it issues a paper currency as a substitute for a metallic one, and it advances money in the way of loan to merchants and others.

That these two operations of banking have no necessary connection will appear obvious from this—that they might be carried on by two separate bodies without the slightest loss of advantage, either to the country or to the merchants who receive accommodation from such loans.

Suppose the privilege of issuing paper money were taken away from the Bank and were in future to be exercised by the State only, subject to the same regulation to which the Bank is now liable of paying its notes on demand in specie, in what way would the national wealth be in the least impaired? We should then, as now, carry on all the traffic and commerce of the country with the cheap medium, paper money, instead of the dear medium, metallic money; and all the advantages which now flow from making this part of the national capital productive in the form of raw material, food, clothing, machinery and implements, instead of retaining it useless in the form of metallic money, would be equally secured.

The public, or the Government on behalf of the public, is indebted to the Bank in a sum of money larger than the whole amount of Bank notes in circulation; for the Government not only owes the Bank fifteen millions, its original capital, which is lent at 3 per cent. interest, but also many more millions which are advanced on Exchequer bills, on half-pay and pension annuities, and on other securities. It is evident, therefore, that if the Government itself were to be the sole issuer of paper money instead of borrowing it of the Bank, the only difference would be with respect to the interest: the Bank would no longer receive interest and the Government would no longer pay it; but all other classes in the community would be exactly in the same position in which they now stand. It is evident too that there would be just as much money in circulation, for it could make no difference in that respect whether the sixteen millions of paper money now circulating in London were issued by Government or by a banking corporation. The merchants could suffer no inconvenience from any want of facility in getting the usual advances made to them in the way of discount or in any other manner; for, first, the amount of these advances must essentially depend upon the amount of money in circulation, and that would be just the same as before; and secondly, of the amount in circulation the Bank would have precisely the same proportion, neither less nor more, to lend to the merchants.

If it be true, as I think I have clearly proved, that the advances made by the Bank to the Government exceed the whole amount of the notes of the Bank in circulation, it is evident that part of its advances to Government, as well as the whole of its loans to other persons, must be made from other funds possessed or at the disposal of the Bank, and which it would continue to possess after Government had discharged its debt to it, and after all its notes were withdrawn from circulation. Let it not then be said that the Bank charter, as far as regards the issuing of paper money, ought to be renewed for this reason, that if it be not the merchants will suffer inconvenience from being deprived of the usual facilities of borrowing, as I trust I have shown that their means of borrowing would be just as ample as before.

It may however be said that, if the Bank were deprived of that part of its business which consists in issuing paper money, it would have no motive to continue a joint-stock company and would agree on a dissolution of its partnership. I believe no such thing; it would still have profitable means of employing its own funds. But suppose I am wrong and that the company were dissolved, what inconvenience would commerce sustain from it? If the joint stock of the company be managed by a few directors chosen by the general body of proprietors, or if it be divided amongst the proprietors themselves and each share be managed by the individual to whom it belongs, will that make any difference in its real amount or in the efficacy with which it may be employed for commercial purposes? It is probable that in no case would it be managed by the individual proprietors, but that it would be collected in a mass or masses and managed with much more economy and skill than it is now managed by the Bank. A great deal too much stress has always been laid on the benefits which commerce derives from the accommodation afforded to merchants by the Bank. I believe it to be quite insignificant compared with that which is afforded by the private funds of individuals. We know that at the present moment the advances by the Bank to merchants on discount are of a very trifling amount, and we have abundant evidence to prove that at no time have they been great. The whole fund at the disposal of the Bank for the last thirty years is well known. It consisted of its own capital and savings, of the amount of deposits left with it by Government and by individuals who employed it as a banker. From this aggregate fund must be deducted the amount of cash and bullion in the coffers of the Bank, the amount of advances to the holders of receipts for the loans contracted for during each year, and the amount of advances to Government in every way. After making these deductions, the remainder only could have been devoted to commercial objects, and if it were ascertained, would, I am sure, be comparatively of a small amount.

From papers laid before Parliament in 1797, in which the Bank gave a number as unit and a scale of its discounts for different years, it was calculated by some ingenious individual, after comparing this scale with other documents also laid before Parliament, that the amount of money advanced in the way of discount to the merchants for a period of three years and a half previous to 1797, varied from two millions to £3,700,000. These are trifling amounts in such a country as this, and must bear a small proportion to the sum lent by individuals for similar purposes. In 1797 the advances to Government alone by the Bank, exclusive of its capital which was also lent to Government, were more than three times the amount of the advances to the whole body of merchants.

A Committee of the House of Commons was appointed last session of Parliament to inquire into the law of pledges and into the relation of consigners of goods from abroad to consignees. This Committee called before it Mr. Richardson, of the house of Richardson, Overend & Co., eminent discount brokers in the City. This gentleman was asked:—

"Q.—Are you not in the habit occasionally of discounting to a large extent bills of brokers and other persons given upon the security of goods deposited in their hands?

"A.—Very large.

"Q.—Have you not carried on the business of a bill broker and money agent to a very large extent, much beyond that of any other individual in this town?

"A.—I should think very much beyond.

"Q.—To the extent of some millions annually?

"A.—A great many; about twenty millions annually, sometimes more."

The evidence of Mr. Richardson satisfactorily proves, I think, the extent of transactions of this kind in which the Bank has no kind of concern. Can anyone doubt that if the Bank were to break up its establishment and divide its funds among the individual proprietors, the business of Mr. Richardson and of others who are in the same line would considerably increase?

On the one hand they would have more applications made to them for money on discount, on the other many who would have money to dispose of would apply to them to obtain employment for it. The same amount of money and no more would be employed in this branch of business, and if not employed by the Bank or by the individual proprietors if they had the management of their own funds, it would inevitably find its way, either by a direct or circuitous channel, to Mr. Richardson or to some other money agent, to be employed by him in promoting the commerce and upholding the trade of the country, for in no other way could these funds be made so productive to the parties to whom they would belong.

If the view which I have taken of this subject be a correct one, it appears that the commerce of the country would not be in the least impeded by depriving the Bank of England of the power of issuing paper money, provided an amount of such money equal to the Bank circulation was issued by Government, and that the sole effect of depriving the Bank of this privilege would be to transfer the profit which accrues from the interest of the money so issued from the Bank to Government.

There remains, however, one other objection to which the reader's attention is requested.

It is said that Government could not be safely entrusted with the power of issuing paper money; that it would most certainly abuse it; and that on any occasion when it was pressed for money to carry on a war it would cease to pay coin on demand for its notes, and from that moment the currency would become a forced Government paper. There would, I confess, be great danger of this if Government—that is to say, the Ministers—were themselves to be entrusted with the power of issuing paper money. But I propose to place this trust in the hands of Commissioners not removable from their official situation but by a vote of one or both Houses of Parliament. I propose also to prevent all intercourse between these Commissioners and Ministers by forbidding every species of money transaction between them. The Commissioners should never, on any pretence, lend money to Government, nor be in the slightest degree under its control or influence. Over Commissioners so entirely independent of them the Ministers would have much less power than they now possess over the Bank directors. Experience shows how little this latter body have been able to withstand the cajolings of Ministers, and how frequently they have been induced to increase their advances on Exchequer bills and Treasury bills at the very moment they were themselves declaring that it would be attended with the greatest risk to the stability of their establishment and to the public interest. From a perusal of the correspondence between the Government and the Bank previous to the stoppage of Bank payments in 1797, it will be seen that the Bank attributes the necessity of that measure (erroneously in this instance, I think) to the frequent and urgent demands for an increase of advances on the part of Government. I ask then whether the country would not possess a greater security against all such influence over the minds of the issuers of paper as would induce them to swerve from the strict line of their duty, if the paper money of the country were issued by Commissioners on the plan I have proposed, rather than by the Bank of England as at present constituted If Government wanted money it should be obliged to raise it in the legitimate way, by taxing the people, by the issue and sale of Exchequer bills, by funded loans, or by borrowing from any of the numerous banks which might exist in the country; but in no case should it be allowed to borrow from those who have the power of creating money.

If the funds of the Commissioners became so ample as to leave them a surplus which might be advantageously disposed of, let them go into the market and purchase publicly Government securities with it. If on the contrary it should become necessary for them to contract their issues without diminishing their stock of gold, let them sell their securities in the same way in the open market. By this regulation a trifling sacrifice would be made, amounting to the turn of the market which may be supposed to be gained by those whose business it is to employ their capital and skill in dealing in these securities, but in a question of this importance such a sacrifice is not worth considering. It must be recollected that from the great competition in this particular business, the turn of the market is reduced to a very small fraction, and that the amount of such transactions could never be great, as the circulation would be kept at its just level by allowing for a small contraction or extension of the treasure in coin and bullion in the coffers of the Commissioners. It would be only when, from the increasing wealth and prosperity of the country, the country required a permanently increased amount of circulation that it would be expedient to invest money in the purchase of securities paying interest, and only in a contrary case that a part of such securities would be required to be sold. Thus then we see that the most complete security could be obtained against the influence which, on a first and superficial view, it might be supposed Government would have over the issues of a National Bank, and that by organising such an establishment, all the interest which is now annually paid by Government to the Bank would become a part of the national resources.

I would propose, then, some such plan as the following for the establishment of a National Bank:—

1. Five Commissioners shall be appointed in whom the full power of issuing all the paper money of the country shall be exclusively vested.

2. On the expiration of the charter of the Bank of England in 1833 the Commissioners shall issue fifteen millions of paper money, the amount of the capital of the Bank lent to Government, with which that debt shall be discharged. From that time the annual interest of 3 per cent. shall cease and determine.

3. On the same day ten millions of paper money shall be employed by the Commissioners in the following manner:—With such parts of that sum as they may think expedient they shall purchase gold bullion of the bank or of other persons, and with the remainder, within six months of the day abovementioned, they shall redeem a part of the Government debt to the Bank on Exchequer bills. The Exchequer bills so redeemed shall thereafter remain at the disposal of the Commissioners.

4. The Bank shall be obliged with as little delay as convenient after the expiration of its charter, to redeem all its notes in circulation by the payment of them in the new notes issued by Government. It shall not pay them in gold, but shall be obliged to keep always a reserve of the new notes equal in amount to its own notes which may remain in circulation.

5. The notes of the Bank of England shall be current for six months after the expiration of the Bank charter, after which they shall no longer be received by Government in payment of the revenue.

7. Within six months after the expiration of the Bank charter the notes of the country banks shall cease to circulate, and the different banks which shall have issued them shall be under the same obligation as the Bank of England to pay them in Government notes. They shall have the privilege of paying their notes in gold coin if they prefer so to do.

8. For the greater security of the holders of Government notes residing in the country there shall be agents in the different towns, who shall be obliged on demand to verify the genuineness of the notes by affixing their signatures to them, after which such notes shall be exchangeable only in the district where they are so signed.

9. Notes issued in one district, or bearing the signature of an agent in one district, shall not be payable in any other; but on the deposit of any number of notes in the office of the district where they were originally issued or where they were signed, agreeably to the last regulation, a bill may be obtained on any other district payable in the notes of that district.

10. Notes issued in the country shall not be payable in coin in the country; but for such notes a bill may be obtained on London which will be paid in coin or in London notes at the option of the party presenting the bill in London.

11. Anyone depositing coin or London notes in the London office may obtain a bill payable in the notes of any other district, to be named at the time of obtaining the bill. And anyone

depositing coin in the London office may obtain London notes to an equal amount.

12. The Commissioners in London shall be obliged to buy any quantity of gold of standard fineness and exceeding one hundred ounces in weight that may be offered them, at a price not less than £3 17s. 6d. per ounce.

13. From the moment of the establishment of the National Bank the Commissioners shall be obliged to pay their notes and bills on demand in gold coin.

14. Notes of one pound shall be issued at the first establishment of the National Bank, and shall be given to anyone requiring them in exchange for notes of a larger amount if the person presenting them prefers such notes to coin. This regulation to continue in force only for one year as far as regards London, but to be a permanent one in all the country districts.

15. It must be well understood that in country districts the agents will neither be liable to give notes for coin nor coin for notes.

16. The Commissioners shall act as the general banker to all the public departments in the same manner as the Bank of England now acts, but they shall be precluded from filling the same office either to any corporation or to any individual whatever.

On the subject of the first regulation I have already spoken. The Commissioners should be, I think, five in number. They should have an adequate salary for the business which they would have to perform and superintend. They should be appointed by Government but not removable by Government.

The second regulation refers to the mode in which the new paper circulation should be substituted for the old. By the provision here made twenty-five millions of paper money will be issued. That sum will not be too large for the circulation of the whole country, but if it should be, the excess may be exchanged for gold coin, or the Commissioners may sell a portion of their Exchequer bills and thus diminish the amount of the paper circulation. There are other modes by which the substitution of the new notes for the old might be made if the Bank of England co-operated with the Commissioners, but the one here proposed would be effectual. It might be desirable that Government should purchase from the Bank at a fair valuation the whole of its buildings if the Bank were willing to part with them, and also take all its clerks and servants into pay. It would be but just to the clerks and servants of the Bank to provide employment and support for them, and would be useful to the public to have the services of so many tried and experienced officers to conduct their affairs. It is a part of my plan, too, that the payment to the Bank for the management of the National Debt should wholly cease at the expiration of the Bank charter, and that this department of the public business should be put under the superintendence and control of the Commissioners.

The third regulation provides for a proper deposit of gold coin and bullion, without which the new establishment could not act. In fact, there would be fourteen millions instead of ten at the disposal of the Commissioners. It has been seen by one of the subsequent regulations that the Commissioners would act as banker to the public departments, and as it is found by experience that on the average these departments have four millions in their banker's hands, the Commissioners would have these four millions in addition to the ten millions. If five millions were devoted to the purchase of coin and bullion, nine millions would be invested in floating securities. If eight millions were invested in gold, six millions would remain for the purchase of Exchequer bills. Whatever debt remained due to the Bank after this second payment made by the Commissioners must be provided for by loan, or made the subject of a special agreement between the Government and the Bank of England.

The fourth and fifth regulations provide for the substitution of the new paper money for the old, and protect the bank from the payment in specie of the notes which it may have outstanding. This cannot be attended with any inconvenience to the holders of those notes, because the Bank is bound to give them Government notes which are exchangeable on demand for gold coin.

The seventh regulation provides for the substitution of the new notes for the old country bank notes. The country banks could have no difficulty in providing themselves with the new notes for that purpose. All their transactions finally settle in London, and their circulation is raised upon securities deposited there. By disposing of these securities they would furnish themselves with the requisite quantity of money to provide for the payment of their notes, consequently the country would at no time be in want of an adequate circulation. The circulation of the country banks is estimated at about ten millions.

The eighth regulation provides against fraud and forgery. In the first instance paper money cannot be issued from each district but must all be sent from London. It is just, therefore, that some public agent should, in as many places as convenient, be prepared to verify the genuineness of the notes. After a time the circulation of each district would be carried on by notes issued in that district in forms sent for that purpose from London.

The ninth regulation provides every possible facility for making remittances and payments to any district in the country. If a man at York wishes to make a payment of £1,000 to a person at Canterbury, by the payment of £1,000 in notes issued at York to the agent in that town he may receive a bill for

£1,000 payable at Canterbury in the notes of that district.

The tenth regulation provides for the payment of the notes of every district in coin in London. If a man in York wants £1,000 in coin Government should not be at the expense of sending it to him, he ought to be at that expense himself. This is a sacrifice which must be made for the use of paper money, and if the inhabitants of the country are not contented to submit to it, they may use gold instead of paper; they must, nevertheless, be at the expense of procuring it.

The eleventh regulation as well as the ninth provides for making remittances and payments to all parts of the country.

The twelfth regulation provides against the amount of the paper currency being too much limited in quantity by obliging the Commissioners to issue it at all times in exchange for gold at the price of £3 17s. 6d. per ounce. Regulating their issues by the price of gold the Commissioners could never err. It might be expedient to oblige them to sell gold bullion at £3 17s. 9d., in which case the coin would probably never be exported, because that can never be obtained under £3 17s. 10½d. per ounce. Under such a system the only variations that could take place in the price of gold would be between the prices of £3 17s. 6d. and £3 17s. 9d., and by watching the market price and increasing their issues of paper when the price inclined to £3 17s. 6d. or under, and limiting them or withdrawing a small portion when the price inclined to £3 17s. 9d. or more, there would not probably be a dozen transactions in the year by the Commissioners in the purchase and sale of gold, and if there were they would always be advantageous and leave a small profit to the establishment. As it is, however, desirable to be on the safe side in managing the important business of a paper money in a great country, it would be proper to make a liberal provision of gold, as suggested in a former regulation, in case it should be thought expedient occasionally to correct the exchanges with foreign countries by the exportation of gold as well as by the reduction of the amount of paper.

The thirteenth regulation obliges the Commissioners to pay their notes on demand in gold coin.

The fourteenth regulation provides for a supply of one pound notes for the country circulation. On the first establishment of the National Bank, but not afterwards, these are to be issued in London, to be subsequently countersigned in the country. As a check on the country agents every description of note might be sent to them from London, numbered and signed. After receiving them, the agent should countersign them before they were issued to the public, and he should be held strictly responsible for the whole amount sent to him in the same manner as the distributors of stamps are responsible for the whole amount of stamps sent to them. It is hardly necessary to observe that the country agents ought to be in constant correspondence with the London district for the purpose of giving information of all their proceedings. Suppose a country agent has given 100 notes of £1 for a note of £100, he must give information of that fact, sending at the same time the larger note for which he has given them. His account in London would be credited and debited accordingly. If he receive £100 in notes and give a bill on another district he must give advice, both to the London district and to the district on which the bill is given, sending up the note as in the former instance. His account will be credited for this £100, and the agent of the other district will be charged with it. It is not requisite to go farther into details; I may already have said too much, but my object has been to show that the security for the detection of fraud is nearly perfect, as vouchers for every transaction would all be originally issued in London, and must be returned to London, or be in the possession of the country agent.

The fifteenth regulation is only explanatory of some of the former regulations.

The sixteenth regulation directs that the Commissioners shall act as banker to the public departments and to the public departments only.

If the plan now proposed should be adopted the country would probably, on the most moderate computation, save £750,000 per annum. Suppose the circulation of paper money to amount to twenty-five millions and the Government deposits to four millions, these together make twenty-nine millions. On all this sum interest would be saved with the exception of six millions perhaps, which it might be thought necessary to retain as deposits in gold coin and bullion and which would consequently be unproductive. Reckoning interest then at 3 per cent. only on twenty-three millions, the public would be gainers of £690,000. To this must be added £248,000 which is now paid for the management of the public debt, making together £938,000. Now supposing the expenses to amount to £188,000, there would remain for the public an annual saving or gain of £750,000.

It will be remarked that the plan provides against any party but the Commissioners in London making an original issue of notes. Agents in other districts in the country, connected with the Commissioners, may give one description of notes for another; they may give bills for notes or notes for bills drawn on them, but in the first instance, every one of these notes must be issued by the Commissioners in London, and consequently the whole is strictly under their cognizance. If from any circumstances the circulation in any particular district should become redundant, provision is made for the transfer of such redundancy to London, and if it should be deficient a fresh supply is obtained from London. If the circulation of London should be redundant it will show itself by the increased price of bullion and the fall in the foreign exchanges, precisely as a redundancy is now shown, and the remedy is also the same as that now in operation, viz.: a reduction of circulation, which is brought about by a reduction of the paper circulation. That reduction may take place in two ways—either by the sale of Exchequer bills in the market and the cancelling of the paper money which is obtained for them, or by giving gold in exchange for the paper, cancelling the paper as before and exporting the gold. The exporting the gold will not be done by the Commissioners; that will be effected by the commercial operation of the merchants, who never fail to find gold the most profitable remittance when the paper money is redundant and excessive. If, on the contrary, the circulation of London were too low, there would be two ways of increasing it—by the purchase of Government securities in the market and the creation of new paper money for the purpose, or by the importation and purchase by the Commissioners of gold bullion, for the purchase of which new paper money would be created. The importation would take place through commercial operations, as gold never fails to be a profitable article of import when the amount of currency is deficient.

SPEECHES OF SIR ROBERT PEEL ON THE RENEWAL OF THE BANK CHARTER.

In the Edition published at Paris in 1904, Appendix 4 is a translation in French of the Speeches of Sir Robert Peel in the House of Commons, May 6th and 20th, 1844, on the Renewal of the Bank Charter. This has not been reprinted here; students are referred to the following works, easily accessible in any large Public Library, where the Speeches are printed in full:—

Hansard's Parliamentary Debates, Vol. 74, pp. 720, 1330.

Speeches of Rt. Hon. Sir Robert Peel, 1810-1850, Vol. 4.

A Corner in Gold, and our Money Laws. 1904. P. S. King & Son. 2s. 6d.

AUTHOR'S BIBLIOGRAPHY.

A Bank Dialogue between Dr. Hugh Chamberlain and a Country Gentleman. London, 1695.

A Comparison between the proposals of the Bank and the South Sea Company. Wherein is shown that the proposals of the first are much more advantageous than that of the latter. London, 1720.

A copy of the Correspondence between the Chancellor of the Exchequer and the Bank of England relative to the Renewal of the Charter of 1833. London, 1858.

A description of the Office of Credit. With a plain demonstration how a man may trade for six times his stock. London, 1665.

A digest of the evidence on the Bank Charter, taken before the Committee of 1832. London, 1833.

A History of Banking in all Nations. 4 Vols. New York, 1896.

A letter concerning the Bank and the Credit of the Nation. London, 1700.

A letter to a friend concerning the credit of the Nation, and with relation to the present Bank of England, as now established by Act of Parliament. Written by a Member of the said Corporation for the public good of the Kingdom. London, 1697.

A letter to the Governor of the Bank of England. London, 1721.

Arguments against prolonging the Bank with proposals for advancing the revenue of the Excise. In a letter to a Member of Parliament. London, 1708.

A second part of a discourse concerning banks. London (undated, but certainly 1696 or 1697).

ADDISON, RT. HON. J. *The Spectator*, No. 3, March, 1701.

An Account of the constitution and security of the General Bank of Credit. London, 1683.

An Account of the Private League between the late King James II. and the French King. (In State Tracts). London, 1705.

An Essay for the Regulation of the Coin. By A. V. London, 1695.

An Honest Scheme for improving the trade and the credit of the Nation. London, 1727.

ANDERSON, ADAM. An Historical and Chronological Deduction of the Origin of Commerce. 4 Vols. London, 1787-89.

ANSON, SIR WILLIAM. The Law and Custom of the Constitution. 2 Vols. 2nd edition. Oxford, 1896.

BAGEHOT, WALTER. Lombard Street: a description of the Money Market. London, 1873.

BAINES, ED. History of the Cotton Manufacture in Great Britain. London, 1835.

BAKER, A. F. Banks and Banking. London, 1892.

Bank of Credit; or the Usefulness and Security of the Bank of Credit examined in a Dialogue between a Country Gentleman and a London Merchant. London, 1683.

BANNISTER, S. The Writings of William Paterson, with Biographical Notices of the Author. London, 1858. 2nd edition, 1859.

BARING, SIR FRANCIS. Observations on the Establishment of the Bank of England, and on the Paper Circulation of the Country. London, 1797.

Observations on the Publication of W. Boyd, Esq., M.P. London, 1801.

BASTABLE, C. F. Public Finance. 3rd edition. London, 1903.

BÉRARD, VICTOR. L'Angleterre et l'Impérialisme contemporain. Paris, 1900.

BESTA. Lezioni sulla Contabilita di Stato. Venice, 1889.

BŒRE, GIUSEPPE. Storia della conversione alla Chiesa Cattolica di Carlo II., Re d'Inghilterra. Estratto della Civilta Cattolica. Rome, 1863.

BOSANQUET, B. TINDAL. Our Banking System. London, 1892.

BOSANQUET, CHARLES. Practical Observations on the Report of the Bullion Committee. London, 1810.

BOUCARD AND JÈZE. Éléments de science et de législation financière. 2 Vols. Paris, 1902.

BOYD, WALTER. A Letter to the Honourable W. Pitt on the influence of the stoppage of issues in specie at the Bank of England on the prices of provisions and other commodities. London, 1801. (2nd edition, revised by the author, 1811).

BRADBURY, HENRY. On the Security and Manufacture of Bank Notes. London, 1856.

BRISCOE, JOHN. Proposals for supplying their Majesties with money on easy terms, exempting the Nobility, Gentry, etc., from taxes, enlarging the yearly estates and enriching all the subjects of the Kingdom by a National Bank. London, 3rd edition, 1696.

BROOM, HERBERT. Constitutional Law, viewed in relation to Common Law. London, 1866.

BRY, GEORGES. Histoire industrielle et économique de l'Angleterre, depuis les origines jusqu' à nos jours. Paris, 1900.

BURNET (Bishop of Salisbury). History of his own time. 6 Vols. Oxford, Clarendon Press, 1823.

BURTON, J. H. History of Scotland. 2nd edition, 8 Vols. Edinburgh, 1873.

BUXTON, SYDNEY. Finance and Politics; An Historical Study, 1783-1885. 2 Vols. London, 1888.

CARLYLE, THOMAS. Cromwell's Letters and Speeches. 5 Vols. London, 1882.

CARY, JOHN. An Essay towards the Settlement of the National Credit in the Kingdom of England. London, 1696.

CANNING, RT. HON. GEORGE. Substance of two speeches delivered on the 8th and 13th of May, 1811, on the Report of the Bullion Committee. London, 1811.

CAUWÈS. Cours d'économie politique. 3rd edition, 4 Vols. Paris, 1893.

CHALMERS, A. The British Essayists. With Prefaces Historical and Biographical. 3rd edition, 45 Vols. London, 1817.

CHALMERS, G. An estimate of the comparative strength of Great Britain. 3rd edition. London, 1804.

CHAMBERLAIN, DR. HUGH. A brief narrative of the nature and advantages of the Land Bank, as proposed by Dr. Hugh Chamberlen. London, 1695.

A proposal by Dr. Hugh Chamberlayne, in Essex Street, for a bank of secure current-credit, to be founded upon land, in order to the general good of landed men, to the increase of the value of Land, and the no less benefit of trade and commerce. London, 1695.

CHAMBERS, R. Domestic Annals of Scotland. Edinburgh, 1858. (2nd edition, 3 Vols., 1859-61).

History of the Rebellion in Scotland in 1745-1746. 2nd edition. London, 1869.

CHILD, SIR JOSIAH. Brief Observations concerning trade and interest of money by J. C. London, 1668.

CHRISTIE, W. D. A Life of Anthony Ashley Cooper, first Earl of Shaftesbury. 2 Vols. London, 1871.

CLARE, GEORGE. A Money-Market Primer and Key to the Exchanges. 2nd edition. London, 1903.

CLARENDON, EDWARD HYDE (first Earl of). History of the Rebellion and Civil Wars in England. 6 Vols., edit. Macray. Oxford, 1888.

The Life of Edward, Earl of Clarendon, and a Continuation of the same, written by himself. 2 Vols. Oxford, 1857.

CLARK, HYDE. On the Debts of Sovereign and Quasi-Sovereign States. Journal of the Royal Statistical Society, Vol. XLI.

COBB, A. STANLEY. Banks' Cash Reserves. London, 1891.

Metallic Reserves and the Meeting of Parliament. London, 1892.

COBBETT, W. A Collection of State Trials. 33 Vols. London, 1809-1826.

COLLIER, J. Ecclesiastical History of Great Britain. 9 Vols. London, 1852.

COLLINS, C. M. The History, Law, and Practice of Banking. London, 1882.

CONANT, CH. A History of Modern Banks of Issue; with an account of the economic crises of the present century. New York, 1896.

COPERNICUS, NICOLAS. Traité de la Monnaie (1526). Latin text with French translation and notes, edited by L. Wolowski. Paris, 1864.

COQ, PAUL. La Monnaie de Banque, ou l'Espèce et le Portefeuille. Paris, 1863.

Corporation Credit; or a Bank of Credit made current by common consent in London, more useful and safe than money. London, 1682.

COTTON, SIR ROBERT. A Speech touching the alteration of coin. London, 1641.

COURCELLE-SENEUIL, J. G. Traité théorique et pratique des opérations de banque. 4th edition. Paris, 1864.

COURTOIS, ALPHONSE FILS. Histoire de la Banque de France et des principales institutions financières de crédit depuis 1716. 2nd edition. Paris, 1881.

COXE, W. Memoirs of Walpole, with original correspondence, etc. 3 Vols. London, 1798.

CRADOCKE, FRANCIS. An expedient for taking away all impositions and for raising a revenue without taxes by creating Banks, for the encouragement of Trade. London, 1660.

CULPEPER, SIR THOMAS. A tract against the high rate of usurie. London (?), 1621.

CUNEO, CARLO. Memorie sopra l'antico debito publico mutui, compere e banche di San Giorgio in Genova. Genoa, 1842.

CUNNINGHAM, W. The Growth of English Industry and Commerce. (Vol. I., Early and Middle Ages; Vol. II., Modern Times). Cambridge, 1890-1892.

DALRYMPLE, SIR J. Memoirs of Great Britain and Ireland. 3 Vols. London, 1771-1788.

DANSON, J. T. On the account of the Bank of England under the operation of the Act 7 and 8 Vict., c. 32. The Journal of the Royal Statistical Society, Vol. X.

DARTIGUENAVE, AYMARD. Relations de la Banque de France avec le Trésor. Paris, 1902.

DAVENANT, CHARLES. Works, Political and Commercial. Edit. Sir C. Whitworth. 5 Vols. London, 1771.

DEFOE, DANIEL. Essay upon Projects. London, 1697.
The History of the Union of Great Britain. Edinburgh, 1709.

Dictionary of Political Economy. Edited by R. H. Inglis Palgrave. 3 Vols. London, 1894-1899.

DILLON, MALCOLM. The History and Development of Banking in Ireland. London, 1889.

DISRAELI, ISAAC. Usurers of the Seventeenth Century. In Curiosities of Literature. 3 Vols. London, 1842.

DOWELL, STEPHEN. History of Taxation and Taxes in England. 2 Vols. London, 1854, 2nd edition, 1888.

DUBOIS, A. Précis de l'histoire des doctrines économiques. Paris, 1903.

DUDLEY, DUD. Metallum Martis; or iron made with pit coale, sea coale, etc. London, 1665.

DUMOULIN. Tractatus contractarum et usurarum. Paris, 1546.

DUNBAR, C. F. The Bank of Venice. The Quarterly Journal of Economics. April, 1892.

DUPONT DE NEMOURS, P. S. Rapport sur la Banque de France et les causes de la crise qu'elle a éprouvée. Paris, 1806; London, 1811.

EDGEWORTH, F. Y. Sir Josiah Child. In Palgrave's Dictionary of Political Economy, Vol. I.

England's Glory, or the great improvement of trade by a Royal Bank. By H. M. London, 23rd June, 1694.

England's Interest, or the great benefit to the trade by the banks or offices of credit in London as it hath been considered and agreed upon by a committee of Aldermen and Commons appointed by the Right Honourable the Lord Mayor. London, 1682.

ERNOUF. Maret, duc de Bassano. Paris, 1878.

EVANS, D. MORIER. The Commercial Crisis, 1847-1848. London, 1848.

The History of the Commercial Crisis, 1857-1858. London, 1859.

EVELYN, JOHN. Diary and Correspondence. 4 Vols. London, 1850-1852.

Extraits des enquêtes parlementaires anglaises. (Publiés par ordre du gouverneur et du conseil de régence de la Banque de France et sous la direction de MM. Coullet et Juglar). 8 Parts. Paris, 1865.

FAIRBAIRN, SIR W. Iron; its history, properties and process of manufacture. Edinburgh, 3rd edition, 1869.

FLEETWOOD, W. A sermon (on Genesis xxiii., 16) against clipping; preached before the Lord Mayor. London, 1694.

"Chronicon Pretiosum," or an account of English gold and silver money, the price of corn and other commodities for the last 600 years. London, 1707.

FILON, AUG. Profils anglais. Paris, 1892.

FOLKES, MARTIN. A table of silver coins from the Norman Conquest. London, 1745.

FORBES, SIR WILLIAM. Memoirs of a Banking House. Edinburgh, 1860.

FOX, CHARLES JAMES. Speeches. 6 Vols. London, 1815.

FOXWELL, H. S. Mr. Goschen's Currency Proposals. Economic Journal, March, 1892.

FRANCIS, JOHN. The History of the Bank of England. 3rd edition. London, 1848.

FRANÇOIS, G. M. Goschen et la Banque d'Angleterre. Journal des Économistes. January, 1892.

FRENCH, G. J. The Life and Times of Samuel Crompton. 3rd edition. Manchester, 1862.

FROUDE, J. A. History of England from the Fall of Wolsey to the Defeat of the Spanish Armada. 12 Vols. London, 1875.

FULLARTON, J. On the Regulation of Currencies and the Working of the New Bank Act. London, 1844.

GARDINER, SAMUEL. History of England, 1603-1642. 10 Vols. London, 1883-1884.

History of the Commonwealth and Protectorate. 1894.

GAIRDNER, CHARLES. Mr. Goschen's Scheme for Reform of the Bank Act. Glasgow, 1892.

The Making of the Gold Reserves. Glasgow, 1891.

GASSART, DU HAYS DU. Des prêts consentis aux Etats par les banques de circulation. Paris, 1902.

GERBIER, BALTHAZAR. Some considerations on the two great staple commodities of England, and on certain establishments wherein the publick good is very much concerned. Humbly presented to the Parliament. London, 1651.

GILBART, J. W. Works, 6 Vols. London, 1865.

History, Principles and Practice of Banking. Revised by E. Sykes, B.A. London, 1907.

GIBBINS, HENRY DE BELTGENS. Industrial History of England. London, 1890.

GIDE, CHARLES. Principes d'économie politique. 6th edition. Paris, 1898.

GIFFEN, SIR ROBERT. Essays in Finance (second series). 2nd edition. London, 1886.

GLADSTONE, W. H. Speech of 8th May, 1854.

GLASSON, E. Histoire du droit et des institutions d'Angleterre. 6 Vols. Paris, 1881-1883.

GODFREY, MICHAEL. A Short Account of the Bank of England. London, 1694. Reprint by Francis, 1848.

GODWIN, WILLIAM. History of the Commonwealth of England. 4 Vols. London, 1824-28.

GOSCHEN, LORD. Speech at Leeds on the Insufficiency of our Cash Reserves and of our Central Stock of Gold. London, 1891.

Address to the London Chamber of Commerce on the Metallic Reserve. London, 1891.

GRELLIER, J. J. Terms of all the Public Loans; with an Appendix by R. W. Wade. 1799. 2nd edition, London, 1802.

GRENVILLE, LORD. Essay on the Supposed Advantages of a Sinking Fund. London, 1828.

GUIZOT, F. P. G. Histoire de la Révolution d'Angleterre, 1625-1660. 2 Vols. Paris, 1854.

HAMILTON, E. W. An Account of the Operations under the National Debt Conversion Act, 1888, and the National Debt Redemption Act, 1889. London, 1889.

HAMILTON, ROBERT. Inquiry Concerning the Rise and Progress, the Redemption and Management of the National Debt of Great Britain and Ireland. London, 1813.

HANKEY, THOMAS. The Principles of Banking; its Utility and Economy, with Remarks on the Working and Management of the Bank of England. London, 1867. 4th edition, 1887.

HARRISON, FREDERIC. Oliver Cromwell. London, 1887.

HAWKINS, EDWARD. The Silver Coins of England. London, 1887.

HOLST, H. VON. The Constitutional History of the United States. English translation by Lalor. 7 Vols. Chicago, 1877-92.

HUTCHESON, ARCHIBALD. A Collection of Calculations and Remarks Relating to the South Sea Scheme and Stock. London, 1720.

Some Calculations Relating to the Proposals made by the South Sea Company and the Bank of England to the House of Commons. London, 1720.

Is not the hand of Joab in all this? or an Enquiry into the grounds of a late pamphlet entitled, "The Mystery of the New-Fashioned Goldsmiths." London, 1676.

JACKSON, FRED. HUTH. To what extent has the position of the Bank of England changed in recent years in comparison with (*a*) similar institutions, and (*b*) London Clearing Bankers? London, Political Economy Club, June, 1903.

The Life of James II., King of England. 2 Vols. London, J. S. Clarke, 1816.

JAUVELLE, E. LEMERCIER DE. Réforme des services de la Trésorerie. Angers, 1887.

JESSOP, AUGUSTUS. The Lives of the Norths. London, 1890.

JEVONS, STANLEY. Investigations in Currency and Finance. London, 1884.

JOPLIN, T. Supplementary Observations to the 3rd edition of an Essay on Banking. London, 1823.

JUGLAR, CLEMENT. Les crises commerciales et leur retour périodique en France, en Angleterre et aux Etats-Unis. 2nd edition. Paris, 1889.

JUSTICE, ALEXANDER. General Treatise on Moneys and Exchanges. London, 1707.

KENETT, WHITE. The Wisdom of Looking Backward. London, 1715.

KING, LORD. Thoughts on the Restriction of Payments in Specie at the Banks of England and Ireland. London, 1804.

KNOX, JOHN JAY. United States Notes. 2nd edition. London, 1885.

LAING, MALCOLM. History of Scotland from the Union of the Crowns to the Union of the Kingdoms. 2nd edition. 4 Vols. London, 1804.

LAMBE, SAMUEL. Seasonable Observations humbly offered to his Highness the Lord Protector. London, 1651.

LANG, ANDREW. Prince Charles Edward. London, 1900.

LASSALLE, J. H. Des finances de l'Angleterre. Paris, 1803.

LATTES, ELIA. La liberta delle banche a Venezia dal secolo XIII. al XVII. Milan, 1869.

LAW, JOHN. Mémoires sur les Banques. In "Économistes et Financiers du xviiie siècle." Paris, 1843.

LAWSON, W. J. History of Banking. 2nd edition. London, 1855.

Le Marché de Londres en temps de crise. Journal des Économistes. February, 1900.

LEAKE, S. M. Nummi Britannici historia; or an Historical Account of English Money. London, 1626. 2nd edition, 1745.

LECKY, W. E. H. History of England in the Eighteenth Century. 8 Vols. London, 1883-1890.

LEROY-BEAULIEU, PAUL. L'Etat moderne et ses fonctions. 3rd edition. Paris, 1900.

Science des Finances. 2 Vols. 6th edition, 1899.

Traité théorique et pratique d'économie politique. 4 Vols., 3rd edition. Paris, 1900.

LETI, GREGORIO. Historia e Memorie sopra la vita di Ol. Cromvele. Amsterdam, 1692.

LEVASSEUR, EMILE. Recherches historiques sur le système de Law. Paris, 1854.

LEVI, LEONE. The History of British Commerce and of the Economic Progress of the British Nation, 1763-1878. London, 1880.

LEWIS, MARK. Proposals to the King and Parliament; or a Large Model of a Bank. London, 1678.

LINGARD, JOHN. History of England. 5th edition, 10 Vols. London, 1849.

LOCKE, JOHN. Some Considerations on the Lowering of Interest and Raising the Value of Money.

Some Observations on a Printed Paper entitled, "For Encouraging the Coining of Silver Money in England."

Further Considerations concerning Raising the Value of Money.

London Journal, 11th June and 12th November, 1720.

LOUBET, PAUL. La Banque de France et l'Escompte. Paris, 1900.

LOUIS XIV. Œuvres de Louis XIV. 6 Vols. Paris, 1806.

LOWNDES. A Report containing an Essay for the Amendment of Silver Coins. London, 1695.

LUTTRELL, N. A Brief Relation of State Affairs from September, 1678, to April, 1714. 6 Vols. Oxford, 1857.

LYON-CAEN, AND RENAULT. Traité des Sociétés commerciales. Paris, 1892.

MACAULAY, LORD. Essays Critical and Historical. 3 Vols. London, 1843.

History of England from the Accession of James II. 5 Vols. London, 1849-1861.

MACHIAVELLI. Le Istorie Fiorentine. Florence, 1537. (French translation by Giraudet. Paris, an VII. 9 Vols.).

MACCARTHY, J. A History of Our Own Times, from the Accession of Queen Victoria to the General Election of 1880. 4 Vols. 2nd edition. London, 1882.

MCCULLOCH. A Select Collection of Scare and Valuable Tracts on Money. London, 1856.

A Select Collection of Scarce and Valuable Tracts on the National Debt and the Sinking Fund. London, 1857.

A Descriptive and Statistical Account of the British Empire. 2 Vols., 4th edition. London, 1854.

Essay on Manufactures. In Treatises of Economical Policy. London, 1853.

Historical Sketch of the Bank of England. London, 1831.

MACKAY, CH. Memoirs of Extraordinary Popular Delusions. 2 Vols. 2nd edition. London, 1892. 1st edition, 1845.

MACLEOD, H. D. Dictionary of Political Economy. 1st Vol. London, 1863.

Theory and Practice of Banking. London. 2 Vols., 1855. 5th edition, 1892-1893.

Theory of Credit. 2 Vols. London, 1893-1897.

MACPHERSON, D. Annals of Commerce. 4 Vols. London, 1805.

MAHON, LORD. *see* STANHOPE, LORD.

MAITLAND. History of London. 2 Vols. London, 1756.

MARNIÈRE, J. H. Essai sur le crédit commercial considéré comme moyen de circulation. Paris, 1801.

Considérations sur la facilité d'établir à Paris une Banque égale à celle de Londres. Paris, 1802.

MARSHALL, J. The Life of George Washington. 5 Vols. Philadelphia, 1804-1807.

MARTIN, JOHN BIDDULPH. The Grasshopper in Lombard Street. London, 1892.

MARTINUZZI, PIETRO. La Banca d'Inghilterra nei riguardi del servizio del Tesoro. Leghorn, 1891.

MAVOR, JAMES. The Call for Currency and Mr. Goschen's Response. London, 1892.

MAZURE. Histoire de la Révolution d'Angleterre. 3 Vols. Paris, 1825.

MEES, W. C. Proeveener geschiedenis van het Bankwezen in Nederland. Rotterdam, 1838.

MENTET DE SALMONET. Histoire des troubles de la Grand' Bretagne. Paris, 1661.

METEYARD, ELIZA. Life of Josiah Wedgwood. 2 Vols. London, 1865-66.

MIGNET. Histoire des Négociations relatives à la succession d'Espagne. 2 Vols. Paris, 1835. Dans la collection des Documents inedits sur l'histoire de France.

MILL, J. S. The Principles of Political Economy. th edition. 2 Vols. London, 1865.

MORLEY, JOHN. Walpole. London, 1889.

Oliver Cromwell. London, 1900.

MOXON, T. B. Our Banking System and its Effects upon Commerce. Transactions of the Manchester Statistical Society, 1891.

MURRAY, H. Proposal for Advancement of Trade. London, 1676.

NEWENHAM, THOMAS. A View of the Natural, Political and Commercial Circumstances of Ireland. London, 1809.

NEWMARCH, W. On the Loans Raised by Mr. Pitt during the First French War. London, 1855.

NOEL, OCTAVE. Les Banques d'émission en Europe. Paris, 1888.

NORMAN, GEO. WARDE. Remarks on Some Prevalent Errors with Respect to Currency and Banking. London, 1838.
A Letter to C. Wood, Esq., M.P., On Money and on the Means of Economising it. London, 1841.

NORTH, ROGER. Life of Dudley North. London, 1744.

Observations upon the Constitution of the Company of the Bank of England, with a Narrative of their late Proceedings. London, 1694.

OVERSTONE, LORD. Tracts and other Publications on Metallic and Paper Currency. London, 1858.

PAGAN, W. The Birthplace and Parentage of William Paterson. Edinburgh, 1865.

PAINE, TOM. The Decline and Fall of the English System of Finance. Philadelphia, 1796. French translation by F. Lanthenas. Paris, 1796.

PALGRAVE, R. H. INGLIS. Notes on Banking. London, 1873.
Bank Rate and the Money Market. London, 1903.

PALMER, J. H. The Causes and Consequences of the Pressure upon the Money Market. London, 1837.

PARKER, CH. STUART. Sir R. Peel from his Private Papers. 3 Vols. London, 1891-99.

Parliamentary History of England from 1066 to 1803. Hansard's Debates. 36 Vols. London, 1806-1820.

Parliamentary Debates from 1803 to the present time. Hansard.

PASQUIER, MAURICE. Sir William Petty. Ses idées économiques. Paris, 1903.

PATERSON, WILLIAM. A Brief Account of the Intended Bank of England. London, 1694.
Memorial to George I. London, 1714.
An Enquiry by the Wednesday's Club in Friday Street. London, 1717.

PEEL, SIR ROBERT. Memoirs, edited by Earl Stanhope and Lord Cardwell. 2 Vols. London, 1856-1857.
Speeches of the Rt. Hon. Sir Robert Peel in the House of Commons. 4 Vols. London, 1853.

PEPYS, S. Diary and Correspondence. 5 Vols. London, 1848-1849.

PERAZZI, C. Memorie intorno alla contabilita dello stato in Inghilterra (Supplement to the project of Quintino Sella). Florence, 1865.

PETTY, SIR WILLIAM. Quantulumcunque concerning money (1682). London, 1695.

PHILLIPS, J. A General History of Inland Navigation, Foreign and Domestic. London, 1803.

PIERSON, DR. N. G. Principles of Economics. Translated from the Dutch by A. A. Wotzel. London, 1902.

POOR, HENRY V. Money and its Laws; embracing a History of Monetary Theories and a History of Currencies in the United States. New York, 1877.

POPE. Epistle to Allen, Lord Bathurst. London, 1732.

PORTER, G. The Progress of the Nation in its Social and Commercial Relations, from the Nineteenth Century to the Present Day. London, 1838-1843. 3rd edition, 1851.

POWNALL, G. H. The Insufficiency of our Cash Reserves and of our Central Stock of Gold. Economic Journal, 1892.

POSTLETHWAYT, J. The History of the English Revenue, from the Revolution in 1688 to Christmas, 1758. London, 1759.

PRICE, BONAMY. Chapters on Practical Political Economy. London, 1878.

PRICE, F. G. HILTON. A Handbook of London Bankers, with some account of their predecessors the early goldsmiths, together with a list of bankers from the earliest one printed in 1677 to that of the London Post Office Directory of 1876. London, 1876. 2nd edition, 1891.

Proposals for Restoring Credit, for Making the Bank of England more Useful and Profitable, and for Relieving the Sufferers of the South Sea Company. London, 1721.

RAFFALOVICH, A. Le Bilan de la Banque d'Angleterre. Journal des Economistes. June, 1893.

Reasons offered Against the Continuation of the Bank. In a Letter to a Member of Parliament. London, 1707.

Remarks on the Bank of England. Humbly addressed to the Hon. House of Commons; by a Merchant of London and a true lover of our Constitution. 2nd edition. London, 1706.

Remarks on the Proceedings of the Commissioners for putting in Execution an Act passed last Session establishing a Land Bank. London, 1696.

Report with the Evidence and Accounts from the Select Committee, on the High Price of Gold Bullion. Parliamentary Paper. London, 1810.

REYNEL, C. The True English Interest. London, 1674.

REZASCO. Dizionario di linguagio italiano storico e amministrativo. Florence, 1881.

RHODES, JAMES FORD. History of the United States from the Compromise of 1850. 3 Vols. New York, 1893-1895.

RICARDO, D. The high price of bullion a proof of the depreciation of money. London, 1809.

A reply to Mr. Bosanquet's Practical Observations on the Report of the Bullion Committee. London, 1811.

Essay on the Funding System. Encyclopædia Britannica. 1821.

Plan for a National Bank. London, 1824.

RICKARDS, SIR G. The Financial Policy of War. London, 1855.

ROBINSON, H. England's Safety in Trade Increased. London, 1641.

ROGERS, THOROLD. The First Nine Years of the Bank of England. Oxford, 1887.

The Industrial and Commercial History of England. London, 1892.

ROSCHER, W. Nationalokonomik des Handels und Gewerbfleiszes. 2nd edition. Stuttgart, 1892.

ROSEBERY, LORD. Pitt. London, 1891.

ROTA, P. Storia delle banche. Milan, 1874.

ROUSSET, CAMILLE. Histoire de Louvois. 4 Vols. Paris, 1862-1863.

RUDING, R. Annals of the Coinage of Great Britain. 3 Vols. London, 1840.

SAVARY. Le Parfait Négociant. 2 Vols. Paris, 1757.

SCOBELL, HENRY. A Collection of Acts and Ordinances of General Use, 1640-1656. London, 1658.

SCOTT, SIR W. Letters of Malachi Malagrowther, Esq., on the Currency. Edinburgh, 1826.

SEELEY, SIR J. R. The Growth of British Policy. 2 Vols. Cambridge, 1895.

Several Objections sometimes made against the Office of Credit fully answered. London, 1682.

SHAW, W. A. The History of the Currency, 1252-1894. London, 1895. French translation by A. Raffalovich. Paris, 1896.

SINCLAIR, SIR JOHN. Letters written to the Governor and Directors of the Bank of England in September, 1796. London, 1797.

The History of the Public Revenue of the British Empire. London, 1785-1790. 3rd edition. With an Examination of the Financial Administration of W. Pitt, 1803-1804.

SMILES, SAMUEL. Lives of the Engineers. 3 Vols. London, 1861-1862.

SMITH, ADAM. Wealth of Nations. Edinburgh, 1863.

SMITH, JOHN. England's Improvement Revived. London, 1673.

SMOLLETT, T. G. History of England from the Revolution to the Death of George II. London.

Some Account of the Transactions of Mr. W. Paterson in Relation with the Orphans' Fund. London, 1695.

STANHOPE, LORD. Life of the Right Hon. W. Pitt. 4 Vols. London, 1861-1862.

History of Queen Anne's Reign. London, 1870.

History of England from the Peace of Utrecht. 7 Vols. London, 1839-54.

STEELE, F. E. On the Changes of the Bank Rate; First their Causes, and Secondly their Effect. London, 1891.

STEPHENS, T. A. A Contribution to the Bibliography of the Bank of England. London, 1897.

STEWART, SIR J. An Enquiry into the Principles of Political Economy. 2 Vols. London, 1767.

STOURM, RÉNÉ. Systèmes généraux d'impôts. Paris, 1893, 2nd edition, 1905.

STOW, J. A. A Survey of the Cities of London and Westminster. 2 Vols. London, 1720.

SUMNER, W. G. A History of American Currency. New York, 1884.

SWIFT. Works. 19 Vols. Edinburgh, 1824.

SWARTE, V. DE. Les vingt premières années de la Banque de France. Paris, 1900.

TAINE, H. A. Histoire de la littérature anglaise. 4 Vols. Paris, 1863-1864.

Les Origines de la France contemporaine. 1899.

TAYLOR, W. COOKE. Life and Times of Sir Robert Peel. 3 Vols. London, 1846-1848.

TENNANT, CHARLES. The Bank of England and the Organisation of Credit. 3rd edition. London, 1867.

The Arguments and Reasons for and against engrafting upon the Bank of England with taillies, as they have been debated at a late General Court of the said Bank. London, 1697.

The Bank of England and their Present Method of Paying Defended. London, 1697.

The Case of the Bank Contract. London, 1735.

The Crisis of 1890. Economic Journal, Vol. I.

The History of the Bank of England from the Establishment of that Institution to the Present Day. London, 1797.

The Life and Adventures of the Old Lady of Threadneedle Street. London, 1832.

The Mystery of the New-Fashioned Goldsmiths or Bankers Discovered. London, 1676.

The Quarterly Journal of Economics published by the Harvard University. Boston, U.S.A.

The Schemes of the South Sea Company and the Bank of England, as proposed to the Parliament for the Reducing of the National Debts. London, 1720.

The Statutes at Large from Magna Charta to 1869. 110 Vols. London, 1762-1869.

The Villany of Stock-Jobbers Detected and the Causes of the late Run upon the Bank Discovered and Considered. London, 1701.

THÉRY, EDMOND. Europe et États Unis d'Amerique. Paris, 1899.

THIERS, A. Histoire de Law. Paris, 1858.

THORNTON, H. An Enquiry into the Nature and Effects of the Paper Credit of England. London, 1802.

THURLOE, J. A Collection of State Papers from 1638 to the Restoration. 7 Vols. London, 1742.

TINDAL, N. History of England from the Revolution to the Accession of King George II. London, 1743.

TODD, ALPH. Parliamentary Government of England. 2 Vols. 2nd edition. London, 1887.

TOOKE, THOMAS. History of Prices. 6 Vols. London, 1838-1857.

An Inquiry into the Currency Principle. London, 1844.

TORRENS, ROBERT. A Letter to the Rt. Hon. Viscount Melbourne on the Causes of the recent derangement of the Money Market. London, 1837.

The Principles and Practical Operation of Sir Robert Peel's Act of 1844, explained and defended. 3rd edition. London, 1858.

TRAILL, H. D. Social England. 6 Vols. London, 1893-97.

TUCKER, JOSIAH. A Letter to a Friend concerning Naturalizations. London, 1753.

TURNOR, TH. The Case of the Bankers and their Creditors, more fully stated and examined. London, 1675.

VAN RANKE, LEOPOLD. History of England principally in the Seventeenth Century. Oxford, 1875.

VAUGHAN, RICE. A Discourse of Coin and of Coinage. London, 1675.

VOLTAIRE. Histoire de Charles XII.

WALPOLE, HORACE. Letters to Sir Horace Mann. 9 Vols. London, 1857-1859.

WAGNER, A. Kredit und Banken. In Schönberg Handbuch d. Pol. Ockon: Italian translation, Biblioteca dell' Economista. 3rd series, Vol. XII. Turin, 1886.

WATSON, ROBERT. The Life of Lord George Gordon, with a Philosophical Review of his Political Conduct. London, 1795.

WILFREDO-PARETO. Cours d'Economie Politique professé a la Faculté de Lausanne. 2 Vols. Lausanne, 1896.

WILSON, JAMES. Capital, Currency and Banking. 2nd edition. London, 1859.

WILLIAMS, BASIL. The Foreign Policy of England under Walpole. English Historical Review, 1901.

WISZNIEWSKI, ADAM. La méthode historique appliquée a la réforme des banques. Histoire de la Banque Saint-George de la République de Gênes. Paris, 1865.

WOLF, LUCIEN. The Resettlement of the Jews in England. London, 1888.

WOLOWSKI, L. F. M. R. La Banque d'Angleterre et les Banques d'Écosse. Paris, 1867.

La Question des Banques. Paris, 1864.

YOUNG, ARTHUR. Political Arithmetic. 2 Parts. London, 1774-1779.

INDEX.